United States Edition RNAB

2012 Year B

Workbook for Lectors, Gospel Readers, and Proclaimers of the Word

Graziano Marcheschi, MA, DMIN

with Nancy Seitz Marcheschi

LTP
LITURGY
TRAINING
PUBLICATIONS

New American Bible readings are taken from *Lectionary for Mass* for Use in the Dioceses of the United States of America, second typical edition © 1998, 1997, 1970 by the Confraternity of Christian Doctrine, Washington, D.C., and are reproduced herein by license of the copyright owner. All rights reserved. No part of *Lectionary for Mass* may be reproduced in any form without permission in writing from the Confraternity of Christian Doctrine, Washington, D.C.

WORKBOOK FOR LECTORS, GOSPEL READERS, AND PROCLAIMERS OF THE WORD 2012, UNITED STATES EDITION © 2011 Archdiocese of Chicago. All rights reserved.

Liturgy Training Publications, 3949 South Racine Avenue, Chicago IL 60609, 1-800-933-1800, fax 1-800-933-7094, orders@ltp.org, www.LTP.org.

Editor: Lorie Simmons
Production Editor: Kris Fankhouser
Typesetter: Jim Mellody-Pizzato
Original book design: Jill Smith
Revised design: Anna Manhart and Jim Mellody-Pizzato
Cover art: Barbara Simcoe
Interior art: Anna Manhart

LTP now prints the text of *Workbook for Lectors, Gospel Readers, and Proclaimers of the Word* with ink that contains renewable linseed oil on paper that is 100% recycled and contains a minimum of 40% postconsumer waste. The paper for this product was de-inked by a process that uses PCF (Processed Chlorine Free) technologies, unlike many de-inking proesses that use toxic bleach. The printing process used to manufacture this book uses a non-heatset process that significantly reduces emission of volatile organic compounds (VOCs) into the atmosphere.

Printed in the United States of America.

ISBN: 978-1-56854-975-0
WL12

CONTENTS

The Authors

Graziano Marcheschi is the Director of Ministerial Resource Development in the Archdiocese of Chicago and recently completed 18 years as the Archdiocesan Director of Lay Ministry Formation. He is a former advisor to the Subcommittee on Lay Ecclesial Ministry of the United States Conference of Catholic Bishops and speaks frequently at national gatherings on ministry and catechesis. Among Graziano's publications are several editions of LTP's *Workbook for Lectors, Gospel Readers, and Proclaimers of the Word* and commentaries on the books of the Pentateuch and Gospels in *The Catholic Bible, Personal Study Edition* (Oxford University Press). Graziano is a host and contributor to local archdiocesan radio and television programming. He holds a Master of Arts in Theater from the University of Minnesota, a Master of Divinity from Loyola University in Chicago, and a Doctor of Ministry from the University of St. Mary of the Lake in Mundelein, Illinois.

Nancy Marcheschi, choreographer and co-director of the Anawim Players, teaches music and performing arts, and is the school liturgist at Pope John XXIII School in Evanston, Illinois.

Dedication

To the young men of Indiana University's singing group, *Straight, No Chaser,* whose music delights the ear, lifts the heart, and evokes a grateful "Hallelujah."

In accordance with c. 827, permission to publish was granted on April 21, 2011, by Reverend Monsignor John F. Canary, Vicar General of the Archdiocese of Chicago. Permission to publish is an official declaration of ecclesiastical authority that material is free from doctrinal and moral error. No legal responsibility is assumed by the grant of this permission.

INTRODUCTION

We who use this book are ministers of the word, whether lectors or readers. (A lector is a layman who has been instituted by a bishop to read from the Lectionary at Mass. A reader is any lay woman or man who reads from the Lectionary. Readers are not instituted by the bishop.) As ministers of the word, we are part of a very important process in the life of the Church. "In Sacred Scripture, the Church constantly finds her nourishment and her strength, for she welcomes it not as a human word, 'but as what it really is, the word of God' (1 Thessalonians 2:13; cf. *Dei Verbum* 24). 'In the sacred books, the Father who is in heaven comes lovingly to meet his children, and talks with them'" (*Dei Verbum* 21) (CCC, 104). In fact, "the Church has always venerated the Scriptures as she venerates the Lord's Body. She never ceases to present to the faithful the bread of life, taken from the one table of God's Word and Christ's Body' (cf. *Dei Verbum* 21). We play a role in helping to present the Word to the people during the liturgy.

We learn from the Constitution on the Sacred Liturgy that Christ "is present in his word, since it is he himself who speaks when the holy Scriptures are read in the Church." We proclaim scripture to experience the Christ present now in our midst and to make present the past events of salvation history. Liturgy allows us to participate in those events, to experience their power, and their ability to transform.

Using This Book

Proclaiming the scriptures is a ministry that involves your whole life, not just your communication skills. So make these scriptures a part of your life every week, and especially during the week prior to the liturgy in which you will proclaim.

Read through all three scriptures for your assigned Sunday in this book. Because all three have been chosen for this day, it is important to look at them together. The Gospel can often teach you much about how the first reading should be proclaimed.

Build your prayer for the week around the scripture passage you will proclaim on Sunday. At some point as you are becoming familiar with your passage, read it directly from your Bible, reading also what comes before and after it to get a clear sense of its context.

Always read all three commentaries. There are suggestions in each that can help you with your own passage. As you read the commentaries, refer to the sections of the scripture passage being discussed and make your own margin notations.

Read the scriptures again using your own margin notes and those printed in the text to remind you of the commentary suggestions.

Always read scriptures aloud taking note of stress and pause suggestions. After several readings, alter the stress markings to suit your style and interpretation.

Using Additional Resources

The better you understand the meaning of your passage, the more effectively you will proclaim it and so help the assembly to understand it. Although the commentaries in this book will help you, lectors may wish to dig deeper. Also, lectors need to develop a lifelong habit of turning to the scriptures for study and prayer. Additional information on resources that will help you to do this are listed at the end of this introduction.

In the beginning was the Word, and the Word was with God, and the Word was God.

Transparency and Drama

In this *Workbook for Lectors, Gospel Readers, and Proclaimers of the Word*, you will read about oral interpretation, dramatic pauses, and about creating characters. Good lectors use these techniques from the world of theater, not to draw attention to themselves, but to draw attention to the word. When people experience good proclamation, they forget the lector in front of them and they hear the scripture in a powerful way. That goal is best achieved by skillful use of all the available reading techniques. Of course, lectors who are overly dramatic, who become more focused on how they proclaim than on what they proclaim may find that their listeners stop believing them. Artifice (an imitation of artfulness) can become an obstacle to good proclamation.

Avoiding artifice does not mean settling for mediocrity. Often the failure to use appropriate techniques leads to a kind of mediocre reading that guarantees the scripture will not be heard. Lectors who cannot differentiate one character in a reading from another, who read too fast or too slow, who have too little energy and don't use the colorful words of a passage, who read in a monotone without rising and falling dynamics and pacing—these readers only draw attention to themselves. The assembly cannot see beyond them. But really good proclaimers—who utilize appropriate techniques for the material being read—draw the assembly into the reading.

True Humility

All lectors need a model of true humility as they work toward excellence in their proclamation. We look to Christ who "emptied himself, taking the form of a slave . . . [and] humbled himself, becoming obedient to death, even death on a cross" (Philippians 2:7–8). Jesus, the Word, humbles himself each Sunday by making himself dependent on us who proclaim him in the assembly. He depends on us to communicate him as a living and vital word. Jesus, alive in every line of scripture, is indeed, obedient "unto death."

This Sacred Ministry

God's word is "living and effective" (Hebrews 4:12) and it "goes forth from [God's] mouth . . . achieving the end for which [he] sent it" (Isaiah 55:11), yet we

God so loved the world that he gave his only Son, so that everyone who believes in him might not perish but might have eternal life.

know that doesn't happen automatically. People must receive and embrace the word and allow it to become a transforming influence in their lives. Before they can do that, lectors must help them to hear it.

Reading as Interpretation

Reading is a form of interpretation. The same word spoken by two lectors will not be "heard" in exactly the same way. Pacing, the words stressed, pauses, volume, tone color, and intensity are all elements that interpret the text. Your responsibility is to make sure your interpretation upholds the plain sense of the text, the author's clear intent, and that you enable the text to speak to everyone.

Conveying the Full Content of a Passage

God's word can also lose its power, beauty, and spiritual import if a reader fails to communicate the full content of a passage, which clearly consists of more than the words. In fact, every text contains three kinds of content: intellectual/theological, emotional, and aesthetic.

The author makes certain points or shares specific details, or tells a specific story, behind which is a theological teaching or spiritual insight. That is the intellectual/theological content. Much of what we encounter in scripture also contains emotional content. We usually call this tone, and it is as much a part of the message as is the cognitive component. If Paul is urgent or peremptory in one of his letters but the assembly is unaware of it because the lector has not communicated that part of the content, then the assembly has not heard Paul's message in its entirety. Finally, every passage contains aesthetic dimensions—elements that make it beautiful. Rhythm, suspense, picturesque language, and imagery all add to the pleasure we take in fine literature. As lectors, we must help our assemblies experience the beauty of the fine literature we call scripture.

To acquire the intellectual/theological content, begin by reading the scripture and the commentary. Next, search the text for the emotion the author is expressing—the emotional content. Finally, look for the aesthetic devices the author employs—repetition, simile, metaphor, irony, and so forth—the aesthetic content.

Tools of the Trade

Margin Notes. Notes may introduce new ideas or repeat information in the commentary. Often they address you as the reader ("Slowly. Tenderly. Build in intensity.") or offer hints about a character's feelings.

Build. "Build" refers to increasing vocal intensity as you speak a certain word or sentence. That could be done by speaking louder, but a quieter voice might produce the same effect. Sometimes "build" is achieved by speaking faster and sometimes by speaking slower. The point is to show more intensity of feeling, greater urgency, or concern. Lack of intensity is one of the great "sins" of proclamation.

Stress (Bold Print). Some words are more important than others. Some are more expressive and carry more emotion. The bolding used within the scripture texts in this book attempts to identify the operative words in a sentence, the ones which convey the meaning.

Echoes. Some words are "echoes" of words that went before. For example, "You shall be a glorious crown

This is my commandment: love one another as I love you.

a royal diadem" (Isaiah 62:3). Here "diadem" echoes "crown" so it needs no stress. In such cases, emphasize the new idea: royal.

Words that Sound Like What They Mean. "Pop," "fizz," and "gulp" are obvious. Some are more subtle: "smashed," "vast," "in haste," "implore," "gleamed." These words usually require special emphasis. The author (or translator) has chosen them carefully to convey the desired meaning. Let them do their work.

Word Value. "Shock" is always a more interesting word than "bean." "Shock" sounds like what it means and immediately conjures up vivid images. "Bean" won't even make your mouth water. Word value is also determined by context. The words "one, two, three . . ." are neutral by themselves, but put in context they intensify: "Three seconds until lift-off! One . . . two . . . !" If, in reading that sentence, "One, two . . ." sounds the same as when followed by "buckle my shoe" you've got work to do. Words are your medium, like a painter's brush or a sculptor's chisel. You must understand the words before you can communicate them. Most words have a dictionary meaning (denotative) and an associational meaning (connotative). "House" and "home" both mean "dwelling," yet they communicate different feelings. Be alert to subtle differences in connotative meanings and express them.

Separating Units of Thought with Pauses. Running too many words together blurs meaning and fails to distinguish ideas. Punctuation does not always indicate clearly what words to group together or where to pause. Identify the units of thought and use your voice to distinguish one from another. The listener depends on you for this organization of ideas. With the letters of Paul, in particular, you must carefully identify individual ideas and share them one at a time.

Scripture in this book is set up in sense lines—one complete idea per line of text. Typically, there will be at least a slight pause at the end of each line. But good reading will require you to look for other needed pauses within individual lines. Moving from one thought unit to another within a paragraph requires shifts in mood and pacing. Don't rush these transitions but honor them with a healthy pause, letting the silence "speak."

Pauses are never "dead" moments. Something is always happening during a pause. Practice will teach you how often and how long to pause. Too many pauses make a reading choppy; too few cause ideas to run into one another. Too long a pause breaks the flow. If pauses are too short, your listeners will be struggling to keep up with you. A substantial pause always follows "A reading from . . ." and both precedes and follows "The word [Gospel] of the Lord."

Ritardando. *Ritardando,* an Italian word, refers to the practice, common in music, of becoming gradually slower as you approach the end of a piece. On the last line of a song you automatically slow down and expand the words. Many readings end this way—with a decreased rate but increased intensity.

Characters. Usually several characters populate the scripture passages you will read. Do your best to distinguish one from another. Be in touch with each character's thoughts, feelings, and motivations, and suggest differences through subtle changes in pitch, pacing, or by subtly expressing each character's emotion. Differentiating between characters is the mark of a fine reader. But don't ever confuse proclamation with stage theatrics. You are suggesting characters, not "becoming" them.

Narrator. The narrator is often the pivotal role of a passage. Timbre, pitch, rate, and energy can make the same words convey very different moods or meaning. Sometimes the narrator is objective: "Jesus took Peter, James and John . . ." (Matthew 17:1; Mark 9:2). But often the narrator has great interest in the events and characters of a story: "And he was transfigured before them and his clothes became dazzlingly white" (Mark 9:2–3). Know the narrator's point of view.

Openings and Closings. First, establish eye contact with the assembly and announce, from memory, "A reading from . . . ." Then take a pause (three full beats!) before starting the reading. The correct pronunciation is "A [uh] reading from . . ." instead of "A [ay] reading . . . ." Do not vary from the prescribed introductory formula. Names of characters are often the first word of a reading. Highlight names so listeners don't miss who the subject is. Pause again (three beats!) at the end of the reading and establish eye contact before announcing (again, from memory) "The word [Gospel] of the Lord." Always pronounce "the" as "thuh" except before words beginning with a vowel as in "'thee' Acts of the Apostles." Your inflection of the last line of the reading should always signal that the reading is about to end. Then, after a pause to establish eye contact with the assembly, add "The word of the Lord." Maintain eye contact while the assembly makes its response.

Follow the custom of your parish, but it is recommended that a substantial period of silence follow each of the readings. Both approach and departure from the ambo should be made with reverence, neither too fast nor too slow.

Eye Contact and Eye Expression. Eye contact is your means of connecting with those to whom you minister. You should look at the assembly during the middle and at the end of every thought or sentence. That means you look down at the beginning, look up in the middle, look down quickly as you approach the end, and then look up again as you finish the sentence. This "down, up, down, up" pattern must not appear mechanical or choppy. Through meaningful "eye expression" you help the listeners enter the story.

Magnify the LORD with me; let us exalt his name together.

Blessed are the poor in spirit, for theirs is the kingdom of heaven.

Pace. The larger the church, the larger the assembly, and the more complex the text, the slower you must read. It's better to be too slow than too fast. Your listeners have not spent time with this reading as you have. They need time to absorb it—to catch your words and comprehend what they mean.

However, too slow can also be deadly. Besides being boring and making every text sound the same, this method robs the material of its natural cadences and makes it impossible to communicate the energy or passion of the author.

You'll read more naturally if you read ideas rather than words, if you share images rather than sentences. Dialogue, because of its need to imitate real conversation, often moves at a faster pace than the rest of the passage.

Using the Microphone. Know your public address system. If it echoes, speak even more slowly than usual (but without losing a natural cadence or the inherent energy of the text). If you hear "popping," you're probably standing too close to the microphone. If you are the first reader, go to the ambo before the start of Mass to adjust the height of the microphone. If you are proclaiming the second reading or Gospel, adjust the microphone position when you reach the ambo.

Gestures and Posture. It is hard to imagine a text that requires the use of gestures. They can be distractions and should be used rarely if ever. Whether you like it or not, your body posture speaks. Make sure it says what you want it to. Don't let your face or body contradict the good news you announce. Remember, lectors are allowed to smile!

Pronunciation. Pronunciation aids are provided in the margin notes (see the key at the end of this introduction). You may also find it helpful to consult the LTP publication, *Pronunciation Guide to the Lectionary*. Various internet pronunciation guides allow you to hear the word spoken aloud. Do a simple search like: "Bible pronunciation guide."

Literary Forms

Each literary form demands a different approach.

Stories. Stories must be "told," not "read." You don't have to memorize them, but you do have to tell them. You are the storyteller. Make the story yours, then share it with your listeners.

Know the story and its context—what precedes and follows it. Know the significance of the events for the characters involved. Understand the chronology of the plot. Identify the climax and employ your best energy there. Use the language. Don't throw away any good words.

Settings give the context in which the action unfolds and usually appears at the beginning of a reading. Don't rush the description.

Characters must be believable. Understand their motivation—why they feel, act, and speak as they do. Characters are often identified by their relationship to another character ("the parents of the one who had gained his sight," says John 9:18). Give stress to those identifying words. Create the characters as distinct individuals, changing the inflection and tone of your voice for each one.

Dialogue reveals characters. What a character says and how are nearly infallible clues to personality. Besides subtly distinguishing one character from another with your voice, learn to let the speakers listen to and answer one another as in real conversation. Bring the dialogue to life and build suspense in the story, revealing one detail at a time.

Epistles. The epistles are simply letters. Know who wrote the letter and who received it. Many biblical resources explain the circumstances around a particular letter. Whether addressed to an individual or to all the faithful of a particular city, each epistle is also addressed to the faithful gathered in your church.

The tone of each letter may vary, but the delivery is always direct. Letters are like conversations between the writer and the person or community addressed.

The purpose or intent of each letter dictates the tone. Very often Paul is the writer. As teacher and spiritual leader, he is motivated by multiple concerns: to instruct, console, encourage, chastise, warn, settle disputes, and more. When reading from one of his letters, be aware of what he's trying to accomplish. Paul is always direct and earnest; even when he

The LORD's word is true; all his works are trustworthy.

exhorts, he never stops loving his spiritual children.

Go slowly in the epistles. It takes time for the assembly to catch the ideas you toss at them. Paul's theology can be tricky, and the style is often a tangle of complex sentences. Many times his mood and purpose change within a single passage. Thinking of Paul's role as teacher, disciplinarian, or "companion on the journey" will help keep you from rushing. Love your listeners and desire their good as much as Paul and the other letter writers do.

Prophetic Writing. The intensity of emotion and degree of urgency required in proclaiming the writing of the prophets make some lectors uncomfortable. But the urgency has to be there.

A pervasive theme in the Old Testament is that we are chosen. With election comes responsibility. Prophets were to remind the Chosen People about those responsibilities—not a popular task. Though not shown in the text, prophetic words are spoken with vocal exclamation points. One must work up courage to tell people what they don't want to hear.

In addition to troubling the comfortable, prophets comforted the troubled. With equal passion, the great seers spoke threat and consolation, indictment and forgiveness. You must do the same for the chosen people you call "parish."

As with the epistles, use resources to learn the situation in which a prophet ministers. Prophets vary. Be attentive to style as well as content. Beware of fast transitions, the instant climaxes, and the frequent lack of conclusions. Often a prophet abruptly stops.

Willingly or reluctantly the prophets were compelled to speak for God. Don't rob them of their intensity. We still need to hear their words.

Poetry. The Old Testament contains much poetry—a marvelously effective and economical form of communication. Rich with imagery and emotions, poetry makes special demands on the proclaimer.

Take time. Poetry is gourmet food, eaten slowly and savored. Go slowly with readings like this passage from Baruch for the Second Sunday of Advent, Year C (Baruch 5:8–9):

> The forests and every fragrant kind of tree
> 　　have overshadowed Israel at God's command;
> for God is leading Israel in joy
> 　　by the light of his glory,
> with his mercy and justice for company.

You need to respond to images by letting yourself "smell" and "feel" as well as "see" the "forests" and "fragrant . . . tree." Word choice in poetry affects meaning more than in any other writing because it affects *sound* and *rhythm.*

Sound and meaning go hand-in-hand in poetry. Even in a language that you don't understand, poetry recited well should touch your emotions.

Rhythm is what distinguishes poetry from prose. It's what makes words sound like music. Compare these two verses: "In times past, God spoke in partial and various ways to our ancestors through the prophets" (Hebrews 1:1), and "For Zion's sake I will not be silent, for Jerusalem's sake I will not be quiet" (Isaiah 62:1). The first line is smooth and flat, but the second has a rhythmic beat flowing through it that makes it exciting.

Repetition abounds in poetry. Yet instead of feeling redundant, repetitions intensify our emotional experience. In Hebrew poetry, *parallelism* is a technique used to repeat, balance, and develop ideas in a poem. For example, this is the first verse of Psalm 19:

> The heavens declare the glory of God;
> 　　the sky proclaims its builder's craft.

Two parallel images express one idea. Since the two thoughts mean the same thing, this is *synonymous parallelism. Antithetic parallelism* uses opposing images to express one idea. Proverbs 15:15 says:

Every day is miserable for the depressed,
but a lighthearted person has a continual feast.

Contrasting ideas make a similar point. Look for these and other forms of parallelism.

A New Opportunity

The third edition of *The Roman Missal*, from which we begin to pray on the First Sunday of Advent, encourages ministers of the word to chant the introduction and conclusion to the readings ("A reading from . . . "; "The word of the Lord."). For those parishes wishing to use these chants, they are demonstrated in audio files that may be accessed either through the QR codes given here (with a smart phone) or through the URL indicated beneath the code.

The first QR code contains the tones for the First Reading in both a male and a female voice.

http://bit.ly/l2mjeG

The second QR code contains the tones for the Second Reading in both a male and a female voice.

http://bit.ly/krwEYy

The third QR code contains the simple tone for the Gospel.

http://bit.ly/iZZvSg

The fourth QR code contains the solemn tone for the Gospel.

http://bit.ly/lwf6Hh

A fuller explanation of this new practice, along with musical notation for the chants, is provided in a downloadable PDF file found at http://www.ltp.org/t-productsupplements.aspx.

Pronunciation Key

bait = bayt	thin = thin
cat = kat	vision = VIZH*n
sang = sang	ship = ship
father = FAH-ther	sir = ser
care = kair	gloat = gloht
paw = paw	cot = kot
jar = jahr	noise = noyz
easy = EE -zee	poison = POY-z*n
her =her	plow = plow
let = let	although = ahl-THOH
queen = kween	church = cherch
delude = deh-LOOD	fun = fun
when = hwen	fur = fer
ice = is	flute = floot
if = if	foot = foot
finesse = fih-NES	

Recommended Works

Find this list of recommended reading in a downloadable PDF file at http://www.ltp.org/t-product supplements.aspx.

1ST SUNDAY OF ADVENT

Lectionary #2

READING I   Isaiah 63:16b–17, 19b; 64:2b–7

Isaiah = ī-ZAY-uh

A reading from the Book of the Prophet Isaiah

You, LORD, are our **father**,
    our **redeemer** you are named **forever**.
Why do you let us **wander**, O LORD, from your **ways**,
    and harden our **hearts** so that we fear you **not**?
Return for the sake of your **servants**,
    the tribes of your **heritage**.
Oh, that you would **rend** the heavens and come **down**,
    with the mountains **quaking** before you,
while you wrought **awesome** deeds we could not **hope** for,
    such as they had not **heard** of from of **old**.
No **ear** has ever **heard**, no **eye** ever **seen**, any God but **you**
    doing such deeds for those who **wait** for him.
Would that you might **meet** us doing **right**,
    that we were **mindful** of you in our **ways**!
Behold, you are **angry**, and we are **sinful**;
    all of us have become like **unclean** people,
    all our good **deeds** are like polluted **rags**;
we have all **withered** like leaves,
    and our **guilt** carries us away like the **wind**.

Ask the question with pained remorse.
It's not an accusation against God, but a
woeful self-recrimination: "Why did you
let us *do* this?"!
Express your own longing for God's
coming to set things right in your life.
This potent poetry should be read with
the passion and sincerity of a runaway
pleading to come home again.

The text alternates between expressions
of God's greatness ("no ear has
heard . . .") and expressions of guilt
before God who is justifiably angry.
Honest admission of sin.

Aware that "we've made our own beds"!
Requires extra sensitivity to imagery and
to the *sound* of words.

READING I — The turning of the seasons brings us back to Advent with its call to step back, examine, and start again. Isaiah reminds us that we are people who lose our shape and need the "potter's" hands to refashion us into the people we are called to be. Advent heralds that message perfectly because, while it joyfully remembers the first coming of Christ, it also reminds us to prepare for his Second Coming, making Advent both a time of repentance and of joyful anticipation.

Honesty and longing fill Isaiah's text, which opens with a penitent's hushed voice making a humble statement of faith. Israel's infidelity has led them into exile. Aware of their sinfulness, they plead with God to "return" to them. In the very midst of their sinfulness, Israel pleads, convinced that God is truly a "father" who loves even his unfaithful children unconditionally.

The words "rend," "quaking," and "awesome deeds" are part of an earnest prayer that invites God to call the errant people to account. Two emotions prevail: awe at God's greatness, and remorse and guilt that they have become "like polluted rags." Some modern hymnals change the classic lines "Amazing Grace how sweet the sound that saved a wretch like me," to read, ". . . that saved *and set me free* . . . ." But scripture doesn't shy from the occasional acknowledgment of wretchedness before God. Today that sentiment rings out in lines like "We have all withered . . . our guilt carries us away . . . you have hidden your face" and delivered us up "to our guilt."

"Yet . . ." becomes a powerful declaration of God's love. The people aren't groveling but claiming their birthright: "you are our *father*" gives us the right to

There is **none** who calls upon your **name**,
who **rouses** himself to **cling** to you;
for you have **hidden** your **face** from us
and have delivered us up to our **guilt**.
Yet, O LORD, you are our **father**;
we are the **clay** and you the **potter**:
we are **all** the work of your **hands**.

This is a sudden reversal. Claim the love of a merciful parent.

READING II   1 Corinthians 1:3–9

A reading from the first Letter of Saint Paul to the Corinthians

Corinthians = kohr-IN-thee-uhnz

Deliver the greeting from memory, making clear eye contact.

Brothers and sisters:
Grace to you and **peace** from God our Father
and the Lord Jesus **Christ**.

Sustain a joyful tone even as you move slowly through the distinct ideas: Paul thanks God because of the graces God has given them, namely gifts of discourse and knowledge; his witness to Christ has been so confirmed among them that now they lack no spiritual gift as they wait for the Lord's return.

I give **thanks** to my God **always** on your account
for the **grace** of God **bestowed** on you in Christ **Jesus**,
that in **him** you were enriched in **every** way,
with all **discourse** and all **knowledge**,
as the testimony to Christ was **confirmed** among you,
so that you are not **lacking** in any spiritual **gift**
as you wait for the **revelation** of our Lord Jesus **Christ**.

This is a comforting promise.

He will keep you **firm** to the **end**,
irreproachable on the day of our Lord Jesus **Christ**.
God is **faithful**,

You are reading climaxes here. Proclaim with tenderness.

and by **him** you were called to **fellowship** with his **Son**,
Jesus **Christ** our **Lord**.

---

expect a child's due from a loving parent—the guidance and protection that come from a parent's nurturing hands.

READING II Scripture never lets us become complacent. No chapter, book, or even Testament captures the full message. Anytime you think you've heard it all, you flip a page and discover there's a whole lot more to hear. Isaiah's text proclaimed a God who saved "a wretch like me," but a very different mood dominates Paul's text. Here we rejoice over "the grace of God bestowed on [us]," we

marvel that we are "not lacking in any spiritual gift," for Christ strengthens us to be "irreproachable on the day of our Lord Jesus Christ." That's obvious good news, especially welcome on a day when the Gospel warns: "Be watchful! Be alert!" The interplay of today's readings—Paul contrasting with Isaiah and the Gospel—establishes the paradox of comfort and threat, darkness and light, that defines the heart of Advent.

The first line is a formal salutation, but immediately Paul becomes personal and emotional. A long sentence comprised

of seven clauses, each expressing a distinct idea, communicates his affection for the people, so go slow and look right at the assembly, giving thanks for each of them. When he speaks of the "testimony to Christ [that] was confirmed among you," it's his own preaching he's referring to. He planted the seeds and they've taken root.

This season of joy leads us on a journey of conversion, so it's fitting that we hear God "will keep [us] firm to the end" (that is, the Day of Judgment). You must believe this before you proclaim it, so recall your own experiences of God's

GOSPEL   Mark 13:33–37

A reading from the holy Gospel according to Mark

Jesus said to his **disciples**:
"Be **watchful**! Be **alert**!
You do not **know** when the time will **come**.
It is like a man traveling **abroad**.
He **leaves** home and places his **servants** in charge,
    each with his own **work**,
  and orders the **gatekeeper** to be on the **watch**.
Watch, therefore,
  you do not **know** when the lord of the house is **coming**,
  whether in the **evening**, or at **midnight**,
    or at **cockcrow**, or in the **morning**.
May he not come **suddenly** and find you **sleeping**.
What I say to **you**, I say to **all**: '**Watch**!' "

Address the "disciples" in your pews.

This is a sobering, even frightening, thought.

The traveler is diligent about getting his house in order.

Don't rush the words here; each creates a different mood and together they remind us that all our expectations are unfounded.
Jesus' warning is motivated by love.

---

faithfulness and let those memories fuel your conviction.

GOSPEL   Advent's early weeks focus on Christ's Second Coming, while the later weeks focus on his birth at Bethlehem. Today, it's Jesus' universal call for watchfulness, punctuated by a brief parable, that opens the Advent season. If the tone seems a bit terrifying, it's meant to be: "You do not know when the time will come." The new liturgical year begins as the last one ended—with a call to readiness and vigilance! Mark, terse and direct, is our primary evangelist this year. This text, so tinged with urgency and drama, is closely connected with Mark's passion narrative: the shadow of the cross falls constantly across Jesus' path.

Deliver the brief parable in a serious tone. The "servants" are placed in charge, but the task of watchfulness is given to the gatekeeper. Each of us is gatekeeper to the home of our souls, so we must be vigilant for we know not the day of the Lord's coming. Gradually increase your energy from "Watch, therefore . . ." to the parable's end, stressing the danger of being unprepared. The divisions of the night ("evening, midnight, cockcrow, morning") help emphasize the unexpected nature of the master's arrival. The urgency is greatest in the final exhortation. Jesus knows we are prone to sleep and likely to be caught off guard. So he warns. Jesus' first followers expected his return in their lifetime. They were wrong. Our generation seems certain he won't return soon. What if we, too, are wrong? Surely, each day draws us closer to the master's return.

2ND SUNDAY OF ADVENT

Lectionary #5

READING I Isaiah 40:1–5, 9–11

Isaiah = ī-ZAY-uh.
Remember, in poetry, sound and meaning are often synonymous.

"Tenderly" sets the tone. God is the speaker, consoling the people after their time of trial.

With hushed intensity, convince us!

The "voice" is Isaiah. Don't rush, but avoid a too-slow, labored delivery. Such energetic lines demand a brisk delivery. These are images, not literal predictions so the joyful *sound* you make is more important than the individual words you use to make it.
Our "rugged" and "rough" hearts will be transformed.

Believe it, you say, "for the mouth of the *Lord* has spoken."

Again, it's God's voice we hear. Now, "Zion" and "Jerusalem" are your assembly.

A reading from the Book of the Prophet Isaiah

Comfort, give **comfort** to my people,
  says your God.
Speak **tenderly** to Jerusalem, and **proclaim** to her
  that her **service** is at an **end**,
  her **guilt** is **expiated**;
indeed, she has **received** from the hand of the LORD
  double for all her sins.

  A **voice** cries out:
In the desert **prepare** the way of the LORD!
  Make **straight** in the **wasteland** a **highway** for our **God**!
Every **valley** shall be filled **in**,
  every **mountain** and **hill** shall be made **low**;
the **rugged** land shall be made a **plain**,
  the **rough** country, a broad **valley**.
Then the **glory** of the LORD shall be **revealed**,
  and all **people** shall see it **together**;
  for the **mouth** of the LORD has **spoken**.

Go up on to a high **mountain**,
  Zion, **herald** of glad **tidings**;
cry out at the top of your **voice**,
  Jerusalem, herald of **good news**!

READING I Here is a marvelous example of Isaiah's poetry. In poetry, sound and meaning are bonded. Meaning is communicated by the *sound* of the words when spoken (joyful, consoling, angry, rousing). The text itself tells you how to read: "O comfort my people . . . Speak tenderly . . . ."

Peter's warnings in today's Second Reading about fiery destruction might overwhelm were they not balanced by the tenderness of this passage. Isaiah was announcing the end of Israel's captivity. An era of redemption was about to dawn, so Isaiah's images are of newness and fresh starts. That calls for a tone of joy and consolation.

From the tenderness of the first paragraph, build to a muted intensity in the "voice" (Isaiah himself) that "cries out . . . prepare the way." Marvel, even as you speak, that these events will occur. These are poetic images and not literal prophecies of what will happen to mountains, but of what will happen to human hearts.

Today's Gospel echoes these words and applies them to the Baptist; speak briskly, but without rushing. Isaiah insists you "cry out at the top of your voice." Do that with *intensity* rather than volume, *belief* rather than decibels. Only if you truly believe God renews hearts can you become a "herald of glad tidings."

Isaiah interweaves images of strength with images of tenderness: God's "strong arm" also "gathers the lambs"; God's "reward" and "recompense" (stressed

Images of power and divine tenderness blend

Emphasize the nouns, not the prepositions.

This is a much cherished image which the New Testament applies to Christ, the Good Shepherd; it blends tenderness and strength!

Fear **not** to cry out
　　and say to the cities of **Judah**:
　　Here is your **God**!
Here comes with **power**
　　the Lord **God**,
　　who **rules** by his strong **arm**;
here is his **reward** with him,
　　his **recompense** before him.
Like a **shepherd** he feeds his **flock**;
　　in his **arms** he gathers the **lambs**,
carrying them in his **bosom**,
　　and leading the **ewes** with **care**.

READING II　2 Peter 3:8–14

A reading from the second Letter of Saint Peter

Establish eye contact with the "beloved."
By stretching "years" and "thousand," your use of these words will suggest the length of time described.

Speak like a kind teacher here.

Begin slowly, then increase rate and volume.

Do not **ignore** this one **fact**, beloved,
　　that with the **Lord** one **day** is like a thousand **years**
　　and a **thousand** years like one **day**.
The Lord does not **delay** his promise, as **some** regard "delay,"
　　but he is **patient** with you,
　　not wishing that **any** should perish
　　but that **all** should come to **repentance**.
But the **day** of the Lord will come like a **thief**,
　　and then the heavens will pass **away** with a mighty **roar**
　　and the **elements** will be dissolved by **fire**,
　　and the **earth** and everything **done** on it will be found **out**.

instead of prepositions "with" and "before") is the comfort of "his bosom." Together, these images become the fabric of consolation and vibrant hope Isaiah's Lord wants to wrap around us.

READING II　A letter is a personal and direct form of communication requiring a personal and direct tone. Certainly a passage addressed to one who is "beloved" requires increased eye contact and a tone suggesting intimacy with

those addressed. Peter is addressing the belief that Christ's return in glory has been delayed, reasoning that what looks like "delay" is instead God's generous patience giving us time to repent, lest we "perish."

But despite that patience, the "day of the Lord will come" and it will be a great and terrible day. Holding back on the cataclysmic imagery would surely defeat the writer's (and the Lectionary's!) purpose.

We've already been reassured of God's love, but now the focus shifts to the flip side of the coin. Love requires that we not shield people from this other truth: behavior has consequences; we have time to repent, but the time is limited. Eventually, everything on the earth will dissolve, our layers of cover-ups will be removed, and everything we have done "will be found out." That's a message our assemblies are meant to hear and you mustn't dilute it.

Imagine a question mark after "ought you to be"; then answer the question with the rest of the sentence.

Since everything is to be **dissolved** in this way,
  what sort of **persons** ought you to **be**,
    conducting yourselves in **holiness** and **devotion**,
    waiting for and **hastening** the coming of the day of **God**,
    because of which the **heavens** will be dissolved in **flames**
    and the **elements** melted by **fire**.

Keep the tone upbeat and hope-filled.

But according to his **promise**
  we await **new** heavens and a new **earth**
  in which **righteousness** dwells.

"Be eager" is encouragement to work and struggle to be found ready.

Therefore, beloved, since you **await** these things,
  be **eager** to be found without **spot** or **blemish** before him,
    at **peace**.

GOSPEL   Mark 1:1–8

A reading from the holy Gospel according to Mark

The **beginning** of the **gospel** of Jesus **Christ** the Son of **God**.

Here begins Mark's account of the Gospel—of "*good* news." Make sure your tone doesn't contradict your words. Just because this was heard in the First Reading doesn't mean you can rush. Quote Isaiah with a slow, deliberate delivery.

As it is written in **Isaiah** the **prophet**:
  *Behold, I am sending my **messenger** ahead of you;*
    *he will **prepare** your way.*
  *A **voice** of one crying out in the **desert**:*
    *"Prepare the way of the **Lord**,*
      *make **straight** his paths."*
John the **Baptist** appeared in the **desert**

Pause briefly after "desert," then increase the intensity.

  proclaiming a baptism of **repentance** for the forgiveness of **sins**.

The author's message doesn't stop with warning, but continues by considering, "what sort of persons *ought* you to be." We must be holy and devout, not only anticipating "the day of God" but trying to hasten it. The image of fiery destruction is intended to be unsettling. But comfort retakes the stage as you explain *why* everything must melt in flames: so that

new heavens and a new earth can replace the old! Here the tone is joyful, as if watching that new world, like a baby, being born.

GOSPEL   Mark's Gospel account begins, not in a manger but in the desert where John lives out Isaiah's centuries-old prophecy of the messenger who is sent to "prepare the way of the Lord." The Second Sunday of Advent always

focuses on John the Baptist, and for good reason. In Matthew, Jesus says that no man born of woman is greater than John the Baptist.

When you quote Isaiah, know that you are identifying Isaiah's "messenger" with John the Baptizer. In John, Old and New Testaments meet. So speak Isaiah's prophecy with excitement and joy, as if alerting a crowd to a long awaited hero's arrival.

Judean = <u>joo</u>-DEE-un
Jerusalem = juh-R<u>OO</u>-suh-lem

Narrate this section with joyful amazement.

Despite these oddities, people eagerly came to him.

Proclaim in John's voice. Don't rush.

Contrast "water" (not much) with "the Holy Spirit" (everything!).

People of the **whole** Judean countryside
　　and all the inhabitants of **Jerusalem**
　　were going **out** to him
　　and were being **baptized** by him in the Jordan **River**
　　as they acknowledged their **sins**.
John was clothed in **camel's** hair,
　　with a leather **belt** around his waist.
He fed on **locusts** and wild **honey**.
And **this** is what he **proclaimed**:
　　"One **mightier** than I is coming **after** me.
I am not **worthy** to stoop and **loosen** the **thongs** of his **sandals**.
I have baptized you with **water**;
　　he will baptize you with the Holy **Spirit**."

John's preaching and his "baptism of repentance" stirred the imagination of the people to the point that they dared to hope that the Messiah was finally among them. Describe with humble awe the success of this strange man's ministry: "The *whole* Judean countryside . . . *all* the inhabitants . . . acknowledged their sins!" Even the fascination with his clothing and odd diet accentuates his success,

for your tone insinuates: "How could such a man attract such crowds?"

Of course, Mark uses John to cast light on Jesus. When John speaks, he is insistent, as if to convince the adoring crowds that he is *not* who they think he is. John need not be the raving lunatic of some biblical films; instead give his voice a humble, self-abasing quality as he asserts his unworthiness to "untie his sandal straps." The reading climaxes as John

gives the first public witness to Jesus: I have given you a glass of water, he says, but he will serve you the wine of the Spirit!

IMMACULATE CONCEPTION

Lectionary #689

READING I   Genesis 3:9–15, 20

A reading from the Book of Genesis

After the man, **Adam**, had **eaten** of the **tree**,
  the LORD God **called** to the man and **asked** him,
    "Where **are** you?"
He answered, "I **heard** you in the **garden**;
  but I was **afraid**, because I was **naked**,
  so I **hid** myself."
Then he asked, "Who **told** you that you were naked?
You have **eaten**, then,
  from the **tree** of which I had **forbidden** you to eat!"
The man **replied**, "The **woman** whom **you** put here with me—
  she **gave** me fruit from the tree, and so I **ate** it."
The LORD God then asked the **woman**,
  "Why did you **do** such a thing?"
The woman **answered**, "The **serpent tricked** me into it,
    so I **ate** it."

Then the LORD God said to the **serpent**:
  "Because you have **done** this, you shall be **banned**
    from all the **animals**
    and from all the wild **creatures**;
  on your **belly** shall you **crawl**,
    and **dirt** shall you eat
    all the **days** of your **life**.

Genesis = JEN-uh-sis

Don't let the familiarity of this "classic" story rob your reading of nuance or reduce it to caricature.

The narrator's tone suggests the wrongness of Adam's deed even as you begin.

God is unaware of any transgression, so God's first question is objective.

Caught "in the act," and needing to cover up, Adam responds. Is he panicked, coolly controlled, or remorseful?

Adam's reference to his nakedness alerts God to his misdeed, so stress it.

Contrast the defensive responses of the Man and Woman: who is more assertive, more defensive? Does one exhibit remorse or shame, is one more afraid?

God's rebuke of the serpent contrasts in tone with comments to Adam and Eve: God is not parental here—a judgment is handed down, uncompromising and severe.

READING I   On this solemnity honoring Mary, we re-encounter our first parents. Why? Because in Mary we recognize God's mercy; we see the God of second chances restoring creation to balance and right order. Mary is the one through whom God's grace begins the work of salvation. Unlike our first mother, Eve, Mary is in harmony with the divine will. She undoes the consequences of Adam and Eve's original disobedience. Through her "yes", she initiates a stunning reversal: from the new *Eve* comes the new and eternal Adam, Jesus the Christ. In the new world Christ has made possible, our Advent is always a pilgrimage from the rebellion of Adam and Eve to the obedience of Mary. In your delivery, let us recognize ourselves in our first parents.

Notice the profound insight into the origin of sin: it was born the moment man and woman desired their own will over the will of God. Its effects are immediate: the creatures hide from God in shame and soon turn on each other. Adam and Eve should not sound like children hiding fault from a stern parent. They are adults who know-ingly rebelled and brought upon them-selves and all humans serious penalties.

In "I will put enmity . . ." we find the Bible's earliest assurance that the Creator will deliver humanity from sin's conse-quences by providing, eventually, an off-spring who will strike down the serpent that represents sin. The verse is often referred to as the *protevangelium*, or "the first Gospel." On this great solemnity, we identify Mary with "the woman" and Christ with her "offspring." Take time with this section and reveal the contrast between the snake's futile strikes at "his heel" and

These lines are central to today's solemnity.

Slowly contrast the snake's *futile* strikes at "his heel" with the offspring's *damaging* blows to the serpent's "head."

Pause, then read slowly. A reminder that Eve is mother of us all.

I will put **enmity** between you and the **woman**,
  and between **your** offspring and **hers**;
he will strike at your **head**,
  while **you** strike at his **heel**."

The man called his wife **Eve**,
  because she became the **mother** of **all** the **living**.

READING II Ephesians 1:3–6, 11–12

Ephesians = ee-FEE-zhuhnz

A reading from the Letter of Saint Paul to the Ephesians

Brothers and **sisters**:

Don't just talk about "blessing" God, do it!

Blessed be the **God** and **Father** of our **Lord** Jesus **Christ**,
  who has **blessed** us in Christ
  with every spiritual **blessing** in the **heavens**,
    as he **chose** us in him, before the **foundation** of the world,
    to be **holy** and without **blemish** before him.

Help the listeners understand what it is they are to be grateful for.

Take a slight pause after the phrase so listeners understand what is God's motivation.

In **love** he destined us for **adoption** to himself
    through Jesus **Christ**,
  in accord with the **favor** of his **will**,
  for the **praise** of the **glory** of his **grace**
  that he **granted** us in the **beloved**.

**"In him" means in Christ.
"The One" refers to God the Father.**

In **him** we were also **chosen**,
  destined in accord with the **purpose** of the One
  who **accomplishes** all things according to the intention
    of his **will**,
  so that we might **exist** for the praise of his **glory**,
  we who **first hoped** in Christ.

Ritardando (that is, gradually slowing to the end) is called for here.**

---

the offspring's damaging blows to the serpent's "head." The ending establishes Eve as a sign of hope, not loss, for she becomes "mother of all the living," as Mary is Mother of all who live in Christ.

READING II Wars rage, marriages end, children suffer abuse, illness takes loved ones, and natural disasters abruptly end human lives. And yet, a classic Christian hymn asks boldly: "How can I keep from singing?" This Pauline text is also a hymn, and it dares to sing of God's goodness and to proclaim God's wonderful

deeds. Exuberant joy explodes in the rhythmic opening sentence. Like the First Reading, Paul's focus is on beginnings, but with a new perspective: now it's not original sin we ponder, but original blessing, God's loving initiative to make us, and call us, and claim us as daughters and sons.

In various forms, the expression "in Christ" is repeated here and throughout Ephesians: "in him," "before him," "in the beloved." The cumulative effect of these phrases is to assert our oneness under the leadership of Christ. Pay special attention to these expressions, giving extra time

when you speak them so they can make their impact.

God's plan of salvation has been accomplished in us who believe and have accepted "adoption" through Christ Jesus. And adoption means we become heirs of a rich inheritance—the opportunity to live our lives as a song of praise to the God who loves us.

On this solemnity of Mary who was chosen from all time to be the immaculate vehicle of God's will, words and phrases like "chose," "before the foundation of the world," "holy and without blemish," and

A reading from the holy Gospel according to Luke

The angel **Gabriel** was sent from **God**
  to a town of **Galilee** called **Nazareth**,
  to a **virgin** betrothed to a man named **Joseph**,
  of the house of **David**,
  and the virgin's name was **Mary**.
And **coming** to her, he said,
  "**Hail**, full of **grace**! The **Lord** is with you."
But she was greatly **troubled** at what was said
  and **pondered** what sort of greeting this might be.
Then the angel **said** to her,
  "Do not be **afraid**, Mary,
  for you have found **favor** with God.
Behold, you will **conceive** in your womb and bear a **son**,
  and you shall name him **Jesus**.
He will be **great** and will be called **Son** of the Most **High**,
  and the Lord God will give him the **throne** of **David**
    his **father**,
  and he will **rule** over the house of Jacob **forever**,
  and of his **Kingdom** there will be **no end**."
But **Mary** said to the **angel**,
  "How can this **be**,
  since I have no relations with a **man**?"
And the angel said to her in **reply**,
  "The Holy **Spirit** will come upon you,
  and the power of the Most **High** will **overshadow** you.
Therefore the **child** to be born
  will be called **holy**, the **Son** of God.

There's a lot to say here, and it's all important, so careful attention to pacing and pauses is essential.

Lift out Mary's name as you proclaim.

Mary's distress should be heard in the narration that speaks of it.

The angel's voice can be energetic and authoritative without being melodramatic. Don't rush the words "Do not be afraid."

Lift out the "royal" language that accentuates the greatness of the "son."

Note that Mary is asking "how"—not "if"—it will happen.

Proclaim solemnly, yet joyfully.

"destined" are especially significant and require extra emphasis. The repeated references to Christ, which require repeated stress, remind us that in the beginning when things went wrong, there also existed the One who would make them right again.

The second paragraph reprises the first. Read slower here, but with the awareness that among the "chosen" is each of us, and also Mary, who truly was the first to hope in Christ and who, therefore, will forever stand as the model of

what it means to be a disciple and what it means to be Church.

GOSPEL The meaning of this solemnity is much misunderstood, and the selection of this Gospel is the likely reason. Many confuse Mary's conception without the stain of original sin with her own virginal conception of Jesus. With one loaded sentence you set the scene for this poignant story of huge consequence: a divine messenger "from God" comes to a nowhere town (Nazareth: what good can come from there?) to a virgin (the

makings of a miracle?) betrothed to Joseph, of the house of David (the *royal* house). A lot to say in one sentence, and all of it is important. After naming Gabriel, Nazareth, Joseph, and David, speak of "Mary" with extra tenderness, so her name isn't lost among the others.

The angel greets Mary with unparalleled salutations. But rather than flatter, they trouble and puzzle her. The uniqueness of this moment is not lost on Mary and its familiarity should not cause it to be lost on your assembly. God is doing something incredibly new, revolutionary, shocking!

News of Elizabeth is meant to reassure; speak of it with confidence and joy.

Even if spoken softly, Mary's words convey strength and amazing boldness

Pause, then announce the angel's departure.

And behold, **Elizabeth**, your relative,
   has **also** conceived a son in her old **age**,
   and this is the **sixth** month for her who was called **barren**;
   for **nothing** will be **impossible** for **God**."
Mary said, "**Behold**, I am the **handmaid** of the **Lord**.
May it be **done** to me according to your **word**."
Then the angel **departed** from her.

And it sets off tremors in Mary's heart. "Greatly troubled," she ponders the meaning of the greeting. Her distress should color the narration that speaks of it.

"Do not be afraid" is a formula that often precedes an announcement of divine intervention, but the angel's words seem to generate more puzzlement than reassurance. The rest of the angel's message is filled with royal, dynastic imagery—"throne . . . rule . . . house of Jacob . . . Kingdom"—reinforcing his initial assertion of the great dignity of Mary's

child. But Mary's response to all this reveals her inner turmoil.

The tone of Mary's question is difficult to guess. But we have a clue in the angel's response: If Mary had doubted like Zechariah, she too might have been struck dumb. Her question seems to ask, not "if" but "how" the angel's declaration will be achieved. Gabriel reassures by asserting God's, not Mary's, role in the conception, and by offering Elizabeth's pregnancy as a pledge that God can accomplish what is promised. Take time with these references to divine intervention and to Elizabeth's

conception, giving them your most careful and solemn, yet tender reading.

Mary's "fiat" ("May it be done"), whether whispered or strongly confident, is central to this solemnity and season, for it reminds us of the posture to which every disciple is called. In surrendering to God's will, Mary makes possible the Incarnation. Our own "yes" also makes God present in the world.

Lectionary #8

Isaiah = Ī-zay-uh

In Luke's Gospel account, Jesus speaks these words in the Nazareth synagogue at the start of his public ministry. Speak humbly, but with growing energy and joy.

Don't make this a "laundry list": visualize each group to whom the prophet (you!) announces good news.

Pause, perhaps envisioning all you've announced coming true, then launch into the expression of joy that comprises the second half of the reading.

The clothing images are metaphors of the kind of life the Messiah will bring, but the prophet experiences it in the present—with energetic joy.

The fruitfulness of the earth is compared to the fruitfulness of God's mercy.

A reading from the Book of the Prophet Isaiah

The **spirit** of the Lord GOD is upon me,
  because the LORD has **anointed** me;
he has **sent** me to bring glad **tidings** to the **poor**,
  to **heal** the **brokenhearted**,
to proclaim **liberty** to the **captives**
  and **release** to the **prisoners**,
to announce a year of **favor** from the LORD
  and a day of **vindication** by our **God**.

I rejoice **heartily** in the LORD,
  in my **God** is the joy of my **soul**;
for he has **clothed** me with a robe of **salvation**
  and **wrapped** me in a mantle of **justice**,
like a **bridegroom** adorned with a **diadem**,
  like a **bride** bedecked with her **jewels**.
As the **earth** brings forth its **plants**,
  and a **garden** makes its **growth** spring up,
so will the Lord GOD make **justice** and **praise**
  spring **up** before all the **nations**.

READING I Spoken by the prophet to announce the restoration of Zion following her exile in Babylon, today's prophecy is filled with hope and joyous anticipation. Unfortunately, verses 2 to 9, which give *details* about what God will accomplish, are left out of our passage.

But the text resounds with good news, and appropriately so on this Gaudete (Rejoice!) Sunday. In the middle of Advent, we pause to rejoice "heartily" because the marvelous work of salvation and restoration that God accomplished for Israel, God also works in our own lives. Therefore, the first eight lines of the text can tell the "poor" and "brokenhearted" in your assembly that God *still* accomplishes marvelous deeds. Speak as the prophet when you assert "the spirit of the Lord God is upon me," but speak humbly, as if you've been shaken to your core by the experience. The prophet knows his selection was the result not of his own worthiness but of God's mercy, the same mercy God extends through *you* to all who listen.

Take the time to understand the depth of joy the prophet heralds. Your sincerity and joy should persuade anyone in the assembly who isn't convinced that God *can* be this generous. Few things are more pathetic than a reader who says "I rejoice" with a lifeless, glum expression! Instead, communicate nuptial joy, and exploit the rich imagery of "diadems," jewels, and new life springing from a fertile earth. It's all beautiful and glowing and too wonderful to hold in. So don't.

READING II Notice when and how Paul says we should rejoice: "always . . . without ceasing . . . in all circumstances." Not just in good times or

short reading = slow reading
Thessalonians = thes-uh-LOH-nee-unz

**Don't rush. Recall the times it's difficult
to follow these instructions.**

**Contrast the negative and positive
admonitions.**

**There is a shift in the mood here. Make
eye contact and speak this as a prayer.**

**First place your own trust in God, then
you can (boldly!) ask us to do the same.**

**John is a most significant character in
salvation history. Give him his due.**

Stress the word "testify."

READING II 1 Thessalonians 5:16–24

A reading from the first Letter of Saint Paul to the Thessalonians

Brothers and sisters:
Rejoice always. Pray without **ceasing.**
In **all** circumstances give **thanks,**
     for this is the will of **God** for you in Christ **Jesus.**
Do not **quench** the Spirit.
Do not **despise** prophetic utterances.
Test everything; retain what is **good.**
Refrain from every kind of **evil.**

May the God of **peace** make you perfectly **holy**
     and may you **entirely, spirit, soul** and **body,**
     be preserved **blameless** for the coming of our **Lord** Jesus **Christ.**
The one who **calls** you is **faithful,**
     and he will also **accomplish** it.

GOSPEL John 1:6–8, 19–28

A reading from the holy Gospel according to John

A man named **John** was sent from God.
He came for **testimony,** to testify to the **light,**
     so that all might **believe** through him.
He was not the light,
     but came to **testify** to the light.

success, but always. Paul doesn't ask us to wear blinders or to ignore life's trials. Instead, he expects us to keep our eyes wide open and rejoice anyway. He dares (and so must you) to ask that we rejoice even if a loved one has recently died, to give thanks even if we are unemployed, to keep praying even as we dine on the bitter dish of failure. Paul's life was marked by the kind of trials that could challenge anyone's faith. Yet he clung to his and boldly asks we do the same. Perhaps, asking the near impossible is best done in a hushed and humble voice.

Deliver Paul's negative commands ("Do not quench . . . despise") with a sense of urgency, as if you sense imminent danger that your hearers might do precisely what you're asking them to avoid. The positive imperatives ("Test . . . retain . . . refrain") should flow from your awareness of the importance of testing everything and avoiding anything that can distract us from the ways of God.

Paul now trades in his teacher's hat for that of a pastor. Again he's asking the impossible, only now of God, who is to make us "perfectly holy." You have two

challenges: speak with great compassion, but with conviction that God can accomplish these things, even in us. The final sentence justifies our hope. Why can you ask for the impossible? Because the One who calls us "is faithful . . . [and] will accomplish it."

GOSPEL **Twice in as many weeks John stands as a symbol of the season we celebrate. An ascetic who shunned the fineries of the world, John emerges from the desert and stands in stark contrast to the garish excesses that**

Levites = LEE-vits.

Stress only the first "admitted."

Let the priests' frustration build as they question him.

Elijah = ee-LĪ-juh

His self-identification requires strength and conviction.

Thinking they've caught him in a trap.

There is strength in John's voice, and no regret. Speak slowly, for there is much important matter here.

Bethany = BETH-uh-nee

And **this** is the testimony of John.
When the Jews from Jerusalem sent **priests** and **Levites** to him
to ask him, "Who **are** you?"
he **admitted** and did not **deny** it,
but admitted, "I am **not** the **Christ**."
So they **asked** him,
"What **are** you then? Are you **Elijah**?"
And he said, "I am **not**."
"Are you the **Prophet**?"
He answered, "**No**."
So they said to him,
"Who **are** you, so we can give an **answer** to those who **sent** us?
What do you have to **say** for yourself?"
He said:
"I am *the **voice** of one crying out in the **desert**,
'Make **straight** the way of the LORD,'*
as Isaiah the **prophet** said."
Some **Pharisees** were also sent.
They asked him,
"Why then do you **baptize**
if you are not the **Christ** or **Elijah** or the **Prophet**?"
John **answered** them,
"**I** baptize with **water**;
but there is one **among** you whom you do not **recognize**,
the one who is coming **after** me,
whose **sandal** strap I am not worthy to **untie**."
This happened in **Bethany** across the **Jordan**,
where John was **baptizing**.

each year, during this holy time, compete for our attention. Initially, John is mistaken for the messiah—he who came to testify to the light, is mistaken for it! Not unlike the way the superficial secular trappings of Advent time (lights, parties, shopping) are often mistaken for the essence of this preparatory season.

John's self-identification announces the true purpose of Advent—not frenzied activity, but making "straight the way of the Lord," preparing minds and hearts for the Lord who came in history and will come again in judgment, and whose return

will render meaningless all those things that distract us from him. John's voice is as needed today as it was two thousand years ago, for there is still "one among [us] whom [we] do not recognize."

Focus on the leaders' efforts to identify the Baptist, who was as mystifying as he was mesmerizing. As the priests attempt to solve the riddle named John, their frustration and curiosity mount with each question. John begins with denials: he is not the light, the Messiah, Elijah, nor the prophet. Unsatisfied, the priests ask adamantly: "Who are you?" But while the

priests become increasingly frustrated, John remains strong and unemotional.

John's feelings finally emerge when he tells who he is—a witness, a voice heralding the need to prepare for one who will be far greater than himself. John recognizes the magnitude of this responsibility, and it should be evident in your voice. But the leaders, missing or ignoring his point, keep questioning with barely concealed hostility. Minimizing his own ministry, he urges them to look about and recognize the disguised God who walks among them.

4TH SUNDAY OF ADVENT

Lectionary #11

READING I   2 Samuel 7:1–5, 8b–12, 14a, 16

A reading from the second Book of Samuel

Speak with David's confident attitude.	When King **David** was settled in his **palace**,
	     and the LORD had given him **rest** from his **enemies**
	          on every **side**,
	     he said to **Nathan** the prophet,

He's genuinely distressed by the imbalance.	"Here **I** am living in a house of **cedar**, while the ark of **God** dwells in a **tent**!"

Nathan sincerely approves the plan.	Nathan **answered** the king,
	     "**Go**, do **whatever** you have in mind,
	     for the **LORD** is with you."

The narration signals God's rejection of the plan.	But that **night** the LORD spoke to **Nathan** and said:
	     "**Go**, tell my servant **David**, 'Thus says the **LORD**:
	     Should you build **me** a house to dwell in?

There is no anger or reproach here. Instead, the tone of a teacher with one more lesson to impart.	" 'It was **I** who took you from the pasture
	     and from the care of the **flock**
	     to be **commander** of my people Israel.
	I have **been** with you **wherever** you went,
	     and I have destroyed all your **enemies** before you.

Now we have what God *will* do—with love for this impetuous king.	And I will make you **famous** like the **great** ones of the earth.
	I will fix a **place** for my people **Israel**;
	     I will **plant** them so that they may **dwell** in their place
	          without further **disturbance**.

Before Israel had kings, "judges" were charismatic leaders God raised up in times of peril for the nation.	Neither shall the **wicked** continue to **afflict** them as they did
	          of **old**,
	     since the time I first appointed **judges** over my people Israel.

READING I Because the compilers of the Lectionary establish an intentional link between the First Reading and the Gospel, it is always best to read the Gospel first. In the Gospel, Gabriel tells Mary she has found favor with God who, through her, will bring forth a ruler to reign from David's throne forever. God is the initiator, God the one who makes the promises. Awed into silence, Mary simply listens to Gabriel's guarantees of future blessings. But David's is quite another story. *He* initiates and proposes to do something for *God*. God demurs and,

through the prophet, questions David instead, declaring that the initiative has been God's all along and that all which has unfolded in David's life has come from God's merciful hand. Like Mary, David has no choice but to stand in humbled silence and hear a listing of all the blessings he has already received.

David is not so much prideful as he is naïve. Surveying his comfortable kingdom, David is genuinely scandalized that he lives in a "house of cedar" while the "ark of God" remains "in a tent." He knows his place in relation to God, and he knows

things are out of balance. The prophet Nathan agrees, believing God will bless David's efforts. But what David fails to understand is that God cannot be outdone in generosity; the scales will always be off balance, for it is God's nature to provide bountifully and ask only for love in return.

God rejects David's plan, reminding him that he is where he is because of divine favor. I gave you your military victories, says the Lord. It was I who turned a boy shepherd into a mighty king. The listing of what God *did* is soon followed by a listing of what God *will* do. With energy,

I will give you **rest** from all your enemies.
The LORD **also** reveals to you
   that he will establish a house for **you.**
And when your **time** comes and you rest with your **ancestors,**
   I will raise up your **heir** after you, sprung from your **loins,**
   and I will make his kingdom **firm.**
I will be a **father** to him,
   and he shall be a **son** to me.
Your **house** and your **kingdom** shall endure **forever** before me;
   your **throne** shall stand firm **forever.**' "

READING II   Romans 16:25–27

A reading from the Letter of Saint Paul to the Romans

Brothers and sisters:
To him who can **strengthen** you,
   according to my **gospel** and the proclamation of Jesus **Christ,**
   according to the revelation of the **mystery** kept secret
      for long **ages**
but now **manifested** through the prophetic **writings** and,
   according to the **command** of the eternal **God,**
   made known to all **nations** to bring about the **obedience**
      of **faith,**
   to the only **wise** God, through Jesus **Christ**
   be **glory** forever and **ever. Amen.**

enthusiasm, and even pride, God enumerates other blessings that will fall into David's life. It is as if a teacher whom a student wants to honor, would say, "No, you won't honor me, I'm going to honor you . . . *and* I'm going to get you into the finest university . . . *and* I'm going to get you a scholarship!" The final sentence holds the greatest revelation: "your throne shall stand firm forever." Pause before you begin the important last line, which echoes throughout today's Gospel.

READING II The message is simple: to God be glory forever! Yet it's presented in one tortuous sentence of 73 words. Why such complexity? Because in their effort to render the ancient texts more literally, Bible translators sometimes end up crafting passages that are difficult to understand. Certainly that's the case today. The translators might have served us better, but the writing is Paul's and translators can only do so much. Taken from the end of Paul's letter to the Romans, this text will require much practice in order for you to grasp what Paul is saying as he closes

his epistle. Some texts are more about "tone" than about content. This is one of them, for the content is summarized in the five words above; the other 68 can be used to create a *tone* of gratitude and praise to the God who is the source of all that is good in our lives and in the Church.

   By mentally (not actually) inserting a few words that are clearly implied in the text, Paul's words cohere with greater meaning: "*To him* [God] *who can strengthen you, according to my gospel and the proclamation of Jesus Christ,* [and] *according to the revelation of the mystery* [that was]

GOSPEL Luke 1:26–38

A reading from the holy Gospel according to Luke

The angel **Gabriel** was sent from **God**
  to a town of **Galilee** called **Nazareth**,
  to a **virgin** betrothed to a man named **Joseph**,
  of the house of **David**,
  and the virgin's **name** was **Mary**.
And **coming** to her, he said,
  "**Hail**, full of **grace**! The **Lord** is with you."
But she was greatly **troubled** at what was said
  and **pondered** what sort of **greeting** this might be.
Then the angel said to her,
  "Do not be **afraid**, Mary,
  for you have found **favor** with God.

"Behold, you will **conceive** in your womb and bear a **son**,
  and you shall name him **Jesus**.
He will be **great** and will be called **Son** of the Most **High**,
  and the Lord **God** will give him the **throne** of David
    his **father**,
  and he will **rule** over the house of Jacob **forever**,
  and of his **kingdom** there will be no **end**."
But **Mary** said to the angel,
  "How can this **be**,
  since I have no relations with a **man**?"
And the angel said to her in **reply**,
  "The Holy **Spirit** will come upon you,
  and the power of the Most **High** will **overshadow** you.

Don't rush here. There is much information in the first sentence.

Let the words be comforting, not frightening: "Hail [pause, then slowly], full of grace! [pause, then gently] The Lord is with you."

Still gently and slowly to counter her fear: "Do not be afraid . . . with God." Note that "Blessed are you among women" is not found in the current translation.
This is the announcement of the fulfillment of ancient prophecy. Give it proper dignity.

Mary believes, but asks to be told "how?"

Reassuring, but with great conviction and awareness of God's power.

kept secret for long ages but [is] *now manifested through the prophetic writings and, according to the command of the eternal God,* [is] *made known to all nations* [that it might] *bring about the obedience of faith— to* [him] *the only wise God, through Jesus Christ, be glory forever and ever. Amen."* Only the italics represent Paul's direct statement; everything else is parenthetical. Seeing this may help you proclaim the given text with more understanding.

While winding round the multiple clauses, remember where you're headed. Don't rush toward the goal or you'll create more confusion. Focus your energy on the nature of this locution, which is both a short hymn of praise (doxology) and a prayer of blessing (benediction). The object of both is God, who has fulfilled in the life, ministry, death, and Resurrection of Jesus the promises made to the prophets of old. That is a strong theme in Romans: what was first revealed to the prophets, God has now made known to all people.

Speak with a smile, deep joy, and awareness that you are singing praise to the God who loves deeply all those gathered before you.

GOSPEL Consult the commentary for the Immaculate Conception Gospel for further insights into this reading.

On this final Sunday of Advent, the First Reading and this Gospel focus on David and Mary, two different characters who, nonetheless, share a striking similarity because through their life stories they demonstrate the remarkable power of God. In the life of this inconsequential young woman, as in the life of King David, we see God in control, we discover that only when we yield humbly to God's sovereignty can

If further evidence were needed, here it is!

Emphasize the word "nothing" (not even a virgin birth).
Mary's words suggest a total surrender to the divine will.

Therefore the **child** to be born
    will be called **holy**, the Son of **God**.
And behold, **Elizabeth**, your relative,
    has **also** conceived a son in her old **age**,
    and this is the **sixth** month for her who was called **barren**;
    for **nothing** will be **impossible** for **God**."
Mary said, "**Behold**, I am the **handmaid** of the Lord.
May it be **done** to me according to your **word**."
Then the angel **departed** from her.

God's power be released and lead us to glory.

On the solemnity of the Immaculate Conception, this Gospel highlighted the theme of Mary's election—this nobody from a nowhere town becomes the Mother of God through the will of God and the working of the Holy Spirit. But today, Advent's last Sunday, Luke's Gospel account serves another purpose. This text might have been chosen for the earlier weeks of Advent, but those Sundays are focused on Christ's return in glory, not his birth as a human being. It's nearly

Christmas, so this last Sunday focuses on Christ's first coming and how that was made possible by Mary's fiat during this encounter with the angel.

There's another aspect to this text: who better than Mary illustrates Advent's pervasive theme of waiting? Waiting often involves periods of fear and comfort cycling within us until the anticipated event arrives. Mary is immediately "troubled" by the angel's greeting and his announcement that she will bear a child. Her question ("How can this be . . . ?") is unlike Zechariah's similar question when

told of John's impending birth, for Mary seems to ask not "if" but "how" the angel's declaration will be achieved. Place ample stress on the angel's comforting reassurances: "Do not be afraid . . ." and "The Holy Spirit will come upon you . . . ." In fact, the effort to allay Mary's fear begins with the angel's salutation. Without understanding all that will flow from it, Mary speaks her "yes" in a bold and stunning declaration (probably not void of fear) that clearly understands that obedience is what it means to be God's "handmaid."

NATIVITY OF THE LORD: VIGIL

Lectionary #13

READING I — Isaiah 62:1–5

Isaiah = ĭ-ZAY-uh

This is long-awaited news announced loudly with great energy, or softly with real but muted zeal.

Several times an idea stated in the first of a pair of lines is immediately repeated, in slightly different words, in the second: "not be silent" / "not be quiet"; "vindication . . . like the dawn" / "victory like a burning torch"; "Nations shall behold your vindication" / "kings your glory"; "glorious crown" / "royal diadem.") Use this literary device to build emphasis by increasing energy from the first to the second expression.

diadem = DĪ-uh-dem

Contrast the words "Forsaken" and "Desolate"—the former times that will be no more, with "My Delight" and "Espoused"—Israel's new status.

Note the spousal imagery of the last four couplets: in each pair of lines the second line receives greater stress. The passionate, tender marriage language suggests God's enduring covenant with the chosen people whose repeated infidelities are transformed into the innocence of a "virgin" bride.

A reading from the Book of the Prophet Isaiah

For **Zion's** sake I will not be **silent**,
    for **Jerusalem's** sake I will not be **quiet**,
until her **vindication** shines forth like the **dawn**
    and her **victory** like a burning **torch**.

Nations shall **behold** your vindication,
    and all the **kings** your **glory**;
you shall be called by a **new** name
    pronounced by the mouth of the LORD.
You shall be a glorious crown in the hand of the LORD,
    a royal **diadem** held by your God.
No **more** shall people call you "**Forsaken**,"
    or your land "**Desolate**,"
but you shall be called "My **Delight**,"
    and your **land** "**Espoused**."
For the LORD **delights** in you
    and makes your land his **spouse**.
As a young **man** marries a **virgin**,
    your **Builder** shall marry **you**;
and as a **bridegroom** rejoices in his **bride**
    so shall your **God** rejoice in **you**.

READING I — Isaiah the prophet and poet dominates the Christmas solemnities, appearing at each of its four Masses—vigil, midnight, dawn, and day. With imagery both rich and earthy, Isaiah signals not only the new relationship God will craft with the chosen people once their time of captivity comes to an end, but he also suggests the revolutionary change in God's relationship with humanity that will be accomplished through the Messiah, whom we know as Jesus the Christ, and who came in the flesh to make us all sons and daughters of God.

Although centuries would pass before Israel's deliverance would actually arrive, and even more before her messiah would come, joyful hope explodes from Isaiah's poetry. Decades of destruction and exile at the hands of foreign invaders don't keep Isaiah from insisting that the people dream of the glorious events that will accompany the messianic era. He builds that hope with images of joy and triumph—a wedding feast, a grand coronation.

Note that Isaiah doesn't just speak for God; he assumes God's own voice: Israel's deliverance is decreed by God, her new name "pronounced by the mouth of the Lord." Isaiah's images are personal and intimate: bride and bridegroom, lover and beloved, husband and wife. With these images of intimacy between young lovers, Isaiah conveys the depth of God's commitment and the possibility of Israel's healing and reconciliation. Despite her infidelity and disobedience, Israel will shed her former names ("Forsaken" and "Desolate") and take on the new names ("My Delight," "Espoused") that reveal God's infinite mercy. By changing her name, God changes Israel's very identity. No longer will she be

Antioch = AN-tee-ahk
Pisidia = pih-SID-ee-uh

"Motioned with his hand . . ." means he's asking them for silence.

Paul speaks with authority. Setting is important here: Paul is in a synagogue, a setting not unlike yours.

Recount the history, keeping in mind where you're headed: Jesus! It's not history for its own sake.

Speak of David with affection and pride, but remember, he's not the main focus of the passage.

This is the climax of the text. Greater energy. Take a pause before "Jesus."

Imagine John trying to convince his followers he is not what they "suppose." Then as if watching Jesus standing on the opposite shore, speak the last line simply and sincerely.

READING II   Acts 13:16–17, 22–25

A reading from the Acts of the Apostles

When **Paul** reached **Antioch** in **Pisidia** and entered
      the **synagogue**,
   he **stood** up, motioned with his **hand**, and said,
      "Fellow **Israelites** and you **others** who are God-fearing, **listen**.
The God of this people **Israel** chose our **ancestors**
      and **exalted** the people during their sojourn
         in the land of **Egypt**.
With uplifted **arm** he led them **out** of it.
Then he removed **Saul** and raised up **David** as **king**;
      of him he **testified**,
      'I have found **David**, son of **Jesse**, a man after my own **heart**;
      he will carry out my every **wish**.'
From this man's **descendants** God, according to his **promise**,
      has brought to Israel a **savior**, **Jesus**.
John **heralded** his coming by proclaiming a **baptism** of **repentance**
      to all the people of **Israel**;
      and as John was **completing** his course, he would say,
      'What do you suppose that I **am**? I am not **he**.
Behold, one is coming **after** me;
      I am not **worthy** to unfasten the **sandals** of his **feet**.' "

shunned and cast aside, but cherished and protected, held in God's own hands.

READING II One of the great figures of Advent makes an unexpected appearance in tonight's liturgy, courtesy of Saint Paul. In his address in the synagogue, Paul speaks of John the Baptist who bridges the Old and New Testaments. Paul embodies the spirit of the Israelite prophets and shines their collective spotlight on Jesus, who fulfills all the messianic promises that had sustained the people through centuries of trial, oppres-

sion, and endless waiting. In the First Reading, Isaiah's images of healing and forgiveness fill us with hope. Paul's words build on Isaiah's momentum, summarizing the nation's history with one deft rhetorical gesture: God led us out of slavery in Egypt, then raised up David as king. From David's descendants God has now raised up a savior for Israel. John prepared the way for him through his baptism of repentance, insisting that he himself was not the messiah, for one would come after him whose sandals he was not worthy to unfasten.

It's no accident that Paul cites such specifics in making his case, for he was keenly aware of the embarrassingly concrete and particular historical aspects of God's interaction with humanity. To put it bluntly, God makes *choices*—one nation (Israel) from among others, one king (David) over another (Saul). God works in *history*—through human events and through the lives of individual human beings. Playing favorites and getting very involved in human events may not fit a modern notion of appropriate divine behavior, but it is an integral part of the

GOSPEL Matthew 1:1–25

A reading from the holy Gospel according to Matthew

The book of the **genealogy** of Jesus **Christ**,
  the son of **David**, the son of **Abraham**.

Abraham became the father of **Isaac**,
  Isaac the father of **Jacob**,
  Jacob the father of **Judah** and his brothers.
Judah became the father of **Perez** and **Zerah**,
  whose **mother** was **Tamar**.
Perez became the father of **Hezron**,
  Hezron the father of **Ram**,
  Ram the father of **Amminadab**.
Amminadab became the father of **Nahshon**,
  Nahshon the father of **Salmon**,
  Salmon the father of **Boaz**,
  whose **mother** was **Rahab**.
Boaz became the father of **Obed**,
  whose **mother** was **Ruth**.
Obed became the father of **Jesse**,
  Jesse the father of **David** the **king**.

David became the father of **Solomon**,
  whose **mother** had been the wife of **Uriah**.
Solomon became the father of **Rehoboam**,
  Rehoboam the father of **Abijah**,
  Abijah the father of **Asaph**.
Asaph became the father of **Jehoshaphat**,
  Jehoshaphat the father of **Joram**,
  Joram the father of **Uzziah**.

Don't rush the "litany" of names. Be sure to rehearse the pronunciations.

Renew energy every few lines.
Isaac = Ī-zik; Judah = JOO-duh

Perez = PAYR-ez
Zerah = ZEE-ruh
Tamar = TAY-mahr: Genesis 38.
Hezron = HEZ-ruhn
Ram = ram
Amminadab = uh-MIN-uh-dab
Nahshon = NAH-shun
Salmon = SAL-muhn
Boaz = BOH-az
Rahab = RAY-hab: Joshua 2:1–7
Obed = OH-bed
Ruth was the great-grandmother of King David.
Uriah = yoo-RĪ-uh. His "wife" is Bathsheba: 2 Samuel 11:1–27.

Rehoboam = ree-huh-BOH-uhm
Abijah = uh-BĪ-juh
Jehoshaphat = jeh-HOH-shuh-fat
Asaph = AY-saf
Joram = JOHR-uhm
Uzziah = uh-ZĪ-uh: struck with leprosy for usurping the role of priests (see 2 Chronicles 26:16–20).

---

divine portrait presented by the Judeo-Christian scriptures.

Today's text introduces an address Paul delivers in the verses that follow this selection. We don't hear those words today, but this introduction is very important on its own. By citing slavery in Egypt, Paul reminds the people that God has always been a savior. The monarchy, exercised by such imperfect individuals as Saul and David (and many far worse that followed) illustrates God's ability to protect and sustain the people even through a flawed political institution like kingship.

Paul is presenting more than a history lesson; he is expounding profound theology that sees God woven into the fabric of all of life. When Paul finally focuses on Jesus and John the Baptist, we encounter, once again, the concreteness of God—taking on human flesh in a *particular person* and at a *particular time* and *place* in human history.

Such, too, is the scandal of the Incarnation, for Jesus was not male *and* female, Jew *and* Gentile, first *and* twenty-first century. But out of that particularity comes a universalism that Paul also heralds, for in Christ male and female, Gentile and Jew no longer matter since all are made one in him.

GOSPEL If the Second Reading from Acts didn't make the point that God works through the "scandal" of particularity, then surely this Gospel passage will. God *chose* not only a *people* from whom to draw the messiah, but a particular *family* as well, and that family lineage is boldly presented here. Its inclusion serves Matthew's theological agenda by asserting that Jesus is all that Israel is—descended from Abraham, descended from David,

Jotham = JOH-thuhm

Ahaz = AY-haz

Hezekiah = hez-eh-KĪ-uh

Manasseh = muh-NAS-uh: Israel's worst king.

Josiah = joh-SĪ-uh: one of Israel's best kings; a reformer.

Jechoniah = jek-oh-NĪ-uh

The exile was the nation's greatest trial.

Shealtiel = shee-AL-tee-uhl

Zerubbabel = zuh-ROOB-uh-b*l

Abiud = uh-BĪ-uhd

Eliakim = ee-LĪ-uh-kim

Azor = AY-zohr

Zadok = ZAD-uhk

Achim = AY-kim

Eliud = ee-LĪ-uhd

Eleazar = el-ee-AY-zer

Matthan = MATH-uhn

"Fourteen" is a deliberate redundancy. Stress each recurrence.

Uzziah became the father of **Jotham**,
   Jotham the father of **Ahaz**,
   Ahaz the father of **Hezekiah**.
Hezekiah became the father of **Manasseh**,
   Manasseh the father of **Amos**,
   Amos the father of **Josiah**.
Josiah became the father of **Jechoniah** and his brothers
   at the time of the Babylonian **exile**.

After the Babylonian exile,
   Jechoniah became the father of **Shealtiel**,
   Shealtiel the father of **Zerubbabel**,
   Zerubbabel the father of **Abiud**.
Abiud became the father of **Eliakim**,
   Eliakim the father of **Azor**,
   Azor the father of **Zadok**.
Zadok became the father of **Achim**,
   Achim the father of **Eliud**,
   Eliud the father of **Eleazar**.
Eleazar became the father of **Matthan**,
   Matthan the father of **Jacob**,
   Jacob the father of **Joseph**, the husband of **Mary**.
Of her was born **Jesus** who is called the **Christ**.

Thus the total number of **generations**
   from **Abraham** to **David**
   is **fourteen** generations;
   from **David** to the Babylonian **exile**,
   fourteen generations;
   from the Babylonian exile to the **Christ**,
   fourteen generations.

descended from saints and sinners, people who have borne the burden of their "election" for many centuries and generations.

In addition, the genealogy proclaims that God can use anyone to accomplish the divine plan—Jew and Gentile, insider and outsider, women as well as men. That last point is obvious to us, but it wasn't then. Five women populate the list of Jesus' ancestors, all of them Gentiles (except Mary), and one is a harlot! All marry under unusual circumstances and all exhibit amazing initiative, playing significant roles in the unfolding of God's plan.

In regard to proclamation, this genealogy presents one of the great challenges in the Lectionary, tempting some to opt for the shorter reading. But consider what you lose by excluding it. Matthew begins with the genealogy because, like Paul in the passage from Acts, he wants to recall the whole of salvation history, suggesting that knowing Jesus requires knowing the story and characters of the Old Testament. Liturgically, the lengthy listing conjures up the protracted, often painful waiting that preceded the time of fulfillment.

Although the genealogy lists Jesus' lineage, Matthew is presenting more than the history of a single family; this is the ancestry of all people of faith who descend from Abraham, the father of all believers (see Romans 4:13–25). Read with that awareness. Any family tree will include names that provoke a smile of recognition while others leave one unmoved. In reading this list, you need not lift out each and every name. In fact, the opposite is better. Use the rhythm of the repetitions to achieve a chant-like litany, although you'll want to slow down at the *familiar* names,

Matthew stresses details of Jesus' conception and the role of Joseph.

Deliver the words "before they lived together" with care about the "delicacy" of the situation.

Stress "righteous man." Insert a brief pause before the word "quietly."

The angelic encounter asserts Jesus' divine origin and his messianic destiny.

Take time with the translation of the name "Emmanuel," which climaxes the reading.

Make a subtle vocal shift for the quotation.

Sustain eye contact after speaking "Jesus."

Now this is how the **birth** of Jesus Christ came about.
When his mother **Mary** was betrothed to **Joseph**,
  but before they **lived** together,
  she was found with **child** through the Holy **Spirit**.
Joseph her **husband**, since he was a **righteous** man,
  yet unwilling to expose her to **shame**,
  decided to divorce her **quietly**.
Such was his **intention** when, **behold**,
  the **angel** of the Lord appeared to him in a **dream** and said,
  "**Joseph**, son of **David**,
  do not be **afraid** to take Mary your **wife** into your **home**.
For it is through the Holy **Spirit**
  that this child has been **conceived** in her.
She will bear a **son** and you are to name him **Jesus**,
  because he will **save** his people from their **sins**."
All this took place to **fulfill**
  what the Lord had said through the **prophet**:
    *Behold, the **virgin** shall **conceive** and bear a **son**,*
      *and they shall name him **Emmanuel**,*
  which means "**God** is **with** us."
When Joseph **awoke**,
  he **did** as the angel of the Lord had **commanded** him
  and took his **wife** into his **home**.
He had no **relations** with her until she bore a **son**,
  and he **named** him Jesus.

[Shorter: Matthew 1:18–25]

as images from that character's life color the way you speak the name.

The birth narrative changes the mood entirely. Here is a *story* (that should *sound* like one!) of divine activity: Mary conceives through "the *Holy Spirit*" and Joseph is counseled by an "*angel*." Matthew's careful attention to the details of the conception ("when . . . betrothed . . . but before they lived together") betrays knowledge of contemporary disputes over Jesus' legitimacy.

Luke highlights Mary's role in the birth of Jesus, but Matthew spends more time on Joseph, through whom Jesus derives his Davidic lineage—another reason for proclaiming the genealogy! Joseph is "righteous" from the start, but not till the angelic intervention is he able to fully embrace God's plan. Here, it's Joseph, not Mary, who is told "do not be afraid," a formula that often accompanies an announcement of God's saving intervention. The angel's words to Joseph do much more

than reassure a shaken fiancé; they reassert Jesus' divine origins and his messianic destiny, in which Joseph is now given a central role.

A quote from the prophet Micah announces the coming of "Emmanuel," a name that means "God is with us." Matthew's well-designed text reminds us that, in Jesus, God came among us in a unique and unimaginable way, but that miracle was made possible by generations of believers who never lost faith and never abandoned hope.

NATIVITY OF THE LORD: MIDNIGHT

Lectionary #14

READING I   Isaiah 9:1–6

Within the context of tonight's liturgy, we view the truth of this passage through the special lens of Christian faith.

"Light" is the operative word. Contrast it with "darkness" and "gloom" as your energy and pacing slowly increase.

The meaning is clearer if you imagine the line without the first "as."

Slowly.

Slowly.

Slowly.

Faster now. "Smashed," "tramped," and "burned" sound like what they mean.

Slowly.

Slowly.

Faster.

Proclaim this line tenderly. Know of whom you speak here.

Give titles either a bold or quiet energy.

The sense of this sentence (see also next page) is: his dominion, which he exercises from David's throne and over David's kingdom and which he confirms and sustains by judgment and justice both now and forever, is vast and forever peaceful.

A reading from the Book of the Prophet Isaiah

The people who walked in **darkness**
  have seen a great **light**;
upon those who dwelt in the land of **gloom**
  a **light** has **shone**.
You have brought them abundant **joy**
  and great **rejoicing**,
as they rejoice before you as at the **harvest**,
  as people make **merry** when dividing **spoils**.
For the **yoke** that **burdened** them,
  the **pole** on their **shoulder**,
and the **rod** of their **taskmaster**
  you have **smashed**, as on the day of **Midian**.
For every **boot** that tramped in **battle**,
  every **cloak** rolled in **blood**,
  will be **burned** as fuel for **flames**.
For a **child** is born to us, a **son** is given us;
  upon his shoulder **dominion** rests.
They name him **Wonder-Counselor, God-Hero,**
  Father-Forever, Prince of **Peace.**
His dominion is **vast**
  and forever **peaceful**,

READING I Isaiah's hymn-like text looks forward to the coronation of a future messianic king who will bring Israel's time of trial and subjugation to an end. At this future time, when the messiah reigns over Israel, all burdens and yokes will be removed and the taskmaster's menacing rod will be forever "smashed." In their place, this great king will bring great rejoicing, the kind of rejoicing that accompanies harvest festivals and the division of the plunder of war—not images *we* might use to excite

the imagination, but the inspired images of that time that are meant to rouse the hearts of Isaiah's readers and fill them with hope of a better future.

Isaiah's words paint a vivid picture of this festive future by contrasting it with a dire former time when boots trampled to war and cloaks were stained with the blood of battle. Your contrast of odious past and hopeful future in this reading will be critical to communicating its message. Ironically, the messianic king who ushers in a reversal of fortune both total and awe-inspiring is introduced as "a child . . . a

son" who will be clothed with the royal titles reserved to kings at their time of coronation: "Wonder-Counselor . . . Prince of Peace."

On this holy night, we hear in Isaiah's words a prophecy *fulfilled,* a promise kept in the person and ministry of Jesus. We realize that we, too, are in the vast assembly of those who "walked in darkness" and on whom light "has shone." Sin is the darkness that claimed us; Christ, the light that banished the night. In this liturgy, we become one with all the hopes of Israel,

from **David's** throne, and over his **kingdom**,
    which he **confirms** and **sustains**
by **judgment** and **justice**,
    both **now** and **forever**.
The **zeal** of the LORD of **hosts** will **do** this!

READING II   Titus 2:11–14

A reading from the Letter of Saint Paul to Titus

Beloved:
The **grace** of **God** has appeared, saving **all**
    and **training** us to reject **godless** ways and **worldly** desires
    and to live **temperately**, **justly**, and **devoutly** in this age,
    as we await the blessed **hope**,
    the **appearance** of the **glory** of our great **God**
    and **savior** Jesus **Christ**,
    who **gave** himself for us to **deliver** us from all **lawlessness**
    and to **cleanse** for himself a people as his **own**,
    eager to do what is **good**.

GOSPEL   Luke 2:1–14

A reading from the holy Gospel according to Luke

In those days a **decree** went out from Caesar **Augustus**
    that the whole **world** should be **enrolled**.
This was the **first** enrollment,
    when **Quirinius** was governor of **Syria**.

Titus = TĪ-tuhs

The word "Beloved" sets the tone.

This is a joyous announcement. "The grace of God" is Isaiah's "great light."

Keep the tone joyful, not scolding.

Stress the word "appearance" to parallel the opening line.

The word "cleanse" is a baptismal reference.
The word "eager" characterizes the tone of your delivery—and our discipleship!

Take notice of the details and contrasts that over-familiarity with the story may cause you to overlook.
This is an elegant and momentous beginning.

Quirinius = kwih-RIN-ee-us

rejoicing in their fulfillment in a "son" who indeed sits forever on David's throne, establishing justice over his vast dominion and peace in every heart. Don't doubt it, for the "zeal," the *passion* of the Lord our God *will* do it.

READING II   All the Christian mysteries are present in every Christian feast. That's why no celebration of the coming of Christ is ever isolated from celebration of his life and death, or from awareness of his future coming in glory. In a single, 75-word sentence, Paul manages to allude to Christ's human birth ("the grace of God has appeared"), his saving death at Calvary ("who gave himself for us") and his anticipated return in glory ("we await the . . . appearance of the glory of our great God"). The start, like a joyous birth announcement, heralds the appearance of God's grace in human form, Jesus, who in the flesh at Bethlehem, is now born in spirit in the heart of anyone who seeks him.

Such divine initiative is not without consequences, for receiving God's grace requires allowing it to "train" us to live in the light and to reject everything that's born of darkness. We are able to abandon "lawlessness" because of the one who "gave himself for us to deliver us" from sin. Just as we anticipate Christ's Second Coming while celebrating the first, we also anticipate the sacrificial death of this manger child as we celebrate his birth. Paul's mood is suggested by the word "eager" in the final line, which tells us not only how

Jesus' royal lineage comes through his adoptive father, Joseph. Don't rush the names. Syria = SEER-ee-uh; Galilee = GAL-ih-lee; Judea = joo-DEE-uh.

So all went to be **enrolled**, **each** to his own **town**.
And **Joseph** too went up from **Galilee** from the town of **Nazareth**
    to **Judea**, to the city of **David** that is called **Bethlehem**,
    because he was of the **house** and **family** of David,
    to be enrolled with **Mary**, his **betrothed**, who was with **child**.
While they were there,
    the **time** came for her to have her **child**,
    and she gave **birth** to her firstborn **son**.
She wrapped him in **swaddling** clothes and laid him in a **manger**,
    because there was no **room** for them in the **inn**.

Speak slowly and simply so the words can do their work.

Cherish these familiar, but tender images.

Use a bit faster pacing to suggest the sudden appearance and the shepherds' fearful reaction. Though lowly in social status, many biblical heroes are shepherds.

Now there were **shepherds** in that region living in the **fields**
    and keeping the **night** watch over their **flock**.
The **angel** of the Lord **appeared** to them
    and the **glory** of the Lord **shone** around them,
    and they were struck with great **fear**.
The angel **said** to them,
    "Do not be **afraid**;
    for **behold**, I proclaim to you good **news** of great **joy**
    that will be for **all** the people.

The angel calms fear by announcing "good news of great joy." What does that suggest about your tone and energy?

For **today** in the city of **David**
    a **savior** has been born for you who is **Christ** and **Lord**.
And this will be a **sign** for you:
    you will find an **infant** wrapped in **swaddling** clothes
    and lying in a **manger**."

Stress "savior," "Christ," and "Lord."

And **suddenly** there was a **multitude** of the heavenly host
    with the angel,
    praising God and saying:

Don't rush. You don't want to waste a single word!

    "**Glory** to God in the **highest**
        and on **earth peace** to those on whom his **favor** rests."

Help your listeners hear the connection between these words and the "Glory to God" sung in the liturgy.

to read, but how to respond to the "appearance of grace."

GOSPEL   This beloved text encompasses the mundane details of a worldwide census and the extraordinary manifestation of an angelic host singing God's praises. Contrasts abound as royal personages like Caesar and Quirinius share the spotlight with Joseph, Mary, and the shepherds who alone are told of Jesus' birth. The obscure village of "Nazareth" in

the no-respect district of Galilee contrasts with Judea and Bethlehem, the birthplace of the Davidic dynasty. Such contrasts add color to the story and a proper reading will require you to draw attention to them.

No other event in scripture is as peopled with angelic beings as is the Incarnation. Announcing, comforting, heralding, warning—angels surround this most extraordinary event in the history of God's dealings with humanity. Here, an angel appears to shepherds who, surrounded by the "glory of the Lord," respond with appropriate fear. But using a familiar

formula that invariably signals the announcement of God's saving intervention, the angel says, "Do not be afraid" and then tells them where to find the "savior" who, not meriting a room in the inn, found shelter instead in a manger. In this passage, only angels herald the good news of the savior's birth, but throughout Luke's narrative, that angelic chorus echoes in the author's voice—the voice of a faithfilled believer.

NATIVITY OF THE LORD: DAWN

Lectionary #15

READING I   Isaiah 62:11–12

A reading from the Book of the Prophet Isaiah

See, the LORD proclaims
　　to the **ends** of the **earth**:
say to daughter **Zion**,
　　your **savior** comes!
Here is his **reward** with him,
　　his **recompense** before him.
They shall be called the **holy** people,
　　the **redeemed** of the LORD,
and you shall be called "**Frequented**,"
　　a city that is **not forsaken**.

READING II   Titus 3:4–7

A reading from the Letter of Saint Paul to Titus

Beloved:
When the **kindness** and generous **love**
　　of God our **savior** appeared,
not because of any righteous **deeds** we had done
　　but because of his **mercy**,
he **saved** us through the **bath** of **rebirth**
　　and **renewal** by the Holy **Spirit**,

Pause after the word "Spirit" above and vocally build from one clause to the other, slowing on the words "hope of eternal life."

Make your joy and gratitude apparent.

whom he richly **poured** out on us
    through Jesus **Christ** our **savior**,
so that we might be **justified** by his grace
    and become **heirs** in hope of eternal **life**.

You're not announcing clouds vanishing in the sky. This is miraculous!

Speak the shepherds' dialogue with eagerness and energy!

Pause after "Mary and Joseph," and then speak "and the infant" as if suddenly seeing him. (It's only the baby who's lying in the manger!)

Don't rush: speak as if these words are still sinking into and astonishing you.

An earlier translation rendered "kept" as "treasured". Give "kept" that nuance, and don't rush the line. Pause between "these things" and "reflecting."

The shepherds' mood is joyous.

Differentiate "heard" (expectation) and "seen" (fulfillment).

GOSPEL   Luke 2:15–20

A reading from the holy Gospel according to Luke

When the **angels** went **away** from them to **heaven**,
    the **shepherds** said to one another,
    "Let us **go**, then, to **Bethlehem**
    to **see** this thing that has taken place,
    which the Lord has made **known** to us."
So they went in **haste** and found **Mary** and **Joseph**,
    and the **infant** lying in the **manger**.
When they **saw** this,
    they made known the **message**
    that had been **told** them about this child.
All who heard it were **amazed**
    by what had been **told** them by the shepherds.
And Mary **kept** all these things,
    reflecting on them in her **heart**.
Then the shepherds **returned**,
    glorifying and **praising** God
    for all they had **heard** and **seen**,
    just as it had been **told** to them.

"hope," and "eternal life." You are proclaiming Christ's birth in this text just as surely as if you were reading today's Gospel from Luke. But you are also reminding us that God's grace is constantly transforming us—today and everyday. Can you announce that good news with anything less than joy and profound gratitude?

| GOSPEL | Consider first the end of the reading, where all are "amazed," Mary reflects quietly "in her heart," and shepherds glorify God's name— all in response to a baby lying in a manger. |

The sight is familiar to us from countless crèches, but world-stopping in its significance and quite unexpected by those who waited centuries for the messiah.

Shepherds stand at either end of this brief text, hearing, responding, witnessing and announcing. With Mary-like faith, they believe that the angels' word to them will be fulfilled. They recognize the child lying on a bed of hay and readily embrace what they have been told about him. From the beginning, Christ's coming turns the world upside down. These lowly shepherds (often despised and mistrusted in their day) are not only chosen to be the first told of the messiah's birth, they prove themselves to be exemplary disciples who don't hesitate or doubt, but rush to share what they have heard and believed about this child. The shepherds' awe at the sight of the heavenly host is now shared by "all," for these simple witnesses not only hear, but *understand* the angels' announcement that this is the Christ. On this day of light we contemplate the miracle of God among us. Announce it with the conviction and awe of those first witnesses!

Lectionary #16

READING I   Isaiah 52:7–10

Isaiah = ī-ZAY-uh

Proclaim slowly, with mounting energy. "Feet" is a *synecdoche*, a poetic device using a part to represent the whole person.

Once again, read slowly: Distinguish each separate thought by visualizing a different image for "peace," "good news," and "salvation."

Pause briefly before and after the word "Hark," but don't overstress it.

The words "directly" and "before their eyes" are an intentional redundancy. Stress *both* expressions.

The chorus of joy widens. Stress "ruins" and "redeems" instead of "Jerusalem."

The last four lines are a summary and a promise, reminding us of what God has done and what God will do. Remember, "salvation" is the child in the manger. That should color your tone.

A reading from the Book of the Prophet Isaiah

How **beautiful** upon the **mountains**
    are the **feet** of him who brings glad **tidings**,
announcing **peace**, bearing good **news**,
    announcing **salvation**, and saying to **Zion**,
    "Your **God** is **King**!"

Hark! Your sentinels raise a **cry**,
    together they shout for **joy**,
for they see **directly**, before their **eyes**,
    the LORD **restoring** Zion.
Break out together in **song**,
    O **ruins** of Jerusalem!
For the LORD **comforts** his people,
    he **redeems** Jerusalem.
The LORD has **bared** his holy arm
    in the sight of all the **nations**;
all the ends of the **earth** will behold
    the **salvation** of our **God**.

READING I | A striking image of a swift and nimble messenger bounding the mountains begins this triumphant hymn that celebrates the Exile's end and God's restoration of Israel. In his wake, the runner leaves only footprints and the good news of "peace" and "salvation." The poet/prophet Isaiah invites us to exult with him at the sight of the Lord leading a jubilant Israel back to a ruined Jerusalem that will soon be restored to its former glory.

The mighty hand of God is at work healing, redeeming, restoring. That's Isaiah's message and the message of this Christmas day liturgy: In the person of Jesus, God's healing and restoring power has taken on flesh; God's salvation is personified, and echoes of that ancient messenger's news resound in the voices of angels who hover over a manger. Christian faith enables us to recognize the coming of Christ as the ultimate act of salvation, surpassing even deliverance from the Exile. In Christ, we are delivered from the exile of sin. In him, every human heart can be redeemed, restored, and comforted. In this liturgy, Isaiah's words foretell the beginning of God's eternal reign, which dawns with the birth of Christ.

Such news must be shared with vibrant faith. The tidings are so wonderful that even the herald is made beautiful by them. The messenger's joy is picked up by the "sentinels" who recognize that God is indeed restoring Zion (Jerusalem). Then, even the scattered stones of ruined Jerusalem are urged to join the jubilation which, eventually, spreads even to "the ends of the earth." God is doing something we could not do for ourselves. His salvation is pure gift. God bares "his holy arm"

READING II Hebrews 1:1–6

A reading from the Letter to the Hebrews

Brothers and sisters:
In times **past**, God spoke in **partial** and **various** ways
    to our **ancestors** through the **prophets**;
in these **last** days, he has spoken to us through the **Son**,
    whom he made **heir** of all **things**
    and **through** whom he created the **universe**,
who is the **refulgence** of his **glory**,
     the very **imprint** of his **being**,
and who **sustains** all things by his mighty **word**.
When he had accomplished purification from **sins**,
he took his **seat** at the **right** hand of the **Majesty** on high,
as far **superior** to the **angels**
as the **name** he has inherited is more **excellent** than theirs.

For to **which** of the angels did God ever say:
    You are my **son***; this day I have* **begotten** *you?*
Or again:
    I will be a **father** *to him, and he shall be a* **son** *to me?*
And again, when he leads the **firstborn** into the world, he says:
    Let all the **angels** *of God* **worship** *him.*

"Partial" means "incomplete."
Distinguish "partial" from "various."
Contrast "in these last days" with "In times past" and "prophets" with "Son."

Probably based on a liturgical hymn of praise. Continue building intensity to the end of the paragraph.

"Accomplished purification" means he accomplished *our* **salvation, not** *his* **purification.**
Assert the superiority of Christ over the angels.
Jesus' "inherited" name is "Son." Assert the uniqueness of that relationship to God.
Speak with love. Don't let the ending sound anticlimactic.

---

and all nations behold the salvation only God can bring. Just like Isaiah's messenger, we too can be made beautiful when we proclaim (at the ambo and through our lives) the good news that God is among us!

READING II Some have speculated that what led the angelic hosts to join with Satan in rebelling against the majesty of God was primordial knowledge of exactly what the author of Hebrews reports today: a human being "superior to the angels" who takes his rightful seat at God's right hand wearing a name far "more

excellent than theirs." In this text, we encounter one of the chief themes of the unknown author of the Letter to the Hebrews: the superiority of Christ and of the work he accomplished. No other being in heaven or on earth surpasses Christ. His work, before as well as after the Incarnation, is unparalleled and singular. In this theologically and spiritually rich letter, the writer explains that God has spoken to humanity in various ways. Previously, God spoke through the prophets, but now God has used the most excellent way—the Son, whom God made "heir

of all things," through whom God created the "universe," who is the "refulgence," that is, "brilliance" of God's glory, and who "sustains all things by his mighty word."

On this day when we contemplate a helpless child, born in time and cradled in his mother's arms, the author of Hebrews focuses us on the full and true identity of this "Son." He is the eternal Christ who, having accomplished the work of salvation by offering his life for our sins, now sits at the right hand of the heavenly throne. Though the conviction that Christ is fully human and fully divine is settled dogma

GOSPEL John 1:1–18

A reading from the holy Gospel according to John

In the **beginning** was the **Word**,
> and the **Word** was with **God**,
> and the Word **was** God.

He was in the **beginning** with God.

All things came to be **through** him,
> and without him **nothing** came to be.

What came to be through him was **life**,
> and this life was the **light** of the human race;

the light **shines** in the **darkness**,
> and the darkness has not **overcome** it.

A man named **John** was sent from **God**.

He came for **testimony**, to testify to the **light**,
> so that all might **believe** through him.

He was not the light,
> but came to **testify** to the light.

The **true** light, which enlightens **everyone**,
> was coming into the world.

He was **in** the world,
> and the world came to **be** through him,
> but the world did not **know** him.

He came to what was his **own**,
> but his own people did not **accept** him.

Using staircase parallelism (where the last word of one phrase becomes the first word of the next) this text introduces the dominant themes of this Gospel: Christ's preexistence, life, light and darkness, the world, and witness. Stress those topics which will dominate the life and ministry of the Word made flesh.

Give these classic lines your best reading. The echoes of Genesis are obvious.

"Life" indicates all of life, including your own.

Shift the tone to signal a new subject.

Stress the word "testimony" but not "testify." Testimony inspires faith.

Speak without judgment. Stress in awe what Christ made possible: becoming children of God.

today, that belief was often challenged, even at the time of this letter's writing. The final paragraph contains only one question: Did God ever say the following about any of the angels? Then come three statements (all declarative sentences, not themselves questions) that contrast Christ with the angels: "You are my son . . ."; "I will be a father . . ."; "Let all the angels . . . ." By citing these three different scripture passages, the author of Hebrews drives home the point that the human child whose birth we celebrate enjoys singular status as God's divine son—to whom even angels must bow down and worship.

GOSPEL Occasionally, the awesome mystery we call God comes into sharper focus. Christmas day can be such a time. Saints and mystics who devoted their lives to better understanding God went about it in two ways—by saying what God is like or by saying what God is not like. We have little choice but to compare God whom we do not know to those things we do—an ocean, a gentle breeze, a mighty warrior.

But when we do, we quickly realize that no comparison is adequate, and we must conclude, "God is not an ocean, nor a breeze, nor a mighty warrior."

Then comes Christmas. And we realize that the mystery of God is most fully revealed in the human life that began that day. Yes, God is partially revealed in all of Creation and in the history of Israel, but God's fullest self-revelation is the person of Jesus. We don't need a picture of Jesus to understand God. Just as people are revealed by what they do rather than by

There should be a growing intensity on the "not," "nor," and "but" phrases.

But to those who **did** accept him
  he gave power to become **children** of **God**,
  to those who **believe** in his name,
  who were born not by **natural** generation
  nor by human **choice** nor by a **man's** decision
  but of **God**.
    And the **Word** became **flesh**

Speak as if you were witnessing the birth. Perhaps the feeling is the joy mixed with fear we call "awe," or maybe it is assertive testimony declaring God's willingness to live "among us."

      and made his **dwelling** among us,
      and we saw his **glory**,
      the glory as of the Father's only **Son**,
      full of **grace** and **truth**.

This is another aside. Speak with conviction, but slowly.

John **testified** to him and cried out, saying,
  "**This** was he of whom I said,
  'The one who is coming **after** me ranks **ahead** of me
  because he existed **before** me.'"
From his **fullness** we have **all** received,

Recall gratefully the "fullness" of which you and your parish have partaken.

  grace in place of **grace**,
  because while the **law** was given through **Moses**,

"Law" and "Moses" contrast with "grace" and "Jesus." Don't sound didactic; instead, stress the good fortune of having received the revelation of God in Jesus.

  grace and **truth** came through Jesus **Christ**.
No one has ever **seen** God.

The closing speaks of the deep relationship between the Father and Son.

The only **Son**, **God**, who is at the Father's **side**,
  has **revealed** him.

[Shorter: John 1:1–5, 9–14]

what they look like, God is revealed in the life and *activity* of Jesus.

Christmas alone, of course, doesn't tell the whole story. We also need Easter and everything before and after it. Focusing only on the helpless babe yields a distorted image. But recalling that the child who was born in humble poverty eventually carried the wood of the manger on his back and let himself be nailed to it, is to begin to understand the mysterious love we call God.

Like the passage from Hebrews, this Gospel text heralds Christ's preexistence

and God's self-revelation in him. The text rings with praise, and even the asides about John the Baptist assert Christ's supremacy. He came into a darkened world, and though his own did not accept him, his light prevails over the world's darkness, and those who accept him he makes "children of God." This text stresses the Baptist's role as a witness to Christ, reminding us that our calling and John's are one: through our lives calling others to Christ. The second mention of John reinforces the importance of witness and testimony.

The evangelist speaks of the Word becoming flesh as if he were watching the birth of a child. Whether you speak this section with joy, pride, or gratitude, use the same emotion later to characterize the Baptist's assertion that "the one . . . coming after me ranks ahead of me."

Great poetry invites us back into its chambers over and over again. The poetry of this prologue loses nothing from being familiar; only our lack of confidence in its power and beauty could diminish its ability to move and inspire.

MARY, THE MOTHER OF GOD

Lectionary #18

READING I   Number 6:22–27

This reading is short, so don't start till the assembly is well settled. Don't rush. God speaks to Moses who is to speak to "Aaron and his sons."

Allow yourself to *pray* this cherished text. That will keep you from reading too fast or too slowly. Too slow a reading robs the words of power as surely as too fast a delivery. Keep in mind that each invocation is distinct.

Deliver the words "and give you peace" slowly, as when ending a song.

Stress the word "name," not "my." The delivery of "I will bless them" should slow down, as when ending a song.

A reading from the Book of Numbers

The LORD said to Moses:
    "Speak to **Aaron** and his **sons** and **tell** them:
    This is how you shall **bless** the Israelites.
Say to them:
    The LORD **bless** you and **keep** you!
    The LORD let his face **shine** upon you,
        and be **gracious** to you!
    The LORD look upon you **kindly**
        and give you **peace**!
So shall they invoke my **name** upon the Israelites,
    and I will **bless** them."

READING I   This prayer was already ancient when Mary herself heard it spoken in synagogue services. No doubt it often touched Jesus' ears as well, and today it blesses us as we begin the New Year. The blessing formula thrice invokes God's divine name in unintended but striking anticipation of our Trinitarian invocations. For the ancient Jews, such a blessing expressed great reverence and awe. For them, person and name were one, so a name captured and conveyed all a person was and had done. Speaking God's name in blessing invoked God's presence

among those blessed. What an appropriate reading for this most ancient honoring of Mary, whose "yes" made possible God's presence among us in human form.

God instructs Moses to teach the blessing to Aaron and his sons, from whom all of Israel's priests will be descended. As you speak the blessing, imagine how Mary might have prayed it for her son Jesus, or how you would pray it over a child leaving home, or for a friend facing hardship. Note the subtle differences in the invocations: the first asks the Lord to shelter and sustain. The second asks that God's face shine

its saving light upon us, and the last asks again for God to "look" upon us and to grant a "peace" only God can give. Avoid a slow monotone or over-articulated delivery of this classic prayer. The lines that introduce and follow the blessing reinforce the prevailing mood of graciousness and compassion.

READING II   Paul tells the Jesus story most succinctly here, and his every detail is important. What was Paul trying to say, and what is the Church teaching us by selecting this reading for

Galatians = guh-LAY-shuhnz

"Fullness of time" means God's timing.
Pause after "Son" and mentally insert
"who was born . . . ."

Jesus was human and subject to the
law, all for the sake of *saving* us from
the law.

Don't read this as a courtroom argument,
but gently and slowly to surprise us again
with this amazing truth.

Pause between the words "Abba" and
"Father," and use the same inflection for
both words.

READING II   Galatians 4:4–7

A reading from the Letter of Saint Paul to the Galatians

Brothers and sisters:
When the fullness of time had **come**, God sent his **Son**,
    born of a **woman**, born under the **law**,
    to **ransom** those under the law,
    so that we might receive **adoption** as **sons**.
As **proof** that you are sons,
    God sent the **Spirit** of his Son into our **hearts**,
    crying out, "**Abba**, **Father**!"
So you are no longer a **slave** but a **son**,
    and if a **son** then also an **heir**, through **God**.

today? Two points are quickly apparent: Jesus is "born of a woman" (Mary), becoming one like us and sharing our human frailty. He is also "born under the law" and lived subject to it, as we see by his submission to circumcision in today's Gospel. But neither of these key points— that deserve stress—is the main point of the reading.

That is found in Paul's announcement, probably borrowed from an early creed, that "God sent his Son . . . that we might receive adoption as sons." Therein lies the meaning of this solemnity and of the entire

Christmas season. Christ's coming through Mary transformed us from slaves to children of God. Now, Paul enthuses, we can even call God "Abba!" (Note the exclamation point, and remember "Daddy" is a better translation of Abba than "Father.") This text is less about who Christ is than about what God did for us *through* Christ.

Paul seeks to teach and inspire. His teaching occurs in that somewhat torturous first sentence where five clauses require slow reading and careful attention to commas and pauses. The inspiration arrives in the final sentence: formerly we

were slaves, but now each has been made a member of the family, a "son" and "heir" who receives an equal share of God's bountiful inheritance. Sadly, overexposure has inoculated us to this amazing news. But your enthusiastic tone can make this "news" once again.

GOSPEL   (For additional insights on this reading please refer to the commentary from the Christmas Mass at Dawn.) Shepherds find what was announced by angels. Filled with amazement, they make known to others what

Review the commentary for Christmas Mass at Dawn.

The text contains three scenes with key words: a) arrival of the shepherds who "saw" and "made known"; b) Mary who quietly "kept . . . reflecting"; c) the eighth day when the child is given his "name."

Proclaim slowly here. Suggest the depth of her reflecting.

Increase energy for the words "Then the shepherds . . ." with a faster pace on middle lines and a slower pace at the end.

Pause here. Time has elapsed. The accent should be on the "name" given him.

GOSPEL Luke 2:16–21

A reading from the holy Gospel according to Luke

The shepherds went in **haste** to Bethlehem
    and found **Mary** and **Joseph**,
    and the **infant** lying in the **manger**.
When they **saw** this,
    they made known the **message**
    that had been **told** them about this child.
All who heard it were **amazed**
    by what had been **told** them by the shepherds.
And Mary **kept** all these things,
    reflecting on them in her **heart**.
Then the shepherds **returned**,
    glorifying and **praising** God
    for all they had **heard** and **seen**,
    just as it had been **told** to them.

When eight days were **completed** for his circumcision,
    he was named **Jesus**, the name given him by the **angel**
    before he was **conceived** in the **womb**.

was told them about this child, and all who hear it are amazed. In the midst of this seeing and announcing and amazement sits Mary, keeping all these things in her heart.

A new year calls us to reflect, sort out, and understand. Today's text from Galatians helps us understand that our lives are fundamentally changed by Christ. Here, the shepherds quickly understand that the world is radically changed, and Mary can't help but ponder the drastic changes her son will bring to her life and maybe even her world. If God becoming human were not a world-altering event, would it be worth

the bother? God comes for our sakes, not God's, to change the world forever. That's what all the amazement is about.

Mary, the focus of this solemnity, sits serenely at the heart of this reading. She is serene not from a lack of awareness, but despite it. That's why extra time is needed for the short line that tells of her musings. Mary doesn't sit oblivious to what has happened in her world and the world beyond. Let the line invite your assembly to realize how much they, too, have to contemplate and treasure.

By introducing the theme of Jesus' name, the last paragraph connects the Gospel with the First Reading. The Book of Numbers announced the wonder of God's presence shining down upon us like the sun. Jesus' name reminds us that God doesn't shine on us from afar, but from within and among us. To dwell among us and save us: that was God's plan long before Jesus "was conceived in the womb" of the one who was to become the mother of Emmanuel, God among us.

EPIPHANY OF THE LORD

Lectionary #20

READING I   Isaiah 60:1–6

Highlight and *contrast* references to light and darkness. Notice the synonymous parallelism (see the Introduction) used in almost every couplet (paired lines) in which the second line of the couplet repeats, balances, or develops what was stated in the first. Though ideas are repeated, they are not redundancies; each time, build energy from the first to second line.

Don't let the series of couplets lure you into a singsong delivery. Focus on each line's meaning to avoid that trap.

These are tender images. Don't waste them.

Pause here, then start this section with renewed energy. "Riches . . . wealth" require growing intensity for variety.

Dromedaries are single-humped camels.

Midian = MID-ee-uhn

Ephah = EE-fuh

"Gold and frankincense" tie this text to the Gospel. The reading begins and ends in joyful praise!

A reading from the Book of the Prophet Isaiah

Rise up in **splendor**, Jerusalem! Your **light** has **come**,
   the **glory** of the Lord **shines** upon you.
See, **darkness** covers the earth,
   and thick **clouds** cover the **peoples**;
but upon **you** the LORD **shines**,
   and **over** you appears his **glory**.
Nations shall walk by your **light**,
   and **kings** by your shining **radiance**.
Raise your eyes and **look** about;
   they all **gather** and **come** to you:
your **sons** come from **afar**,
   and your **daughters** in the arms of their **nurses**.

Then you shall be **radiant** at what you see,
   your **heart** shall throb and **overflow**,
for the **riches** of the sea shall be emptied out **before** you,
   the **wealth** of nations shall be **brought** to you.
Caravans of camels shall **fill** you,
   dromedaries from **Midian** and **Ephah**;
all from **Sheba** shall come
   bearing **gold** and **frankincense**,
   and proclaiming the **praises** of the LORD.

READING I   An epiphany manifests something previously hidden. Today's solemnity celebrates the manifestation of Christ to the nations, but it is only the first of other "epiphanies" that will manifest the divinity of Jesus. The Church also celebrates Jesus' Baptism in the Jordan and his changing water into wine at Cana as manifestations of the divine made human in Christ.

Isaiah's joyful prophecy announces to Jerusalem that her time of exile will come to an end and that a new and glorious day of hope, light, and victory has dawned. In the midst of darkness and murky clouds, says Isaiah, a light has begun shining—and the light shines directly upon those who had been cowering in fear.

The manifestation of God in our lives can both terrify and relieve us. If we've spent enough time in the darkness of fear, it takes courage to look at the light. Its blinding radiance frightens us. But if we open our eyes and look, fear can disappear as quickly as the shadows that helped create it. Isaiah calls the people of Israel to open their eyes and see what God is doing for them. He calls them to believe in the impossible—that their hearts will "throb and overflow"; that their children will be carried to Israel by the Gentiles in whose lands they had been exiled; that within the land of Israel, foreigners will sing the praises of Israel's God.

On this day, Isaiah's words have special meaning for us. We are being roused from sleep to hear God's message of hope. We, too, can expect the unexpected and see in the darkness. God has taken human flesh; the impossible has been made possible, and there is nothing God cannot do.

Ephesians = eeFEE-zhuhnz

Paul is saying: For your benefit, I was given a grace from God to care for; that is, a *mystery* was *revealed to* me. Read slowly or this sentence will become obscure at best.

Use "namely" to draw focus on what follows.

The "revelation" isn't named yet. Former generations were denied it, but now apostles (such as Paul) have glimpsed it.

These last three lines name the hidden truth that's now revealed. Three distinct images: "coheirs," "same body," "copartners." Distinguish them by speaking slowly and deliberately.

READING II Ephesians 3:2–3a, 5–6

A reading from the Letter of Saint Paul to the Ephesians

Brothers and sisters:
You have **heard** of the **stewardship** of God's **grace**
  that was **given** to me for your **benefit**,
    namely, that the **mystery** was made **known** to me
      by **revelation**.
It was not made known to people in **other** generations
  as it has **now** been revealed
  to his holy **apostles** and **prophets** by the **Spirit**:
  that the **Gentiles** are **coheirs**, **members** of the same **body**,
  and **copartners** in the promise in Christ **Jesus**
    through the **gospel**.

GOSPEL Matthew 2:1–12

A reading from the holy Gospel according to Matthew

When **Jesus** was born in **Bethlehem** of **Judea**,
  in the days of King **Herod**,
    behold, **magi** from the **east** arrived in **Jerusalem**, saying,
    "Where is the newborn **king** of the **Jews**?
We saw his **star** at its **rising**
  and have come to do him **homage**."
When King Herod **heard** this,
  he was greatly **troubled**,
    and all Jerusalem **with** him.

Before anything else, this is a story. Proclaim it as such.

"East" suggests the magi's foreign, exotic identity. They are astrologers and their dialogue is spoken with eagerness and sincerity.

"Herod" introduces an undercurrent of threat.

Your task is to believe that, and announce it with conviction.

READING II The ancient solemnity of the Epiphany of the Lord celebrates the manifestation of God in Christ and the extension of God's saving love to all people. This revelation of God's saving action is not just a past event we gather to remember, but a present and ongoing reality the Church is charged to announce.

Paul says the universal availability of salvation was part of God's secret plan, unknown in former ages but now revealed by the Spirit. This is a startling revelation. The very strangers Israel feared are made family members. Those considered "other" have become part of "us." God planned this from the start. While we thought ourselves different and special, Paul says, God was planning a family so big no one could count it. God has made Jew and Gentile coheirs—not only members of the same family, but "members of the same body!"

If all can become "copartners in the promise . . . through the *gospel*," as Ephesians states, then sharing the Gospel takes on new urgency. The life of the Church and of every Christian is an epiphany—a manifestation of the saving Lord in our midst yesterday, today, and everyday.

Paul received this knowledge as a direct "revelation" from God. He shares it boldly with people reluctant to embrace that truth. Now, you must boldly proclaim that the living Christ came to sanctify and save *all* people.

GOSPEL As he does throughout his Gospel, Matthew quotes the prophets to demonstrate that Jesus is

This comes from Micah 5:1, but it is altered slightly by Matthew.

A note of danger sounds again. Speak the line in Herod's voice.

King Herod is cunning, but don't overdo it in your delivery.

Here is familiar, comforting imagery.

"House" is unexpected. They find him with Mary.

Note that they don't kneel but rather "prostrate."

Express both the relief and derision found in this sentence: in the nick of time (relief!) the necessary information was kept from Herod (delight!).

Assembling all the chief **priests** and the **scribes** of the people,
  he **inquired** of them where the **Christ** was to be **born**.
They said to him, "In **Bethlehem** of **Judea**,
  for thus it has been written through the **prophet**:
    And **you**, Bethlehem, land of **Judah**,
      are by no means **least** among the rulers of Judah;
    since from you shall come a **ruler**,
      who is to **shepherd** my people **Israel**."
Then Herod called the magi **secretly**
  and **ascertained** from them the **time** of the star's appearance.
He sent them to **Bethlehem** and said,
  "**Go** and search **diligently** for the child.
When you have **found** him, bring me **word**,
  that I **too** may go and do him **homage**."
After their **audience** with the king they **set** out.
And **behold**, the **star** that they had seen at its rising
    preceded them,
  until it came and **stopped** over the place where the **child** was.
They were **overjoyed** at seeing the star,
  and on entering the **house**
  they saw the **child** with **Mary** his **mother**.
They **prostrated** themselves and did him **homage**.
Then they opened their **treasures**
  and offered him gifts of **gold**, **frankincense**, and **myrrh**.
And having been **warned** in a dream not to **return** to Herod,
  they **departed** for their country by another **way**.

the fulfillment of prophecy and the object of divine intervention. This story speaks of more than Gentile kings worshipping a child. It speaks of effort and quest, of signs observed and followed, of risk and danger, deception and narrow escape; and it says that through all these a child became the revelation of God to the world. Ironically, it is foreigners who strive and seek and find; who open treasures and offer gifts, and who go forth to distant lands announcing the good news of God among us.

But then, the details of Matthew's story differ strikingly from the angels and

shepherds we typically associate with Jesus' birth. Threat immediately enters this story, for while shepherds rejoice at the announcement of the Savior's birth, Herod "and all Jerusalem" are "greatly troubled." The magi come to the capital and its palace seeking the newborn king, only to learn his birth was prophesied to occur in a humble village. Herod lets the foreigners go to seek him, while he plots the demise of the potential rival.

Although many of Matthew's words offer comforting familiarity ("magi,"

"Bethlehem," "east," "star," "child," "shepherd," "gold, frankincense, and myrrh," other words disturb because they are unexpected ("King Herod," "house," "prostrated"). We anticipate *kneeling*, not *prostrated*, magi who enter a *stable* not a *house*; Herod should loom over the end of Jesus' life, not its beginning. Herod's presence gives a sense of impending danger. His deceit and plotting portend the threat that will haunt Jesus all his days; they foreshadow his Passion. By paying close attention to the familiar *and* the disturbing, you'll reveal the rich texture of this story.

2ND SUNDAY IN ORDINARY TIME

Lectionary #65

READING I   1 Samuel 3:3b–10; 19

A reading from the first Book of Samuel

Samuel was **sleeping** in the **temple** of the LORD
　　where the **ark** of God was.
The LORD **called** to Samuel, who answered, "**Here** I am."
Samuel ran to **Eli** and said, "**Here** I am. You **called** me."
"**I** did not call you," Eli said. "Go back to **sleep**."
So he **went** back to sleep.
Again the LORD called Samuel, who **rose** and went to **Eli**.
"**Here** I am, " he said. "You **called** me."
But Eli answered, "I did **not** call you, my son. Go back to **sleep**."

At **that** time **Samuel** was not **familiar** with the LORD,
　　because the LORD had not **revealed** anything to him as yet.
The LORD called Samuel **again**, for the **third** time.
Getting **up** and going to **Eli**, he said, "Here I am. You **called** me."
Then Eli understood that the **LORD** was calling the youth.
So he **said** to Samuel, "Go to **sleep**, and if you are **called**, reply,
　　'**Speak**, LORD, for your servant is **listening**.'"
When Samuel went to **sleep** in his place,
　　the LORD **came** and revealed his **presence**,
　　calling out as before, "**Samuel**, **Samuel**!"
Samuel answered, "**Speak**, for your servant is **listening**."

Samuel **grew** up, and the LORD was **with** him,
　　not permitting any **word** of his to be without **effect**.

Start slowly so the setting and characters can be established clearly.

Since we don't hear the call, let your careful narration suggest God's summons.
Here, the pacing is brisk, as if Samuel thinks there is an urgent need.

Speak the line as if Eli is convincing the boy he's only dreaming.
This important line suggests Samuel's spiritual immaturity.

Samuel might be more insistent here, perhaps even a bit whiny.
The reading turns on the line "Eli understood."

Speak with great reverence and more energy on the second "Samuel."

Speak the line in a way that suggests the great transformation this encounter will accomplish in Samuel's life.

READING I | Dedicated to the Lord's service before he was born, Samuel lives now under the tutelage of the temple priest, Eli. He began his service at a very early age and now, possibly aged thirteen, he experiences a divine encounter that will set the trajectory of his life. Samuel will become a prophet who, like John the Baptist, uncompromisingly speaks God's word. He will straddle the age of judges—military leaders who led in times of peril—and the age of kings, the first of which, Saul and David, Samuel himself anointed.

A listening and obedient heart distinguishes this young boy, and the discernment of his master, Eli, helps set the stage for the divine encounter you will be privileged to narrate. Often, a pivotal event seems quite ordinary when it occurs; only later does its profound significance strike us. As narrator, you understand the significance for Samuel's life, and the life of Israel, of this divine call. But Samuel is not aware and Eli is slow to catch on.

Proclaim the text as the story it is, mindful of its important elements: the setting—the magnificent temple where a young boy is easily overwhelmed and where Eli recognizes the special presence of God; the characters—Samuel, young, naive, and sleepy, and Eli, tired but patient, then suddenly aware; the suspense—the Lord calls and calls again; Eli understands (the turning point), and God finally speaks (the climax).

When Samuel first approaches Eli, he speaks with the sleepy awareness of a child doing what he thinks he's told. Eli is calm and gentle. But the third time Samuel

Corinthians = kohr-IN-thee-uhnz

A blunt message like this requires sustained eye contact and love for those addressed.

Contrast the word "immorality" with the word "Lord."

Present Paul's reasoning with energy and conviction.

Look at the assembly as you give this injunction.

Once again, use Paul's reasoning to persuade, not intimidate.

For Paul, "A" ("you have been purchased") leads to "B" ("glorify God").

READING II 1 Corinthians 6:13c–15a, 17–20

A reading from the first Letter of Saint Paul to the Corinthians

Brothers and sisters:
The body is not for **immorality**, but for the **Lord**,
   and the **Lord** is for the **body**;
   God **raised** the Lord and will also raise **us** by his **power**.

Do you not **know** that your bodies are **members** of **Christ**?
But whoever is **joined** to the Lord becomes one **Spirit** with him.
Avoid immorality.
Every **other** sin a person commits is **outside** the body,
   but the **immoral** person sins against his own **body**.
Do you not **know** that your body
   is a **temple** of the Holy **Spirit** within you,
   whom you have from **God**, and that you are not your **own**?
For you have been **purchased** at a **price**.
Therefore **glorify** God in your **body**.

might be more insistent. Suddenly, Eli comprehends and responds with clear instructions. God's voice must be authoritative, yet kind. Samuel responds in a child's awed and humble voice. After a pause, convince us this favored child grew into a sturdy tree that bore good fruit.

READING II Sometimes strong words are best, and rarely Paul shies from using them. The Corinthians, even some who had turned to Christ, embraced sexual immorality with great license, so Paul steps in to set things

straight. But instead of scolding, he offers persuasive arguments for moral behavior based on his respect for the body's sacredness.

Paul makes his point clearly and forcefully: any lewd conduct is incompatible with the dignity we are given by oneness with Christ. Fornicators sin against their own bodies and against the Spirit who dwells within them. Bad enough! Worse is that we don't have a right to violate ourselves for we are not our own; at great "price," God has "*purchased*" us. The Word of God became flesh and all bap-

tized in him are now his body. Sexual sin is therefore never private, for it injures all the members of the body. The reading has a very colloquial feel, as if Paul were standing before the community chiding, encouraging, warning. Address his double "Do you not know . . ." directly at the assembly, making good eye contact.

Hard sayings don't need to be spoken in anger, but they also don't need to be laced with honey. What you speak is offered for the good of your listeners. How might you speak to a younger sibling you found abusing drugs or cheating on a

GOSPEL John 1:35–42

A reading from the holy Gospel according to John

John was standing with two of his **disciples**,
and as he watched **Jesus** walk by, he said,
"**Behold**, the **Lamb** of **God**."
The two disciples **heard** what he said and **followed** Jesus.
Jesus turned and **saw** them following him and **said** to them,
"What are you **looking** for?"
They said to him, "**Rabbi**"—which translated means **Teacher**—,
"where are you **staying**?"
He said to them, "**Come**, and you will **see**."
So they went and **saw** where Jesus was staying,
and they **stayed** with him that day.
It was about **four** in the afternoon.
Andrew, the brother of Simon **Peter**,
was one of the two who **heard** John and **followed** Jesus.
He first found his own brother **Simon** and told him,
"We have found the **Messiah**"—which is translated **Christ**—.
Then he **brought** him to Jesus.
Jesus **looked** at him and said,
"You are **Simon** the son of **John**;
you will be called **Cephas**"—which is translated **Peter**.

Speak of the characters and locations with familiarity and care.

Try to render this familiar line as if it were fresh and new.
The two disciples "heard" Jesus with more than their ears.
Let this dialogue sound like Jesus is enjoying the exchange.

Here, let your tone suggest they found something worth staying for.

The pacing can quicken a bit here as you narrate how Andrew eagerly sought out his brother.

Let the words "Jesus looked at him" convey the depth with which Jesus saw Peter.

---

spouse? Today, you address brothers and sisters in the pews who deserve no less concern or candor.

GOSPEL Some authors write about locations as if all their readers had been there. They haven't, of course, but the author writes with a familiarity that assumes a common understanding of the place. Scripture sometimes assumes a familiarity with certain geographical sites that your reading tone must not contradict. So here, speak of Bethany and the Jordan as you might about your home town and a nearby river.

John speaks of Jesus with such intensity and certitude, with such a fixed and reverent gaze that his five words become persuasion enough to turn Andrew and his friend into John's *ex*-disciples. A fascinating exchange ensues between Jesus and the disciples; each speaks coyly, revealing less than the other wants to know. Don't over-dramatize Jesus' invitation. It has a playful quality, teasing the young men's curiosity. Relate the episode (even the time of day is remembered!) from the viewpoint of the evangelist who may well have heard about the event from both men (unless *he* was the unnamed disciple).

The identity of Andrew is given, and he goes off to proselytize his brother Peter with astounding testimony that combines certainty and disbelief, familiarity and awe. This extraordinary moment is dressed in everyday garb, for Jesus' address to Peter contains no dramatic overtones. There is no way Peter could have imagined at that time that by changing his name, Jesus would forever change his destiny.

3RD SUNDAY IN ORDINARY TIME

Lectionary #68

Jonah = JOH-nuh

Jonah is a two page book. Consider reading it all to get a better sense of the context.

Nineveh = NIN-uh-vuh

Speak this line with the authoritative voice of God urging Jonah to obey.

Your narration here can suggest Jonah's reluctance to be God's instrument of intervention.

Speak the warning with Jonah's eagerness.

The people's reaction can be narrated with the attitude of the repentant citizens who experience an instant change of heart.

Speak as the narrator, not as Jonah, of the great marvel of God's generous mercy.

READING I   Jonah 3:1–5, 10

A reading from the Book of the Prophet Jonah

The **word** of the LORD came to **Jonah**, saying:
    "**Set** out for the great city of **Nineveh**,
    and **announce** to it the message that I will **tell** you."
So Jonah made **ready** and **went** to Nineveh,
    according to the LORD's **bidding**.
Now Nineveh was an enormously **large** city;
    it took three **days** to go through it.
Jonah began his **journey** through the city,
    and had gone but a **single** day's walk announcing,
    "**Forty** days more and Nineveh shall be **destroyed**,"
when the people of Nineveh **believed** God;
    they proclaimed a **fast**
    and **all** of them, **great** and **small**, put on **sackcloth**.

When God **saw** by their actions how they **turned**
        from their evil way,
    he **repented** of the evil that he had **threatened** to do to them;
    he did **not** carry it out.

READING I Actually this is the *second* time "The word of the Lord came to Jonah." His encounter with the whale made him more disposed to heed God's directive to "set out." Initially, Jonah disobeyed God's command because he had no desire to be a vehicle of conversion and repentance for the Ninevites. Knowing what preceded and follows this episode will enable you to tell this story with more color and variety.

"Jonah made ready" only because of the whale of an incentive God provided, and though his close call moved Jonah's

feet, it didn't move his heart. Let that knowledge color your narration. Jonah does the Lord's "bidding," but he hopes the Ninevites won't listen! You can describe the city's enormity from Jonah's perspective—dreading the prospect of walking through it for "three [long!] days." But Jonah doesn't hold back on the message of destruction, for he believes the Ninevites so deserve the threatened punishment that he can't wait to see it fall upon them. Announce his threats forcefully. Then speak with Jonah's incredulity as you recount the people's repentance.

Later, Jonah will much lament this manifestation of God's mercy upon the Ninevites, for his sense of justice excluded such compassion. So speak the lines from the perspective of one of the kneeling Ninevites upon whom it gradually dawns that the promised destruction is averted, and that instead of fire, it's the gentle rain of God's forgiveness that falls upon them.

READING II Christ's coming changed everything. The world in its present form is passing away. That's more a spiritual than a physical reality that

Corinthians = kohr-IN-thee-uhnz

With a short reading, always take extra time to ensure all are settled and listening.

Speak the line solemnly, with eye contact. Then pause and sustain the eye contact.

The individual activities (weeping, rejoicing, buying, and so forth) are not as important as the idea that *all* the things of this world will eventually pass away. Keep the pacing brisk, suggesting urgency rather than emphasizing the specific life situations.

Pause after "not using it fully," and then deliver the final line from memory, making eye contact with assembly.

READING II 1 Corinthians 7:29–31

A reading from the first Letter of Saint Paul to the Corinthians

I **tell** you, brothers and sisters, the **time** is running **out**.
From **now** on, let those having **wives** act as **not** having them,
 those **weeping** as **not** weeping,
 those **rejoicing** as **not** rejoicing,
 those **buying** as **not** owning,
 those **using** the world as **not** using it **fully**.
For the world in its **present** form is passing **away**.

---

saints and poets sense better than the rest of us. Yes, physical realities change too— governments collapse, species disappear, friends and relatives die, we don't inhabit the same world we were born in, and when we die it will be different still.

Paul announced this truth to a community expecting the end of the world and Jesus' imminent return in glory. Does that make his words meaningless for us who still await Christ's return? Of course not!

Paul knew that once we are in Christ, our relationship to the world must change. We are to be in the world but not of it. Paul

was telling his readers not to change their social and/or marital status. But we don't proclaim this text to remember what Paul told believers 2,000 years ago. We share it for contemporary believers who still must learn that the things of this world are fleeting, their value transitory, and that we must hold lightly to the world's goods lest they hold on to us and distract us from what really matters.

In today's Gospel, Jesus calls fishermen to leave everything and follow him. In the text from Jonah, God used a whale to convince Jonah to embrace his mission.

All three texts speak a clear message: it matters little if we weep or rejoice, profit or not from use of the world's goods. What matters is our relationship with Christ. Time grows short to proclaim that message. Some who hear it today will not live to hear it again.

GOSPEL Here, "Good News" is preceded by bad. "After John had been arrested" is a foreboding opening that casts a deliberate shadow and hints that as Jesus follows John in ministry, so will he follow him in death. Awareness of

GOSPEL Mark 1:14–20

A reading from the holy Gospel according to Mark

After **John** had been **arrested,**
  Jesus came to **Galilee** proclaiming the gospel of **God**:
    "**This** is the time of **fulfillment**.
The kingdom of **God** is at **hand**.
Repent, and **believe** in the **gospel**."

As he passed by the Sea of **Galilee**,
  he saw **Simon** and his brother **Andrew** casting their **nets**
    into the sea;
  they were **fishermen**.
Jesus **said** to them,
  "Come after **me**, and I will make you fishers of **men**."
Then they **abandoned** their nets and **followed** him.
He walked along a little **farther**
  and saw **James**, the son of **Zebedee**, and his brother **John**.
They **too** were in a boat mending their **nets**.
Then he **called** them.
So they **left** their father **Zebedee** in the **boat**
  along with the hired **men** and **followed** him.

John's arrest colors the mood of the opening.

Give Jesus' words a vibrant energy that would inspire men to abandon their livelihoods to follow him.

Take time with the names and the description of their profession.

Jesus is inviting, but the words are in the form of an imperative.

Once again, make sure the assembly understands who the characters are.

Emphasize the familial relationship of sons and father.

Pause briefly after the words "the hired men." Then, with admiration, announce their decision.

John's death also sets the mood for Jesus' proclamation of the kingdom—he does it fully aware of the cost involved, an awareness that steels and sobers the delivery of his proclamation.

The kingdom comes upon the unsuspecting fishermen in the person of Jesus. A literal reading of this text seems far-fetched. Could practical men so quickly and easily abandon everything to follow a man who has even less then they do? Last week's Gospel from John that revealed some of the men were already disciples of the Baptist (Andrew, maybe John), lends credence to the immediacy of their response, but it doesn't lessen the marvel of that instant decision.

A less literal reading robs the text of its power and meaning, for the one who calls is no less than the Son of God. Mark uses the two sets of brothers to spotlight the price of discipleship: it costs everything—livelihood, as with Simon and Andrew, and family, as with James and John. Let that tell you where to place your stress: in the first instance on the references to "sea," "nets," and "fishermen"; in the second on the mention of "Zebedee" and the "hired men."

To win their allegiance, Jesus must first capture the men's imaginations, so his words must ring with zeal and strength and excitement. In preparing to proclaim, it may be helpful to recall how Christ first won your heart and allegiance.

4TH SUNDAY IN ORDINARY TIME

Lectionary #71

READING I   Deuteronomy 18:15–20

Deuteronomy = doo-ter-AH-nuh-mee

Only the first line is spoken by the narrator, the rest is spoken in Moses' voice. Give Moses an authoritative tone and go slowly so the multiple clauses don't become a confusing muddle.

Moses is recalling the people's encounter with God at Horeb and how they feared meeting the Lord face to face. He's telling them: This is exactly what you asked for.

Here, Moses is quoting the Lord who promises a future prophet. Speak again with great authority.

The mood darkens a bit here. God warns of the pitfalls that come with intermediaries. Don't blunt the shock value of these strong lines. Careful attention to the words marked for stress will assist your delivery.

A reading from the Book of Deuteronomy

Moses spoke to all the **people**, saying:
"A **prophet** like me will the LORD, your **God**, raise **up** for you
from among your own **kin**;
to **him** you shall **listen**.
This is exactly what you **requested** of the LORD, your God,
      at **Horeb**
on the day of the **assembly**, when you **said**,
'Let us not **again** hear the voice of the LORD, our **God**,
nor see this great **fire** any more, lest we **die**.'
And the LORD said to me, 'This was **well** said.
I will raise up for them a **prophet** like you from among their **kin**,
and will put my **words** into his mouth;
he shall tell them **all** that I **command** him.
Whoever will not **listen** to my words which he speaks
      in my name,
I **myself** will make him **answer** for it.
But if a prophet **presumes** to speak in my name
an oracle that I have **not** commanded him to speak,
or speaks in the name of **other** gods, he shall **die**.'"

READING I   The institution of prophecy tells us much about God's relationship with the chosen people. A sure sign of love in any relationship is communication—the initiative to open one's mind and heart to another. Through the prophets, God was in constant communication with the people—encouraging, warning, comforting. A later chapter of Deuteronomy (34:10) says "Since then no prophet has arisen in Israel like Moses, whom the Lord knew face to face." Moses could handle that kind of intimacy, but apparently the people could not.

At Horeb, the Israelites had been so intimidated by the Divine Presence manifested in fire and thunder that they had actually asked God not to "speak" directly to them again, but use a human intermediary instead. Pleased, God granted the request.

Here Moses announces God's decision to send a prophet like himself whom they need not fear, for the people believed a direct encounter with God would result in death, since no mortal could survive God's Presence. But God warns that intermediaries can bring problems, for some may ignore the words the prophet speaks

in God's name. If anyone shows such disrespect, God says sternly, "I myself will make him answer." But more serious is the prophet who abuses his office and speaks "an oracle that I have not commanded." God's remedy is uncompromising and blunt: that prophet "shall die."

Originally, the passage referred to the whole line of prophets who would succeed Moses, but eventually this text was taken to refer to a final, messianic prophet. The selection of this text for today's liturgy identifies Jesus with that prophet and links the authority with which Jesus

Corinthians = kohr-IN-thee-uhnz

Paul's first sentence sets the tone for what follows.

Contrast what each is "anxious about" and who each wants to "please."

Note the balance in the advice given to women and men. Paul is not suggesting any imparity between male and female. Each has responsibilities and legitimate rights.

Make eye contact as you share these lines. Here, Paul is solicitous and flexible, seeking only the good of his readers.

Read this entire chapter in 1 Corinthians to get a better sense of the context and Paul's intent.

READING II   1 Corinthians 7:32–35

A reading from the first Letter of Saint Paul to the Corinthians

Brothers and sisters:
I should like you to be free of **anxieties**.
An **unmarried** man is anxious about the things of the **Lord**,
   how he may **please** the Lord.
But a **married** man is anxious about the things of the **world**,
   how he may please his **wife**, and he is **divided**.
An unmarried **woman** or a **virgin** is anxious about the things
      of the **Lord**,
   so that she may be holy in both **body** and **spirit**.
A **married** woman, on the other hand,
   is anxious about the things of the **world**,
   how she may please her **husband**.
I am telling you this for your own **benefit**,
   not to impose a **restraint** upon you,
   but for the sake of **propriety**
      and **adherence** to the Lord without **distraction**.

---

teaches to the charismatic authority demonstrated by Moses and his successors.

READING II Paul is answering the Corinthians' questions about practical matters like marriage and sexuality. But taken out of context, this passage makes little sense and may even alienate some listeners. Paul's true intent is best seen in the first and last sentences where his tone is quite pastoral. Paul wants to be helpful by offering good advice for hard times. He and his contemporaries are expecting the end of the world, so he

takes a practical approach, urging the Corinthians to focus on the essentials, to simplify their lives and avoid what is unnecessary. Who could disagree that a less complicated life appears easier to live than one laden with the responsibilities of children, home, and spouse?

Paul is concerned that time is running out, so he encourages stability—maintaining their current state of life rather than embracing new situations that may heighten anxiety. The first sentence sets Paul's premise; pause, then, like a wise teacher, share Paul's advice stressing his

contrasts between the commitments and constraints of the married and unmarried. This is a simple message, but he doesn't deal with it simplistically. Paul is pointing to higher things, ideal values, while remaining firmly rooted in reality. He is solicitous, fatherly, and unusually flexible in his options, for he's not legislating restrictions, only offering options for how best to be ready for the Lord's return.

GOSPEL It's intriguing to find an unclean spirit right in the midst of the synagogue where Jesus

GOSPEL   Mark 1:21–28

A reading from the holy Gospel according to Mark

Then they came to **Capernaum**,
    and on the **sabbath Jesus** entered the synagogue and **taught**.
The people were **astonished** at his teaching,
    for he taught them as one having **authority**
        and not as the **scribes**.
In their synagogue was a man with an **unclean spirit**;
    he cried out, "What have you to **do** with us, Jesus of **Nazareth**?
Have you come to **destroy** us?
I **know** who you **are**—the **Holy** One of **God**!"
Jesus **rebuked** him and said,
    "**Quiet**! Come **out** of him!"
The unclean spirit **convulsed** him and with a loud **cry**
    came **out** of him.
All were **amazed** and asked one another,
    "What **is** this?
A new **teaching** with **authority**.
He commands even the unclean **spirits** and they **obey** him."
His **fame** spread **everywhere** throughout the whole region
    of **Galilee**.

Capernaum = kuh-PER-nee-*m

Give us a sense of Jesus' spellbinding authority.

Start this section slowly, then increase the energy and rate as the spirit cries out and protests.
Don't overdo it, but suggest the man's uncontrolled exclamations and the spirit's fear.
Pause between Jesus' "Quiet!" and "Come out of him!"

Read the narration ("all were amazed . . .") slowly, but then deliver the onlooker comments at a brisker, energetic pace.

Pause after the third comment, then narrate with obvious satisfaction the news of his growing fame.

---

teaches and leaves the assembly "astonished." The people sense the authority with which he teaches, an authority that perhaps evokes memories of the great prophets of their tradition. Certainly the "spirit" knows with whom he's dealing and bluntly calls Jesus out. But his tactic serves only to demonstrate further the remarkable character of this rabbi. The exorcism also serves Mark's purpose of demonstrating the authority of Jesus, though it's not the power to do miracles that Mark wants to highlight; rather the depth and power of Jesus' teaching.

Driving out the spirit simply validates the supremacy of that teaching. The miracle says: Here is one whose authority is manifest in both word *and* deed.

Speak the first paragraph with the authoritative tone that characterized Jesus' teaching, for it sets the mood for the action that follows. The possessed man "cries out" to Jesus. Without exaggerating, suggest the compulsion with which he speaks and the uncontrolled flow of his exclamations. The man is loud, fast, and intense, apparently on the offensive and defensive at the same time, and clearly

afraid. Jesus matches his intensity, but in contrast to the possessed man, we see (reflected on your face) the "authority" that set Jesus apart from the scribes.

Narrate the exorcism as if you were watching it, conveying the terrible energy of this bizarre event. Sustaining the energy, narrate the amazement of the onlookers. Don't try for three different onlooker voices, but vary the energy, intensity and rate of the three comments. As you inform us of Jesus' growing "fame," your tone acknowledges the propriety and predictability of that notoriety.

5TH SUNDAY IN ORDINARY TIME

Lectionary #74

READING I   Job 7:1–4, 6–7

A reading from the Book of Job

Job spoke, saying:
   Is not man's life on **earth** a **drudgery**?
      Are not his days those of **hirelings**?
   He is a **slave** who longs for the **shade**,
      a **hireling** who waits for his **wages**.
   So **I** have been assigned months of **misery**,
      and **troubled** nights have been **allotted** to me.
   If in **bed** I say, "When shall I **arise**?"
      then the night **drags** on;
   I am filled with **restlessness** until the **dawn**.
   My days are **swifter** than a weaver's **shuttle**;
      they come to an end without **hope**.
   Remember that my life is like the **wind**;
      I shall not see **happiness again**.

Job = johb
The tone of the reading is plaintive.
Subtly stretching key words will help
create that effect.
Make eye contact and don't try to soften
the negative tone of these lines.

You need not speak with anger;
Job seemed resigned to this fate.

Contrast the long, restless *nights* with
the swiftly passing *days*.

Pause after "without hope," then make
eye contact and speak the final line with
great resignation.

READING I Put bluntly, the chief message of the book of Job is: God is God and we are not. As he faces stunning calamities, Job wonders why such evil has befallen him. The old assumptions—that misfortune was God's punishment for wrongdoing—can't apply here because Job is clearly a righteous man. In the end, he must accept that human suffering is a mystery and even the noblest cannot demand an explanation from God.

But when our pain becomes so great that all we can *do* about it is to *talk* about it, we discover that talking *can* make a difference. In the face of great trials, a healthy option is simply to acknowledge how awful the situation is while trusting God will be with us in the darkness and pain. Plumbing the depths of misery is a human quality, and this passage is a marvel of misery—oozing with pain, anxiety, and depression—which Job expresses without embarrassment.

Today's Gospel will offset this reading with images of healing and hope. But here, with license to accent the negative emotions, you focus on the futility of life: as demeaning as forced military service ("drudgery"), as dehumanizing as menial labor ("hirelings"), as hopeless as slavery.

For Job, life has become "months of misery" filled with restless nights and days that vanish as quickly as his "hope." When you speak of the lonely nights and desperate days, imagine someone gravely ill who is overcome by depression, and deliver the despair of the last line with quiet resignation. Surely, at some time, such an emotion has tried to rule your heart: let that memory color your delivery. Then the Gospel will surprise us all the more with the saving works of Christ.

READING II   1 Corinthians 9:16–19, 22–23

A reading from the first Letter of Saint Paul to the Corinthians

Brothers and sisters:
If I preach the **gospel**, this is no reason for me to **boast**,
    for an **obligation** has been imposed on me,
    and **woe** to me if I do **not** preach it!
If I do so **willingly**, I have a **recompense**,
    but if **unwillingly**, then I have been entrusted
        with a **stewardship**.
What then is my **recompense**?
That, when I **preach**,
    I offer the gospel free of **charge**
    so as not to make full use of my **right** in the gospel.

Although I am **free** in regard to all,
    I have made myself a **slave** to all
    so as to win over as **many** as **possible**.
To the **weak** I became **weak**, to win **over** the weak.
I have become **all** things to **all**, to save at least **some**.
All this I do for the sake of the **gospel**,
    so that I **too** may have a **share** in it.

This reading is taken out of context, so read slowly to give your hearers a chance to enter Paul's argument.

Speak in a positive tone of the "obligation . . . imposed" on him.

Here, Paul is saying, "Even if I preach unwillingly, I am nonetheless entrusted with a responsibility."
Paul is referring back to the "recompense" mentioned above. Speak in a positive tone; he is proud that he does not claim his legitimate rights.

There are a number of balances which must be stressed: "*free* in regard to all" balances "a *slave* to all"; "all things to *all*" balances "to save at least *some*."

Note Paul's final motivation: by giving away the Gospel, he gets to share in its blessing.

READING II Paul acknowledges a compulsion to speak the word of God. The word "obligation," here suggests more a burden than a privilege. But for Paul, proclamation of the Gospel is pure privilege. When he says "woe to me if I do not preach it," he's not fearing divine reprisal, but speaking like an athlete about the need to exercise or a poet about the need to write—they would stop being who they are if they terminated those activities, and Paul would not be Paul if he became mute about the Gospel.

His talk of recompense might seem indulgent, but keep in mind that he was criticized by opponents who thought his refusal to accept money for preaching reflected lack of confidence in his own authority. False teachers would soon appear in Corinth who all too eagerly accepted financial support. Paul doesn't want to be mistaken for someone like that. His goal is simple: do everything in his power to win at least some to Christ. Hence his famous declaration that he became "all things to all people." For the sake of Christ, he will be "weak" to win over the weak and become a "slave" to win over as many as possible. That Paul feels strongly and that these are intensely personal issues for him are the keys to your proclamation. Paul is not bragging, but persuading skeptics. Preaching the Gospel "willingly" is its own reward, but even if he were unwilling he couldn't escape the fact that he's been "entrusted with a stewardship," a responsibility he simply can't avoid.

Paul's freedom allows him to *choose* the slavery of willing service. His service to the weak and to all is a sign of great love

GOSPEL   Mark 1:29–39

A reading from the holy Gospel according to Mark

On leaving the **synagogue**
  Jesus entered the house of **Simon** and **Andrew**
    with **James** and **John**.
Simon's **mother-in-law** lay sick with a **fever**.
They immediately **told** him about her.
He **approached**, **grasped** her hand, and helped her **up**.
Then the fever **left** her and she **waited** on them.

When it was **evening**, after **sunset**,
  they brought to him all who were **ill** or possessed by **demons**.
The whole **town** was gathered at the **door**.
He cured **many** who were sick with various **diseases**,
  and he **drove** out many **demons**,
    not permitting them to **speak** because they **knew** him.

Rising very **early** before **dawn**, he **left**
  and went off to a **deserted** place, where he **prayed**.
Simon and those who were **with** him **pursued** him
  and on **finding** him said, "Everyone is **looking** for you."
He told them, "Let us go **on** to the nearby **villages**
  that I may preach there **also**.
For this **purpose** have I **come**."
So he went into their **synagogues**,
  preaching and driving out **demons** throughout the **whole**
    of **Galilee**.

Speak with familiarity of Simon's mother-in-law and the details of her healing ("grasped her hand," "she waited on them"). Note that time references begin each segment of this text.

Suggest Jesus' gentleness and compassion with these words. Pause before starting the next section.

The mood here is less intimate, for the whole city is gathering. Stress the apparent power with which Jesus healed.

Here is another mood shift. Jesus rises in the quiet of the morning to pray alone. Stress the words "pursued" and "finding."

Jesus is roused from his prayer, but he eagerly embraces his mission: to preach God's word. Share the final sentence with joy, for what Jesus did then you also do this day.

---

which you should convey throughout. Paul is not good enough to love, he's smart enough to love, for he knows that service without love offers no "share" in the Gospel's blessings.

| GOSPEL | Mark's Gospel account is distinctive in its simplicity. |

He says much with few words and makes the amazing events of the kingdom appear commonplace. Mark's style calls for an unembellished reading where understatement speaks with its own eloquence. If you don't rush and you use all the words to tell the story, Mark's images will come to life and weave their magic.

This is a very different world from Job's. Here the sick are healed and demons are expelled. But note that *"all"* who were ill or possessed came to Jesus and the *"whole"* town gathered at his door, yet not all, but *"many"* of the sick and possessed were healed and cleansed. Again, God is God and we can only wonder why some were healed and others not. Yet divine power is manifest clearly, powerfully, almost routinely in Jesus' ministry. As the narrator, speak as someone who knew and loved Jesus. Tell of his miracles with familiarity and great respect.

Mark's time references deserve attention: "evening" and "sunset" suggest the tired part of a day suddenly made tumultuous by the arrival of the sick and possessed. "Early before dawn" signals a change of mood as well as time. Suddenly, the rapt silence of Jesus' prayer is broken by the disciples' exclamation. But Jesus is re-energized and sets out resolutely to bring the miraculous abundance of the kingdom to all of Galilee.

6TH SUNDAY IN ORDINARY TIME

Lectionary #77

READING I   Leviticus 13:1–2, 44–46

Leviticus = lih-VIT-ih-kuhs

Note that God is the speaker throughout.
Aaron = AYR-uhn
leprosy = LEP-ruh-see

Go for a dispassionate, not a matter of fact delivery. This is a matter of greatest importance for the health of the community.

Stress words like "rent," "bare," and "muffle" to stress the seriousness of the topic. Cry out "unclean" with about half the energy expected of the leprous person.

The order given in the last sentence is necessarily unyielding. Allow some pathos to color your voice so we can long, with the Gospel's leper, for Jesus' words: "I *do* will it."

A reading from the Book of Leviticus

The LORD said to **Moses** and **Aaron**,
  "If someone has on his **skin** a **scab** or **pustule** or **blotch**
  which appears to be the sore of **leprosy**,
  he shall be brought to **Aaron**, the **priest**,
  or to one of the priests among his **descendants**.
If the man **is** leprous and unclean,
  the priest shall **declare** him unclean
  by reason of the **sore** on his head.

"The one who **bears** the sore of leprosy
  shall keep his garments **rent** and his head **bare**,
  and shall muffle his **beard**;
  he shall cry out, '**Unclean, unclean**!'
As long as the sore is **on** him he shall **declare** himself unclean,
  since he is in **fact** unclean.
He shall dwell **apart**, making his abode **outside** the camp."

READING I Often the First Reading helps set the stage for the drama that will unfold later in the Gospel. That is certainly the case today. The First Reading presents a difficult and distressing situation and starts us longing for a remedy; it stirs us and makes us uncomfortable. The Gospel will address that tension and offer the solution for which our hearts have begun to yearn.

This text may seem harsh to modern ears, but only if its true intent is missed. The leprosy cited here is both the same as and different from what we know as that disease today and included other skin maladies that could be temporary in nature. What's important to understand is that such diseases presented a double threat to the community. In addition to their contagion—a serious enough issue in a world lacking medical remedies—there was also a spiritual component: exposure to the disease rendered people spiritually unclean and disqualified them from participating in the community's worship. God is the speaker throughout the passage giving instructions meant for the safety and *survival* of the community, so they *must* be obeyed. Your tone must be authoritative, but speak dispassionately, the way the medical director of a hospital might enunciate new procedures for preventing infection. More recent experience with viruses like SARS and H1N1 helps us better understand what might otherwise appear to be remarkable insensitivity or even cruelty. Because these are directions that must be heard and understood to be heeded, stress details like "scab or pustule or blotch" and

Corinthians = kohr-IN-thee-uhnz

Don't catch your listeners off-guard by rushing the opening lines. Stress "*eat* or *drink* or *whatever*" in order to contrast with "do *everything* . . . of God."

Paul is alluding to dietary laws, the violation of which might give scandal to others. This is a variation of "When in Rome . . . ."

Paul holds himself up as a model, not to elevate himself but to instruct others.

Memorize this line and deliver it while sustaining good eye contact.

READING II · 1 Corinthians 10:31—11:1

A reading from the first Letter of Saint Paul to the Corinthians

Brothers and sisters,
whether you **eat** or **drink**, or **whatever** you do,
    do **everything** for the glory of **God**.
Avoid giving **offense**, whether to the **Jews** or **Greeks**
    or the church of **God**,
    just as **I** try to please **everyone** in every **way**,
    not seeking my **own** benefit but that of the **many**,
    that they may be **saved**.
Be **imitators** of **me**, as **I** am of **Christ**.

---

the injunction to cry out "unclean" to warn others of possible danger.

READING II You may have heard the adage: "There are no small parts, only small actors." This passage may look "small" but it is no less a privilege to enliven these words that exude Paul's personal energy and his signature self-disclosure.

It goes without saying that you must read slowly and sustain eye contact from start to finish. The energy level is high from

the beginning and grows steadily to the end. Paul's instructions are brief and follow one upon the other in close succession, so be careful not to run them together. He counsels the Corinthians (and us) to do everything for God; to give no offense to either Jew or Greek or the church; and he asks that all imitate him.

Last week Paul told the Corinthians he became all things to all people, to save at least some. Now he says, "I try to please *everyone* in every way" as a reminder that he is willing to do any lawful thing to win their salvation. And in his willingness to

put his "own benefit" behind that of others, he is bold enough to ask them to imitate him. Paul is seldom shy about talking about himself and when such talk is for the benefit of others, he's downright fearless: Imitate me, he says with great passion, for by doing so you imitate Christ.

GOSPEL Mark is typically the most economical storyteller among the evangelists, stating facts and quickly moving on. But of the three evangelists who tell today's story, Mark not

GOSPEL Mark 1:40–45

A reading from the holy Gospel according to Mark

A **leper** came to **Jesus** and kneeling **down begged** him and said,
  "If you **wish**, you can make me **clean**."
Moved with **pity**, he stretched out his **hand**,
  touched him, and **said** to him,
  "I **do** will it. Be made **clean**."
The leprosy left him **immediately**, and he was made **clean**.
Then, warning him **sternly**, he **dismissed** him at **once**.

He **said** to him, "See that you tell **no** one **anything**,
  but **go**, **show** yourself to the **priest**
  and **offer** for your cleansing what Moses **prescribed**;
  that will be **proof** for them."

The man went **away** and began to **publicize** the whole matter.
He **spread** the report **abroad**
  so that it was **impossible** for Jesus to enter a town **openly**.
He remained **outside** in **deserted** places,
  and people kept **coming** to him from **everywhere**.

The introduction is brief, but important, so take time with the details.

Stress the "pity" that motivates Jesus' response and highlight the physical contact of Jesus with the leper.

Narrate these lines with the amazement of the crowd or of the healed leper himself.

Deliver Jesus' injunctions with authority. Jesus wants the man to observe the requirements of the law. The "proof" doesn't refer to Jesus' miracle but to the man's being healed and thus rendered able to reenter society.

Speak with the man's joy and gratitude.

"He" is Jesus who, unsuccessfully, seeks refuge for quiet and prayer.

---

only delivers the most detail, but also the most vivid and human telling.

Commentators say we may have two stories dovetailed here: one which shows Jesus' pity toward the leper and another showing his anger toward the *spirit* of leprosy. The dismissal statement ("warning him sternly, he dismissed him at once") they claim, is directed at the spirit, not the leper. If that's the case, it would explain why Jesus, after apparently sending him away, is suddenly addressing the leper again and instructing him "tell no one anything."

Whatever the case may be, the heart of this Gospel lies in the encounter between Jesus and the leper, who pleads, "If you wish . . . ." The man makes a claim on Jesus' compassion and Jesus reaches out and touches the man, thus rendering himself unclean and making himself ineligible to enter the synagogue. But Jesus has now bonded himself to this outcast and puts the leper's needs ahead of his own. Levitical law required a return visit to the priests to document one's healing, and while Jesus wants the leper to comply he also asks the impossible of him: tell no one by whom or

how he was healed. The leper disregards the order and instead boldly announces his good news to the entire village. Mark seems to be telling us that the presence of God in Jesus is so great that it cannot be hidden, it will be found out and must be made manifest—just as Jesus himself is found by the masses who came to him from "everywhere."

7TH SUNDAY IN ORDINARY TIME

Lectionary #80

READING I   Isaiah 43:18–19, 21–22, 24b–25

Isaiah = ī-ZAY-uh

A reading from the Book of the Prophet Isaiah

These are positive, joy-filled imperatives. Even the Exodus will be exceeded by what God is doing now!

You are almost chastising the people for not being alert enough to "see."

See the commentary for help with this awkward sentence.

Jacob and Israel are both metaphors representing the nation.

Note the repetition of "I." Of course, the second "I" receives the greater stress. God offers forgiveness not because the people deserve it, but "for my own sake."

Thus says the LORD:
Remember **not** the events of the **past**,
    the things of long **ago consider** not;
see, I am doing something **new**!
    Now it springs **forth**, do you not **perceive** it?
In the **desert** I make a **way**,
    in the **wasteland, rivers**.
The **people** I formed for **myself**,
    that they might **announce** my **praise**.
Yet you did not **call** upon me, O **Jacob**,
    for you grew **weary** of me, O **Israel**.
You **burdened** me with your **sins**,
    and **wearied** me with your **crimes**.
It is I, **I**, who wipe **out**,
    for my **own** sake, your **offenses**;
    your **sins** I remember no **more**.

READING I Israel's Exile and their deliverance from that punishment remained for the chosen people a primary sign of God's active intervention in their lives. Today's text alludes to the approaching end of the Exile and the glorious return to the promised land. God is the speaker who boldly announces a divine amnesia: "Your sins I remember no more." Begin with that end in mind. The good news of this text is that God is a forgiving God who blots out our sins and renews and restores us. God announces "something new," and urges the people to open their eyes to "perceive it." Ask "Do you not perceive it?" with a sense of urgency and an expectation that your assembly, too, should sense newness all around.

In the Gospel, we'll see Jesus extend healing and forgiveness to a paralytic. It is Jesus, the Messiah, who ushers in the ultimate fulfillment of the something new promised here. The "things of long ago" is a reference to the Exodus from Egypt. God's promise of a *new* Exodus—the return from Exile—anticipates the ultimate deliverance (from sin) that will be achieved in Christ's death and Resurrection.

"The people I formed" is the second half of the verse from which that sentence is taken. It actually reads: "I put water in the desert and rivers in the wasteland for my chosen people to drink, the people I formed . . . ." To make sense of the text as it stands, pause after "people" as if there were a comma, then finish the sentence.

READING II 2 Corinthians 1:18–22

A reading from the second Letter of Saint Paul to the Corinthians

Brothers and sisters:
As **God** is **faithful**,
    our **word** to you is not "**yes**" and "**no**."
For the Son of **God**, Jesus **Christ**,
    who was **proclaimed** to you by **us**, **Silvanus** and **Timothy**
        and **me**,
    was not "**yes**" and "**no**," but "**yes**" has been **in** him.
For however **many** are the promises of God, their **Yes** is in **him**;
    therefore, the **Amen** from us also goes through **him** to God
        for **glory**.
But the one who gives us **security** with you in Christ
    and who **anointed** us is **God**;
he has also put his **seal** upon us
    and given the **Spirit** in our **hearts** as a first **installment**.

Imagine the word "Just" at the start of the second sentence, that is, "Just as God is faithful . . . ."

Silvanus = sil-VAY-nuhs

Speak with the authority of a chosen Apostle exercising his teaching role.

Here, stress the word "and" then the second "yes."

In the phrase "their yes," "their" refers to God's promises whose "yes" flows through Christ as does our "Amen," flowing from us through Christ to God.

Speak the final sentence with conviction, including the assembly among those who have received "his seal" and "spirit."

GOSPEL Mark 2:1–12

A reading from the holy Gospel according to Mark

When Jesus returned to **Capernaum** after some **days**,
    it became **known** that he was at **home**.
Many gathered together so that there was no longer **room**
        for them,
    not even around the **door**,
    and he preached the **word** to them.

Capernaum = kuh-PER-nee-*m

Narrate briskly till you reach the word "door," then slow down to emphasize his preaching of the "word."

READING II | Paul had some tense moments with the Corinthian community that led to several changes regarding his plans to visit them. His vacillation resulted in bad feelings and accusations of being indecisive and unreliable. Here he makes his response, asserting that just as God is faithful and reliable, his word is reliable. He is and always has been consistent, for he came to proclaim the positive Gospel of Christ, and he has been as positive as the Gospel he preached. The Christ preached to them by Paul and his companions, he asserts, was not of two minds—"yes and no"; Christ is always *single*-minded, for nothing but "yes" resides in him.

The wording is a bit awkward and the meaning somewhat obscure, but when you speak of "the promises of God" you are saying that it was in Jesus that all of God's promises were fulfilled; the "yes,"—the grace of those promises—flowed *to* us through Jesus, therefore the *Amen* that flows *from* us to God is also channeled through Christ. The final sentence is also a bit abstruse: Paul is validating his own ministry to the Corinthians, claiming that it is God who "gives us security with you . . . and anointed us." But he goes further: what God has done for Paul and his companions, God has done also for the Corinthians—that is, God has sealed them with the Holy Spirit as the beginning of his transforming work in them.

GOSPEL | In all of human history, no one like Jesus ever walked the earth. What the crowds shouted 2,000 years ago following the healing recounted

The scene shifts to the friends and paralytic. Speak slowly and with emphasis of the size of the crowd and the inability to reach Jesus.

Pause before you begin this line, as if Jesus were marveling at the descending mat.

The scribes are offended by his audacity to forgive sins.

Narrate Jesus' thoughts with a tone of frustration. But let the dialogue suggest a concern for the scribes as well as the paralytic and crowd.

Speak Jesus' commands slowly: there are three of them—"rise . . . pick up . . . go."

Make eye contact with those in your assembly so they understand that this affirmation still holds true today.

They came **bringing** to him a **paralytic** carried by **four men**.
Unable to get near **Jesus** because of the **crowd**,
  they opened up the **roof** above him.
After they had broken **through**,
  they let down the **mat** on which the paralytic was **lying**.
When Jesus saw their **faith**, he **said** to the paralytic,
  "**Child**, your **sins** are **forgiven**."
Now some of the **scribes** were sitting there **asking** themselves,
  "Why does this man **speak** that way? He is **blaspheming**.
Who but God **alone** can forgive **sins**?"
Jesus immediately **knew** in his mind
  what they were **thinking** to themselves,
  so he said, "Why are you **thinking** such things in your **hearts**?
Which is **easier**, to say to the paralytic,
  'Your **sins** are **forgiven**,'
  or to say, '**Rise**, **pick** up your mat and **walk**'?
But that you may **know**
  that the Son of Man has **authority** to forgive sins on earth"
  —he said to the paralytic,
  "I **say** to you, **rise**, pick up your **mat**, and go **home**."
He **rose**, picked up his mat at **once**,
  and went **away** in the sight of **everyone**.
They were all **astounded**
  and **glorified God**, saying, "We have **never** seen **anything**
    like **this**."

here, still holds true: "We have never seen anything like this." The large crowd that gathered at Capernaum came to hear Jesus' preaching; the healing was an unexpected benefit that lent authority to his words. Of course, the remarkable aspect of this story is the initiative of the paralytic's companions. What drove them through the roof is the same thing that claims Jesus' compassion: "their faith." Usually, Jesus requests a verbal affirmation of faith before he heals, but here he sees it enacted by this industrious little band.

Jesus reads the minds of the scribes whose judgment that Jesus' words are blasphemous, seems rather reasonable. Apparently, however, an open heart should have sensed the authority in Jesus' words and teaching, so Jesus does reproach them mildly for their questioning and doubting spirit. But the healing seems to be performed as much for the sake of the doubting scribes as for the paralytic. That might temper the tone of the line: "that you may know . . . to forgive sins on earth." Jesus wants all to come to faith, even these judgmental leaders. When he speaks

to the paralytic, Jesus' tone must blend authority and compassion. Take ample time to give the command to "rise," "pick up" and "go." It's not just the miracle, but the teaching with authority that astounds the crowd and moves them to praise.

ASH WEDNESDAY

Lectionary #219

READING I   Joel 2:12–18

Joel = JOH-*l

Establish eye contact and speak the line slowly, so your assembly understands these words are "now" meant also for them.

God is saying, don't make a show of your repentance by tearing your garments, instead tear your hearts.

Slow your pace as you speak "slow to anger." A hopeful tone colors "Perhaps he will."

After a pause, launch into these imperatives ("proclaim," "call," "Gather") with a lively and urgent tone.

Your tone here says: "Yes, even bride and groom must forsake their pleasure to join the priests in petitioning God."

A reading from the Book of the Prophet Joel

Even **now**, says the LORD,
   return to me with your **whole heart**,
   with **fasting**, and **weeping**, and **mourning**;
Rend your hearts, not your **garments**,
   and **return** to the LORD, your **God**.
For **gracious** and **merciful** is he,
   slow to anger, **rich** in kindness,
   and **relenting** in **punishment**.
Perhaps he will **again** relent
   and leave behind him a **blessing**,
Offerings and **libations**
   for the LORD, your **God**.

Blow the **trumpet** in **Zion**!
   proclaim a **fast**,
   call an **assembly**;
Gather the **people**,
   notify the congregation;
Assemble the elders,
   gather the **children**
   and the **infants** at the **breast**;
Let the bridegroom **quit** his room,
   and the **bride** her **chamber**.

READING I
The people of Israel often saw natural disaster as a sign of God's disfavor and experienced it as punishment for their behavior or as warning to amend their ways. At the time of the prophet Joel, a devastating plague of locusts ravaged the land of Judah. He immediately sensed in this calamity a sign of danger, a clear omen that the fearful "Day of the Lord" was drawing near. His response was to rouse the people and call them to repentance, urging them to turn to God with fasting and weeping.

The prophet Joel's words ring out on every Ash Wednesday calling God's people to repentance and conversion. The Church does not depend on disasters—natural or human made—to spark a call to renewal. That call is built into the liturgical cycle because human nature is sufficiently predictable that the need for repentance is as sure as the change of seasons. Like prodigal children, we wander from the Lord and often return only when some trial or tragedy pulls us back. That was the constant pattern in the life of Israel: disobedience and infidelity led to some impending dan-

ger, which led the people to repentance, which resulted in God's merciful pardon. The pattern perdures and so God's voice calls out again: "return to me."

Joel calls for all the people—nursing infants, children, elders, even honeymooners—to follow the lead of their priests in begging God's mercy. But notice that the opening paragraph offers an image of a "gracious and merciful" God who is "slow to anger" and abounding in love. It is this God to whom the people must turn, a God who may "relent" and leave a blessing instead of chastisement. There is great

Between the **porch** and the **altar**
    let the **priests**, the **ministers** of the Lord, **weep**,
And say, "**Spare**, O Lord, your **people**,
    and make not your **heritage** a **reproach**,
    with the nations **ruling** over them!
Why should they say among the **peoples**,
    '**Where** is their **God**?'"

Then the Lord was stirred to **concern** for his land
    and took **pity** on his people.

> Speak the question, "Where is their God?" in the mocking voice of the foreign nations.
> After a pause, announce God's decision to forgive.

READING II   2 Corinthians 5:20—6:2

A reading from the second Letter of Saint Paul to the Corinthians

Brothers and sisters:
We are **ambassadors** for **Christ**,
    as if **God** were **appealing** through us.
We **implore** you on behalf of **Christ**,
    be **reconciled** to God.
For **our** sake he made him to **be** sin who did not **know** sin,
    so that we might become the **righteousness** of God in **him**.

Working **together**, then,
    we **appeal** to you **not** to receive the **grace** of God in **vain**.

> Establish good eye contact and speak directly to the assembly.
>
> Memorize this line and speak it with great sincerity.
>
> Paul stresses this point: the one with *no* sin took *all* sin upon himself.
>
> Paul is urging us not to waste the gift purchased at so great a price!

---

urgency in the lines that begin "Blow the trumpet . . . ." All these are imperatives, but no individual command is as important as their cumulative effect. Joel calls for a communal response and the plea is "spare your people," not "spare me." God is the speaker, instructing the people how to pray; they are even told to appeal to God's pride by saying, Why should foreigners look at us and wonder where our God is!

The last two lines are spoken by the prophet who heralds God's mercy. Let the word "pity" tell you how to speak of the compassionate God who forgives.

READING II We have a mission—you and I, and all Christians. We didn't always know that as clearly as we do today. Before the Second Vatican Council, laity were thought to participate in the mission of the *clergy* to whom Christ had entrusted his mission of sanctifying the world. But now we understand that Christ's mission is ours as well: each of us—lay, religious, and clergy—is to be an ambassador for Christ. We represent Christ to a world that little knows him. We speak, through our *actions*, on behalf of Christ, and what the world will know of him it will know because of us. What credential do we need for this important role? Simply this: "be reconciled to God." We cannot wallow in sin and claim to speak for God. We cannot hate our sister or brother and represent the Lord of love and mercy. "Be reconciled to God" is the heart of the Lenten message. Speak it boldly.

Paul provides the model: he *"implores,"* a strong word but commensurate with the importance of the task it calls us to. We must become "the righteousness"—the very holiness and justice—"of God." But God never forces anyone's conversion.

For he **says**:

> In an **acceptable** time I **heard** you,
>   and on the day of **salvation** I **helped** you.

Behold, **now** is a very **acceptable** time;
  behold, **now** is the **day** of **salvation**.

This line, too, could be memorized. The assembly must understand that "now" means "today."

Remember to avoid an overly harsh or judgmental tone.

Throughout, the text achieves emphasis through contrast, juxtaposing the behavior of hypocrites with that of true disciples ("you").

Is Jesus speaking from anger or frustration?

Don't vary the stress on this thrice-repeated refrain, but emphasize those same three words each time.

GOSPEL   Matthew 6:1–6, 16–18

A reading from the holy Gospel according to Matthew

Jesus said to his **disciples**:
  "Take **care** not to perform righteous **deeds**
  in order that people may **see** them;
    otherwise, you will have no **recompense**
      from your heavenly **Father**.
When you give **alms**,
  do not blow a **trumpet** before you,
    as the **hypocrites** do in the **synagogues**
      and in the **streets**
  to win the praise of **others**.
Amen, I **say** to you,
  they have **received** their reward.
But when **you** give alms,
  do not let your **left** hand know what your **right** is **doing**,
    so that your **almsgiving** may be **secret**.
And your **Father** who **sees** in secret will **repay** you.

Thus Paul "appeals." If we *don't* respond, it may be that, for us, Christ's work was done in vain. Here, Paul touches on one of the great mysteries of the Incarnation: Jesus not only became part of sinful humanity, he took all human sin onto himself and paid sin's price that we might attain that righteousness only God can bestow on us. Paul wants us to reap the benefits of that sacrifice. Quoting Isaiah, he applies the prophet's words to the present: *"now is a very acceptable time . . . ."* That "now" refers even to the moment of proclamation. As you speak, God calls; as the

assembly sits and listens the time to respond is upon them!

This text is sometimes referred to as the "Lector's Prayer," an appropriate enough designation that accurately names the proclaimer's role as God's spokesperson. But, of course this text is for your entire assembly who need to better understand that the work Christ left for his Church is squarely in their hands.

GOSPEL   The pattern repeats three times: When you "give alms . . . pray . . . fast" do not do it like

"the hypocrites." They do it for the sake of the crowds and their own exaltation. Instead, when you pray, fast, or give alms do it in secret so that your Father "who sees in secret will repay you."

The advice of Jesus contrasts quite markedly with the advice given by Joel in the First Reading. The prophet called for communal and public demonstration of repentance, but Jesus instructs the believer to pray "secretly." Jesus himself points to the reason for the disparity: by Jesus' time Joel's way had become so

Resist the temptation to adopt the superior attitude of the hypocrites as you speak these lines.

"When **you** pray,
   do not be like the **hypocrites**,
   who love to **stand** and pray in the **synagogues**
     and on **street** corners
   so that others may **see** them.
Amen, I say to you,
   they have **received** their reward.
But when **you** pray, go to your **inner** room,
   close the door, and pray to your Father in **secret**.
And your Father who **sees** in secret will **repay** you.

Here, Jesus offers the better way.

Stress the same words as before.

"When **you** fast,
   do not look **gloomy** like the **hypocrites**.
They **neglect** their appearance,
   so that they may **appear** to others to be **fasting**.
Amen, I say to you, they have **received** their reward.
But when **you** fast,
   anoint your head and **wash** your face,
   so that you may **not** appear to be fasting,
   except to your **Father** who is **hidden**.
And your Father who **sees** what is hidden will **repay** you."

Do you hear sarcasm or regret in these lines?

Once again, be sure you don't sound as arrogant as the hypocrites and note the third recurrence of "Father sees/repays" refrain.

Slow down as you speak the words "who sees . . . will repay you."

institutionalized that it became the insincere approach of hypocrites whose elaborate demonstrations of generosity and mortification were calculated more to earn the crowd's applause than God's mercy.

Jesus wants sincerity because anything less is useless. As T. S. Eliot observes in *Murder in the Cathedral*, "The last temptation is the greatest treason: To do the right thing for the wrong reason." If you want to please God, Jesus says, perform your religious acts *only* for God. The acts he names are the three traditional Lenten practices: prayer, fasting, and almsgiving.

Doing them is always important, but *why* we do them is even more so. Spiritual growth results less from external changes we manage to affect and more from internal changes experienced while doing good works. Seek others' recognition through good deeds and you'll forsake God's approval. Instead Jesus urges: "go to your inner room," pray "in secret," "wash your face." Jesus' private piety contrasts with the hypocrites' *false* piety. Such show-offs are already paid in full.

Of course we can't call others to abandon insincerity and pride using a tone of judgment or sarcasm. Humility begets humility, so first we must remove any plank from our own eye. Jesus is instructing, not condemning, for he loves even the hypocrites and desires their conversion. He laments their self-inflicted blindness and so warns all disciples that even religion can become a trap. If Jesus is frustrated here, it is because hypocrites are hurting themselves while giving others a bad example. Jesus cares about the spiritual welfare of *all* his listeners, so his advice is for all who are willing to listen and heed—even the hypocrites.

1ST SUNDAY OF LENT

Lectionary #23

READING I   Genesis 9:8–15

A reading from the Book of Genesis

Your tone for the introduction should signal that good news is coming.

God said to **Noah** and to his **sons** with him:
"**See**, I am now establishing my **covenant** with you
    and your descendants **after** you
    and with every living **creature** that was **with** you:
    all the **birds**, and the various tame and wild **animals**
    that were **with** you and came out of the **ark**.

Don't rush this section. The naming of the creatures reveals God's compassion for all Creation.

I will establish my **covenant** with you,
    that **never** again shall all bodily creatures be **destroyed**
    by the **waters** of a **flood**;
    there shall not be **another** flood to **devastate** the earth."

The voice of God is strong and loving.

God **added**:

Speak slowly and with great emphasis: "There shall not be another flood!"

"This is the **sign** that I am giving for all ages to **come**,
    of the **covenant** between **me** and **you**
    and every living creature **with** you:

The sign of the "bow" is offered as if to remove any doubt.

    I set my **bow** in the clouds to serve as a **sign**
    of the covenant between **me** and the **earth**.

The words "I set my bow" are offered as a guarantee.

When I bring **clouds** over the earth,
    and the bow **appears** in the clouds,
    I will recall the **covenant** I have made

As throughout the Old Testament, God is given human qualities here.

    between **me** and **you** and **all** living beings,

Let your earnest voice and attitude become the "bow" promising unending fidelity.

    so that the **waters** shall never **again** become a **flood**
    to **destroy** all mortal **beings**."

READING I The flood waters have receded. Noah and his family, and their vast menagerie, are back on solid ground. But God doesn't simply watch the crew disembark and go their way. God addressees this small band and his words are full of hope and promise. At the start of the penitential time of Lent, we begin not with the flood story itself—a tale of God's response to human sin which should make us mindful of our own failings and shortcomings. Instead, we read of

God's promise to never repeat this form of chastisement. Unlike the narrower, more demanding covenants God will make with Abraham and Moses, the covenant with Noah embraces all humankind and asks nothing in return for God's promise. This 'first' covenant between God and people is a key moment in human history which the Genesis author wants to embed in the mind of the reader, so he employs the technique of repetition to aid the memory.

The presence of repetition signals that we are dealing with a kind of writing that requires appreciation of language, for there is more language than content here. Having wiped the slate clean, God wants to start fresh. God's dialogue is peppered with the word "covenant"—the key word of the passage and a word that points to today's Gospel, which heralds Jesus as the ultimate fulfillment of all God's promises. In all the talk of covenant, God's *initiative* is blatant and God's good will palpable; the

READING II   1 Peter 3:18–22

A reading from the first Letter of Saint Peter

Beloved:
Christ **suffered** for **sins** **once**,
    the **righteous** for the sake of the **unrighteous**,
    that he might **lead** you to **God**.
Put to **death** in the **flesh**,
    he was brought to **life** in the **Spirit**.
In it he **also** went to preach to the **spirits** in **prison**,
    who had once been **disobedient**
    while God patiently **waited** in the days of **Noah**
    during the building of the **ark**,
    in which a **few** persons, **eight** in all,
    were **saved** through **water**.
This prefigured **baptism**, which saves you **now**.
It is not a removal of **dirt** from the body
    but an **appeal** to God for a clear **conscience**,
    through the **resurrection** of Jesus **Christ**,
    who has gone into **heaven**
    and is at the right hand of **God**,
    with **angels**, **authorities**, and **powers subject** to him.

The text opens like a hymn of praise. Give it that elevated quality.

Contrast "put to death" with "brought to life."

"It" refers to the "Spirit" in which he was brought to life.

Emphasize the Noah reference to make explicit the connection with the First Reading.

Noah's salvation from the waters of the flood prefigures Baptism.

Give the final lines an exalted quality befitting the one who reigns over the angelic host.

repetitions serve only to reinforce that. That the various mentions of covenant say the same thing over and over is no reason to rush them. In songs, refrains receive the same amount of time each time they recur. Use the repetitions to stroke God's people with tenderness, to persuade them with unadorned sincerity of God's forgiveness and unending fidelity.

READING II The reading opens with a declaration of the saving benefits of Christ's sacrifice, telling us that the *"righteous"* one suffered for us who are

"unrighteous" in order to lead us to God. Another rhetorical balance follows the first: Christ died in the *"flesh,"* but was brought to life *"in the Spirit."* In that same Spirit, he went to the "spirits in prison"—a cryptic reference that may indicate the souls of sinful people who died in the flood, or more likely, may suggest the angelic spirits who had turned against God from time immemorial. The mention of Noah and the flood—a clear connection with today's First Reading—links that ancient event of

sin and salvation with Christian Baptism, though it does it through contrast, since the destructive waters of the flood now become the saving waters of Baptism. On this first Sunday of Lent, this apt allusion focuses us on the baptismal "bath" that cleansed us of sins and also reminds us of our need for constant cleansing and renewal. Of course, Baptism does not remove bodily "dirt," but the grime that sullies our poor consciences.

This text begins and ends with lines that could be taken from an ancient Christological hymn. The ending speaks of

A short reading requires slow reading.

Use all of Mark's words to establish color, texture, and mood.

Contrast the words "beasts" and "angels."

Pause before this next section. The word "arrested" contrasts with the rest of the paragraph.

There is a sense of urgency in Jesus' words. Give them adequate emphasis and shift focus to different parts of the assembly on each line.

GOSPEL   Mark 1:12–15

A reading from the holy Gospel according to Mark

The **Spirit** drove **Jesus** out into the **desert**,
    and he **remained** in the desert for **forty** days,
        tempted by **Satan**.
He was among wild **beasts**,
    and the **angels ministered** to him.

After **John** had been **arrested**,
    Jesus came to **Galilee** proclaiming the gospel of **God**:
    "This is the time of **fulfillment**.
The **kingdom** of God is at **hand**.
Repent, and **believe** in the **gospel**."

the risen Christ who, ascended to the Father, reigns at God's right hand, as the heavenly multitudes sing his endless glory!

GOSPEL This bare bones Gospel clearly demonstrates why Mark is the most economical storyteller among the four evangelists, though sometimes he provides details the longer-winded evangelists leave out. But that's not the case today. In contrast to the adage that asserts "less is more," today less is

actually less. In other years, we begin Lent with Luke and Matthew relating the dramatic clash of personalities and kingdoms which occurs in the desert. But Mark relates all that by simply saying he was "tempted by Satan."

What to do with such meager fare? Try what every good cook who has been caught short of food for unexpected guests learns to do: serve less but serve it well. Each of the first five lines tells something important: Jesus was in the *desert* for *forty days*, *tempted* by Satan, and in the company of *beasts* and *angels*.

A pause precedes the mention of John's arrest and Jesus' Galilean ministry. Jesus' three-line proclamation is packed with news of God's saving action and an urgent call for appropriate response: God's kingdom is now among you, so "repent, and believe!"

2ND SUNDAY OF LENT

Lectionary #26

READING I   Genesis 22:1–2, 9a, 10–13, 15–18

A reading from the Book of Genesis

God put **Abraham** to the **test**.
He **called** to him, "**Abraham**!"
"**Here** I am!" he replied.
Then God said:
     "Take your son **Isaac**, your **only** one, whom you **love**,
          and go to the land of **Moriah**.
There you shall **offer** him up as a **holocaust**
     on a **height** that I will point **out** to you."

When they **came** to the place of which God had **told** him,
     Abraham built an **altar** there and arranged the **wood** on it.
Then he **reached** out and **took** the knife to **slaughter** his son.
But the LORD's **messenger called** to him from heaven,
     "**Abraham, Abraham**!"
"**Here** I am!" he answered.
"Do not lay your **hand** on the boy," said the messenger.
"Do not do the least **thing** to him.
I know now how **devoted** you are to God,
     since you did not **withhold** from me your own beloved **son**."
As Abraham looked **about**,
     he spied a **ram** caught by its **horns** in the **thicket**.
So he went and **took** the ram
     and **offered** it up as a **holocaust** in **place** of his **son**.

This is a story, so be sure to pay attention to setting, characters, plot, and dialogue.

Abraham responds with a naive and ironic "Here I am" to God's terrible request to "Take your *son*;" made all the more gut-wrenching by the powerful emphasis: "your *only* one, whom you *love*."

Don't embellish; these words alone can speak the horror of God's command.

Stress the word "came" to suggest the passage of time.

Suggest Abraham's silent struggle to comply.

Narrate the action with the "knife" one phrase at a time; speaking it in one breath would make Abraham seem heartless.

The pace of narration quickens here. Increase your intensity (not necessarily your volume) when calling Abraham's name—and stress the second "Abraham" more than the first. God's dialogue is spoken with authority.

Pause before this section to suggest the passage of time.

READING I   God puts Abraham to the "test," and it is no ordinary test. Passing is near impossible: would anyone offer up a son, even if God asked? And what kind of God would make such a request? The homilist will need to wrestle with such questions to help the modern mind deal with the contours of this story. But as proclaimer, you must present the tale within the biblical context from which it comes. God is God, and God can ask

anything of his creatures. While today obedience may seem passé to some, an old-fashioned virtue that somehow demeans the adult individual, the Bible highly esteems that virtue, holding it up—as it does here—as a primary component of a relationship with God.

What you proclaim here is an important story that establishes Abraham as our father in faith. Because of this great trial, Abraham has been held up throughout history as a model of faith. Isaac, too, becomes a "type," or image, of Christ in his exemplary willingness to accept God's will,

even if it means his death. Much rests on the proclamation of this story. Your primary goal must be to tell it sincerely and convincingly, which means simply, without melodrama or exaggerated theatrics. But "simple" telling does not mean void of emotion or suspense. Both are clearly present, though understated. We can only assume Abraham's inner struggle as he packs wood and knife to "slaughter his son." His silent struggle can be suggested as you speak—almost numbly—of the building of the altar and the binding of Isaac.

The voice of God is still authoritative, but pride and compassion are also blended in.

Again the LORD's messenger called to Abraham
　　from heaven and said:
"I **swear** by **myself**, declares the LORD,
that because you **acted** as you **did**
in not **withholding** from me your beloved **son**,
I will **bless** you **abundantly**

Make eye contact as you speak of this blessing, which includes the members of your assembly.

and make your **descendants** as **countless**
as the **stars** of the sky and the **sands** of the seashore;
your descendants shall take **possession**
of the **gates** of their **enemies**,
and in your **descendants** all the nations of the **earth**
　　shall find **blessing**—
all **this** because you **obeyed** my **command**."

READING II　　Roman 8:31b–34

A reading from the Letter of Saint Paul to the Romans

The first question and the implied "No" that answers it is the most powerful declaration of this text.

Brothers and sisters:
If **God** is for us, who can be **against** us?
He who did not spare his own **Son**
　　but handed him **over** for us **all**,
　　how will he not **also** give us everything **else** along with him?

The first two lines of this sentence establish the identity of the one who will "give us everything else." Pause before "how will he . . ."

These are strongly stated questions. There is an implied "so . . ." before "who will condemn?"

Who will bring a **charge** against God's chosen ones?
　　It is **God** who **acquits** us, who will **condemn**?
Christ Jesus it is who **died**—or, rather, was **raised**—
　　who also is at the **right** hand of God,
　　who indeed **intercedes** for us.

Stress Christ's constant intercession before the Father.

God's true compassion is revealed in "Do not lay your hand . . ." and the promise that follows, while Abraham's shocked "Here I am" resolves into relief as he spies and prepares the ram. Abraham's reward is blessing for himself and, through him, for all nations who become his heirs in faith.

| READING II | The words of this text are among the most comforting in all of scripture: "If God is for us, who can be against us?" The answer, of course, is no one! Just as no one will bring a

charge and no one will condemn us. This is a text we all might want to memorize (and add on the verse that follows this segment) to quote to ourselves and to others in times of distress. Uncharacteristically, today's First Reading has greater consonance with this Second Reading than with the Gospel. "He who did not spare his own son . . ." is an apt description of Abraham. That is why Isaac—Abraham's son, his *only* one—is such a clear prefiguration of Christ who, as *God's* only begotten son, is not spared but handed over for the sake of us all.

The questions Paul poses constitute a powerful rhetorical device. They invite and require a brief pause before and after each is asked. Let each question settle into the assembly before you pose the next. The final sentence is not a question, but a declaration of faith in the one who "died—or, rather, was raised" and who ceaselessly makes intercession with the Father on our behalf. It is he who makes it possible for us to live with confidence and without fear—a reality worth proclaiming boldly.

GOSPEL   Mark 9:2–10

A reading from the holy Gospel according to Mark

Jesus took Peter, James, and John
    and led them up a high mountain apart by themselves.
And he was transfigured before them,
    and his clothes became dazzling white,
    such as no fuller on earth could bleach them.
Then Elijah appeared to them along with Moses,
    and they were conversing with Jesus.
Then Peter said to Jesus in reply,
    "Rabbi, it is good that we are here!
Let us make three tents:
    one for you, one for Moses, and one for Elijah."
He hardly knew what to say, they were so terrified.
Then a cloud came, casting a shadow over them;
    from the cloud came a voice,
    "This is my beloved Son. Listen to him."
Suddenly, looking around, they no longer saw anyone
    but Jesus alone with them.

As they were coming down from the mountain,
    he charged them not to relate what they had seen to anyone,
    except when the Son of Man had risen from the dead.
So they kept the matter to themselves,
    questioning what rising from the dead meant.

Make sure the players in this drama are carefully named.

Mountaintops were often biblical sites of divine revelation.

Speak of the transformation as if you had witnessed it and now relate it for the first time.

Pause before naming Elijah and speak the names of these heroes with a gravity that suggests their importance in Israel's history.

Peter's exclamation is spontaneous and earnest. His talk of tents can be fast and frenzied, which you explain by naming their fear.

Proclaim this episode slowly and with great dignity. The cloud represents the divine and the voice speaks with love and authority.

Time has elapsed. Narrate Jesus' instructions as if they were actual dialogue.

Speak progressively slower as you say, "what rising from the dead meant."

GOSPEL   An incredibly significant event narrated in very few words means every word must be used to its fullest. Just days after his first prediction of the Passion, Jesus takes his three closest confidants "up a high mountain" (the only words you have to set the scene) where he is revealed in all his glory. If Mark's disciples were not so consistently obtuse, we might think it unfair that these three were given a revelation that could ready and steel them against the ignominy and scandal of the Passion. But even these privileged ones will soon come down the mountain wondering "what rising from the dead meant."

The purpose of this narrative is clear: it balances the dire prediction that precedes it. Christ will usher in the kingdom of God, but it won't be from the back of a white charger. It will be from the wood of the cross. This incident excites a hope within these select disciples that the glory they see manifest also awaits Jesus on the other side of the tomb. There are four parts to this episode: the Transfiguration; the appearance of Moses and Elijah; Peter's exclamation and suggestion; the appear-ance of the cloud and the divine voice. Each part adds a significant theological dimension to this story: the dazzling, white garments suggest the presence of the divine; Moses and Elijah represent the law and prophets of the Old Testament; Peter is overwhelmed but can recognize that it is good for them to be there; the voice provides divine validation of Jesus' sonship and instructs all to listen to him. You must go slowly so that each scene can come to life. A careful, unhurried reading will allow you to communicate the rich content of this dramatic revelation of divine glory.

3RD SUNDAY OF LENT

Lectionary #29

READING I   Exodus 20:1–17

A reading from the Book of Exodus

God reminds the people that he is a God of salvation and liberation who brought them out of slavery. That's an important context for the commandments that follow.

The voice of God is full of authority and dignity, but the motivation is love.

Let your voice express great disdain for false idols and all they represent.

In those days, **God** delivered all these **commandments**:
   "**I**, the LORD, am your **God**,
   who **brought** you out of the land of **Egypt**, that place
      of **slavery**.
You shall not have **other** gods besides **me**.
You shall not carve **idols** for yourselves
   in the shape of **anything** in the sky **above**
   or on the earth **below** or in the waters **beneath** the earth;
   you shall not **bow** down before them or **worship** them.
For **I**, the LORD, your **God**, am a **jealous** God,
   inflicting **punishment** for their fathers' **wickedness**
   on the **children** of those who **hate** me,
   down to the **third** and **fourth** generation;
   but bestowing **mercy** down to the **thousandth** generation
   on the children of those who **love** me
      and **keep** my commandments.

Don't hold back on the words "jealous" and "punishment." They express God's concern for the people who need to know their behavior *will* have consequences.

Sustain the tone of noble authority even on the elaborations or commentaries that follow this and other commandments.

"You shall not take the **name** of the LORD, your God, in **vain**.
For the LORD will not leave **unpunished**
   the one who **takes** his name in **vain**.

As you elaborate, let your tone say: "This is reasonable. It's not too much to ask."

"**Remember** to keep **holy** the **sabbath** day.
Six days you may **labor** and do all your **work**,
   but the **seventh** day is the **sabbath** of the LORD, your **God**.

READING I Experience teaches us that legitimate limits can be expressions of love; children crave them and, knowingly or not, sense the love that undergirds them. Good parents and teachers know this and make rules because they love these children who rely on their experience and wisdom. God does the same. In scripture, the Law is not seen as a source of confinement, but of liberation from the tyranny of our own weaknesses. God's *love*, not God's anger, shows us the better way. Let the first sentence, where a concerned and loving God offers a reminder

that "I . . . brought you out of . . . slavery," set the tone for the proclamation.

The injunction against worshipping "other gods" expresses God's awareness that worshipping other gods means adopting their *value systems*, rather than the law of love contained in the commandments. The word "jealous" may be a surprising and too human an attribute to ascribe to God. But God's jealousy is for the people's *welfare* and that motivates the stern admonition to resist the allurements of false gods and idols. The mention of punishment visited on children for the sins of their

fathers may seem to be beneath God's dignity. How do we understand this? By realizing that God doesn't relish threatening "punishment," but does want us to understand that all actions have consequences. Although God is eager to shower "mercy down to the *thousandth* generation," your tone must warn that God won't shy from giving us what we *deserve*.

God who made us knows our needs, and resting and communing with our God is foremost among them. Like a loving mother telling her children to eat what's good for them, you command Sabbath

Sabbath rest is extended to all God's creatures.

Your pacing on "In six days . . . is in them" can be rapid and intense; but slow down suddenly and read "but on the seventh" in a calmer tone.

Use the words "blessed" and "holy" to express the very sacred nature of the Sabbath.

Don't rush the consequence of honoring father and mother.

The "shall not" commandments can be delivered, without rushing, at a faster pace. Note the stress is almost exclusively on the final word of each line.

Slow down here. Your tone suggests: "Don't waste your time coveting these things."

No **work** may be done then either by **you**, or your
　　son or **daughter**,
　or your male or female **slave**, or your **beast**,
　or by the **alien** who lives with you.
In **six days** the LORD made the **heavens** and the **earth**,
　the **sea** and all that is **in** them;
　but on the **seventh** day he **rested**.
That is why the LORD has **blessed** the sabbath day
　　and made it **holy**.

"**Honor** your **father** and your **mother**,
　that you may have a long **life** in the land
　which the LORD, your God, is **giving** you.
You shall not **kill**.
You shall not commit **adultery**.
You shall not **steal**.
You shall not bear **false** witness against your **neighbor**.
You shall not **covet** your neighbor's **house**.
You shall not **covet** your neighbor's **wife**,
　nor his male or female **slave**, nor his **ox** or **ass**,
　nor anything **else** that **belongs** to him."

[Shorter: Exodus 20:1–3, 7–8, 12–17]

observance, noting that God's concern extends even to the "slave," the "beast," and the "alien."

　God links respect for father and mother to a long life. Look at the parents before you in the assembly and call us to that respect.

　The "shall not" commandments call us to live in a way that frees us from fear of each other and frees us to love one another. Slow your rate for the two final injunctions, letting your tone suggest the futility of desiring what is not ours. This is not God's *wish* list—these are God's commands, which if followed, we will discover to be God's gifts for our lives.

READING II　Sometimes there's no better way to say something than to say it bluntly. The stark language of such communication grabs us and makes us listen, and the unadorned clarity penetrates in a way that more nuanced language might not. Paul is stark and unadorned here. Some want to see magic while others expect clever speech or fascinating new ideas, he says. But from the life of Christ, he highlights neither his miracles nor his unique teaching. To "Jews" demanding "signs" and "Greeks" seeking logic, Paul offers only the baffling sign of the cross. Paul preaches Christ's Crucifixion knowing full well that Jews will stumble and Gentiles laugh at the ignominious end to Jesus' life.

　Paul doesn't care. He cares about teaching the truth—truth so surprising, foolish, and sometimes blinding that it causes one to stumble. But, Paul asserts, those who are "called," whether Jew or Gentile, will recognize Christ as the power and wisdom of God; they won't be blinded

READING II 1 Corinthians 1:22–25

Short readings always require a slower pace and extra time before you begin to ensure that all are listening.
Contrast "signs" and "wisdom."

Contrast "stumbling" with "foolishness" and "Jews" with "Gentiles."

Imagine the word "is" between "Christ" and "the power of God."
Deliver this line slowly and, if possible, from memory.

A reading from the first Letter of Saint Paul to the Corinthians

Brothers and sisters:
Jews demand **signs** and **Greeks** look for **wisdom**,
    but **we** proclaim Christ **crucified**,
    a **stumbling** block to **Jews** and **foolishness** to **Gentiles**,
    but to those who are **called**, Jews and Greeks **alike**,
    Christ the **power** of God and the **wisdom** of God.
For the **foolishness** of God is **wiser** than human **wisdom**,
    and the **weakness** of God is **stronger** than human **strength**.

GOSPEL John 2:13–25

The opening tone is upbeat, giving no hint of what's to come.

Let your voice begin to tense here. The details of "oxen" and "sheep" are important.
The scene is surprisingly violent. Don't soften it. Read with energy and passion. Jesus' anger has become like a runaway train no one could stop.

This is the key line of the confrontation.

A reading from the holy Gospel according to John

Since the **Passover** of the Jews was **near**,
    Jesus went up to **Jerusalem**.
He found in the **temple** area those who sold **oxen**, **sheep**,
    and **doves**,
    as well as the **money** changers seated there.
He made a **whip** out of **cords**
    and **drove** them all **out** of the temple area,
    with the **sheep** and **oxen**,
    and spilled the **coins** of the **money** changers
    and **overturned** their **tables**,
    and to those who sold **doves** he said,
    "Take these **out** of here,
    and **stop** making my Father's **house** a **marketplace**."

by the truth, but walk by its light. The predictable response is that of the Jews and Greeks; that God's grace has allowed us a different response is something to be cherished and celebrated.

Paul concludes with a verse that should be memorized—for proclamation and for life: The foolishness of God outshines human wisdom, and the weakness of God overwhelms human strength. Use Paul's clarity, his skillful use of balance, and his masterful paradox to grab and penetrate the hearts of your listeners.

GOSPEL Without warning, Jesus decides to clean house. Following on the heels of the miracle at Cana, Jesus comes to Jerusalem for Passover and suddenly he's knotting cords to make a whip and driving money changers from their stalls. Remembering that this is the great feast of Passover sheds some light on this odd behavior. The holy city becomes a magnet at this special time, drawing pilgrims from many parts of the world, all coming to observe a sacred feast that reminds them of God's provident care, of God's power and majesty, and of the

right relationship between God and his people. What Jesus encounters in the temple area contradicts all that. The power and majesty of God have taken a back seat to the commercial interests of the vendors. The people's gratitude and worship are turned into opportunities for greed, and right relationship with God has become but a business transaction.

Jesus' relationship with God is that of son to father, so he has no patience for the travesty that greets him. His disciples will later recall the words of scripture that

Relate this detail with a sense of pride.

His **disciples** recalled the words of **Scripture**,
> ***Zeal*** *for your house will* ***consume*** *me.*
At this the Jews **answered** and said to him,
> "What **sign** can you show us for **doing** this?"
Jesus **answered** and said to them,
> "**Destroy** this temple and in **three days** I will raise it **up**."
The Jews said,
> "This **temple** has been under construction for **forty-six years**,
> and **you** will raise it up in **three days**?"
But **he** was speaking about the temple of his **body**.
Therefore, when he was raised from the **dead**,
> his disciples **remembered** that he had said this,
> and they came to **believe** the Scripture
> and the **word** Jesus had spoken.

The Jewish leaders respond with anger and disdain, trying to eyeball Jesus into retreat. He holds his ground and dares them to destroy this temple. "Go ahead," he seems to say, "I dare you."

Once again, this aside is delivered as if by an insider confiding in fellow constituents.

While he was in **Jerusalem** for the feast of **Passover**,
> many began to **believe** in his name
> when they saw the **signs** he was doing.
But Jesus would not **trust** himself to them because he **knew**
> them all,
> and did not need **anyone** to testify about human **nature**.
He **himself** understood it **well**.

Let your tone suggest the superficiality of this belief.

These lines contain caution, anger, and sadness.

explain Jesus' action, but the religious leaders will need much more than that. What "sign" will you offer for doing this, they ask. His response is as bold as it is cryptic. Of course, they have no idea of his real intent. Taking him literally, they can do no more than scoff at his nonsense. The narrator's aside that follows this encounter fills us in on Jesus' real intent, but it does so without giving any ground to those who questioned and failed to understand.

Apparently, Jesus did perform some signs during his Passover stay, for we are told that many came to believe in him because of those signs. Yet it seems Jesus may have performed the signs with some reluctance. He seems to understand that with crowds one is only as good as his last sign. It was to call forth faith and to change hearts that Jesus came; those who depend on signs often stop believing when the signs stop. Three times in this text we see Jesus behave in a way that utterly contradicts the overly pious images we sometimes concoct from our inadequate imaginations: first is the surprising violence of the cleansing, second is his confrontational response regarding a "sign,"

and the third is here. As much as he gives himself to the crowds, letting them take his time and spend his energy, still we are told he is cautious and does "not trust himself to them." The reason for his caution is his understanding of "human nature"—and he understands it "well." This sobering ending should remind us that Jesus did what he did with his eyes wide open and it should make us grateful that despite his intimate knowledge of us, Jesus still went willingly to the cross.

3RD SUNDAY OF LENT, YEAR A

Lectionary #28

READING I   Exodus 17:3–7

A reading from the Book of Exodus

In those days, in their **thirst** for **water**,
   the people **grumbled** against Moses,
   saying, "**Why** did you ever make us **leave** Egypt?
Was it just to have us **die** here of **thirst**
   with our **children** and our **livestock**?"
So Moses **cried** out to the LORD,
   "What shall I **do** with this people?
A little **more** and they will **stone** me!"
The LORD **answered** Moses,
   "Go over there in front of the **people**,
   along with some of the **elders** of Israel,
   holding in your **hand**, as you go,
   the **staff** with which you struck the **river**.
I will be **standing** there in front of you on the rock in **Horeb**.
Strike the rock, and the **water** will **flow** from it
   for the people to **drink**."
This Moses **did**, in the presence of the **elders** of Israel.
The place was called **Massah** and **Meribah**,
   because the Israelites **quarreled** there
   and **tested** the LORD, saying,
   "Is the LORD in our **midst** or **not**?"

Start slowly. "Thirst for water" sets up the whole reading.

Recall the sound of your own grumbling. Do you express great anxiety by becoming more strident or more quietly intense?

Moses is angry, but at whom—the people, God, or both?

Like a frustrated parent, be angry at first, but then your words should melt into a tone of loving reassurance. "Staff . . . river" is a reference to the plague that changed the Nile river to blood. The staff that deprived Egypt of water will provide for Israel. The words "in front of the people" convey the public nature of God's reassurance made "in the presence of the elders" who witness the saving miracle.

Speak the words "This Moses did" in a tone that suggests the miracle occurred.

Massah = MAS-uh means "the place of the test."

Meribah = MAYR-ih-buh means "the place of the quarreling."

The question can be read with the anxiety of the people or with the narrator's regret at their apparent lack of faith.

READING I The First Reading tells a story of physical thirst, anticipating the Gospel story of the Samaritan woman's who thirst for "living water." The words "thirst," "water," and "drink" introduced here become central images in John's story of Jesus' encounter with the woman at the well. Water, so essential to human survival, serves as a powerful symbol of our need for God. Deserts, then—where water is scarce and our thirst great—reinforce this important biblical symbolism. The grumbling Israelites thirst not only for water but also

for reassurance that God is "in [their] midst." The entire passage is an affirmative response to their final question.

   The grumbling of the Israelites, although surprising after the miracles they've witnessed, demonstrates the very human tendency to blame someone else for difficulties. It's an understandable response, but annoying nonetheless. Moses reacts with near despair. You have just two questions with which to express the people's intimidating anger: "Why did you . . . Was it just . . . ?" Their tone leaves little room for our sympathy. Moses

calls out loudly to God, genuinely fearing the people's wrath, but also frustrated that he's been put in this situation. God is surely sad and angry at the people's lack of faith. Yet God is merciful. God meets the people's needs, threatens no punishment, and shows sensitivity both to Moses' situation and the people's wants. Your hopeful tone as you narrate "This Moses did" lets us know he succeeded in making the water flow.

   The final narration rings with regret. The people should have known better. The way you speak the names "Massah" and

Don't read this like abstract theology, for the text announces hope, love, and joy!

Paul describes the workings of faith, hope, and love, moving effortlessly from one to the other. Faith brings peace and access to grace, which leads to a hope that will not disappoint. Note: we don't "speak" of hope; we "boast" of it!

There are three distinct ideas in this sentence.

Assume the diction of a teacher making an important point.

It *would* be unusual to willingly die for a just person, but even *more* unusual is what God did—dying for us while we were still in sin! Proclaim with joy and awe.

READING II   Romans 5:1–2, 5–8

A reading from the Letter of Saint Paul to the Romans

Brothers and sisters:
Since we have been **justified** by **faith**,
  we have **peace** with God through our **Lord** Jesus **Christ**,
  through whom we have gained **access** by faith
  to this **grace** in which we **stand**,
  and we boast in **hope** of the **glory** of **God**.

And **hope** does not **disappoint**,
  because the **love** of God has been poured **out** into our **hearts**
  through the Holy **Spirit** who has been **given** to us.
For **Christ**, while we were still **helpless**,
  died at the appointed time for the **ungodly**.
Indeed, only with **difficulty** does one **die** for a **just** person,
  though perhaps for a **good** person one **might** even
    find **courage** to die.
But God **proves** his love for us
  in that while we were still **sinners** Christ **died** for us.

Narrate as if you were one of the Samaritans who is converted at the end of the story: It's your own town you're describing; the woman is your neighbor; this incident changed your life.

Samaria = suh-MAYR-ee-uh

Sychar = SĪ-kahr

Slower pacing helps suggest Jesus' tiredness.

GOSPEL   John 4:5–42

A reading from the holy Gospel according to John

(1) **Jesus** came to a town of **Samaria** called **Sychar**,
  near the plot of **land** that **Jacob** had given to his son **Joseph**.
Jacob's **well** was there.
Jesus, **tired** from his journey, sat **down** there at the well.
It was about **noon**.

"Meribah" should tell us this was not a proud moment in Israel's history.

READING II Paul's words shed light on both the First Reading and the Gospel, explaining why God is so patient and merciful in the other two readings: "While we were still helpless," God's love was "poured out into our hearts through the Holy Spirit." God saves weak sinners, not the strong and the righteous.

"Justified by faith," the Christian believer is no longer *separated* from God but instead receives "*access* by faith" to

God's presence. God's forgiving love is so great that we can even "boast" that one day we will share in God's own glory. This hope is God's free gift which, though tasted, is not fully attained, for it can be wholly realized only in the Resurrection. Our hope is sure; it awaits its time of completion, but God *will* fulfill the promise because it is anchored in his love for us.

Without experiencing the in-pouring of God's love, it is impossible to turn Paul's theology into words to live by. A story like the one in today's Gospel bridges that gap between theology and experience. Once she experiences Christ's love, the Woman

at the Well knows how to respond. In our lives, too, it is always God who initiates, who moves us toward reconciliation, who gives us the grace we need to apologize or forgive when relationships fracture. How can we not rejoice? God has adopted us and we did nothing to deserve it! God has lavished us with gifts and expects nothing in return but our love.

Paul describes this generosity of scripture in a rather awkward sentence: Look, he argues, always trying to persuade, when is anyone willing to die for even a good person? Well, alright, maybe

She is stunned that he would ask her for a favor.

(2) A **woman** of Samaria came to draw **water**.
Jesus **said** to her,
  "**Give** me a **drink**."
His **disciples** had gone into the **town** to buy **food**.
The **Samaritan** woman said to him,
  "How can **you**, a **Jew**, ask **me**, a **Samaritan woman**,
    for a **drink**?"
—For **Jews** use nothing in **common** with **Samaritans**.—
Jesus **answered** and said to her,

Keep the dialogue conversational, not theological.

(3) "If you **knew** the **gift** of God
  and **who** is saying to you, 'Give me a drink,'
  you would have asked **him**
  and he would have given **you living** water."
The woman **said** to him,

She bluntly challenges him and his *chutzpah*.

  "**Sir**, you do not even have a **bucket** and the cistern is **deep**;
  where then can you **get** this living water?
Are you **greater** than our father **Jacob**,
  who **gave** us this cistern and **drank** from it **himself**
  with his **children** and his **flocks**?"
(4) Jesus **answered** and said to her,

Contrast his tone with the woman's.

  "Everyone who drinks **this** water will be **thirsty** again;
  but whoever drinks the water **I** shall give will **never** thirst;
  the water **I** shall give will become in him
  a **spring** of water **welling** up to eternal **life**."
The **woman** said to him,

She's eager for this amazing water.

  "Sir, **give** me this water, so that I may not be **thirsty**
  or have to keep **coming** here to **draw** water."

Speak evenly, with no hint of judgment.

(5) Jesus said to her,
  "**Go** call your **husband** and come **back**."
The woman **answered** and said to him,

Is her tone wholly transformed, or is this a final brusque reply?

  "I do not **have** a husband."

---

for a *really* good person, but Christ died while we were still helpless and steeped in sin. There's all the proof we need! Let your own experience of that great mercy help you compensate for the awkward phrasing and persuade your listeners that *they* are among those for whom Christ willingly died.

GOSPEL Today's Gospel, with its powerful baptismal allusions, speaks to the elect, and to all of us, through the encounter between Jesus and his boundary-breaking future disciple.

This story is always offered as an option during Years B and C because of its unique power. If you choose it, tell it in its entirety because the shorter version is weaker. Scholars debate whether John's story relates an actual encounter between Jesus and a Samaritan woman or includes Johannine embellishment meant to express important Christological themes. As Gospel reader, your only concern is John's story.

There are three uneven acts to this drama: first, the repartee between Jesus and the woman; second, the return of the

apostles, characterized by their surprise and confusion and Jesus' urgency; third, the enthusiastic response of the Samaritan townspeople.

(1, 2) Faithful Jews bypassed the shortest route from Judea to Galilee because it passed through Samaria. Let your tone signal that Samaria was not a destination for observant Jews; then Jesus' decision to pass through, for theological, not geographical reasons, will stand out all the more. "Jacob's well" was an ancient holy place that you should name with familiarity. In the noontime sun, Jesus approaches

Jesus is blunt here, but not harsh.

Jesus answered her,
  "You are **right** in saying, 'I do not have a **husband**.'
For you have had **five** husbands,
  and the one you have **now** is not your **husband**.
What you have said is **true**."
(6) The woman said to him,

His prescient knowledge impresses her, but she abruptly changes the subject.

  "Sir, I can **see** that you are a **prophet**.
Our **ancestors** worshiped on this **mountain**;
  but **you** people say that the place to worship is in **Jerusalem**."
Jesus said to her,

Here, too, despite the teaching, maintain a conversational tone.

  "**Believe** me, woman, the hour is **coming**
  when you will worship the **Father**
  neither on this mountain **nor** in Jerusalem.
You people worship what you do not **understand**;

Don't let these words sound accusatory or prideful.

  we worship what we **understand**,
  because **salvation** is from the **Jews**.
But the hour is **coming**, and is now **here**,
  when **true** worshipers will worship the Father
    in **Spirit** and **truth**;
  and **indeed** the Father **seeks** such people to worship him.
God is **Spirit**, and those who **worship** him
  must worship in **Spirit** and **truth**."
(7) The woman **said** to him,

She begins to sense who stands before her.

  "I know that the **Messiah** is coming, the one called the **Christ**;
  when he **comes**, he will tell us **everything**."
Jesus said to her,

His self-identification is a gesture of love to the woman.

  "I am **he**, the one **speaking** with you."

The second act begins here. The return of disciples shatters the mood. They seem suspicious.

(8) At that moment his disciples **returned**,
  and were **amazed** that he was talking with a **woman**,
  but **still** no one said, "What are you **looking** for?"
  or "Why are you **talking** with her?"

The woman undertakes her missionary journey. Speak the phrase "Could he be . . . ?" with expectant joy.

The woman **left** her water jar
  and went into the **town** and said to the **people**,

the well and he is tired, hot, and thirsty. The woman is surprised that a man, and a rabbi at that, would speak to a woman in public, especially a ritually unclean Samaritan! She, however, has nothing to lose. She, too, is countercultural—and an outcast: after all, she has lived with more than one man to whom she was not married, so she doesn't shy from pointing out their religious differences.

(3) Jesus refers to himself as "the gift of God," insinuating his identity as the source of "living water," but the woman misses that cloaked reference and takes

him literally. This exchange is central. Jesus means "water of life," but she hears, "flowing water" as opposed to still well water. She mocks Jesus, but only mocks herself, for what she presumes impossible, that Jesus could be greater than Jacob, is the very truth she'll soon learn.

(4) Jesus becomes persuasive. The Woman becomes excited, but only because she misunderstands. Contrast is the key to Jesus' dialogue: Everyone who drinks *this* water will thirst *again*; but those who drink the water *I* shall give will *never* thirst. Jesus will be water that

requires no cup to drink, for he will bubble up like a "spring" within the believer's heart. With her naiveté exposed, the stage is set for the disarming crisis that follows.

(5) When Jesus tells her to "Go call your husband," he is calmly preparing the way for her conversion. Her admission is surprising in one so contentious. Remarkably, Jesus' blunt naming of her sinfulness fails to drive her away; obviously, his honesty is tempered with compassion.

(6) Jesus' knowledge of her private life shocks the woman into acknowledging Jesus as "prophet." But immediately she

They're prodding: "Rabbi...EAT!" His response summarizes his ministry.

Note the ample harvest imagery.

Jesus is urging them to open their eyes and see.

This is the final act. The woman's testimony generates high energy. They are urging him to remain with them.

There should be joy and gratitude in their comment to the woman who is responsible for their faith. Place special emphasis on the title given to Jesus.

"**Come** see a **man** who told me **everything** I have **done**.
Could he possibly be the **Christ**?"
They went out of the town and **came** to him.
(9) Meanwhile, the disciples **urged** him, "Rabbi, **eat**."
But he said to them,
"I have **food** to eat of which you do not **know**."
So the disciples **said** to one another,
"Could someone have **brought** him something to eat?"
Jesus said to them,
"My **food** is to do the **will** of the one who **sent** me
and to **finish** his work.
(10) Do you not say, 'In four months the **harvest** will be here'?
I **tell** you, look **up** and see the fields **ripe** for the **harvest**.
The **reaper** is already receiving **payment**
and gathering crops for eternal **life**,
so that the **sower** and **reaper** can rejoice **together**.
For here the saying is verified that 'One **sows** and another **reaps**.'
I sent you to **reap** what you have not **worked** for;
others have done the work,
and **you** are sharing the **fruits** of their work."

(11) Many of the **Samaritans** of that town began to **believe** in him
because of the **word** of the **woman** who testified,
"He told me **everything** I have **done**."
When the Samaritans **came** to him,
they invited him to **stay** with them;
and he **stayed** there two **days**.
Many **more** began to believe in him because of his **word**,
and they **said** to the woman,
"We no longer believe because of **your** word;
for we have heard for **ourselves**,
and we **know** that this is **truly** the **savior** of the **world**."

[Shorter: John 4:5–15, 19b–26, 39a, 40–42]

shifts to a less embarrassing subject. Jesus' answer surprisingly minimizes the importance of where one worships ("mountain" vs. "Jerusalem"). Instead, he announces a new universalism where worship transcends place.

(7) Jesus' words awaken dreams of the Messiah in the woman. When she speaks with confidence of the Messiah's coming, Jesus rewards her by revealing himself to her. Echoes of the divine "I am" sound in his self-identification.

(8) When the disciples return, the mood changes. They are surprised at what they find. The tone of their unasked questions can suggest confusion, or even disapproval. But the transformed woman, now freed of shame, runs to share her discovery with the townspeople.

(9, 10) Now it is the disciples who misunderstand, taking literally Jesus' reference to food. Their confusion may best be spoken in a hushed tone, contrasting with the urgency of their appeal to "eat." But Jesus explains that his "food," is doing the will of God. What better summary of his ministry and of our mission? Utilizing rich harvest imagery, Jesus speaks urgently on the theme of evangelization.

(11) In this narration we learn of the woman's success as a missionary, for the Samaritans believed "because of the word of the woman." Stress that point and speak "who told me everything . . . " in her excited voice. But many townspeople hear Jesus' words directly and recognize him as "savior." Let their profession of faith sound on your lips as if it were your own!

4TH SUNDAY OF LENT

Lectionary #32

READING I   2 Chronicles 36:14–16, 19–23

Chronicles = KRAH-nih-k*ls

Speak these words with head-shaking frustration.

A reading from the second Book of Chronicles

In **those** days, all the **princes** of **Judah**, the **priests**, and the **people**
    added **infidelity** to **infidelity**,
    practicing all the **abominations** of the nations
    and **polluting** the LORD's **temple**
    which he had **consecrated** in **Jerusalem**.

Here, your frustration can turn to disdain.

Early and **often** did the LORD, the God of their **fathers**,
    send his **messengers** to them,
    for he had **compassion** on his people and his **dwelling** place.

Your tone is insistent that God did everything possible to warn the people.

But they **mocked** the messengers of God,
    despised his warnings, and **scoffed** at his prophets,
    until the **anger** of the LORD against his people was so **inflamed**
    that there was no **remedy**.

As narrator, you can hardly believe this yourself.

Their enemies **burnt** the house of God,
    tore down the walls of **Jerusalem**,
    set all its **palaces afire**,
    and **destroyed** all its precious **objects**.

Your tone announces that they brought this fate upon themselves.

Those who **escaped** the sword were carried **captive** to **Babylon**,
    where they became **servants** of the king of the **Chaldeans**
        and his **sons**
    until the kingdom of the **Persians** came to power.

Slow your pacing here to emphasize the significance of the exile.

All this was to **fulfill** the word of the LORD spoken by **Jeremiah**:
    "Until the land has **retrieved** its lost **sabbaths**,
    during all the time it lies **waste** it shall have **rest**
    while **seventy** years are **fulfilled**."

Let your tone suggest: If only they had listened! The land will rest for 70 years to compensate for the desecrated Sabbaths.

READING I   The author of Chronicles is frustrated and pained over his people's refusal to keep the covenant, and their rejection of God's "messengers." Imagine how you might speak about legislators who ignored years of admonitions to prepare for a natural disaster you knew was inevitable? How would you declare, "they mocked," our messengers, "despised" our warnings, "and scoffed at" our prophets? The mood of this text reflects the conviction that this fate was self-generated. The "anger of the Lord" is a *consequence* of freely chosen behavior.

The Chaldean atrocities are intentionally listed to make explicit the consequences of the people's infidelity. Don't gloss over them, but let them do their work of shocking us with graphic detail. Speak with regret of the destruction of people, places, and "precious objects" as if it were your relatives slaughtered or your childhood home that was pillaged. During the exile, Jeremiah had prophesied that Israel's stay in Babylon would last 70 years. Repeated here, Jeremiah's words are not angry or righteous, but an echo in

which we now recognize the truth, bitter as it is to swallow.

When Cyrus finally came on the scene, he fulfilled Jeremiah's words. This pagan king, it turns out, was more responsive to God's prompting than was Israel. God did not forget the covenant and mercifully restored the land through Cyrus, whose voice is charged with sincerity, not pomposity. The last phrase is a blessing, undeserved, but generously imparted.

READING II   Today is Laetare Sunday, a day when the violet vest-

Suggest the great king's military power and the divine mandate he was given.

In the **first** year of **Cyrus**, king of **Persia**,
in order to **fulfill** the word of the LORD spoken by **Jeremiah**,
the LORD **inspired** King Cyrus of Persia
to issue this **proclamation** throughout his kingdom,
both by word of **mouth** and in **writing**:
"Thus says **Cyrus**, king of **Persia**:
All the kingdoms of the **earth**
the LORD, the God of **heaven**, has **given** to me,
and he has also **charged** me to build him a **house**
in **Jerusalem**, which is in **Judah**.

Cyrus is sincerely seeking to do God's will.

Speak this last sentence as a blessing.

Whoever, therefore, among you belongs to any **part** of his **people**,
let him go **up**, and may his **God** be **with** him!"

READING II Ephesians 2:4–10

Ephesians = ee-FEE-zhuhnz

A **reading from the Letter of Saint Paul to the Ephesians**

Brothers and sisters:
God, who is **rich** in **mercy**,

The heart of the passage is in this first line.

because of the great **love** he had for us,
even when we were **dead** in our **transgressions**,
brought us to **life** with **Christ**—by **grace** you have
been **saved**—,
raised us up with him,
and **seated** us with him in the **heavens** in Christ **Jesus**,
that in the ages to **come**

God's motive is to share the "riches of his grace" with us.

he might show the immeasurable **riches** of his grace
in his **kindness** to us in Christ **Jesus**.
For by **grace** you have been **saved** through **faith**,

Stress the fact that our salvation is not our own doing.

and this is not from **you**; it is the **gift** of **God**;
it is not from **works**, so no one may **boast**.

---

ments are set aside and our Lenten penances lessened. We pause at this midpoint in Lent and heed the entrance antiphon: "Rejoice, oh Jerusalem." Typically, the Second Reading has little connection with the First Reading and Gospel, but in Lent the Second Reading is chosen to reinforce the message of the other two texts. Today, all three readings offer reason to rejoice.

Paul proclaims his good news from the very first line: "God . . . is rich in mercy." Even when we were "dead" in our sinfulness, God took the initiative to raise us to life in Christ. Paul is clear about the

source of salvation: Yes, he says, we were "created in Christ Jesus for the *good works*," but it is by God's *favor* that we were saved, not through any merit of our own. To make sure we understand, Paul reiterates: "by *grace* you have been saved through *faith*, and this is not from *you*." Grace is God's free gift, pure and simple. That announcement of God's mercy sets the tone of the entire passage. Speak with tender gratitude of a God who lavishes on us the richest gift of all, salvation. Express the concern and caring of a God who sought us in the midst of our "transgressions" to

give us new life. God's "great love" motivates this generous initiative. Express that love in every sentence, in every pause; and let it glow from your eyes each time you look at the assembly.

This divine love resembles that of a parent, the kind of love that convinces children they are lovable even when they fail. Paul was the first to declare that salvation is free and unmerited. Let yourself experience the joy and peace that comes from knowing it, then share that truth with persuasive conviction.

We are the works of God's hands.

End with an upbeat tone.

For we are his **handiwork**, created in Christ **Jesus**
for the good **works**
that God has prepared in **advance**,
that we should **live** in them.

GOSPEL John 3:14–21

A reading from the holy Gospel according to John

Nicodemus = nik-uh-DEE-muhs

Address the assembly as if they were Nicodemus.

Speak this classic verse extra slowly so all have time to recognize and absorb it.

Your pacing might quicken a bit here.

This is a sobering truth; don't soften it.

More hard words here. Don't hesitate to speak these truths bluntly.

The text ends on a note of hope.

Jesus said to **Nicodemus**:
"Just as Moses lifted up the **serpent** in the **desert**,
so must the Son of **Man** be **lifted** up,
so that everyone who **believes** in him may have eternal **life**."

For God so **loved** the world that he gave his only **Son**,
so that everyone who **believes** in him might not **perish**
but might have eternal **life**.
For God did not **send** his Son into the world
to **condemn** the world,
but that the world might be **saved** through him.
Whoever **believes** in him will **not** be condemned,
but whoever does **not** believe has **already** been condemned,
because he has not believed in the **name** of the only Son of **God**.
And this is the **verdict**,
that the **light** came into the **world**,
but people preferred **darkness** to light,
because their **works** were **evil**.
For everyone who does **wicked** things **hates** the light
and does not come **toward** the light,
so that his **works** might not be **exposed**.
But whoever lives the **truth comes** to the light,
so that his **works** may be clearly **seen** as done in **God**.

GOSPEL It's important to remember that "God so loved [and loves!] the world." Good abounds and the world is not evil; God sent the Son not to condemn the world but to save it. Jesus' words are meant to offer assurance and comfort, which is all the more apparent in the context of the conversation between Jesus and the confused Nicodemus. We all puzzle over questions regarding judgment and salvation, and your assembly would likely welcome the same assurance.

Jesus tells Nicodemus that, like Moses' serpent, he must be "lifted up," a

reference to his death, and he connects his tragic fate to God's love for the world. His mission is not to condemn humanity, but to be a bridge between God and us that "the world might be saved." State this truth with confidence and love.

Jesus speaks hard words when he asserts that some prefer the darkness of sin. The notion that salvation and condemnation are a choice each of us gets to make is a concept we tend to stubbornly resist, for we prefer to deny our responsibility and pin the blame squarely on God. Speak Jesus' reasoning slowly and clearly, with-

out harshness, but suggesting the pain Jesus must have felt at knowing that some do prefer "darkness," and the "evil" deeds done in it, to the "light" he freely offers. Try a different tone on each of the last two sentences. A furrowed brow might accompany your explanation that anyone who "hates the light" cannot "come toward the light." But with genuine joy make the final declaration that true believers are happy to disclose that their works are "done in God."

4TH SUNDAY OF LENT, YEAR A

Lectionary #31

READING I   1 Samuel 16:1b, 6–7, 10–13a

A reading from the first Book of Samuel

The voice of God is resolute and authoritative.

The LORD said to **Samuel**:
  "Fill your horn with **oil**, and be on your **way**.
I am sending you to **Jesse** of **Bethlehem**,
  for I have chosen my **king** from among his **sons**."

Eliab = ee-LĪ-uhb

Speak of Eliab with Samuel's conviction that this is God's anointed.

As Jesse and his sons came to the **sacrifice**,
  Samuel looked at **Eliab** and thought,
  "**Surely** the LORD's **anointed** is here **before** him."
But the LORD said to Samuel:
  "Do not judge from his **appearance** or from his lofty **stature**,
  because I have **rejected** him.

Give God's dialogue the tone of a patient teacher rather than a disciplinarian. God uses this opportunity to teach a valuable lesson about God's ways and ours.

Suggest the tediousness of this lengthy process. Stress "seven."

Not as **man** sees does **God** see,
  because **man** sees the **appearance**
  but the LORD looks into the **heart**."
In the **same** way Jesse presented **seven** sons before Samuel,
  but Samuel **said** to Jesse,
  "The LORD has not chosen any **one** of these."
Then Samuel **asked** Jesse,
  "Are these **all** the sons you have?"

Samuel is confused, perhaps worried, and somewhat exasperated.

Jesse is not hopeful that his youngest will be the one.

Jesse replied,
  "There is still the **youngest**, who is tending the **sheep**."
Samuel said to Jesse,
  "**Send** for him;

In contrast with Jesse, Samuel is immediately hopeful.

  we will not begin the sacrificial **banquet** until he **arrives** here."

READING I   Today's Second Reading and Gospel both deal overtly with the theme of light and darkness. That theme is also evident in this First Reading, where Samuel moves from the darkness of judging from appearance into the light of judging by God's standards instead—a lesson the disciples will also learn in today's Gospel.

Saul has disappointed the Lord by turning to fortune-tellers instead of trusting God, so God sends Samuel to seek and consecrate his successor from among the eight sons of Jesse. Samuel is not in an enviable position: not only must he secretly discern and anoint Saul's successor—knowing full well that he could be put to death if his mission is discovered—but he is also sent "blind" to recognize the one among Jesse's sons whom God has chosen to become Israel's new (and greatest) king. Samuel must somehow discern whom the Lord wants and announce God's choice to the anxious family. The verses missing from this Lectionary selection say the elders of Bethlehem "came trembling to meet" Samuel; considering the circumstances, he may be doing some trembling of his own!

In order to size up the eight brothers, Samuel invites Jesse's family to a "sacrifice" specially arranged so he can survey the young men and select the "Lord's anointed" from among them. The tall and sturdy Eliab fits Samuel's expectations, so the prophet quickly assumes his mission is accomplished. But God's admonition to "not judge from his appearance" keeps Samuel from jumping to conclusions. That admonition, heard elsewhere in the Old Testament, constitutes the heart of the

Speak with great respect and admiration for David.

Jesse **sent** and had the young man **brought** to them.
He was **ruddy**, a youth **handsome** to behold
   and making a **splendid** appearance.
The LORD said,
  "**There**—**anoint** him, for **this** is the one!"

God is pleased with this choice!

Then **Samuel**, with the horn of **oil** in hand,
   anointed David in the presence of his **brothers**;
   and from **that** day on, the **spirit** of the LORD **rushed**
    upon David.

Slowly, as he is anointed, he is filled with the Spirit.

READING II   Ephesians 5:8–14

A reading from the Letter of Saint Paul to the Ephesians

The good news of the opening and closing sentences undergirds the teaching tone in the body of the reading. Speak one line at a time. You must not blur these ideas.

Brothers and sisters:
You were once **darkness**,
  but **now** you are **light** in the **Lord**.
Live as **children** of light,
  for **light** produces every kind of **goodness**
  and **righteousness** and **truth**.

"Goodness," "righteousness," and "truth" are three distinct qualities.

Try to learn what is **pleasing** to the Lord.

"Try" sets the tone of this line: exhortation softened by an understanding that doing right is not an easy process to learn.

Imagine speaking these words to a beloved young person in your charge.

Take no part in the **fruitless** works of **darkness**;
  rather **expose** them, for it is **shameful** even to **mention**
  the things done by them in **secret**;
  but everything **exposed** by the light becomes **visible**,
  for everything that **becomes** visible is **light**.
Therefore, it says:

Hear the cadence in this line. Speak it with joyous hope.

  "**Awake**, O sleeper,
  and **arise** from the **dead**,
  and **Christ** will give you **light**."

---

reading: God's ways are not our ways; we judge from appearance, God judges the heart.

    After a lengthy process of examining and rejecting each of seven sons, Samuel asks if these are "all" of the siblings. Jesse's tone can betray his skepticism about the candidacy of the one remaining son who is off "tending the sheep." But Samuel appears immediately hopeful that this last may be the one, and eagerly commands they send for him! It was God who rejected the first seven brothers and it will be God who chooses the worthy candidate.

David's appearance quickens the tempo of the piece: short, clipped phrases describe the boy who was "ruddy," "handsome," and "splendid." Samuel knows instantly this is God's chosen. Slowly and with dignity, narrate David's anointing in front of his father and brothers. "Rushed" is one of those great words that surprises *and* communicates. But remember, it is the Spirit who rushes, not you.

READING II This text finds a home in Lent because of the baptismal allusions found in its light/darkness

references and in the excerpt from an early baptismal hymn that closes the passage. It also wonderfully complements today's Gospel that proclaims Jesus as "light of the world." In a text that repeats the word "light" six times in the span of a dozen-plus lines, there can be little question where our emphasis must go. Add the double reference to "darkness," and all doubt is removed.

    For those preparing for Baptism, Lent is a period of purification and enlightenment and for them, as for all of us, the passage begins and ends with the same good

GOSPEL John 9:1–41

A reading from the holy Gospel according to John

(1) **Jesus** passed by he saw a man **blind** from **birth**.
His **disciples** asked him,
   "Rabbi, who **sinned**, **this** man or his **parents**,
   that he was born **blind**?"
Jesus answered,
   "Neither **he nor** his parents sinned;
   it is so that the **works** of **God** might be made **visible**
     through him.
We have to **do** the works of the one who sent me while it is **day**.
Night is coming when **no** one can work.
While I am in the **world**, I am the **light** of the world."
(2) When he had said this, he **spat** on the ground
   and made **clay** with the saliva,
   and **smeared** the clay on his **eyes**, and said to him,
   "Go **wash** in the **Pool** of **Siloam**"—which means **Sent**—.
So he **went** and **washed**, and came back able to **see**.

(3) His **neighbors** and those who had **seen** him earlier
   as a **beggar** said,
   "Isn't this the one who used to **sit** and **beg**?"
Some said, "It **is**,"
   but **others** said, "**No**, he just **looks** like him."
He said, "**I am**."
So they said to him, "**How** were your eyes **opened**?"
He replied,
   "The man called **Jesus** made **clay** and **anointed** my eyes
   and told me, 'Go to **Siloam** and **wash**.'
So I **went** there and **washed** and was able to **see**."

Stress "blind from birth" for it is later questioned.

Jesus' answer is unexpected and new. Don't rush.

Enjoy the graphic details!

Siloam = sih-LOH-uhm.
Relate the miracle with a sense of awe.
Pause to shift to this new scene.

The bystanders are of differing opinions.

The man is insistent: "I am!"

He relates the details joyfully.

---

news: once you were darkness, now you are light. Paul's use of metaphor ("you were . . . darkness"; "you are light") makes an important point about the spiritual life: we become what we do consistently. Live in darkness long enough and you will become darkness. Live in the light of Christ and you will be light! Through Baptism each of us has been liberated from fruitless and shameful deeds done in darkness and empowered to live in the light of Christ.

    Because it is possible to move from "light" to "darkness," Paul takes on an exhortative tone to caution us of the real dangers that confront us. Imagine speaking to college freshmen away from home for the first time, urging them to use their newfound freedom responsibly, warning them that shameful behavior eventually comes to light. How would you nuance Paul's exhortation to "take no part in the fruitless works of darkness"? If one of those young people were your own child, might you complement the strong directives ("Try to learn . . . take no part . . . expose them . . .") with underlying compassion so that after focusing on the dangers of living in the dark you could also offer an invitation to embrace the light which is Christ?

    The closing lines, originally sung as part of an early baptismal hymn, conclude with a promise of light. Darkness is sin and separation from Christ, but light symbolizes grace and oneness with him. By stressing "arise from the dead" you'll remind us of the perennial possibility of being overcome by darkness and death; then, by contrast, the final "light" will shine more brightly.

It suddenly dawns on him he doesn't know Jesus' whereabouts. Pause to introduce this new scene.

And they said to him, "Where **is** he?"
He said, "I don't **know**."

As you read "So the Pharisees . . ." your tone should hint at where they're going with this.
Start the phrase "He put clay" in a matter-of-fact tone, but end in a joyful tone.
One of the Pharisees is angry, the other reasonable.

(4) They **brought** the one who was once blind to the **Pharisees**.
Now Jesus had made clay and opened his eyes on a **sabbath**.
So then the Pharisees **also** asked him how he was able to see.
He **said** to them,
    "He put **clay** on my eyes, and I **washed**, and **now** I can **see**."
So some of the **Pharisees** said,
    "This man is not from **God**,
    because he does not keep the **sabbath**."
But **others** said,
    "How can a **sinful** man do such **signs**?"
And there was a **division** among them.
So they said to the blind man **again**,
    "What do **you** have to say about him,
    since he opened **your** eyes?"
He said, "He is a **prophet**."

He must decide if he will make this confession of faith, and he does it boldly.

(5) Now the Jews did not **believe**
    that he had been **blind** and gained his **sight**
    until they summoned the **parents** of the one
        who had gained his sight.
They **asked** them,
    "Is this your **son**, who you say was **born** blind?
How does he now **see**?"
His parents **answered** and said,
    "We **know** that this is our **son** and that he was born **blind**.
We do **not** know how he **sees** now,
    nor do we know **who** opened his eyes.
Ask **him**, he is of **age**;
    he can speak for **himself**."

They feel they've been duped, so they look further.

The parents' speech is guarded, they say only what they must.

GOSPEL
Scholars debate the amount of theology layered onto the kernel of this miracle story. Luckily, John is both a theologian and a storyteller. Rather than subordinate the narrative to his theologizing, John has so integrated his ideas into this story line that deleting any part of the story would destroy aspects of both the artistry and the theology.

The narrator, who is critical in this story, needs a personality to match the tone of the several asides in the text. Perhaps the person is an eyewitness turned believer,

perhaps the apostle; certainly the narrator is an invested, caring observer.

(1) The disciples reflect the accepted wisdom of their culture by assuming the man's blindness is the result of sin. John uses their ignorance to set up one of his misunderstanding/illumination sequences that reveals his key insight into who Jesus is, namely, the light of the world. Jesus' answer surprises the disciples. Contrast their assumption ("Who sinned, *this* man or his *parents*?") with Jesus' assertion that "Neither he nor his parents sinned" but "that God's works might be made visible."

Because he knows the time grows short to do the will of the one who sent him, Jesus speaks of the advance of "night" with urgency.

(2) Jesus is not afraid to touch human pain, so the words used to describe the healing are graphic: "spat," "clay," "saliva," "smeared." Stress these pungent images that accent the "hands-on" nature of this healing. Jesus' instructions to wash may be a test of faith which the man gladly accepts. Note that the meaning of "Siloam" refers back to Jesus' self-description as one "sent" by the Father.

Offer this aside as an excuse for the parents' behavior.

His parents said this because they were **afraid**
of the Jews, for the Jews had already **agreed**
that if anyone **acknowledged** him as the **Christ**,
he would be **expelled** from the **synagogue**.
For this reason his **parents** said,
"He is of **age**; question **him**."

Speak the narration as if through clenched teeth, suggesting the exasperation of the leaders.

(6) So a **second** time they called the man who had been blind
and said to him, "Give **God** the praise!
We **know** that this man is a **sinner**."

He replied,

The man's tone suggests: Don't' entangle me in your politics. All I know is I'm healed!

"If he is a **sinner**, I do not **know**.
One thing I **do** know is that I was **blind** and now I **see**."
So they said to him,
"What did he **do** to you?
How did he open your eyes?"
He answered them,
"I told you **already** and you did not **listen**.

He's becoming impatient—and bold!

Why do you want to hear it **again**?
Do **you** want to become his disciples, **too**?"
They **ridiculed** him and said,
"**You** are that man's disciple;
we are disciples of **Moses**!

The leaders' anger is mounting.

We **know** that God spoke to **Moses**,
but we do not know where this one is **from**."
The man **answered** and said to them,

First he mocks them, and then he instructs them.

"This is what is so **amazing**,
that you do not know where he is **from**,
yet he **opened** my **eyes**.
We know that God does **not** listen to **sinners**,
but if one is **devout** and does his **will**, he **listens** to him.

(3) The crowd's reactions to the miracle span the spectrum of amazement, confusion, doubt, and jealousy. Some speculate about the beggar's identity and how he was healed, while others insist they know the truth. The beggar simply recounts the events without editorial comment. Although his own enlightenment will grow, here his healer is just "the man called Jesus." We sense that he surprises even himself when he realizes he doesn't know the whereabouts of this Jesus—whom he has yet to see.

(4) Speak the aside about healing on the Sabbath in a tone that signals the encounter with the Pharisees will be controversial. Under these intimidating circumstances the beggar's responses are more guarded. The Pharisees seem as divided as the crowd, some calling Jesus "sinful" and others countering that the evidence speaks of godliness. Avoid presenting the Pharisees as uniformly sinister by stressing their sharp division. Mirroring the growth of one coming to faith, the beggar reaches another stage of illumination when he risks the confession that Jesus is a "prophet."

(5) The dramatic scene with the man's parents sets the stage for the judgment Jesus later levels at the religious leaders who refused to believe. The fearful parents play their cards close to the chest, saying only what they must, not taking the risks their son took. Their fear may reflect more the attitude prevalent at the time of John's writing than that of Jesus' day. Later decades did see real animosity develop between Jews and Christians resulting in the Christians' expulsion from synagogues,

It is **unheard** of that anyone ever **opened** the eyes
> of a person born **blind**.
If this man were **not** from **God**,
> he would not be able to **do** anything."
They answered and said to him,
> "**You** were born totally in **sin**,
> and are you trying to teach **us**?"
Then they **threw** him **out**.

They take refuge in the false assumption that his blindness was the result of sin. Pause before the final scene with Jesus.

(7) When **Jesus** heard that they had **thrown** him out,
> he **found** him and said, "Do you **believe** in the Son of **Man**?"
He answered and said,
> "Who **is** he, sir, that I may **believe** in him?"
Jesus said to him,
> "You have **seen** him,
> and the one **speaking** with you is **he**."

As of yet, he has not beheld Jesus, and he's anxious to "see" him.

He said,
> "I **do** believe, Lord," and he **worshiped** him.
Then Jesus said,
> "I **came** into this world for **judgment**,
> so that those who do **not** see **might** see,
> and those who **do** see might become **blind**."

Pause after "he said" to suggest his moment of decision.

Jesus' tone attracts the attention of the Pharisees.

Some of the **Pharisees** who were with him **heard** this
> and said to him, "Surely **we** are not also blind, **are** we?"
Jesus said to them,
> "If you **were** blind, you would have no **sin**;
> but **now** you are saying, 'We **see**,' so your sin **remains**."

This is strong, uncompromising language, but motivated by his desire that they truly "see."

[Shorter: John 9:1, 6–9, 13–17, 34–38]

---

but it was not yet a reality in Jesus' time. But, that detail is well motivated within the context of the story. You might read the parenthetical aside ("His parents said this") as the narrator's attempt to make fear an excuse for the parents' unexpected behavior.

(6) Don't make this second encounter with the religious leaders a carbon of the first. Good literature builds and peaks again and again and varies its rhythm and intensity. The leaders' anger and frustration, even any sincere desire for the truth,

must have intensified by now. They assume that Jesus is a "sinner," but the beggar disagrees with brilliantly animated and witty dialogue. Daringly, he launches into a lecture proclaiming Jesus to be "from God," evoking a swift and harsh response from the leaders.

(7) Notably, Jesus goes looking for the beggar and *invites*, more than questions, his belief in "the Son of Man." Because the beggar has yet to *see* Jesus, a pause before the beggar's response will allow us to imagine him remembering Jesus' voice before he falls down to worship. In his final

speeches, Jesus utters stark and uncompromising truth. But how might a savior who seeks everyone's salvation speak such words of judgment?

Proclaiming this lengthy text well won't be accomplished without adequate practice. You'll know it is worth the time and effort when you realize that good proclamation doesn't recall a past event but makes that saving moment and its graces present and available for the assembly.

5TH SUNDAY OF LENT

Lectionary #35

READING I   Jeremiah 31:31–34

Jeremiah = jayr-uh-MĪ-uh

Let your tone be joyful from the very start.

This is a brief glance back at past wrongdoing. Don't over-emphasize this sentence.

Stress, instead, the new moment coming upon the nation.

Read slowly here, for this is a radically new moment. Speak this as if it were the tenderest gesture of love imaginable.

Emphasize that both the "least" and "greatest" will know the Lord.
Be awed by God's willingness to forgive and forget.

A reading from the Book of the Prophet Jeremiah

The **days** are **coming**, says the LORD,
 when I will make a **new** covenant with the house of **Israel**
 and the house of **Judah**.
It will **not** be like the covenant I made with their **fathers**
 the day I took them by the **hand**
 to lead them **forth** from the land of **Egypt**;
 for they **broke** my covenant,
 and I had to show myself their **master**, says the LORD.
But **this** is the covenant that I will make
 with the house of Israel **after** those days, says the LORD.
I will place my law **within** them and **write** it upon their **hearts**;
 I will be their **God**, and **they** shall be my **people**.
No **longer** will they have need to **teach** their friends and relatives
 how to **know** the LORD.
All, from **least** to **greatest**, shall **know** me, says the LORD,
 for I will **forgive** their evildoing and **remember** their sin
 no **more**.

READING I The final Sundays of Lent make us stand before the compassionate Christ who willingly suffered, died, and rose again for us. It is because of what Jesus accomplished through his death and Resurrection that we can claim the covenant that Jeremiah heralds here: God's law written not on paper but in our *hearts*, healing and restoring our relationship with God.

The drama suggested in this powerful text is often repeated in our own lives: someone wrongs us, but then grace enables us to let go of our hurt and move ahead, and we invite the wrongdoer to move ahead with us. Focused on the future, we might review the past, in order to let what will come stand in stark contrast with what has been.

Like a lover wooing back an unfaithful beloved, God announces miraculous good news: "I will make a new covenant." Then God winces at the memory of Israel's infidelity: "It will not be like the covenant" made at Zion that "they broke." Speak with regret of Israel's sinfulness and the dire punishment (the Exile) it brought upon them.

"But *this* is the covenant" seals shut the door to the past. The clouds of memory part and the sun's new light pours in. Like a lover who carves names onto a tree, God promises to "place my law *within* them" (an *appropriately* stressed preposition) and "write it upon their *hearts*." God says, with profound simplicity: "I will be their God."

Utterly convinced, explaining that teaching will become unnecessary. All will know the Lord without instruction, you announce, because they will be overwhelmed by a God who first forgives and then forgets.

A short reading requires slower reading.

This is a reference to Jesus' agony in the garden where he suffered greatly and prayed fervently to God.

The author offers Jesus as a model for us. Contrast "Son though he was" with "obedience" and "suffered."

This line offers hope to all. Make sure all in your assembly feel included.

READING II   Hebrews 5:7–9

A reading from the Letter to the Hebrews

In the days when Christ **Jesus** was in the **flesh**,
　　he offered **prayers** and **supplications** with loud **cries** and **tears**
　　to the one who was able to **save** him from **death**,
　　and he was **heard** because of his **reverence**.
Son though he **was**, he learned **obedience** from what he **suffered**;
　　and when he was made **perfect**,
　　he became the source of eternal **salvation**
　　　　for all who **obey** him.

Let your tone suggest that this request is unusual.

In John, "seeing" Jesus means recognizing the need for him to undergo the "hour" for which he came.

Speak these lines with simple, unadorned nobility.

Deliver these maxims as if they were words meant to reassure loved ones who are about to lose you.

GOSPEL   John 12:20–33

A reading from the holy Gospel according to John

Some **Greeks** who had come to worship at the **Passover** Feast
　　came to **Philip**, who was from **Bethsaida** in **Galilee**,
　　and **asked** him, "**Sir**, we would like to see **Jesus**."
Philip went and told **Andrew**;
　　then Andrew and Philip went and told **Jesus**.
Jesus **answered** them,
　　"The **hour** has come for the Son of **Man** to be **glorified**.
Amen, **amen**, I say to you,
　　unless a grain of **wheat** falls to the ground and **dies**,
　　it remains just a **grain** of wheat;
　　but if it **dies**, it produces much **fruit**.

READING II   The author of Hebrews alludes to Jesus' agony in the garden and makes it a model for our own life of prayer. Employing the same technique a good parent uses when children are frightened by bad dreams, he tells a story of being in a similar situation. The technique not only distracts the children, it tells them someone else survived such an ordeal and offers hope that they might, too. The author of Hebrews knows this strategy and applies it well for the sake of any who might be reluctant to approach Christ in the midst of human woe, who fear his judgment rather than anticipate his sympathy.

Tell your listeners not to be afraid to do what God's own son did: offer "prayers and supplications with loud cries and tears." Jesus' prayer was heard because of his reverent submission to God's will, through which he learned "obedience." Short passages must be read slowly and require that you set the images in your mind before you speak the first word. This short piece obliges you to believe, like Jesus, that we too can find blessing in suffering as we also seek to be perfected.

GOSPEL   We can only speculate why the Gentile Greeks wanted to see Jesus, but there can be no doubt that if they heard this discourse, they got more than they bargained for. The Greeks approach the only two apostles with Greek names, asking for an audience with Jesus, an unusual request coming from Gentiles. The apostles pass the decision to Jesus, but he makes no direct response, keeping his focus on "the hour" which has "come."

The remainder of the passage is suffused with the paradoxes that distinguish

Here, Jesus seems to be both teaching others and himself about these profound truths.

Whoever **loves** his life **loses** it,
 and whoever **hates** his life in **this** world
 will **preserve** it for **eternal** life.
Whoever **serves** me must **follow** me,
 and where **I** am, there also will my **servant** be.
The **Father** will honor whoever **serves** me.

This is a "mini" garden scene where Jesus' anguish is quite real.

"I am **troubled** now. Yet what should I **say**,
'**Father**, **save** me from this hour'?
But it was for this **purpose** that I **came** to this hour.
Father, **glorify** your name."

Here, Jesus gives his assent to the fate that awaits him.

Then a **voice** came from heaven,
 "I **have** glorified it and will glorify it **again**."

The "voice" is mistaken for thunder, which means it should grab attention and impress those who hear it.

The crowd there **heard** it and said it was **thunder**;
 but others said, "An **angel** has spoken to him."
Jesus answered and said,
 "This **voice** did not come for **my** sake but for **yours**.

A lot of information is contained in these lines: The time of judgment has come; Satan is to be driven from the world; through his death and Resurrection, Jesus will save many.

Now is the time of **judgment** on this world;
 now the **ruler** of this world will be **driven** out.
And when I am **lifted** up from the earth,
 I will draw **everyone** to **myself**."

The last line is not spoken with regret, but with resolve.

He **said** this indicating the kind of **death** he would **die**.

Christian faith: death leads to life; clinging to life is a sure way to lose it; defeat in the world's eyes means glorification in God's.

Being at once both teacher and student, Jesus announces his own passing and the necessity for that "hour" to come, simultaneously teaching and learning about the need to surrender to the will of God. His dialogue is neither flippant nor didactic, for he speaks from his depths with full understanding of what lies ahead, like someone on a death bed consoling the relatives who have gathered, instead of being consoled by them.

At least momentarily, the *reality* of death is overwhelming even for Jesus. "My soul is troubled . . ." is considered John's attempt at a garden scene, so Jesus' anguish, though short lived, is real. Knowing he came for the very crisis he fears, Jesus resolves to accept it by asking God to turn the moment of his death into a paradoxical moment of glory.

The thundering voice "from the sky" gives testimony to Jesus for the sake of the crowd. The crowd responds with animated, though uncomprehending, excitement. Jesus' final words suggest resignation,

inner peace, and excitement over what his being "lifted up" will mean for "everyone." Unlike the crowds, you understand that Jesus' death makes possible salvation for all, so narrate the parenthetical sentence with knowing significance rather than regret. After all, what Jesus said also indicated the sort of *life* he would offer to everyone who follows him.

5TH SUNDAY OF LENT, YEAR A

Lectionary #34

READING I Ezekiel 37:12–14

Ezekiel = ee-ZEE-kee-uhl

There are many ways to suggest the urgent and earnest feelings of this text—with full-throated conviction; with quiet intensity; with subdued emotion, but always as if the events were unfolding right before you. Choose your tone and use it to persuade us.

On the opening sentence, speak the first and third lines at a slower pace than the middle line. Do the same for the second sentence.

Highlighting the word "spirit" will help prepare us for the Second Reading where God's spirit is the central motif.

Imagine looking into the eyes of one who needs these promises. Take a long pause before announcing "The word of the Lord."

A reading from the Book of the Prophet Ezekiel

Thus says the Lord **GOD**:
  O my **people**, I will **open** your **graves**
  and have you **rise** from them,
  and bring you **back** to the land of **Israel**.
Then you shall **know** that I am the **LORD**,
  when I **open** your graves and have you **rise** from them,
  O my people!
I will put my **spirit** in you that you may **live**,
  and I will **settle** you upon your **land**;
  thus you shall know that **I** am the **LORD**.
I have **promised**, and I will **do** it, says the **LORD**.

READING I Today's three texts fit together like the instruments of an ensemble, unique and distinctive, yet blending to make a harmonious statement about the possibility of Resurrection and new life. They propel us toward the climactic events of Holy Week and the Triduum.

God's word is meant to persuade us that the impossible can occur. This text was addressed to the nation of Israel during its time of exile, a situation that was as hopeless as anyone can imagine. It was to awaken the hope of dramatic reversal that this prophecy was spoken then, and now. Uttered on a battlefield over the dry and barren bones of long-dead soldiers, this oracle proclaims the death of despair, the inevitability of the impossible, the advent of new hope: the Exile will end and the dead will rise to life. It is God's voice, not the prophet's, which twice makes that pledge. With great urgency and sincerity, the exclamation "O my people" frames God's promise.

Written long before belief in an afterlife was fully embraced by Israel, the dramatic images of this passage speak eloquently of God's love and protection accompanying us to the grave and beyond. During the Exile, being resettled "upon [their] land" was the only form of resurrection that mattered. "I will put my spirit in you that you may live" is a promise of such restoration, so save your best emphasis for that line. In this text, Ezekiel presents one of scripture's most striking images—the

READING II   Romans 8:8–11

A reading from the Letter of Saint Paul to the Romans

A short text calls for a slow reading. Paul's logic is filled with joy.

The negative tone of "Those who are in the flesh" immediately turns positive on "But you are not." Make eye contact as you proclaim this truth.

The negative tone of "does not belong to him" immediately turns positive on "But if Christ."

Contrast "dead"/"sin" with "alive"/"righteousness."

This is an "if-then" clause, but "then" is implied, not stated. Announce this good news with joy.

Stress Paul's conviction of bodily resurrection.

Brothers and sisters:
Those who are in the **flesh** cannot **please** God.
But **you** are not in the flesh;
    on the **contrary**, **you** are in the **spirit**,
    if only the **Spirit** of God **dwells** in you.
Whoever does not **have** the Spirit of **Christ** does not **belong**
        to him.
But if Christ is **in** you,
    although the **body** is dead because of **sin**,
    the **spirit** is **alive** because of **righteousness**.
If the **Spirit** of the one who raised **Jesus** from the dead **dwells**
    in you,
    the One who raised **Christ** from the dead
    will give **life** to **your** mortal bodies **also**,
    through his **Spirit dwelling** in you.

GOSPEL   John 11:1–45

A reading from the holy Gospel according to John

For the narrator, these are familiar names and places. Speak of the anointing with tenderness.

Bethany = BETH-uh-nee

(1) Now a man was **ill**, **Lazarus** from **Bethany**,
    the village of **Mary** and her sister **Martha**.
Mary was the one who had **anointed** the Lord with perfumed **oil**
    and dried his **feet** with her **hair**;
    it was her **brother** Lazarus who was **ill**.

dead rising from their graves—to offer his message of hope. Speak that message to each individual in the assembly, for many wounded hearts long to hear such words of promise.

READING II   Like Ezekiel, Paul draws a contrast between what is and is not life, and the difference is the Spirit of God. Paul contrasts "Spirit" with "flesh," which for him represents those who have not embraced new life in Christ but live only to please themselves. "Spirit,"

on the other hand, refers to those who have accepted newness of life and live self-lessly, pleasing both God and neighbor.

Paul's readers, he asserts proudly, are in this second group. Although the opening line states bad news ("Those who are in the flesh cannot please God"), Paul immediately qualifies himself: "But you are not . . ." part of that bad news, he tells us. You are living the good news of life in the Spirit! Walk your listeners slowly through the clear logic and nice progression of Paul's reasoning. Contrasting "dead" and "sin" with "alive" and "righteousness" will

clarify Paul's logic all the more. Of course, Paul's statement that "the body is dead" is not meant literally. He's saying that, despite being saved through Christ's Resurrection, the fullness of salvation won't be ours till after death. For now, our bodies are subject to the *signs* of sin and death—illness, aging, pain—because we live in a world that's still under sin's influence. But our spirit already enjoys a foretaste of what will be ours fully in eternity.

Suggest the anxiety of the two sisters when you speak the word "Master."

Don't get philosophical here. Keep the tone low-key and conversational.

Proclaim the words "Jesus loved . . . and Lazarus" slowly. Everything else builds on this.

The disciples are immediately anxious and incredulous: Do you really want to go back there!

Once again, avoid a lofty tone and keep it conversational.

Deliver this line as if you were really going to wake a sleeping friend.

The disciples are suggesting that their Master is not making sense!

Speak with some gravity, but not sadness.

So the sisters sent **word** to Jesus saying,
    "**Master**, the one you **love** is **ill**."
When Jesus **heard** this he said,
    "This illness is **not** to end in **death**,
    but is for the **glory** of **God**,
    that the **Son** of God may be **glorified** through it."
(2) Now Jesus **loved** Martha and her sister and Lazarus.
So when he **heard** that he was ill,
    he **remained** for two **days** in the place where he **was**.
Then **after** this he said to his disciples,
    "Let us go back to **Judea**."
The disciples said to him,
    "**Rabbi**, the Jews were just trying to **stone** you,
    and you want to go **back** there?"
Jesus answered,
    "Are there not **twelve** hours in a day?
If one walks during the **day**, he does not **stumble**,
    because he sees the **light** of this world.
But if one walks at **night**, he **stumbles**,
    because the light is not **in** him."
He said this, and then told them,
    "Our friend **Lazarus** is **asleep**,
    but I am going to **awaken** him."
So the disciples said to him,
    "**Master**, if he is **asleep**, he will be **saved**."
But Jesus was talking about his **death**,
    while **they** thought that he meant **ordinary** sleep.
So then Jesus said to them **clearly**,
    "**Lazarus** has **died**.
And I am **glad** for you that I was not **there**,
    that you may **believe**.

Significantly, Paul's conclusion announces hope of *physical* resurrection for those who possess Christ's spirit. The same spirit who enables Christians to live holy lives now will bring their "mortal bodies" to life on the last day. Resurrection is not a metaphor, it's a promise that should be proclaimed with the same attitude of joy that has pervaded the entire text.

GOSPEL Even a story this good is not worth telling if it doesn't tell us about our own lives—that death still yields to life, that Jesus walks among us ready to repeat the words that beckoned Lazarus from the tomb, that he's still willing to brave the stench of death and call us back to life. We tell and retell the stories of scripture because they can evoke that kind of hope from us. So, as proclaimer, decide what you need to do to make this a proclamation of hope rather than a recitation of history. Perhaps that will mean spending time with these characters till they're as real to you as those from a favorite piece of literature—or as real as people you encounter on your daily rounds. You may need to imagine yourself in the same situation—watching a loved one die, hoping for a remedy that comes too late. You might read the story several times picturing yourself a different character each time—a disciple, one of the sisters, a mourner, Jesus, even Lazarus. Is there someone you know for whom this story has been a source of hope? Could you ask why the story touched them? These strategies will take time, but they'll be worth the effort.

Let us **go** to him."
So **Thomas**, called **Didymus**, said to his fellow **disciples**,
  "Let us **also** go to **die** with him."

When Jesus **arrived**, he found that Lazarus
  had already been in the **tomb** for **four days**.
Now Bethany was **near** Jerusalem, only about two miles **away**.
And many of the **Jews** had **come** to Martha and Mary
  to **comfort** them about their brother.
When Martha **heard** that **Jesus** was coming,
  she went to **meet** him;
  but **Mary** sat at home.
Martha said to Jesus,
  "**Lord**, if you had **been** here,
  my brother would not have **died**.
But even **now** I know that **whatever** you ask of God,
  God will **give** you."
Jesus said to her,
  "Your brother will **rise**."
Martha said to him,
  "I **know** he will rise,
  in the **resurrection** on the last **day**."
Jesus told her,
  "**I** am the resurrection and the **life**;
  whoever **believes** in me, even if he **dies**, will **live**,
  and everyone who **lives** and believes in me will **never** die.
Do **you** believe this?"
She said to him, "**Yes**, Lord.
I have come to believe that you are the **Christ**, the Son of **God**,
  the one who is **coming** into the **world**."

Thomas is willing to pay the price of discipleship.

"Four days" reflects the Jewish belief that the spirit left the body after three days: hence Lazarus is "fully" dead.

Martha exhibits mixed emotions: disappointment and hopefulness.

Martha has missed his point. Jesus' explanation and self-identification are the key points of this Gospel passage.

Deliver these lines slowly. This parallels the "light of the world" pronouncement in last week's Gospel.

Martha's confession is sincere and unreserved.

(1) In the opening lines, the narrator speaks with familiarity and affection about these people and places, about perfume and hair-dried feet. The sisters send for Jesus with confidence that he will hasten to the side of the one "you love." As with the healing of the blind man, Jesus announces the divine purposes to be achieved through "this illness," but demonstrates a surprising lack of urgency.

(2) Although Jesus loves Lazarus' family, he tarries intentionally before setting out for Bethany (the name means "house of the lowly"). The disciples are disturbed and frightened by the prospects of returning to Judea and seem to consider the decision irresponsible. Jesus' reply utilizes a familiar Johannine motif: day and night. "Day" is the time of Jesus' sojourn on the earth—a time for doing God's work freely and unafraid, because "if one walks during the *day*, he does not stumble." Jesus' announcement of Lazarus' death need not be emotional; simplicity better hints at his depth of inner feeling. But the thickheaded disciples misunderstand his use of "asleep." Jesus clarifies and reiter-

ates the divine purpose behind these events. Thomas anticipates Peter's Last Supper grandstanding ("I will lay down my *life* for you!") in his own eagerness for martyrdom.

(3) The physical reality of Lazarus' death is starkly emphasized when Jesus arrives at Bethany and discovers Lazarus has been in the tomb four days. Martha clearly is distressed by Jesus' delay, but while she rebukes him she also confesses her faith that God will grant whatever

Speak in a quieter tone here. Earlier, Martha may have been coaxing Mary to go, but now Mary goes eagerly.

Mary's line echoes Martha's, but vary the delivery for variety.

Jesus experiences genuine sorrow. A note in the New American Bible says that in Greek this is a startling image: "He snorted in spirit."

"Come and see" is the same reply Jesus gives to John's disciples at the start of his ministry.

Convey the contrasting moods of the crowd.

Proclaim these simple but dramatic statements slowly.

Martha's worry about the stench is a very practical concern.

(4)When she had **said** this,
　　she went and called her sister Mary **secretly**, **saying**,
　　"The **teacher** is here and is **asking** for you."
As soon as she **heard** this,
　　she rose **quickly** and **went** to him.
For Jesus had not yet come into the **village**,
　　but was still where Martha had **met** him.
So when the Jews who were **with** her in the house **comforting** her
　　saw Mary get up quickly and go out,
　　they **followed** her,
　　presuming that she was going to the **tomb** to **weep** there.
When Mary came to where **Jesus** was and **saw** him,
　　she fell at his **feet** and said to him,
　　"**Lord**, if you had **been** here,
　　my brother would not have **died**."
When Jesus saw her **weeping** and the Jews who had come
　　　with her weeping,
　　he became **perturbed** and deeply **troubled**, and said,
　　"**Where** have you **laid** him?"
They said to him, "**Sir**, come and **see**."
And Jesus **wept**.
So the Jews said, "See how he **loved** him."
But some of them said,
　　"Could not the one who opened the eyes of the **blind** man
　　have **done** something so that **this** man would not have **died**?"

So **Jesus**, perturbed **again**, came to the **tomb**.
It was a **cave**, and a **stone** lay across it.
Jesus said, "Take away the **stone**."
Martha, the dead man's **sister**, said to him,
　　"Lord, by **now** there will be a **stench**;
　　he has been dead for **four days**."

Jesus asks. Jesus' response is cryptic and not at all what Martha wants to hear. In Jesus' great pronouncement that he is the source of life, this text reaches a climatic high point. In response, Martha declares her full and confident faith in Jesus as the anointed Son of God.

(4) While Martha went to meet Jesus, Mary remained home. Now, Martha (secretly!) tells Mary that Jesus is *asking* for her, so Mary runs to Jesus, falls at his feet and weeps over the loss of her brother,

laying responsibility squarely on Jesus. Mary's sorrow elicits a rare demonstration of emotion from Jesus who becomes "deeply troubled" and asks, "Where have you laid him?" You play this scene each time you visit a funeral home: "Come and see."

(5) As he is led to the tomb, Jesus weeps, causing the bystanders to remark favorably on his love for Lazarus, but others join the Mary/Martha chorus, judging Jesus for doing nothing for this friend though he healed strangers. "It was a cave" is the haunting reference to the tomb

that soon will give up Lazarus. Jesus' bold command to remove the stone is given with authority, but Martha's concern ("there will be a stench") betrays a lack of confidence, so he reproaches her gently.

(6) Before calling Lazarus, Jesus prays—both to thank God and for the sake of "the crowd." He addresses the Father with confidence, asking that the crowds be brought to faith. Throughout, Jesus has been in charge, the master of circumstances, but the full extent of his power

Jesus offers a gentle reproach to Martha.

Jesus said to her,
   "Did I not **tell** you that if you **believe**
   you will see the **glory** of **God**?"
So they **took away** the stone.
(6) And Jesus raised his **eyes** and said,

Jesus prays for others here, not himself.

   "**Father**, I **thank** you for **hearing** me.
I know that you **always** hear me;
   but because of the **crowd** here I have said this,
   that they may **believe** that you **sent** me."
And when he had **said** this,
   he **cried** out in a **loud** voice,

The command is spoken with great authority.

See the commentary for possible phrasing of this line.

   "**Lazarus**, come **out**!"
The **dead** man **came** out,
   tied **hand** and **foot** with **burial** bands,
   and his **face** was wrapped in a **cloth**.
So Jesus said to them,
   "**Untie** him and let him **go**."

Hearing this Gospel should arouse deeper faith in the assembly as it did in the townspeople.

Now **many** of the Jews who had come to **Mary**
   and **seen** what he had done began to **believe** in him.

[Shorter: John 11:3–7, 17, 20–27, 33b–45]

---

and authority is shown nowhere else better than in this dramatic moment. In John, it is this event that finally prompts the religious leaders to move against Jesus.

As you speak "Lazarus," imagine those who are most in need of renewed life—your city's homeless poor, an oppressed country, a friend suffering from depression, a long-dead part of you. Only a unique, divine authority could summon life from the tomb. The emergence of Lazarus can be read without much inflection. The key

is to really *witness* the event in your imagination, then the assembly will see and *feel* it with you. But for that to happen, you must read slower than you've ever read. Try phrasing like this: "The dead man / came out / bound / hand / and foot / with burial bands / and his face / was wrapped in a cloth." Practice until it sounds and feels right.

(7) Build energy on each successive phrase of this final sentence. This great miracle, unlike the healing of the blind man, brings "many" in Bethany to believe in Jesus. Through this dramatic narrative,

you bring your assembly in contact with a side of Jesus' humanity we rarely see. The Lord of life, who healed the blind and raised the dead, was one of us, mourning the death of a friend, comforting his family, shedding real tears.

PALM SUNDAY OF THE LORD'S PASSION

Lectionary #37

GOSPEL AT THE PROCESSION   Mark 11:1–10

Bethphage = BETH-fuh-jee
Bethany = BETH-uh-nee
The geographical references are important code words.

Jesus speaks in a straightforward, confident tone, but don't over emphasize his foreknowledge of events.

Suggest the disciples' surprise at finding the colt as Jesus indicated.

The tone of the bystanders is scolding, while the disciples' response is rather timid. Again they are surprised to see Jesus' words fulfilled.

Don't isolate the three actions narrated here ("brought . . . put . . . sat") but connect them with mounting energy.

A reading from the holy Gospel according to Mark

When **Jesus** and his **disciples** drew near to **Jerusalem**,
    to **Bethphage** and **Bethany** at the Mount of **Olives**,
    he sent two of his **disciples** and said to them,
    "Go into the village **opposite** you,
    and immediately on **entering** it,
    you will find a **colt** tethered on which no one has ever **sat**.
Untie it and **bring** it here.
If anyone should **say** to you,
    'Why are you **doing** this?' reply,
    'The **Master** has **need** of it
    and will send it **back** here at **once**.'"
So they **went** off
    and **found** a colt tethered at a **gate** outside on the **street**,
    and they **untied** it.
Some of the **bystanders** said to them,
    "What are you **doing**, untying the **colt**?"
They **answered** them just as Jesus had **told** them to,
    and they **permitted** them to **do** it.
So they **brought** the colt to Jesus
    and put their **cloaks** over it.
And he **sat** on it.

PROCESSION GOSPEL | **MARK**. The crowds who have been following Jesus have seen a blind man healed and are perhaps expecting additional fireworks. But Jesus is wholly focused on his entry into the city. Mark makes no mention of the prophecy of Zechariah that Christ's entry fulfills, but Jesus' careful attention to details makes the scene an intentional re-enactment of the prophecy, found in Zechariah 9:9, announcing the King who comes riding the foal of a donkey.

Mark's geographical references are significant. "Bethany at the Mount of Olives" not only recalls the home of Mary and Martha and the town where Jesus most often stayed when visiting Jerusalem, but it names the spot that was popularly associated with the coming of the Anointed One, the Mount of Olives. The mention of "Jerusalem," of course, evokes all that will unfold there in a matter of days. Calmly and confidently, Jesus instructs the disciples, making no great show of his foreknowledge of the "colt."

The disciples must have been amazed to find things as Jesus described—his prescience accurate even to the question posed by the bystanders. There is rebuke in that question, so, as narrator, deliver the disciples' reply to suggest both their timidity and your surprise that the bystanders "permitted them to do it."

Mark's narration lacks details regarding the swelling crowd and the energy that was coalescing around Jesus as cloaks start flying and his path is padded with palms. But Jesus was likely engulfed by the crowd, looking behind and before him

Narrate this scene as if watching it unfold with awe and delight.

Increase your energy from one "blessed" statement to the other and sustain the energy for the final "hosanna."

Many people spread their **cloaks** on the **road**,
  and others spread leafy **branches**
  that they had cut from the **fields**.
Those **preceding** him as well as those **following** kept **crying** out:
  "**Hosanna!**
    Blessed is he who comes in the name of the **Lord!**
    Blessed is the **kingdom** of our father **David** that is to **come!**
  Hosanna in the **highest!**"

Or:

GOSPEL AT THE PROCESSION   John 12:12–16

A reading from the holy Gospel according to John

Start slowly, stressing "great crowd" and their instant response to the news of Jesus' coming.

Stress the mention of "palm branches" and the initiative of the crowd.

The crowd's energy should grow from "hosanna" to "king of Israel."

When the great **crowd** that had come to the **feast** heard
  that **Jesus** was coming to Jerusalem,
  they took **palm** branches and went out to **meet** him,
    and cried out:
      "**Hosanna!**
        Blessed is he who comes in the name of the **Lord**,
          the **king** of **Israel**."

Once again, read slowly so these few details don't get lost.

Quote the prophecy with an exalted, formal tone.

Share this information with tolerance for their initial lack of understanding, but excitement about the later realization.

Jesus found an **ass** and **sat** upon it, as is written:
  Fear no **more**, *O daughter* **Zion**;
  see, *your king* **comes**, *seated upon an* **ass's** *colt*.
His disciples did not **understand** this at first,
  but when Jesus had been **glorified**
  they **remembered** that these things were **written** about him
  and that they had **done** this for him.

as the chant swelled around him. The Hosannas are as poignant as they are ironic when we consider that Jesus will soon ask his Father to save him from this same crowd.

JOHN. John's more succinct rendering of the triumphal entry into the holy city is told with a coda that highlights the prophecy of Zechariah that is fulfilled in the events of this day. The disciples are not sent to fetch an animal in preparation for Jesus' royal entrance. Things unfold more spontaneously. We hear nothing of the disciples except that "at first" they did not

"understand." Perhaps they were overwhelmed and lost in the shouts and exaltation of the crowd that impulsively strips branches from the trees to hail Jesus as the "king of Israel." Jesus finds his own donkey here and takes his seat upon it, the only throne he'll ever willingly mount as Israel's king.

John immediately links the event with a messianic prophecy that begins with the admonition to "fear no more." Given the fateful events that will follow in the wake of this day's reverie, it seems necessary to

remind the reader that Jesus entered willingly into the events that would soon engulf him, that just as his regal entry was part of God's plan for his glorification, so too would be the events of Gethsemane and Calvary, where this King of Israel would reign from the throne of the cross.

READING I Removed from their context in the third of Isaiah's Suffering Servant songs, the opening lines of this passage take on a special meaning for those who labor in the ministry of the word. The words constitute a prayer of

Lectionary #38

READING I   Isaiah 50:4–7

A reading from the Book of the Prophet Isaiah

> The Lord **GOD** has **given** me
>   a **well**-trained **tongue**,
> that I might **know** how to **speak** to the **weary**
>   a **word** that will **rouse** them.
> **Morning** after **morning**
>   he **opens** my ear that I may **hear**;
> and I have not **rebelled**,
>   have not turned **back**.
> I gave my **back** to those who **beat** me,
>   my **cheeks** to those who plucked my **beard**;
> my **face** I did not **shield**
>   from **buffets** and **spitting**.
>
> The Lord **GOD** is my **help**,
>   **therefore** I am not **disgraced**;
> I have set my **face** like **flint**,
>   **knowing** that I shall **not** be put to **shame**.

READING II   Philippians 2:6–11

A reading from the Letter of Saint Paul to the Philippians

> Christ **Jesus**, though he was in the form of **God**,
>   did not regard **equality** with God
>   something to be **grasped**.

Let your presence project the gratitude that fills these lines.

Be aware of who the "weary" are in your community.

Communicate a sense of pride and gratitude for the God-given strength to endure.

Don't gloss over these graphic details. Give them their due. "Plucked my beard" is a grave insult.

Here is the voice of hope in the face of adversity.

Speak with rock-like confidence and strength.

Speak the name of the Lord with reverence.

thanks for a ministry that is both privilege and responsibility. Isaiah's Servant speaks these words with gratitude for God's special call—a call that proves both sweet and bitter in the life of the Servant who willingly embraces the divine call but must endure pain and indignity in God's service.

Pride and joy tinge the declaration that God has taught the servant how to speak to the "weary" with a "word" that will "rouse" them. The weary are those weighed down by physical or emotional burdens, those afflicted by life's trials and sorrows. (Do you know who the "weary" in

your community are?) These weary are heartened with nothing more than a word. God's word has the power to heal and bless; it can rouse a listless spirit and reinvigorate a tepid heart. "Rouse" means "encourage," so stir up your listeners more with enthusiasm than increased volume.

Without boasting, the Servant speaks of how he freely endured the abuse of others. The graphic images of being beaten and spat upon anticipate the cruel treatment Jesus himself will endure. But you might also consider thinking of someone

you know who has suffered for doing the right thing (a friend who sacrificed a job rather than integrity). The pain described is intense, but it is spoken of in the past tense: he has allowed his back to be beaten, his face to be slapped, even his beard to be plucked and pulled (a grave insult in that society), but God was with me through it all, says the Servant.

The last four lines acknowledge God's gracious assistance. The Servant was strong in facing opposition because he was filled with God-given confidence that he would not "be put to shame." He stands

The word "rather" helps you put greater emphasis on what Jesus *did* ("emptied . . . humbled . . . obedient . . ."), rather than what he avoided.

Stress his humility and the reality of the pain he endured.

This is the turning point. Let your volume and rate increase.

Once again, speak the name of Jesus with dignity and reverence. The hymn is citing Isaiah 45:23.

Your greatest energy goes to the acclamation of Christ, followed by a slightly lower key delivery of the final line.

Rather, he **emptied** himself,
　taking the form of a **slave**,
　coming in **human** likeness;
　and found **human** in **appearance**,
　he **humbled** himself,
　becoming **obedient** to the point of **death**,
　even death on a **cross**.
Because of this, God greatly **exalted** him
　and **bestowed** on him the **name**
　which is above **every** name,
　that at the name of **Jesus**
　every **knee** should bend,
　of those in **heaven** and on **earth** and **under** the earth,
　and every **tongue confess** that
　Jesus **Christ** is **Lord**,
　to the **glory** of God the **Father**.

PASSION　Mark 14:1—15:47

The Passion of our Lord Jesus Christ according to Mark

The proximity of the festival adds urgency to the chief priests' scheming.

(1) The **Passover** and the Feast of Unleavened **Bread**
　were to take **place** in two days' **time**.
So the chief **priests** and the **scribes** were seeking a way
　to **arrest** him by **treachery** and put him to **death**.
They said, "**Not** during the **festival**,
　for fear that there may be a **riot** among the people."

Utilize the schemer's conspiratorial tone to deliver these lines.

The tone is quite different here; suggest Jesus' desire to enjoy the calm before the storm.

(2) When he was in **Bethany** reclining at **table**
　in the house of **Simon** the **leper**,
　a **woman** came with an alabaster jar of perfumed **oil**,
　costly genuine **spikenard**.

---

strong and solid, like flint, and with a confidence that's ready to make sparks.

READING II　The first part of the verse that begins this elegant text admonishes us to make the attitude of Christ our own. What is that attitude? The balance of the text tells us: though he was God, he did not cling to his equality with God and instead became one of us; not like us mind you, but one of us! The theology of this text is critical to our understanding of the preexistent Christ, but its hymn-like structure (Paul may be quoting an early

Christian hymn) makes it a song of praise more than a theological treatise.

Remember that the text is an entreaty to imitate Christ who humbled himself and became obedient even unto death. But in typical Christian irony, emptying leads to filling; humility to glorification. Yes, Christ accepted death—the most humiliating form of death imaginable, "death on a cross."

But that realization leads to the turning point and climax of the reading: "Because of this . . . ." Speak with a quickened tempo and joyous energy of

Christ's exaltation by God. In striking similarity with Isaiah's Servant Song of Reading I, Christ does not rebel ("he emptied himself") and offers his back for beating (he accepted "even death on a cross") and thus he is not disgraced ("God highly exalted him"). His exaltation is a great reward, greatly deserved, so speak of it with strength and conviction. Don't rush the declaration that the universe, "heaven . . . earth . . . and under the earth," the universe's three levels according to ancient belief) must join the praise. And it's not only Christ who is acclaimed

There is agitation in the voices of those who protest the waste.

She **broke** the alabaster jar and **poured** it on his **head**.
There were some who were **indignant**.
"Why has there been this **waste** of perfumed oil?
It could have been **sold** for more than three **hundred** days' **wages**
 and the **money** given to the **poor**."
They were **infuriated** with her.

Jesus jumps in to defend the woman and instruct the others. His voice is authoritative and persuasive.

Jesus said, "Let her **alone**.
Why do you make **trouble** for her?
She has done a **good** thing for me.
The **poor** you will **always** have with you,
 and whenever you **wish** you can do **good** to them,
  but you will not always have **me**.
She has done what she **could**.
She has **anticipated** anointing my **body** for **burial**.

Don't rush this familiar but significant line.

Amen, I say to you,
 wherever the **gospel** is **proclaimed** to the whole **world**,
 what she has **done** will be told in **memory** of her."

There is a sense of disbelief in relating that "one of the Twelve" did this.

(3) Then Judas **Iscariot**, one of the **Twelve**,
 went off to the chief **priests** to hand him **over** to them.
When they **heard** him they were **pleased**
 and promised to pay him **money**.
Then he looked for an **opportunity** to hand him over.

There is a shift in tone here. The mood is more upbeat and casual.

(4) On the **first** day of the Feast of Unleavened **Bread**,
 when they **sacrificed** the Passover **lamb**,
 his **disciples** said to him,
 "Where do you want us to **go**
 and **prepare** for you to eat the **Passover**?"
He sent two of his **disciples** and said to them,
 "Go into the **city** and a man will **meet** you,
 carrying a jar of **water**.

Jesus speaks with confidence of the details they will find.

Follow him.

---

here, for the glory we give to him is given through him to God our Father.

PASSION | Remembering is at the heart of Catholic liturgy: we remember Jesus and in the remembering *he* is present among us. Storytelling also employs this concept. As teller of the Passion narrative, succumb to the story's power by being the first to feel the fear and tears, the love and hate, the anger and the pathos and the guilt in all its scenes.

The Good Friday Passion will contrast mightily with this account from Mark. John gives us a regal Jesus in charge of his destiny: he reigns from the cross and surrenders his life without outcry or regret. But Mark's tale is full of shadows. Denied, abandoned, accused, rejected, and mocked are the operative words of Mark's narrative. This story describes the Messiah's painful passage before he enters his glory, and in that it closely parallels Matthew's account. Each evangelist has his unique take on the suffering Jesus: Luke presents a healing, compassionate Christ moving toward Calvary; John a sovereign lord; but Mark's Jesus is Isaiah's silent, suffering servant who receives vindication from the unlikeliest source, a Roman soldier who declares him God's Son only when he hangs dead and disgraced from the ignominy of the cross. Don't diminish the strong emotions of this sad, intense, ironic Passion. The severe sorrow of Mark's story will heighten the reversal of Christ's ultimate vindication.

Enlist the parish's best readers for the Passion proclamation. It may be divided into three parts: narrator, Jesus (spoken by the priest), and the other voices in the story. Best practice is to avoid assigning a "role"

Wherever he **enters**, say to the **master** of the house,
  'The **Teacher** says, "Where is my **guest** room
  where I may eat the **Passover** with my **disciples**?"'
Then he will show you a large **upper** room **furnished** and **ready**.
Make the **preparations** for us **there**."
The disciples then **went** off, **entered** the city,
  and **found** it just as he had **told** them;
  and they **prepared** the Passover.

(5) When it was **evening**, he came with the **Twelve**.
And as they reclined at **table** and were **eating**, Jesus said,
  "**Amen**, I say to you, **one** of you will **betray** me,
  one who is **eating** with me."
They began to be **distressed** and to **say** to him, one by **one**,
  "**Surely** it is not **I**?"
He said to them,
  "One of the **Twelve**, the one who **dips** with me
    into the **dish**.
For the Son of Man indeed **goes**, as it is **written** of him,
  but **woe** to that man by **whom** the Son of Man is **betrayed**.
It would be **better** for that man if he had never been **born**."

(6) While they were **eating**,
  he took **bread**, said the **blessing**,
  broke it, and **gave** it to them, and said,
  "**Take** it; this is my **body**."
Then he took a **cup**, gave **thanks**, and **gave** it to them,
  and they all **drank** from it.
He said to them,
  "This is my **blood** of the **covenant**,
    which will be **shed** for **many**.

This line can suggest both the disciples' pleasure at finding things as Jesus said and their desire to care for him through these preparations.

Don't rush past the references to "evening" and "the Twelve." The mood will shift immediately with the reference to the betrayer.

Contrast the panicked denials with Jesus' calm revelation of the betrayer's identity.

Calm pervades the scene. Speak these sacred words as if for the first time, not as ritual prayer but as words shared with friends.

to the assembly. The power of good proclamation is marred when the assembly must follow along in a missal, preoccupied with their part. Find a reliable resource for dividing up the lines, but use this commentary and your prayer to plumb the text, the characters, and their distinct motivations.

(1) **The Conspiracy.** Mention of the upcoming feasts is significant, for it provides incentive for the leaders to act now. These priests and scribes have witnessed Jesus' immense popularity; their devious plotting contrasts sharply with the crowd's affection. Use the fricative sound of words like "priests," "scribes" and "festival" to suggest the sinister intentions of these leaders. Their calculated caution only intensifies the feeling of malice.

(2) **The Anointing at Bethany.** Even this domestic scene is marred by controversy. Sensing the storm that will soon break upon him, Jesus seeks the company of friends and savors the attention and tender ministry given him by the "woman." Your narration of the anointing should be as soothing as the perfume poured upon his head. The "indignant" comments of the onlookers could be whispered, their tone

providing a violent contrast to the comfort of the ointment. The words "indignant" and "waste" suggest motives beyond concern for the poor. Ministry to the poor is a constant responsibility for the disciples, but this is their *last* opportunity to minister to Jesus. The woman seems to know this. In Jesus' voice we may hear gratitude for the kindness done and for the vision and understanding that allow her, and not his disciples, to intuit the path of pain he's about to walk.

(3) **The Betrayer.** "One of the Twelve" (a phrase often paired with Judas' name)

Keep the mood upbeat since Jesus is focused on the coming of the Kingdom.

Don't let their singing go unnoticed.

Jesus' tone is persuasive, but not angry.

Peter really believes he won't fail Jesus and says so adamantly.

Jesus is not trying to convince Peter, but to prepare him for what will surely happen.

Peter is a little hurt, but full of love in these exclamations.

Jesus' grief is contained and muted.

Now Jesus' terror begins to show.

Amen, I **say** to you,
  I shall not **drink** again the fruit of the **vine**
  until the day when I drink it **new** in the kingdom of **God**."

(7) **Then**, after singing a **hymn**,
  they went out to the Mount of **Olives**.

Then Jesus said to them,
  "**All** of you will have your **faith** shaken, for it is **written**:
    I will **strike** the shepherd,
    and the **sheep** will be **dispersed**.
But after I have been **raised** up,
  I shall go **before** you to **Galilee**."
Peter said to him,
  "Even though **all** should have their faith **shaken**,
  mine will not be."
Then Jesus said to him,
  "**Amen**, I say to you,
  this very **night** before the cock crows **twice**
  you will **deny** me **three times**."
But he **vehemently** replied,
  "Even though I should have to **die** with you,
  I will not **deny** you."
And they **all** spoke **similarly**.

(8) Then they came to a place named **Gethsemane**,
  and he **said** to his disciples,
  "**Sit** here while I **pray**."
He **took** with him **Peter**, **James**, and **John**,
  and began to be **troubled** and **distressed**.
Then he **said** to them, "My **soul** is **sorrowful** even to **death**.
Remain here and keep **watch**."

expresses the shame and shock of Jesus' betrayer coming from the ranks of his most inmost circle. We'll never know his true motive, and Mark supplies no hint, but your voice should suggest some turmoil and ambivalence in Judas. The priests promise "money," spiking his determination to find an "opportunity" to betray his master.

(4) Passover Preparations. Unaware of events that soon will engulf them, the disciples inquire calmly about preparations. As in the Procession Gospel, Jesus reveals prescient knowledge regarding details of the celebration. His tone is not emotional but confident; he is "the Teacher" he calls himself instructing his pupils. "The disciples then went off" is spoken at a faster pace, as if by the disciples who are amazed and delighted to find things "just as he told them."

(5) The Betrayal. Waiting till dark, Jesus and friends quietly enter the city. During the intimate meal, Jesus speaks of his betrayer. The disciples panic, and each denies guilt. Without histrionics or self-pity Jesus insists that one is guilty and reveals the action that will identify him. Jesus accepts his fate but laments that it will be one of his own who sets the scene for scripture's fulfillment, speaking a judgment like no other in the Gospel.

(6) The Lord's Supper. Wiping the bitter taste of betrayal from his lips, Jesus gives himself to his friends in a way he never has before: "Take . . . this is my body . . . my blood." He speaks with love, both for his friends and for all who will be drawn to this meal. The cup from which Jesus will "not drink again" brims with fear and sorrow, but he points to a time when drinking and fellowship will be renewed in "the kingdom of God."

He **advanced** a little and **fell** to the ground and **prayed**
that if it were **possible** the hour might **pass** by him;
he said, "**Abba**, **Father**, **all** things are possible to you.
Take this cup **away** from me,
but not what **I** will but what **you** will."
When he **returned** he found them **asleep**.
He said to **Peter**, "**Simon**, are you **asleep**?
Could you not keep **watch** for one **hour**?
Watch and **pray** that you may not undergo the **test**.
The **spirit** is **willing** but the **flesh** is **weak**."
Withdrawing **again**, he **prayed**, saying the **same thing**.
Then he **returned** once more and found them **asleep**,
for they could not keep their **eyes** open
and did not know what to **answer** him.
He returned a **third** time and said to them,
"Are you **still** sleeping and taking your **rest**?
It is **enough**. The hour has **come**.
Behold, the Son of **Man** is to be handed **over** to **sinners**.
Get **up**, let us **go**.
See, my **betrayer** is at **hand**."

(9) **Then**, while he was still **speaking**,
Judas, one of the **Twelve**, **arrived**,
accompanied by a **crowd** with **swords** and **clubs**
who had come from the chief **priests**,
the **scribes**, and the **elders**.
His **betrayer** had arranged a **signal** with them, saying,
"The man I shall **kiss** is the one;
arrest him and lead him away **securely**."
He came and **immediately** went over to him and said,
"**Rabbi**." And he **kissed** him.
At this they laid **hands** on him and **arrested** him.

Margin notes (left column):

Don't make this sound like play-acting. Jesus truly wishes to avoid this fate.

Jesus is clearly disappointed in the three disciples. He warns them, but without anger.

Mark makes a weak excuse for the exhausted disciples.

Jesus is now resigned and ready.

Contrast "one of the Twelve" with "swords and clubs."

Try subtly suggesting a conspiratorial whisper.

Take a slight pause before and after "Rabbi."

---

(7) **Peter's Denial Foretold.** The meal ends in song, but Jesus' joy is muted by his realization that these friends will soon scatter. In an earlier age, David fled to the Mount of Olives and wept over his betrayal by a trusted advisor. Now, in this same place, Jesus prophesies his best friends' cowardice. His voice must convince them that they, in fact, will do what they think inconceivable, but no judgment infects his tone. And he quickly offers hope of resurrection and reunion. Ever impetuous, Peter "vehemently" and naively asserts unwavering fidelity; the others join the chorus.

(8) **Gethsemane.** The garden provides a momentary layover on the way to Calvary. Jesus instructs the disciples to "sit down," while he invites his most trusted friends to enter the inner chambers of his now "troubled and distressed" soul. He doesn't hesitate to confess that he is "sorrowful even to death" and asks these confidants to support him with their presence and watchfulness. When alone, the full weight of his grief thrusts him to the ground. There's no posturing in Jesus' request to avoid his fate, but the word "Abba" signals his willingness to accept it, for Jesus' uniquely intimate relationship with the Father engenders a trust that says "not what I will, but what you will." Jesus returns to find the disciples sleeping. His disappointment showing, Jesus challenges Peter's earlier bravado: You promised fidelity, but you could not even stay awake with me for an hour? Jesus will pray twice more before recovering his resolve, so he needs and asks the disciples' prayer and support. Aware that each person will eventually face "the test," he also urges them to strengthen their weak nature against that time of trial. Mark says, feebly: "they could

Suggest the fury of the "bystander."	One of the **bystanders** drew his **sword**, struck the high priest's **servant**, and cut off his **ear**. Jesus said to them in **reply**,

Jesus speaks with confidence and shames them for their cowardice.	"Have you come out as against a **robber**,
	    with **swords** and **clubs**, to **seize** me?
	Day after **day** I was with you **teaching** in the **temple** area,
	    yet you did not **arrest** me;
	    but that the Scriptures may be **fulfilled**."
	And they all **left** him and **fled**.

This scene, which is unique to Mark's Gospel account, should not be rushed. Another disciple abandons Jesus.	Now a young **man** followed him
	    wearing nothing but a linen **cloth** about his body.
	They **seized** him,
	    but he left the cloth **behind** and ran off **naked**.

Your tone should signal the approaching danger.	(10) They led **Jesus** away to the high **priest**,
	    and all the **chief** priests and the **elders** and the **scribes**
	        came **together**.

The sound of your voice can suggest Peter's hesitance and fear.
Sanhedrin = san-HEE-druhn
	Peter followed him at a **distance** into the high priest's **courtyard**
	    and was seated with the **guards**, **warming** himself at the **fire**.
	The chief **priests** and the entire **Sanhedrin**
	    kept trying to obtain **testimony** against Jesus
	    in order to put him to **death**, but they found **none**.

As narrator, enjoy their frustration and failure to get the witnesses to agree.	Many gave **false** witness against him,
	    but their **testimony** did not **agree**.
	Some took the **stand** and testified **falsely** against him,
	    alleging, "We **heard** him say,

The witnesses quote Jesus in slow cadences.	'I will **destroy** this temple made with **hands**
	    and within **three days** I will build **another**
	    not made with hands.'"
	Even **so** their testimony did not **agree**.

The high priest takes charge, attempts to provoke Jesus, and is amazed by his silence.	(11) The **high** priest **rose** before the assembly and **questioned** Jesus, saying, "Have you no **answer**? What are these men **testifying** against you?"

not keep their eyes open" to explain the disciples' continued stupor, but surprised and ashamed and not knowing what to say, they wisely remain speechless. Steeled by his third time at prayer, Jesus returns to find the disciples "still sleeping." This third failure to "keep watch" with Jesus anticipates Peter's triple denial. But now Jesus is ready to face his "hour," even alone if need be. Without chiding, he says that the "Son of Man" is about to be surrendered into the clutches of sinners. Freed of fear, Jesus calls the disciples and announces calmly, "My betrayer is at hand."

(9) The Betrayal and Arrest. In one sentence we are told that Judas is one of the intimate Twelve and that he arrives with an angry crowd armed with "swords and clubs." Highlight that stark contrast. Judas' whispered instructions to the "chief priests" contrast with his seemingly earnest greeting to Jesus. Pause slightly before speaking "Rabbi" to suggest the effort with which Judas forced the insincere word from his mouth. Following another pause, he envelops Jesus in a traitor's embrace which he punctuates with a kiss.

The pace quickens as Jesus is arrested and a "bystander" responds with swordplay. In contrast to Luke's Gospel account, here Jesus ignores the violence as he ignored Judas' kiss. Instead, he addresses the mob, indicting them for the cowardice that made them seek him under the cover of darkness rather than in the light of day. He accepts the fate foretold by scripture and then watches his friends take flight. The enigmatic young man, found only in Mark, who sheds his linen cloth and runs off naked, represents Christ's *total* abandonment: early on, disciples left every-

Jesus is calm, confident, and regal in his response.

But he was **silent** and answered **nothing**.
Again the high priest asked him and **said** to him,
  "Are you the **Christ**, the son of the **Blessed** One?"
Then Jesus answered, "I **am**;
    and 'you will **see** the Son of Man
      seated at the **right** hand of the **Power**
      and **coming** with the **clouds** of **heaven**.'"

The high priest jumps at the opportunity to make a show of his outrage.

At **that** the high priest **tore** his garments and said,
  "What further **need** have we of **witnesses**?
You have **heard** the blasphemy.
What do you **think**?"
They all **condemned** him as deserving to **die**.
Some began to **spit** on him.

They are all convinced Jesus is a liar and blasphemer.

They **blindfolded** him and **struck** him and **said** to him,
    "**Prophesy!**"
And the **guards** greeted him with **blows**.

There is tension throughout this scene.

(12) While **Peter** was below in the **courtyard**,
  one of the high priest's **maids** came along.
Seeing Peter **warming** himself,
  she looked **intently** at him and said,
  "You **too** were with the **Nazarene**, **Jesus**."

Her first inquiry is sparked by simple curiosity.

But he **denied** it saying,
  "I neither **know** nor **understand** what you are **talking** about."
So he went out into the **outer** court.
Then the **cock** crowed.

Don't rush this reference to the crowing cock.

The maid **saw** him and began again to say to the **bystanders**,
  "**This** man is **one** of them."
Once **again** he **denied** it.
A little **later** the **bystanders** said to Peter once more,
  "**Surely** you are **one** of them; for you **too** are a **Galilean**."

Perhaps insulted, the maid is determined to identify Peter. The bystanders are adamant in their agreement with her. Peter is in a rage, cursing.

He began to **curse** and to **swear**,
  "I do not **know** this man about whom you are talking."

thing to follow Jesus, now they leave everything to desert him.

(10) Jesus before the Sanhedrin. The mood of the priests dominates this section. They've longed for this opportunity to have it out with Jesus, whom they're convinced is a fraud. The tone of the opening sentence should suggest the malice of these leaders. Knowledge of their sinister intentions keeps Peter at a distance from the high priest's house, though he does brave the company of the "guard" and warms himself at the fire. The chief priests and "the *entire* Sanhedrin" gather to convict

Jesus, their frustration and anger building as they fail to gather evidence to condemn. The narrator enjoys commenting on how even the perjured testimony "did not agree." But remember that while the malice is real, it emanates less from evil hearts than from blinded hearts—hearts convinced that Jesus is a charlatan.

(11) The Verdict. Through the narration *and* dialogue, assume the character of the high priest who rises to take charge, thinking he can provoke a response from the silent Jesus. But Jesus won't be forced. His silence provokes more abuse

from the priest. Jesus' reply will seal his fate; so suggest that he *decided* to answer, for his own reasons, not because the priest provoked him. He speaks with dignity, authority, and full awareness. Jesus has exceeded the leaders' expectations. They need not continue making the case: such blatant blasphemy calls for death. Use the verbs "condemned," "spit," "blindfolded," "struck," "prophesy" to suggest the fury with which they attacked this blasphemer who finally revealed himself.

(12) Peter's Denial. Peter's blind fear and his instincts of self-preservation dom-

Deliver these lines as a haunting memory. Underplay the emotions: as if remembering tears, not shedding them.

The story continues to unfold. Tell it as the sympathetic narrator, not as one of the Sanhedrin.

At first, Pilate is more annoyed than curious, but Jesus' calm demeanor captures Pilate's attention.

Jesus' silence is not petulance, but confidence that amazes Pilate.

Your tone betrays the hope that things might turn out differently this time.

Pilate asks a leading question.

And **immediately** a cock **crowed** a **second** time.
Then Peter **remembered** the word that Jesus had **said** to him,
   "Before the **cock** crows **twice** you will deny me **three** times."
He broke **down** and **wept**.

(13) As soon as **morning** came,
   the chief **priests** with the **elders** and the **scribes**,
   that is, the whole **Sanhedrin**, held a **council**.
They **bound** Jesus, led him **away**, and handed him over to **Pilate**.
(14) Pilate **questioned** him,
   "Are you the **king** of the **Jews**?"
He said to him in reply, "**You** say so."
The chief priests **accused** him of **many** things.
Again Pilate questioned him,
   "Have you no **answer**?
See how many things they **accuse** you of."
Jesus gave him no further **answer**, so that Pilate was **amazed**.

Now on the occasion of the **feast** he used to **release** to them
   one **prisoner** whom they **requested**.
A man called **Barabbas** was then in prison
   along with the **rebels** who had committed **murder**
      in a **rebellion**.
The crowd came **forward** and began to **ask** him
   to **do** for them as he was **accustomed**.
Pilate **answered**,
   "Do you want me to release to you the **king** of the **Jews**?"
For he **knew** that it was out of **envy**
   that the chief **priests** had handed him over.
But the chief priests **stirred** up the crowd
   to have him release **Barabbas** for them **instead**.

inate this section. In the courtyard, Peter, too, is put on trial and ends up his own judge and jury. The persistent servant girl clings to him like flypaper, adding to his panic. At first she's simply curious, but she quickly becomes insistent as she and the bystanders penetrate his subterfuge, refusing to be taken for fools. Peter initially *feigns* ignorance and removes himself from the scene. But the girl insists he's one of Jesus' men, prompting a quick denial. When the other bystanders weigh

in, using his background to indict him, Peter responds with panicked cursing and swears no knowledge of Jesus. But the cockcrow catches Peter off guard; it brings him to his senses as Jesus' prophecy echoes in his heart. Imagine him, years later, relating the story in a homily to newly minted Christians, recalling for them the flow of guilt and shame and tears.

(13 and 14a) Jesus before the Sanhedrin and Pilate. Morning brings Jesus before the assembled Sanhedrin who make short shrift of him, knowing they need a higher, civil authority to condemn him to death. Your

tone as narrator resembles that of a court reporter announcing the decision reached by "the *whole* Sanhedrin." In his breathless account, Mark provides no preliminaries, so Pilate's entrance is abrupt. He may have been roused from his bed to deal with this troublesome Jew. His first question ("Are you the king of the Jews?") parrots the accusation leveled against him by the priests and he fully understands the sinister motives that underlie the accusation. Jesus' terse reply surprises the governor;

Pilate is seeking a way out for Jesus.

Pilate **again** said to them in reply,
"Then what do you want me to **do**
with the man you call the **king** of the **Jews**?"
They **shouted** again, "**Crucify** him."

Pilate appears pitiful and indecisive.

Pilate said to them, "**Why**? What **evil** has he done?"
They only shouted the **louder**, "**Crucify** him."

He complies angrily, as if saying: "All right, have it your way!"

So **Pilate**, wishing to **satisfy** the crowd,
released **Barabbas** to them and, after he had Jesus **scourged**,
handed him **over** to be **crucified**.

Without any melodrama, make Christ's pain your own as you narrate the ensuing scenes.

(15) The **soldiers** led him **away** inside the **palace**,
that is, the **praetorium**, and **assembled** the whole **cohort**.
They **clothed** him in **purple** and,
weaving a crown of **thorns**, **placed** it on him.
They began to **salute** him with, "**Hail**, King of the **Jews**!"
and kept **striking** his head with a **reed** and **spitting** upon him.
They **knelt** before him in **homage**.
And when they had **mocked** him,

Your empathy with the mocked Jesus should be evident as you speak these lines.

they **stripped** him of the purple cloak,
dressed him in his **own** clothes,
and led him **out** to crucify him.

Cyrenian = si-REE-nee-un

Rufus = ROO-fuhs

(16) They pressed into **service** a **passer-by**, **Simon**,
a **Cyrenian**, who was coming in from the **country**,
the father of **Alexander** and **Rufus**,
to **carry** his **cross**.

Golgotha = GAWL-guh-thuh

They **brought** him to the place of **Golgotha**
—which is translated **Place** of the **Skull**—.
They gave him **wine** drugged with **myrrh**,
but he did not **take** it.

Contrast "crucified him" with "casting lots."

Then they **crucified** him and divided his **garments**
by casting **lots** for them to see what each should **take**.
It was **nine** o'clock in the **morning** when they **crucified** him.

---

his second inquiry is more insistent. Now, he's interested in this enigmatic figure.

(14b) The Sentence of Death. As narrator, help us hope that here the tide will turn; that Jesus might be the "prisoner whom they requested." Pilate himself seems to hope that the custom he established will provide Jesus' release. And even though he recognizes the "envy" that will keep the priests from choosing Jesus, he makes the offer like a desperate magician trying to force a card on a clever spectator. The priests quickly deflect Pilate's ploy by inciting the crowd to request

Barabbas instead. In Mark, Pilate is less proactive in his efforts to save Jesus than in other gospels. His question, "What evil has he done?" is a sincere (and poignant) attempt to sway the leaders, but he quickly succumbs to pressure and surrenders Jesus. There are no clear lines drawn here between supportive Romans and hostile Jewish crowd: Mark's forsaken Jesus receives support from no one.

(15) Mockery by the Soldiers. The soldiers don't hold back in their revilement of Jesus, so you mustn't hold back in your description of it. Rough-handled and

mocked, Jesus becomes the morning's entertainment for the insensitive group of soldiers who focus their scornful attention on him. Let your tone convey the degradation Jesus endures, rather than anger at the perpetrators. The soldiers eagerly take out on Jesus whatever pent-up hostility they might have preferred to direct at the recalcitrant Jewish population. Words like "salute," "striking," "spitting," "mocked" and "stripped" underscore with onomatopoeic sound the soldiers' violent scorn.

(16) The Way of the Cross. Speak of Simon as of someone known and respected.

Speak the title with the mocking tones of the soldiers.

Crucifixion with "two revolutionaries" is yet another insult.

The **inscription** of the **charge** against him read,
  "The **King** of the **Jews**."
With him they crucified two **revolutionaries**,
  one on his **right** and one on his **left**.
Those passing by **reviled** him,
  shaking their **heads** and **saying**,
  "**Aha**! You who would **destroy** the **temple**
  and **rebuild** it in three **days**,
  save yourself by coming **down** from the cross."

Both the bystanders and the priests feel vindicated thinking that Jesus is an obvious fraud.

Likewise the chief **priests**, with the **scribes**,
  mocked him among themselves and said,
  "He saved **others**; he cannot save **himself**.
Let the **Christ**, the King of **Israel**,
  come **down** now from the cross
  that we may **see** and **believe**."

Share this final detail with sadness.

Those who were **crucified** with him **also** kept **abusing** him.

(17) At **noon darkness** came over the whole **land**
  until **three** in the afternoon.
And at three o'clock Jesus **cried** out in a loud **voice**,
  "*Eloi, Eloi, lema sabachthani?*"
  which is **translated**,
  "My **God**, my **God**, **why** have you **forsaken** me?"

Speak the Aramaic with emotion, but deliver the English translation in hushed, neutral tones.

Some of the bystanders who **heard** it said,
  "**Look**, he is calling **Elijah**."

The bystanders are still derisive.

One of them **ran**, soaked a **sponge** with **wine**, put it on a **reed**
  and **gave** it to him to **drink** saying,
  "**Wait**, let us **see** if Elijah comes to take him **down**."
Jesus gave a loud **cry** and breathed his **last**.

Pause before this line, then announce Jesus' death with great reverence.

[Here all kneel and pause for a short time.]

The **veil** of the **sanctuary** was torn in **two** from top to **bottom**.

In that light, Simon's "pressed" service seems more privilege than burden. Refusing to dull his pain with drugged wine, Jesus is nailed to the cross. In one brief sentence Mark tells us of Jesus' Crucifixion and of the callous soldiers, who gamble for his garments. The brevity and sparse details of Mark's account magnify the sadness and serve Mark's purpose of depicting Jesus' total abandonment.

Mark saves his details for the three groups of detractors who taunt Jesus: the bystanders, the scribes and priests, and the insurgents who hang beside Jesus.

Were it not so awful, one might imagine the detractors as schoolyard bullies suddenly emboldened by their victim's helplessness. But the taunts go beyond insult; there's vindication that Christ's scandalous circumstance only confirms. The cross answers their derisive question: Could this really be the great Messiah?! In Mark, there is no "good thief"; those crucified with him join in the abuse.

(17) The Death of Jesus. Narrate the death from the perspective of one of the appalled women disciples who looks on "from a distance." An unnatural "darkness" brings gloom, hushed tones, and nervousness not known in daylight. Clearly it matches the darkness of this moment when creatures put to death God's Son. Don't soften Jesus' cry of abandonment. The Aramaic line should ring with pathos and loud intensity, but the English translation can be whispered and un-nuanced. The onlookers break the mood with hushed jeers, glad their entertainment isn't over. Even a presumed act of kindness ("soaked a sponge with wine") is just an excuse for a final taunt ("Wait, let us see if Elijah comes"). This mockery, spoken by one who

Suggest the deeper significance of the torn veil: Through Christ all people attain greater access to God.

centurion = sen-TOOR-ee-uhn

The centurion's declaration is sincere but understated.

Speak of these women with familiarity and love.

When the **centurion** who stood **facing** him
   saw how he breathed his **last** he said,
   "**Truly** this **man** was the Son of **God!**"
There were also **women** looking on from a **distance**.
Among them were Mary **Magdalene**,
   Mary the mother of the younger **James** and of **Joses**,
     and **Salome**.
These women had **followed** him when he was in **Galilee**
   and **ministered** to him.
There were also many **other** women
   who had come **up** with him to **Jerusalem**.

Joseph, too, deserves a tone of deference and admiration.

(18) When it was already **evening**,
   since it was the day of **preparation**,
   the day before the **sabbath**, **Joseph** of **Arimathea**,
   a **distinguished** member of the **council**,
   who was **himself** awaiting the **kingdom** of **God**,
   came and **courageously** went to **Pilate**

Admire Joseph's courage as you proclaim.

   and **asked** for the body of **Jesus**.

Only Mark mentions Pilate's surprise.

Pilate was **amazed** that he was already **dead**.
He summoned the **centurion**
   and **asked** him if Jesus had already **died**.

Stress the confirmation of Jesus' death.

And when he **learned** of it from the **centurion**,
   he **gave** the body to Joseph.
Having bought a linen **cloth**, he took him **down**,
   wrapped him in the linen cloth,
   and laid him in a **tomb** that had been **hewn** out of the **rock**.

Let the sound of your words caress the Lord.

Then he rolled a **stone** against the **entrance** to the tomb.
Mary **Magdalene** and Mary the mother of **Joses**

Your tone should hint at hope and Resurrection.

   watched where he was **laid**.

[Shorter: Mark 15:1–39]

---

mistakes "Eloi" for the prophet's name, is the last human voice Jesus will hear.

Allow the "loud cry" to echo within you before you announce Jesus' death. Mark's pacing suddenly quickens. Now you narrate events that vindicate the claims Jesus made about himself: the temple curtain is mysteriously and symbolically torn, a pagan soldier proclaims his faith in Jesus, and faithful disciples are found watching from a distance. The torn veil removes the barrier between God and creatures, signifying greater human access to God while the Gentile centuri-

on's confession hints at the universality of the Gospel. The sorrow of Jesus' death yields to hope as you list these pious women who kept watch and may have been the earliest transmitters of this story.

(18) The Burial. With remarkable courage Joseph comes to tend to the burial and braves the presence of Pilate to request the body of Jesus. Speak with affection, knowing how precious is the privilege Joseph is given in being able to minister to the Lord. Pilate is surprised, or maybe disappointed, that Jesus is so soon dead; his effort to verify will only make more strik-

ing the reversal of the third day and removes any doubt that Jesus' death might have been feigned.

The final moments with a deceased loved one are the hardest. All in us that clings to life resists the closing of the casket or the rolling of the stone. Read slowly and with great care, caressing Jesus with your words as you speak of "linen," "tomb" and "entrance." The two Marys stood attentively and "watched," silent witnesses who, three days hence would return to find an empty tomb, and Resurrection would surprise and overwhelm the world.

HOLY THURSDAY: MASS OF THE LORD'S SUPPER

Lectionary #39

READING I   Exodus 12:1–8, 11–14

A reading from the Book of Exodus

The LORD said to **Moses** and **Aaron** in the land of **Egypt**,
  "This **month** shall stand at the **head** of your **calendar**;
  you shall reckon it the **first** month of the year.
Tell the whole **community** of Israel:
  On the **tenth** of this month every one of your **families**
  must procure for itself a **lamb**, one **apiece** for each **household**.
If a family is too **small** for a whole lamb,
  it shall **join** the **nearest** household in procuring one
  and shall **share** in the lamb
  in **proportion** to the number of **persons** who **partake** of it.
The lamb must be a year-old **male** and without **blemish**.
You may take it from either the **sheep** or the **goats**.
You shall keep it until the **fourteenth** day of this month,
  and **then**, with the whole assembly of Israel **present**,
  it shall be **slaughtered** during the evening **twilight**.
They shall take some of its **blood**
  and **apply** it to the two **doorposts** and the **lintel**
  of every **house** in which they **partake** of the lamb.
That same **night** they shall **eat** its roasted flesh
  with unleavened **bread** and bitter **herbs**.

"This is **how** you are to eat it:
  with your loins **girt**, **sandals** on your **feet** and your **staff**
    in **hand**,
  you shall **eat** like those who are in **flight**.

Israel is still in captivity when they receive these instructions. Let your tone convey the importance of this solemnity, for this night is like no other night; this meal like no other meal.

It is God who speaks here with both authority and compassion.

God's commands don't burden the needy; instead they make community.

Keep your pacing brisk; it's not the specifics that matter here, but the sense of God's providence and the people's obedience.

Slow your pacing for these important details that anticipate the blood of the messianic lamb.

The sense of urgency and preparedness needs to be stressed. It describes the attitude with which we are to await the return of the Messiah.

READING I   Tonight begins the Holy Triduum, the Three Days, when we celebrate the great solemnity of our salvation. It may seem odd, on this night, to recall the minute details of preparations for an ancient meal; odd, until we realize that meal was eaten on the eve of Israel's deliverance from slavery, and that it is the prototype of the ritual meal Jesus shares with his friends on this eve of humanity's salvation. During these three days, Jesus becomes the paschal lamb prophetically presented here, whose blood releases humankind from the bonds of sin.

The details enumerated here ensure the keeping of this ritual meal down through many generations—a point made in the last sentence. These instructions could be delivered literally—as directives about how to purchase, slaughter, and eat a sacrificial animal—or they can be proclaimed in a way that conveys something deeper: this is more than remembrance of a past historical event. By *recalling* this incident we *experience* it here in the present, and the saving grace it made available then is made present and available now.

That is the theology and purpose of all liturgical proclamation: through remembering, God's past saving action is made present in our own day.

So speak of month, day, lamb, and those who share it with the awareness that your speaking makes that moment present in the assembly. All are to share the meal. Households too small for an entire lamb are to combine with larger households so this feast is not a burden, but an occasion for community life and sharing.

Don't shy from these hard words. The tone is one of divine authority and might, not vengeance.

Slow down for these references to "blood" and God's response to seeing it. Speak carefully and with a tone of compassion.

This is a direct command. First, pause and take a breath as you survey the assembly. Then give the divine directive.

It is the **Passover** of the LORD.
For on this **same** night I will go through **Egypt**,
    striking down every **firstborn** of the land, both **man** and **beast**,
    and executing **judgment** on all the **gods** of Egypt—**I**, the LORD!
But the **blood** will mark the **houses** where **you** are.
Seeing the blood, I will pass **over** you;
    thus, when I **strike** the land of **Egypt**,
    no destructive **blow** will come upon **you**.

"This day shall be a **memorial feast** for you,
    which all your **generations** shall celebrate
    with **pilgrimage** to the LORD, as a **perpetual** institution."

Corinthians = kohr-IN-thee-uhnz
Because Paul jumps right in, you'll need to start slowly and read the opening sentence with extra care, especially the reference to Christ's betrayal.
Pause after "handed on to you"; an implied "namely" precedes what follows.

Only Paul and Luke's Gospel record the command "do this . . . ." It expresses strength and love, but no sentimentality.
The words that convey Jesus' actions are important to stress: he "took," gave "thanks," and "broke" the bread.
The final sentence is Paul's great insight. Pause before it, make eye contact, and speak directly to the assembly.

READING II 1 Corinthians 11:23–26

A reading from the first Letter of Saint Paul to the Corinthians

Brothers and sisters:
I **received** from the Lord what I also handed on to **you**,
    that the Lord **Jesus**, on the night he was handed **over**,
    took **bread**, and, after he had given **thanks**,
    broke it and said, "This is my **body** that is for **you**.
Do this in **remembrance** of me."
In the same way also the **cup**, after supper, saying,
    "This **cup** is the new **covenant** in my **blood**.
Do this, as often as you **drink** it, in **remembrance** of me."
For as often as you **eat** this bread and **drink** the cup,
    you proclaim the **death** of the **Lord** until he **comes**.

Express boldly the pungent images of slaughtered lambs and door posts smeared with blood, for they deepen the connection between this meal and Christ, the eternal Lamb. Significantly, the meal is to be eaten "like those who are in flight," that is, with a sense of expectation, the same kind of expectation with which Israel would await the Messiah and with which we await the return of Christ. Israel is in the hands of an awesome and terrifying God who will strike down "every firstborn" and execute judgment. Yet God also protects: "I will pass over you . . . no destructive blow

will come upon you" should be spoken like consoling words uttered in the midst of a terrible storm. Blood is the sign of life; but through the shedding of blood, death will be averted both once and forever.

READING II Tonight's Gospel narrates Jesus' washing of the feet of the apostles, not the institution of the sacred meal that has become the Mass. That narration falls to you as you proclaim these words of Paul that constitute one of the oldest sections of the entire New Testament. Paul's text is brief and

unadorned, relating only the sacred words and actions of Jesus as he sat at table with his friends for the last time. But this is not a nostalgic or melancholy text meant to evoke lugubrious feelings about Jesus' last words or his last moments before death. No, the mood is one of reverence, gratitude, and conviction.

Paul's context—the meal—which occurred "on the night he was handed over" is important, though not because it sets the emotional tone, but because it highlights the depths of God's love and

Set the scene by stressing both Jesus' awareness and the lateness of the "hour."

There is striking juxtaposition between the stress on Jesus' love for "his own" and the mention of Judas' betrayal.

Iscariot = ih-SKAYR-ee-uht

Stress Jesus' fully conscious intentionality.

You might narrate from the perspective of the surprised disciples or with the loving intent in Jesus' heart; either way, pay attention to the details and use the verbs.

Recall that in Luke (5:8) Peter once told Jesus, "Depart from me, Lord, for I am a sinful man." He seems to be speaking out of that same sensibility here. Peter's protests are as sincere as his later compliance.

Jesus is not rebuking him, but teaching.

GOSPEL   John 13:1–15

A reading from the holy Gospel according to John

Before the feast of **Passover**,
    Jesus **knew** that his hour had **come**
    to pass from **this** world to the **Father**.
He loved his **own** in the world and he **loved** them to the **end**.
The **devil** had already induced **Judas**, son of Simon the **Iscariot**,
        to hand him **over**.
So, during **supper**,
    fully **aware** that the Father had put **everything** into his power
    and that he had **come** from God and was **returning** to God,
    he **rose** from supper and took **off** his outer garments.
He took a **towel** and **tied** it around his waist.
Then he poured **water** into a basin
    and began to **wash** the disciples' **feet**
    and **dry** them with the **towel** around his **waist**.
He came to Simon **Peter**, who said to him,
    "**Master**, are you going to **wash** my **feet**?"
Jesus **answered** and said to him,
    "What I am **doing**, you do not **understand now**,
    but you **will** understand **later**."
Peter **said** to him, "You will **never** wash my feet."
Jesus answered him,
    "Unless I **wash** you, you will have no **inheritance** with me."

Jesus' generous self-giving. At the very time he was being betrayed by one of his own, Jesus was giving himself to us in a way that would last for all time. The shadow of the cross isn't absent from this meal and Paul concludes with a clear reminder that what we commemorate is both meal and *sacrifice*. The truth of Christianity is once again ironic, for it is Christ's death that gives us life.

Don't try to sound like Jesus as you speak his words. You are evoking Paul, who is quoting Jesus in order to persuade the Corinthians that what he taught them came

directly from the Lord himself, and that sharing in this sacred meal makes visible and present Jesus' death and Resurrection. "Do this in remembrance of me" is only quoted here and in Luke's Gospel. By hearing it out of order, in the Liturgy of the Word, it may touch us in a new way today. The last sentence unites past and future in the present act of worship: the meal we share is wayfarer's food that sustains us until that day when Christ returns in all his glory.

GOSPEL   In John's Passion narrative, Jesus is in charge of his destiny and walks deliberately toward the fate that awaits him on Calvary. We see elements of that intentionality here as Jesus, fully aware of what lies ahead, sets about purposefully to wash the apostles' feet. He knows that his "hour" has come, that Judas has fallen into the grip of the "devil," and yet he overflows with love for his disciples and is impelled to teach them a final lesson. With towel and basin, he undertakes a task not even a slave could be compelled to do. John's details are important. Like the

Peter's surrender to Jesus is total and unreserved.

Let Jesus' tone convey his love for Peter. There is a baptismal allusion here that suggests one who has received the cleansing of Baptism, like one returning from a bath, is clean and therefore doesn't need another bath, only the washing of feet (cleansing of the grime of daily sin).

This is a new "beat" in the narrative. Don't rush the details. Jesus makes sure his disciples have learned the lesson. Do the same with your assembly.

The pronouns are the key to the meaning of this sentence.

They will need to follow him not only in service to one another, but in laying down their lives.

Simon Peter said to him,
   "**Master**, then not only my **feet**, but my **hands** and **head**
      as **well**."
Jesus said to him,
   "Whoever has **bathed** has no **need**
      except to have his **feet** washed,
   for he is **clean** all **over**;
   so **you** are clean, but not **all**."
For he **knew** who would **betray** him;
   for this **reason**, he said, "Not **all** of you are clean."

So when he had **washed** their feet
   and put his **garments** back on and reclined at **table** again,
   he **said** to them, "Do you **realize** what I have **done** for you?
You call me 'teacher' and 'master,' and **rightly** so, for indeed I **am**.
If **I**, therefore, the **master** and **teacher**, have washed **your** feet,
   you ought to wash one **another's** feet.
I have given you a **model** to follow,
   so that as **I** have done for **you**, you should **also** do."

supper narratives that tell us Jesus took, blessed, broke and gave the bread, here we learn that he "tied," "poured," "wash[ed]" and "dr[ied]." Because here these actions of Jesus replace the institution narrative, you must give them the weight and significance they require, for they point to the very nature of Christian discipleship. However, when Jesus later tells the apostles he has "given [them] a model to follow," he's suggesting more than the humble service he just demonstrated.
   The humiliating nature of washing another's dirty feet points to the even more

humiliating death Jesus is about to willingly undergo. He has demonstrated for his closest friends not just the need to care for one another through humble service, but the need to lay down their lives for one another in the same way he will when he embraces the shame of the cross. Peter seems to sense the deeper meaning of what Jesus is doing and initially demurs. But when Jesus states that Peter can have no part of him without participating in this "bath"—a multi-layered allusion evoking both Baptism and the actual death and

Resurrection that Baptism signifies— Peter responds with characteristic hyperbole, asking Jesus to wash him from head to toe. Fully aware of *whose* he is, Peter unreservedly casts his lot with Jesus. To ensure that the disciples have understood his enacted parable, Jesus questions them directly. Help your listeners understand that this lesson is intended for all believers, not only for those in leadership. Jesus has given a "model" during the supper with his friends, but soon he will give yet another—when he mounts the cross.

GOOD FRIDAY OF THE LORD'S PASSION

Lectionary #40

READING I   Isaiah 52:13—53:12

Isaiah = ī-ZAY-uh

God speaks of the servant with strength and pride. The word "See" calls us to attention!

The mood suddenly shifts as the narration of the suffering of God's servant begins.

The sense of these verses is: In the same way that many were amazed at him— because he was so disfigured he didn't even look human—nations and kings will be startled and astonished by him.

The voice shifts here to that of the foreign nations.

The speakers marvel at their own blindness, yet in their defense, the servant did appear unremarkable and unattractive. However, they rue how they mistreated him.

Contrast his innocence with *our* guilt.

A reading from the Book of the Prophet Isaiah

See, my servant shall **prosper**,
    he shall be raised **high** and greatly **exalted**.
Even as many were **amazed** at him—
    so **marred** was his look beyond human **semblance**
    and his **appearance** beyond that of the sons of **man**—
so shall he **startle** many **nations**,
    because of him **kings** shall stand **speechless**;
for those who have not been **told** shall **see**,
    those who have not **heard** shall **ponder** it.

Who would **believe** what we have heard?
    To **whom** has the arm of the LORD been **revealed**?
He grew up like a **sapling** before him,
    like a **shoot** from the parched **earth**;
there was in him no **stately** bearing to make us **look** at him,
    nor **appearance** that would **attract** us to him.
He was **spurned** and **avoided** by people,
    a man of **suffering**, accustomed to **infirmity**,
one of those from whom people **hide** their faces,
    spurned, and we **held** him in no **esteem**.

Yet it was **our** infirmities that he bore,
    our **sufferings** that he endured,
while we thought of him as **stricken**,
    as one **smitten** by God and **afflicted**.

READING I This Song of the Suffering Servant is indeed a song, a dirge, in fact. It is a long, painful, and repetitive look at the bruised and bleeding face of God's sinless Servant. Isaiah's fine poetry achieves its effects in the way all good verse does, through the *sound* of the proclaimed words, not just their meaning.

Isaiah's original purpose was likely to describe the mission of God's people, Israel, and their role in God's plan of salvation, or even to consider his own role as God's servant and mouthpiece. But on Good Friday we are thinking of Jesus,

God's sinless Servant, as the perfect fulfillment of this prophecy. So today, Isaiah's dirge helps us sing of Jesus. But Isaiah's lament flips the pattern we usually find in a dirge. Typically, dirges speak of past glory and future sorrow; but this song anticipates a glory that flows *from* the wounds of the Suffering Servant. The pain is past; the glory promised! God's voice offers the Servant as one to be praised. Stress the words that announce what the servant will do ("prosper" and "be raised high") and the impact he will have on others ("startle" and render kings "speechless").

What follows is a marvel: the voice shifts ("Who would believe [it]?") to that of the Gentile nations who recognize the Servant (Israel) as God's instrument and confess their guilt for causing his enormous suffering. We hear the terrible regret of looking back and realizing a great opportunity was missed: he grew up in our midst, but there was nothing extraordinary about him. This is a remarkable insight— often repeated in the Bible—that we judge by human standards and miss divinity in our midst.

Don't let this read like a list of injuries done to some stranger. The sense of regret is heightened by the awareness of who paid the price for them.

"Stripes" are the marks left behind from a whipping. Speak of them with gratitude.

Soften your tone here. "Lamb" and "sheep" are the same metaphor, so the pace can quicken on the second image. Your tone should reveal a sense of wonder at the servant's silent acceptance of his fate.

"Oppressed" and "condemned" are two distinct words; don't rush them together.

There is a deep sense of regret, perhaps even anger, over this indignity.

"Pleased" is a word that surprises, but it reveals that the servant's fate is within the will of God. Speak it with resignation.

The voice of God returns. Note the "if . . . then" clause that begins the sentence. Death alone is not what saves, but the intentionality of the one who gives his life. Speak in a quieter, more persuasive tone.

But he was **pierced** for our **offenses**,
    crushed for our **sins**;
upon **him** was the **chastisement** that **makes** us **whole**,
    by his **stripes** we were **healed**.
We had **all** gone astray like **sheep**,
    each following his **own** way;
but the LORD laid upon **him**
    the **guilt** of us **all**.

Though he was **harshly** treated, he **submitted**
    and opened **not** his **mouth**;
like a **lamb** led to the **slaughter**
    or a **sheep** before the **shearers**,
    he was **silent** and opened not his **mouth**.
Oppressed and **condemned**, he was taken **away**,
    and who would have thought any **more** of his **destiny**?
When he was cut **off** from the land of the **living**,
    and **smitten** for the sin of his **people**,
a **grave** was assigned him among the **wicked**
    and a **burial** place with **evildoers**,
though he had done **no wrong**
    nor spoken any **falsehood**.
But the LORD was **pleased**
    to **crush** him in **infirmity**.

If he gives **his** life as an offering for **sin**,
    he shall see his **descendants** in a **long** life,
    and the **will** of the LORD shall be **accomplished** through him.

Because of his **affliction**
    he shall see the **light** in **fullness** of **days**;

Then the people share the painful realization that *his* suffering was for *our* sake: We foolishly thought he was "smitten by God" for his *own* failings, but "he was pierced for *our* offenses, crushed for *our* sins." "Spurned," "suffering," "hide their faces" are strong words that communicate the contempt and ridicule he endured. "Smitten," "afflicted," "pierced," and "crushed" are also powerful words that, with their harsh sounds, suggest the injustice endured by God's servant.

In the next paragraph the servant becomes a sacrificial "lamb," a metaphor strongly identified with the innocent Christ. Speak this section with great intensity, awed that this "lamb" went willingly "to the slaughter," accepting his fate without rancor or protest. Grieve at the final humiliation of being buried "with evildoers." Although the words are heavy and the rhythm intense, the text does not lapse into despair. As narrator, you understand the meaning of these events, that somehow all this was within the will of God; your tone must remain resolute and hopeful.

In the closing paragraphs, Isaiah breaks with prior biblical tradition that viewed suffering as punishment for sin, and asserts instead a positive and expiatory value in suffering. The servant's affliction was neither random nor wasted; it was so valuable, in fact, that it brings reward for the servant and justification and healing for others. These affirmations lay the foundation for Catholicism's understanding not just of Jesus' own suffering, but of the meaning and value of all human suffering. Isaiah gives us a powerful lens through which we view the events of Holy Week. This inspired text describes more

through his **suffering**, my servant shall justify **many**,
   and their **guilt** he shall **bear**.
Therefore I will give him his **portion** among the **great**,
   and he shall divide the **spoils** with the **mighty**,
because he **surrendered** himself to **death**
   and was **counted** among the **wicked**;
and he shall take **away** the sins of **many**,
   and win **pardon** for their **offenses**.

The reading climaxes here. The servant is honored, but notice that it is because he suffered willingly!

Slow your delivery as you read the final sentence, but notice that the reading ends with good news, not sorrow.

READING II   Hebrews 4:14–16, 5:7–9

A reading from the Letter to the Hebrews

Brothers and sisters:
Since we have a **great** high **priest** who has passed
   through the **heavens**,
Jesus, the Son of **God**,
let us hold **fast** to our **confession**.
For we do not have a high priest
   who is **unable** to **sympathize** with our **weaknesses**,
   but one who has **similarly** been **tested** in every **way**,
   yet without **sin**.
So let us **confidently** approach the throne of **grace**
   to receive **mercy** and to find **grace** for timely **help**.

In the days when Christ was in the **flesh**,
   he offered **prayers** and **supplications** with loud **cries** and **tears**
   to the one who was able to **save** him from **death**,
   and he was **heard** because of his **reverence**.

The opening sentence is an if/then construct: *If* (or *since*) "we have a great high priest," *then* "let us hold fast . . . ." Therefore you must read slowly so the if/then connection is not missed. "Great High Priest" is an assertion of Christ's superiority to the priests of the old law.
Jesus was one of us. He understands our suffering and temptations.

Where he was *unlike* us is his total sinlessness.

Distinguish the words "mercy" and "grace."

"Tears and supplications" may allude to Gethsemane and perhaps elsewhere—weeping over Lazarus or mourning Judas' betrayal. His suffering was real, that's why he understands ours.

---

aptly than any other the suffering Messiah we memorialize today.

In the final sentences, God's voice pronounces future glory for the humble servant and deliverance for the "many" for whom his willing and selfless suffering has won "pardon." Ending on a note of sadness would negate Isaiah's message. The darkness of death often becomes the ground in which seeds of new life flourish. Conclude with that realization: what the servant has done will continue to yield life.

READING II God's word declares it: perfection is nurtured in the soil of obedience. In obedience, Isaiah's servant suffers innocently for the sake of his people and saves them from punishment. The author of Hebrews recognizes in Jesus the same exemplary obedience demonstrated by Isaiah's servant.

As in Isaiah, we find in Hebrews a companion in suffering, a brother in pain and rejection, one who has drunk fully of struggle and temptation and who, without shame, wears the mantle of humanity.

Though he was like us, and though he suffered and was "tested in every way," he is also a "great high priest" who has "passed through the heavens." He was *unlike* us in his total innocence and his complete surrender to the will of God, but those qualities now enable Christ to intercede for us before the Father. Therefore, we can "confidently approach" this "high priest" who has endured all that we endure, and more.

The author later calls this letter "a message of encouragement" (13:22). That is what sets this second reading apart from the first. Because Hebrews is a cele-

Take note that Jesus "learned" obedience through his suffering.

God's son modeled obedience. We imitate him and find salvation. Make eye contact on "for all who obey him."

Son though he **was**, he learned **obedience** from what he **suffered**;
and when he was made **perfect**,
he became the **source** of eternal **salvation**
for all who **obey** him.

PASSION　John 18:1—19:42

The Passion of our Lord Jesus Christ according to John

Kidron = KID-ruhn
The garden is a peaceful, familiar place.

(1) **Jesus** went out with his **disciples** across the Kidron **valley**
to where there was a garden,
into which he and his disciples **entered**.

The shadow of Judas suddenly shifts the mood.

Judas his **betrayer also** knew the place,
because Jesus had **often** met there with his disciples.
So Judas got a band of **soldiers** and **guards**
from the chief **priests** and the **Pharisees**

Lanterns are symbolic of the hour of darkness.

Jesus moves forward fully aware and in charge of his destiny.

and went there with **lanterns**, **torches**, and **weapons**.
Jesus, knowing **everything** that was going to happen to him,
went out and said to them, "Whom are you **looking** for?"
They **answered** him, "**Jesus** the **Nazorean**."
He said to them, "**I AM**."
Judas his betrayer was **also** with them.
When he said to them, "**I AM**,"

Jesus' power overwhelms the guards. He'll be taken only when he permits it.

they turned **away** and fell to the **ground**.
So he **again** asked them,
"**Whom** are you looking for?"
They said, "**Jesus** the **Nazorean**."
Jesus answered,

The theological significance of the "I AM" statements should not be ignored.

"I **told** you that **I AM**.

---

bration of what has already occurred, instead of lamentation, it proclaims confident joy over what Christ has accomplished for us. Jesus' sacrifice completely transcends the sacrifices of the old law; he has become our perfect representative before God.

　　"Loud cries and tears" are an allusion to Gethsemane where Jesus pled to be spared the fate that awaited him. But that reference doesn't require a reenactment of the garden agony because the point is that "he was heard," though not by being saved *from* death but by being delivered *through*

it. Jesus "learned obedience" by willingly embracing suffering, and he was "made perfect" by that suffering. In other words, even the Son of God exercised free will; he was not forced to obey God like some automaton, but he obeyed nonetheless, despite temptation and great struggle. The result is "eternal salvation for all," and Hebrews holds out hope that "all who obey him" can move through suffering to perfection. That our own suffering can yield perfection is a great mystery, a hope you are called to share with conviction and joy.

PASSION　John's Passion narrative paints a very intentional portrait of the Christ who makes his way to Calvary. Here Jesus is not a victim, but the author of his own destiny. The story tells of Jesus' irrevocable movement toward glory—the "hour" of which John's Gospel has spoken throughout. All the details John selects serve this purpose of presenting a Jesus who remains sovereign Lord despite his suffering. The synoptic writers depict a sad and sorrowful Christ force-marched to his painful destiny, but John eliminates the episodes that would

Shift your tone slightly to suggest the quoting of scripture.

Violence is expressed with "struck" and "cut off." Malchus = MAL-kuhs

Jesus rebukes Peter here.

Annas = AN-uhs
Caiaphas = KAY-uh-fuhs or KĪ-uh-fuhs

This is a significant quote attributed to Caiaphas.

Is Peter kept out or staying out from fear?

Peter doesn't want to be overheard denying Jesus.

So if you are looking for **me**, let **these** men **go**."
This was to **fulfill** what he had said,
  "I have not lost **any** of those you **gave** me."
(2) Then Simon **Peter**, who had a **sword**, **drew** it,
  struck the high priest's slave, and **cut** off his right **ear**.
The slave's name was **Malchus**.
Jesus said to Peter,
  "Put your **sword** into its **scabbard**.
Shall I not **drink** the cup that the Father **gave** me?"

So the band of **soldiers**, the **tribune**, and the Jewish **guards**
    seized Jesus,
  bound him, and brought him to **Annas** first.
He was the **father-in-law** of **Caiaphas**,
  who was **high** priest that year.
It was **Caiaphas** who had **counseled** the Jews
  that it was better that **one** man should die
    rather than the **people**.

(3) Simon **Peter** and **another** disciple **followed** Jesus.
Now the **other** disciple was **known** to the high priest,
  and he entered the **courtyard** of the high priest with **Jesus**.
But **Peter** stood at the gate **outside**.
So the other **disciple**, the **acquaintance** of the high priest,
  went out and spoke to the **gatekeeper** and brought Peter **in**.
Then the **maid** who was the **gatekeeper** said to Peter,
  "You are not one of this man's **disciples**, **are** you?"
He said, "I am **not**."
Now the slaves and the **guards** were standing
    around a charcoal fire
  that they had made, because it was **cold**,
    and were **warming** themselves.
Peter was also standing there keeping **warm**.

compromise his image of a purposeful Christ in full control of his fate. Gone are the garden agony, the help of Simon, the mourning women, the ridicule hurled at the crucified Christ from religious leaders and bystanders. Passion Sunday presents the abused and abandoned martyr of Matthew, Luke, and Mark, but the Christ of Good Friday is always John's self-possessed and resolute Lord, who moves knowingly toward Calvary where he mounts the cross as a king mounts his throne.

Jesus' fate results from the unholy alliance of Jewish leaders and Roman authorities and, in John, the role of the Romans is introduced earlier than in the synoptic versions. Yet, for some readers, John's persistent use of the term "the Jews" suggests that blame for Christ's death rests solely on Jewish shoulders, a culpability subsequently inherited by each successive generation. Papal and episcopal statements have made it clear that this is not the belief of the Church. When these texts are read, listeners should be made aware that the Church does not hold the Jewish people guilty. Your homily might provide an opportunity to counter any potential misunderstanding.

The power of the story rests in its ability to be new each time we hear it. This is also the hope for every lector who fears proclaiming words that have been heard too often. Read the Passion knowing you can help your listeners experience it again for the first time. You'll do that best if you yourself are drawn in, experiencing the flow of emotions as you imagine the action unfold before you.

Effective proclamation of this lengthy narrative can be achieved in a number of

This is a new scene, so renew your energy here.

(4) The high priest **questioned** Jesus
   about his **disciples** and about his **doctrine**.
Jesus **answered** him,
   "I have spoken **publicly** to the world.
I have always taught in a **synagogue**
   or in the **temple** area where all the Jews **gather**,
   and in **secret** I have said **nothing**. Why ask me?
Ask those who **heard** me what I **said** to them.
They know what I said."

Jesus is strong in his self-defense, showing the weakness of their "case."

When he had **said** this,
   one of the temple **guards** standing there **struck** Jesus and said,
   "Is **this** the way you answer the high **priest**?"

Deliver the line like a slap—fast and hard.

Jesus answered him,
   "If I have spoken **wrongly**, **testify** to the wrong;
   but if I have spoken **rightly**, why do you **strike** me?"

Jesus holds his ground here.

Then Annas sent him **bound** to **Caiaphas** the **high** priest.

Another new scene begins here.

(5) Now Simon **Peter** was **standing** there keeping **warm**.
And they **said** to him,
   "**You** are not one of his **disciples**, **are** you?"
He **denied** it and said,
   "I am **not**."

Peter is getting angry here.

One of the **slaves** of the high priest,
   a **relative** of the one whose **ear** Peter had cut off, said,
   "Didn't I see you in the **garden** with him?"
Again Peter denied it.

The denials are brief, but this line suggests the lasting impact on Peter.

And **immediately** the **cock** crowed.

(6) Then they brought Jesus from **Caiaphas** to the **praetorium**.
It was **morning**.
And they **themselves** did not **enter** the praetorium,
   in order not to be **defiled** so that they could eat the **Passover**.

ways. Although it demands a level of excellence that's rare, a single, gifted reader can deliver a riveting proclamation. Often, parishes opt for assembly participation in the proclamation. This method encourages the assembly to read along with the lectors, which can keep people from entering deeply into the story. Most often, the best option is for three fine readers to divide the lines and share the narration. One reader (a priest) should portray Jesus and the other readers divide the remaining characters—but avoid having

anyone read the dialogue of two characters who are speaking to each other.

More important than the method of proclamation, however, is your relationship with the story. In the liturgical assembly, the proclamation of scripture brings the saving events of the past into the present. That awesome responsibility mustn't be trivialized by lack of preparation or by over-dramatization. The Jesus of the Gospel according to John is so grounded in his identity as God's son and in his relationship with the Father that he can embrace his destiny without wavering. As

you share this story, every syllable of your proclamation should declare that truth.

(1) Jesus seeks the peaceful familiarity of the garden, but Judas penetrates that sanctuary with a noisy crowd of soldiers bearing "lanterns, torches and weapons." What stark irony that those who bring the "hour of darkness" come bearing light, and that so large a cohort comes against the unarmed Jesus. In this Gospel, Jesus has not agonized in the garden. Rather than spent and forlorn, he emerges full of authority and clear awareness of what will unfold. Not waiting on the crowd,

This is a spat among political adversaries. Each is annoyed with the other.

So **Pilate** came out to **them** and said,
"What **charge** do you bring against this man?"
They **answered** and said to him,
"If he were not a **criminal**,
we would not have handed him **over** to you."
At **this**, Pilate said to them,
"Take him **yourselves**, and **judge** him according to your **law**."
The Jews **answered** him,
"We do not have the right to **execute** anyone,"
in order that the word of **Jesus** might be **fulfilled**
that he said indicating the kind of **death** he would die.

The scene shifts here. Pilate is "starting over" and is not presented as a villain.

So Pilate went **back** into the praetorium
and **summoned** Jesus and said to him,
"Are you the **King** of the **Jews**?"
Jesus answered,
"Do you say this on your **own**
or have **others** told you about me?"

Pilate is becoming impatient again.

Pilate answered,
"I am not a **Jew**, **am** I?
Your own **nation** and the chief **priests** handed you over to me.
What have you **done**?"

Jesus is not passive, but engaged in debate.

Jesus answered,
"My **kingdom** does not **belong** to **this** world.
If my kingdom **did** belong to this world,
my attendants would be **fighting**
to **keep** me from being handed over to the Jews.
But as it **is**, my kingdom is not **here**."
So Pilate said to him,
"Then you **are** a king?"

Stress the verb ("are") here, not the noun ("king").

Jesus answered,
"**You** say I am a king.

Jesus challenges the mob with his question. Their response is no match for his confidence, and they are immediately overwhelmed by his regal "I AM." Jesus is still caring for his own; in demanding that they "let these men go," he reveals his willingness to accept the crowd's designs against him, but not against his friends.

(2) Peter responds boldly, risking his own life by taking up the sword. "Struck" and "cut off" convey his rage. But Jesus will have none of this. Matching Peter's energy, he orders him to "Put [his] sword into its scabbard," an echo, perhaps, of

"Get behind me, Satan." Once again, John stresses Jesus' choice to "drink the cup." By noting that it was the Roman soldiers who assisted the Jewish guards in arresting Jesus, John highlights the complicity of the Roman occupiers. Don't let that detail go unnoticed. Announce "that it was better that one man die . . ." in the firm voice of Caiaphas.

(3) Peter's first denial can be underplayed. It would seem he has quickly forgotten his grandiose Last Supper protestations of undying loyalty. That will haunt him soon enough. For now, the courage he displayed

in the garden is gone and we see only the frustration he experiences at being unable to get close to the action. When "the other disciple" gets him through the gate, Peter makes a faint, over-the-shoulder response to the girl's question (perhaps trying to keep the "disciple" from overhearing him).

(4) When interrogated by the high priest, Jesus shows remarkable composure and confronts the injustice of his treatment without fear. But the guard mistakes his confidence for disrespect and responds with violence. Jesus boldly risks another slap by challenging his attacker.

Jesus speaks with confidence here.

For this I was **born** and for this I came into the **world**,
> to **testify** to the **truth**.
Everyone who **belongs** to the truth **listens** to my voice."
Pilate said to him, "What is **truth**?"

(7) When he had **said** this,
> he **again** went out to the Jews and said to them,
> "I find no **guilt** in him.
But you have a **custom** that I release one **prisoner** to you
> at **Passover**.

**Pilate is seeking a quick resolution.
Is he trying to put words in their mouths?**

Barabbas = buh-RAB-uhs

Do you want me to release to you the **King** of the **Jews**?"
They cried out **again**,
> "Not **this** one but **Barabbas**!"
Now Barabbas was a **revolutionary**.

(8) Then Pilate took Jesus and had him **scourged**.
And the soldiers wove a **crown** out of **thorns** and placed it
> on his **head**,
> and clothed him in a **purple** cloak,
> and they came to him and said,

This is a greatly understated scene, but the pain and shame are very real.

> "**Hail**, **King** of the **Jews**!"
And they **struck** him **repeatedly**.
Once **more** Pilate went out and said to them,

Perhaps Pilate is saying, "Look at what you made me do!"

> "**Look**, I am bringing him **out** to you,
> so that you may **know** that I find no **guilt** in him."
So Jesus came out,
> wearing the crown of **thorns** and the purple **cloak**.
And he said to them, "**Behold**, the man!"
When the chief priests and the guards **saw** him they **cried** out,
> "**Crucify** him, **crucify** him!"
Pilate said to them,

When a phrase is repeated, give greater stress to second utterance.

> "Take him **yourselves** and **crucify** him.

The guard's violent anger should color your *narration* as well as his dialogue. Jesus is recovering from the slap when he begins his reply, so his second clause should be spoken with more intensity than the first.

(5) Peter saw Jesus attacked and did nothing, but he reacts quickly when he feels himself attacked. The question, "You are not one of his disciples, are you?" stings him like a sword. His answer is short and quick. The "relative" of the victim of Peter's own violence tries to get an admission from Peter (probably out of revenge). But Peter refuses a third time to

publicly own Jesus. Deliver "And again Peter denied it" not as narration, but as Peter's actual words of denial. Though not predicted in this Gospel account, the cock crows after this third denial. Narrate that painful moment with the regret that must have flooded Peter's heart.

(6) In Pilate's judgment hall, John dramatizes an intense struggle between forces of good and evil. Jesus stands alone before his accusers with Pilate playing the double role of judge and occasional advocate. John devotes more time to the interaction between Pilate and Jesus than do

the synoptic Gospel accounts, giving us additional details, like their exchange about "truth." Pilate clearly appears to be pushed in a direction he is not eager to go. In proclaiming this Passion we must deal with the characters John has created, and it cannot be denied that, in their tug-of-war, Pilate comes off looking better than the religious authorities. The struggle between them lends life and excitement to this part of the narrative. But John's portrait of the Jewish authorities is not one-dimensional. In addition to the men who became chief instigators in the plot

The leaders' energy increases as they sense Pilate weakening.

The priests have pushed the right button in Pilate.

Pilate's frustration turns on Jesus.

Jesus' tone is unapologetic.

"Friend of Caesar" is a title of honor bestowed by Rome on high-ranking officials, which Pilate might lose if he mishandles this situation.

Gabbatha = GAB-uh-thuh

Pilate's words suggest his frustration with both Jesus and the priests.

I find no **guilt** in him."
The Jews **answered**,
   "We have a **law**, and according to that **law** he ought to **die**,
   because he **made** himself the **Son** of **God**."
(9) Now when Pilate **heard** this statement,
   he became even **more** afraid,
   and went back into the **praetorium** and said to **Jesus**,
   "Where are you **from**?"
Jesus did not **answer** him.
So Pilate said to him,
   "Do you not speak to **me**?
Do you not **know** that I have **power** to **release** you
   and I have power to **crucify** you?"
Jesus answered him,
   "You would have **no** power over me
   if it had not been **given** to you from **above**.
·For **this** reason the one who handed me **over** to you
   has the **greater** sin."
Consequently, Pilate tried to **release** him; but the **Jews** cried out,
   "If you **release** him, you are not a **Friend** of **Caesar**.
Everyone who makes himself a **king** opposes **Caesar**."

(10) When Pilate **heard** these words he brought Jesus out
   and **seated** him on the **judge's** bench
   in the place called **Stone Pavement**, in **Hebrew**, **Gabbatha**.
It was **preparation** day for **Passover**, and it was about **noon**.
And he said to the **Jews**,
   "**Behold**, your **king**!"
They **cried** out,
   "**Take** him away, **take** him away! **Crucify** him!"

against Jesus, there are other men of unquestioned integrity and sincerity—Nicodemus and Joseph of Arimathea.

Not only is Pilate roused from his bed at early morning, but, making matters worse, he is awakened in order to hear a religious case brought by Jewish leaders who won't even enter the praetorium for fear of being "defiled." He must go to them, but their exchange suggests there's no love lost between the governor and these Jewish subjects. Only John tells us that the motive for seeking recourse with

Pilate was the fact that the religious leaders lacked "the right to execute anyone."

In his role as reluctant advocate, Pilate questions Jesus, but he is annoyed that this Jew who has disturbed his sleep dares to question him back. Jesus' compelling power seems to draw Pilate to him, but Pilate won't yet take him seriously. So he spars with him: "Then you *are* a king? . . . What is *truth*?"

(7) It's quite possible Pilate sees an opportunity to resolve the problem quickly—and favorably—for Jesus when

he brings up the Passover custom of releasing a prisoner. But to no avail, so he intensifies his efforts: Maybe a good flogging will satisfy these zealots! John shields us from the brutality and horror of the flogging and mockery of Jesus, providing fewer details than the other Gospel writers, but use the narration you have to emphasize the soldiers' contempt as they scourge and crown Jesus with thorns.

(8) After the scourging, Pilate expects the chief priests to be satisfied. His tone seems to say: I've listened to you; I've punished him for you. That's all you get! But

This is a final effort to forestall.

Pilate said to them,
　"Shall I crucify your **king**?"
The chief **priests** answered,
　"We have **no** king but **Caesar**."
Then he **handed** him over to them to be **crucified**.

This is another new scene. Speak slowly.

Golgotha = GAWL-guh-thuh

(11) So they **took** Jesus, and, **carrying** the cross **himself**,
　he went out to what is called the **Place** of the **Skull**,
　　in **Hebrew**, **Golgotha**.
There they **crucified** him, and with him two **others**,
　one on either **side**, with Jesus in the **middle**.
Pilate also had an **inscription** written and put on the **cross**.
It read,

Proclaim the inscription slowly and with authority.

　"**Jesus** the **Nazorean**, the **King** of the **Jews**."
Now **many** of the Jews **read** this inscription,
　because the place where Jesus was **crucified** was near the **city**;
　and it was written in **Hebrew**, **Latin**, and **Greek**.
So the chief **priests** of the Jews said to **Pilate**,
　"Do not **write** 'The **King** of the Jews,'
　but that he **said**, 'I am the King of the Jews.'"
Pilate answered,

Speak deliberately: "What I have written, I / have / written!"

　"What I have **written**, I have written."

(12) When the soldiers had **crucified** Jesus,
　they took his **clothes** and **divided** them into four **shares**,
　　a share for each **soldier**.
They also took his **tunic**, but the tunic was **seamless**,
　woven in one **piece** from the top **down**.
So they said to one another,

The cruel insensitivity of the Roman soldiers should be apparent.

　"Let's not **tear** it, but cast **lots** for it to see whose it will **be**,"

the calls for crucifixion both anger and frighten Pilate. He's being pushed further than he expected and senses his hands will be even bloodier before the day is out. Pilate offers to hand him over while still asserting Jesus' innocence. But for the Jewish leaders the case is clear: Jesus is *guilty*, a blasphemer deserving death.

(9) Pilate is gripped with fear. His growing anger and mounting frustration with the religious leaders he now hurls at Jesus: "Where do you come from? Do you refuse . . . . Do you not *know* . . . ?" Jesus' quiet composure disturbs yet impresses

Pilate. In their conversation about "power," Jesus says the blame for his death will fall less on Pilate than on the leaders who have falsely accused him. The intensity builds, and the chief priests sense trouble.

(10) Seeing Pilate weakening, the religious men pressure him, but Pilate does not surrender Jesus easily. In response to the threats to report him to Caesar, Pilate parades their Jesus before them, with a taunting "Behold your king!" The mob is so caught up in denying Jesus as their king that they claim Caesar instead, the pagan whose occupying forces they so bitterly

despise. A final effort to win pity for Jesus—"Shall I crucify your king?"—is followed by Pilate's capitulation to the evil designs of the mob.

(11) Jesus carries the cross "*himself,*" in this Gospel and John offers no details of the Crucifixion, save that Jesus hung between two anonymous criminals. Don't rush the narration, but avoid an overly somber tone; John isn't interested in presenting the horror of Crucifixion; he spends his time instead on Pilate's inscription that declares Jesus "King of the Jews." Proclaim that inscription as might a herald

Use a tone shift when quoting scripture.

In this new scene the women are much grieved. Probably, *four* women are identified: "his mother's sister" is different from "Mary the wife of Clopas."
Clopas = KLOH-puhs
Magdala = MAG-duh-luh

In this new scene stress Jesus' awareness and control.

hyssop = HIS-uhp

Jesus' "spirit" is the Holy Spirit, the spirit of the new creation. Jesus' death is the giving of the Spirit.

Breaking legs assured a quicker death—by asphyxiation.

in order that the passage of **Scripture** might be **fulfilled**
    that says:
    *They divided my **garments** among them,*
    *and for my **vesture** they cast **lots**.*
This is what the soldiers **did**.
(13) Standing by the **cross** of Jesus were his **mother**
    and his mother's **sister**, **Mary** the wife of **Clopas**,
    and Mary of **Magdala**.
When Jesus **saw** his mother and the **disciple** there whom he **loved**
    he said to his mother, "**Woman**, behold, your **son**."
Then he said to the **disciple**,
    "Behold, your **mother**."
And from **that** hour the **disciple** took her into his **home**.

(14) **After** this, aware that **everything** was now **finished**,
    in order that the **Scripture** might be **fulfilled**,
    Jesus said, "I **thirst**."
There was a **vessel** filled with common **wine**.
So they put a **sponge** soaked in wine on a sprig of **hyssop**
    and put it up to his **mouth**.
When Jesus had **taken** the wine, he said,
    "It is **finished**."
And **bowing** his **head**, he handed **over** the **spirit**.

[Here all kneel and pause for a short time.]

(15) Now since it was **preparation** day,
    in order that the **bodies** might not **remain** on the cross
        on the **sabbath**,
    for the sabbath day of **that** week was a **solemn** one,
    the Jews asked **Pilate** that their legs be **broken**
    and that they be taken **down**.

reading from a scroll. The dialogue between Pilate and priests is animated and angry, but this time Pilate gets the last word.

(12) The Roman soldiers divide his clothing into four even parts. But recognizing the value of his tunic, they gamble for it. Let your tone suggest their insensitivity and selfishness, but the quotation of scripture "they divided my garments" calls for a tone of sadness and resignation, as does the summary statement: "This is what the soldiers did."

(13) John does not present Jesus abandoned on the cross, for the Marys are

keeping watch. Speak of "his mother" and the others in an animated and hopeful tone, as if the women were trying with their own energy to sustain Jesus' failing strength. These holy women are familiar to and revered by the narrator, so your tone should suggest you know them. The dialogue is spoken by the *dying* Jesus who, nonetheless, is still ministering to others. In his words, "behold your son . . . mother" we hear a gripping and singular expression of love.

(14) This death scene is constructed to serve John's purpose of depicting a lord

who goes knowingly to his death. Aware that all is "now finished"—but without anguish or despair—Jesus says, "I thirst." He has mustered his last strength to fulfill scripture. Taking a sip of wine, offered as a gesture of kindness, he utters his last words with strength and full awareness. Pause briefly after "It is finished" and then, imagining Jesus dropping his head in death, quietly, read the narration. In handing over his "spirit," Jesus is both surrendering his life and passing on the Holy Spirit. Take a longer pause here for silence and prayer.

Blood and water are important theological symbols.

So the **soldiers** came and **broke** the legs of the **first**
   and then of the **other** one who was crucified with Jesus.
But when they came to Jesus and saw that he was already **dead**,
   they did **not** break his legs,
     but one soldier thrust his **lance** into his **side**,
     and immediately **blood** and **water** flowed out.

Speak with conviction, stressing the word "eyewitness."

An **eyewitness** has **testified**, and his testimony is **true**;
   he **knows** that he is speaking the **truth**,
   so that you **also** may come to **believe**.
For this **happened** so that the **Scripture** passage might be **fulfilled**:
   *Not a **bone** of it will be **broken**.*
And again **another** passage says:
   *They will **look** upon him whom they have **pierced**.*

Arimathea = ayr-ih-muh-THEE-uh

(16) After **this**, **Joseph** of **Arimathea**,
   secretly a **disciple** of Jesus for **fear** of the **Jews**,
   asked **Pilate** if he could **remove** the body of Jesus.
And Pilate **permitted** it.

Proclaim with tender respect for Joseph and, later, Nicodemus.

Nicodemus = nik-uh-DEE-muhs

So he came and **took** his body.
Nicodemus, the one who had first come to him at **night**,
   also came bringing a mixture of **myrrh** and **aloes**
   weighing about one hundred **pounds**.

myrrh = mer
aloes = AL-ohs

They took the **body** of Jesus
   and bound it with **burial cloths** along with the **spices**,
   according to the Jewish **burial** custom.

Slow your pacing for the final lines.

Now in the **place** where he had been crucified there was a **garden**,
   and in the garden a **new tomb**, in which no one
     had yet been **buried**.

Although the final sentence lacks drama, speak with solemn reverence of the burial of Jesus.

So they laid Jesus **there** because of the Jewish **preparation** day;
   for the **tomb** was close **by**.

(15) The drama is not yet over. First there is talk of "preparation day" and "Sabbath"—significant details that should not be rushed. While the overall tone is subdued, speak of the soldiers who broke the legs and thrust the lance with some intensity, for the men whose legs are being broken are still living. "Blood and water" is a sure biological sign of death, but it is also a powerful theological symbol, traditionally seen to represent Baptism and Eucharist. Speak of it with reverence. Mention of the "eyewitness" is a critical dimension of John's message, which is meant to bolster faith, so narrate with confidence. Remember, you aren't making a courtroom presentation but presenting the faith of a believer.

(16) Speak of Joseph as a now revered member of the community, the secrecy surrounding his discipleship understandable because of "fear of the Jews." He asks a favor of Pilate who, by granting it, is again cast in a positive light. Nicodemus, another secret disciple, now reveals his allegiance to Jesus by coming to care for his body, anointing it with oils and spices, something which does not occur on Friday in the synoptic gospels. Speak of the burial with great reverence and tenderness, but hold the grief in check, as you might if telling a friend about a loved one's funeral that she was unable to attend. Controlling your own sorrow, you would state the facts with obvious love for the deceased. This impromptu tomb was the best they could do for Jesus but, *mirabile dictu!* (wonderful to tell!) it didn't have to do for long.

EASTER VIGIL

Lectionary #41

READING I   Genesis 1:1—2:2

A reading from the Book of Genesis

In the **beginning**, when God created the **heavens** and the **earth**,
the earth was a formless **wasteland**, and **darkness**
covered the **abyss**,
while a mighty **wind** swept over the **waters**.

Then God **said**,
"Let there be **light**," and there **was** light.
God saw how **good** the light was.
God then **separated** the light from the **darkness**.
God called the light "**day**" and the darkness he called "**night**."
Thus **evening** came, and **morning** followed—the **first** day.

Then God said,
"Let there be a **dome** in the **middle** of the waters,
to **separate one** body of water from the **other**."
And so it **happened**:
God **made** the dome,
and it separated the water **above** the dome
from the water **below** it.
God called the dome "the **sky**."
Evening came, and **morning** followed—the **second** day.

Then God said,
"Let the **water** under the sky be gathered into a single **basin**,
so that the dry **land** may appear."

Your first three words set the epic tone of what you relate. Keep in mind the five-part pattern of each day and use the repeated refrains to draw your listeners deeper and deeper into the pattern of God's creative work. The pattern should be obvious, so stress the repetitions rather than hide them with novel readings on each day. Their regularity, familiarity and predictability give the passage much of its power. So don't rush them.

The declaration that Creation is "good" and the accomplishment of God's command are stressed each time they recur.

Renew your energy (and make eye contact) with each "Then God said."

READING I For this great solemnity, the Church reserves her most beautiful ritual and her finest stories. The time of penitence is over. Tonight we start anew. And we begin at the beginning, telling the story of the God who creates and the God who saves, of the God who patiently waits, who chastises, and who requires that we surrender everything to him.

In the Genesis account, God is a sovereign power who creates not with hands but with the spoken word, a divine "fiat."

Yet God's every move is motivated by tender love, by a desire to create an ideal home for the man and woman who will receive dominion over it. Proclaim, therefore, with an intensity and emotional involvement that tells your listeners, not about what was made when, but of the loving God who made it all.

The structure of this narrative contains a pattern of five recurring refrains. Each day of Creation contains 1) an *introduction*: "Then God said"; 2) God's spoken *command*: "Let there be . . ."; 3) an announcement of the *accomplishment* of

the command: "And so it happened"; 4) an *affirmation* of the goodness of each day's work: "God saw how *good* it was"; and 5) an identification of the day: "Evening came and morning followed the first day . . . the second . . ." and so on. The most important refrains are the last two. God's affirmation of the goodness of Creation should be as sincere and tender as parents' affirmation of their child. Don't let the naming of each day sound like a tired worker checking off the day's accomplishment. These refrains are part of the sacred poetry of the text. Use

Identify each of God's creations—"the earth . . . the sea"—with tenderness.

There is a lot of detail here; use the words marked for emphasis to guide you in placing your stress. But here it's the energy and enthusiasm that matter most, not the individual words.

Here as before, emphasizing details is less important than conveying a sense of joy and wonder.

Speak the words "and he made the stars" quickly, with excitement, or slowly, with amazement. Note that the purpose of each of the lights somehow serves humanity.

And so it **happened**:
  the water under the sky was **gathered** into its basin,
  and the dry **land** appeared.
God called the dry land "the **earth**,"
  and the basin of the **water** he called "the sea."
God saw how **good** it was.
Then God said,
  "Let the **earth** bring forth **vegetation**:
  every kind of **plant** that bears **seed**
  and every kind of **fruit tree** on earth
  that bears fruit with its **seed** in it."
And so it **happened**:
  the earth brought forth every **kind** of plant that bears **seed**
  and every kind of **fruit tree** on earth
  that bears fruit with its **seed** in it.
God saw how **good** it was.
Evening came, and morning **followed**—the **third** day.

Then God said:
  "Let there be **lights** in the dome of the sky,
  to separate **day** from **night**.
Let them mark the fixed **times**, the **days** and the **years**,
  and serve as **luminaries** in the dome of the sky,
  to shed **light** upon the earth."
And so it **happened**:
  God made the **two** great lights,
  the **greater** one to govern the **day**,
  and the **lesser** one to govern the **night**;
  and he made the **stars**.
God **set** them in the dome of the **sky**,
  to shed **light** upon the earth,
  to **govern** the day and the night,
  and to separate the **light** from the **darkness**.

the refrains to draw your listeners deeper into the pattern of God's creative work.

Chaos reigned in the "beginning." It is to bring order from that chaos that God sends the wind of the spirit to move over the dark, brooding waters. If you've seen a large lake or the ocean at night you know the kind of water "swept" by that "mighty wind."

The creator God of Genesis is awe-inspiring, a sovereign Lord who creates by merely saying "Let there be . . . ." Find an appropriate level of authority and power that doesn't overdramatize. We should

sense delight in God's work of Creation, so proclaim joyfully.

Each repetition of "*Then* God said" advances us through the days of Creation, so find fresh energy with which to deliver each iteration. After describing the events of each day, announce "And so it happened" with gratitude and awe, the way you might speak if you witnessed the birth of a child. After creating light, God separates the water, so essential for all of life, into separate realms—the sky above and the earth below.

Again by fiat, God separates the earth and sea, causing the dry land to appear. God names them and calls them good. Genesis presents God as intimately involved in the work of Creation, fashioning every detail from the "plant that bears seed" (a pine or oak) to the "fruit tree . . . that bears fruit with its seed in it" (apples and oranges). Such careful and purposive design calls forth our own love of the earth and vigilance towards its God-given resources. Again God blesses Creation with divine goodness, a refrain you must speak with deepening conviction.

Each time it recurs, "Evening came, and morning followed" should convey the end of an epoch of time and Creation. Speak with a sense of accomplishment, joy, and peace.

This "day" teems with life; there is much excitement and energy in these lines.

Notice that God "blesses" the creatures. End this section with calm satisfaction.

Renew energy once again with joy at the thrill of creating life.

The reading reaches a sub-climax here. *All* of Creation is good!

Use a nobler, slower pacing here. Humans are made in God's own likeness! Take note of the plural pronouns. Use, don't rush, the repetitions, for they deepen our sense of these great truths.

God saw how **good** it was.
Evening came, and **morning** followed—the **fourth** day.

Then God said,
  "Let the water **teem** with an **abundance** of living **creatures**,
  and on the **earth** let **birds** fly beneath the **dome** of the sky."
And so it **happened**:
  God created the great **sea** monsters
  and all kinds of **swimming** creatures with which
    the water **teems**,
  and all kinds of winged **birds**.
God saw how **good** it was, and God **blessed** them, saying,
  "Be **fertile**, **multiply**, and **fill** the water of the seas;
  and let the birds **multiply** on the earth."
Evening came, and morning **followed**—the **fifth** day.

Then God said,
  "Let the **earth** bring forth all kinds of living **creatures**:
  cattle, **creeping** things, and wild **animals** of all **kinds**."
And so it **happened**:
  God made all **kinds** of wild **animals**, all kinds of **cattle**,
  and all kinds of **creeping** things of the earth.
God saw how **good** it was.

Then God said:
  "Let us make **man** in our **image**, after our **likeness**.
  Let them have **dominion** over the **fish** of the sea,
    the **birds** of the air, and the **cattle**,
    and over all the wild **animals**
    and all the creatures that **crawl** on the **ground**."
God created **man** in his **image**;
  in the image of **God** he created him;
  male and **female** he created them.

The light of God's own brilliance graces the third day. Speak joyfully of brother sun who nourishes all living things. Extol sister moon who dispels the shadows of the fearful night. And sing of the countless stars dotting the evening sky. Your delivery can be as fresh and novel as each starlit night, keeping your listeners attentive, engaged in the awe-inspiring narrative rather than concluding, "I've heard all this before."

Day five dawns with a flurry of creative energy: "sea monsters . . . swimming creatures . . . winged birds" are the products of God's abundance and delight. The waters teem and the skies are aflutter with spectacular creatures that issue from the mind of God. God blesses them or orders them to "multiply" in the waters and on the earth: a divine command that fills the world with goodness.

The most creative day comes last. Living creatures great and small, "wild" and "creeping" things are brought to jubilant life. God delights like a child watching an endless parade of circus animals of "all kinds." And all of them are good.

Flowing from and exceeding all that went before, comes a creature made "in our image, after our likeness." This creature shares divine life. Let your voice assume a tender and solemn quality. God can't be outdone in lavishing his creatures with gifts. All that the world holds, God bestows on man and woman. God gives "dominion" and blessing and commands them to "Be fertile and multiply." God gives them every plant and tree and all the living creatures. These are caring words of entrustment and generosity, not the commands of an overseer.

God **blessed** them, saying:
"Be **fertile** and **multiply**;
fill the earth and **subdue** it.
Have **dominion** over the fish of the **sea**, the birds of the **air**,
and all the **living** things that **move** on the earth."
God **also** said:
"**See**, I give you every **seed**-bearing plant all over the **earth**
and every **tree** that has seed-bearing **fruit** on it to be your **food**;
and to all the **animals** of the land, all the **birds** of the air,
and all the living creatures that **crawl** on the **ground**,
I give all the **green** plants for **food**."
And so it **happened**.
God looked at **everything** he had made, and he found it
very good.
Evening came, and **morning** followed—the **sixth** day.

Thus the **heavens** and the **earth** and all their array
were **completed**.
Since on the **seventh** day God was **finished**
with the work he had been doing,
he **rested** on the seventh day from all the **work**
he had **undertaken**.

[Shorter: Genesis 1:1, 26–31a]

READING II   Genesis 22:1–18

A reading from the Book of Genesis

God put **Abraham** to the **test**.
He called to him, "**Abraham!**"
"**Here** I am," he replied.

Speak this as a blessing, not an order. All the beauty and goodness that God has created is entrusted to humanity.

This is a summary statement: God's Creation is very *good!*

With a sense of accomplishment and pride, pause after "completed."

"Rested" suggests more than being idle; it means appreciating and delighting in the "work," that is, the beloved Creation, God has now completed.

The opening line both introduces and states the point of the entire story. Pause slightly after "Abraham." His "Here I am" should be spoken eagerly.

God surveys all that has been made and all of it is *very* good.

With joyful pride, declare that the work is completed. Now comes Sabbath rest, another of God's great gifts to his people who are forever called to share in that rest.

READING II Each time we read this story, we are reminded that we belong to a God who demands everything of us. That's a hard and unattractive truth. We prefer a gentle God who understands and patiently endures our weaknesses. Even this story may fail to sway us, for we look at the ending and think God was just fooling. After all, what kind of a God would make so brutal a demand? Such objections make good sense today. But for the culture from which the Genesis author comes the sacrifice of human beings was not unknown. So for Abraham to take God's brutal request seriously is quite believable. You must make it believable to your listeners.

From the start, we know nothing awful will really happen, so it is in Abraham's struggle that we find the true horror of this story, not in Isaac's close call. On this holy night, as we recall the history of our salvation and celebrate the new covenant in Christ, we look back to the beginnings. In Isaac, so innocent and accepting that he lets himself be bound without protest, we find a type, or symbol, of the innocent Christ who willingly let himself be bound to the cross of our salvation. But in Abraham, who unlike us does not know this is a "test," we find another "type," a symbol of the Father God who so loved the world that he sent his only begotten son to die for all. The horror of the story lies in the turmoil

Moriah = moh-RĪ-uh

Don't give away what comes at the end of the sentence. God's voice is solemn, not stern. Emphasize the gravity of God's command by stressing "only" and "love."

Abraham works hard to hide his pain. Don't let this sound like an outing in the country.

This image foreshadows Jesus' carrying his own cross. Don't let it go to waste.

This dialogue is poignant: Isaac is sincerely curious and unaware. Abraham speaks intentionally and his words are pained and weighty.

This is not a throwaway line when you consider what lies ahead.

Proclaim slowly here as the scene grows tense and darker. Share one image at a time. Tying up the boy can't sound like he's buttoning Isaac's jacket.

Don't speak like you're describing a "close call," but as if you were relating the actual slaughter. "But" breaks the mood; speak faster. The second "Abraham" is louder, stronger than the first.

Then God said:
  "Take your son **Isaac**, your **only** one, whom you **love**,
    and **go** to the land of **Moriah**.
There you shall **offer** him up as a **holocaust**
  on a **height** that I will point **out** to you."
Early the next **morning** Abraham saddled his **donkey**,
  took with him his son **Isaac** and two of his **servants** as well,
  and with the **wood** that he had cut for the holocaust,
  set out for the place of which God had **told** him.

On the **third** day Abraham got **sight** of the place from **afar**.
Then he **said** to his servants:
  "Both of you stay **here** with the **donkey**,
    while the **boy** and I go on over **yonder**.
We will **worship** and then come **back** to you."
Thereupon Abraham took the wood for the holocaust
  and laid it on his son **Isaac's** shoulders,
  while he **himself** carried the **fire** and the **knife**.
As the two walked on **together**, Isaac **spoke**
      to his father Abraham:
  "**Father**!" Isaac said.
"**Yes**, son," he replied.
Isaac continued, "Here are the **fire** and the **wood**,
  but where is the **sheep** for the holocaust?"
"**Son**," Abraham answered,
  "God **himself** will provide the sheep for the holocaust."
Then the two **continued** going forward.

When they **came** to the place of which God had **told** him,
  Abraham built an **altar** there and arranged the **wood** on it.
Next he **tied** up his son Isaac,
  and put him on **top** of the wood on the **altar**.

Abraham experiences as he prepares to carry out this gruesome mission. The enduring spiritual value of the story derives from our need to struggle with the emotions of this man preparing to murder his own son—and with the realization that the God who made us requires that we hold nothing back. Abraham's naiveté ("Here I am!") quickly turns to anguish as God's authoritative voice surprises him with the request for a human holocaust. Don't give away the shock in God's directive by making God's voice too powerful or threatening, and pay special attention to the words "your *only* son, whom you *love*."

Abraham's response is immediate and lonely, for he clearly has not hinted to son or family the true nature of the mission he commences the very next morning. It was to be through Isaac that God's promise to make Abraham's descendents as numerous as the stars would be fulfilled. But how could that happen if Isaac is sacrificed? Abraham's faith enables him to trust God despite the contradiction inherent in the divine command. Thus, Abraham becomes another "type"—a model of all believers who put their trust in God.

A man who willingly surrenders what he holds most dear can become a model of faith for us only if you relate convincingly the human dimensions of this chilling story. The unemotional tone of the narration, as Abraham saddles donkey and takes servants, paints for us his stoic face. His controlled dialogue, in particular, with the servants and with Isaac, reveals Abraham's determination to avoid alarming his son. Isaac is confused and says so. His question about the "sheep" requires Abraham to work even harder to maintain his numb calmness. But he covers his pain well

"Here I am" has no sense of relief yet, just terror. The "Do not" commands can be spoken with calm and tender compassion. "I now know . . ." is spoken solemnly. Pause after "beloved son."
This is a new beat; the pace is faster and the mood upbeat. The "ram" is replacement for Isaac. Don't rush.

"Yahweh-yireh" (YAH-way-YEER-ay) means "The Lord will see [to it]."

In a long passage like this, variety in pacing is urgent. Though it is "God" speaking, you must not adopt a monotone or an overly slow delivery. Speak like a parent giving good news to an anxious child—both reassuring and praising.
The fulfillment of these promises is what tonight's readings and tonight's liturgy are all about.

If you've given proper emphasis and not rushed the preceding, the final line will call us all to obedience.

Then he **reached** out and took the **knife** to **slaughter** his son.
But the LORD's **messenger** called to him from **heaven**,
   "**Abraham, Abraham!**"
"**Here** I am," he answered.
"Do not lay your **hand** on the boy," said the messenger.
"Do not do the least **thing** to him.
I **know** now how **devoted** you are to **God**,
   since you did not **withhold** from me your own beloved **son**."
As Abraham looked **about**,
   he spied a **ram** caught by its horns in the **thicket**.
So he went and **took** the ram
   and offered **it** up as a holocaust in **place** of his son.
Abraham **named** the site **Yahweh-yireh**;
   hence people now say, "On the **mountain** the LORD will **see**."

Again the LORD's messenger **called** to Abraham from heaven
   and said:
"**I swear** by myself, declares the LORD,
that because you **acted** as you **did**
in not **withholding** from me your beloved **son**,
I will **bless** you **abundantly**
and make your **descendants** as **countless**
as the **stars** of the sky and the **sands** of the seashore;
your descendants shall take **possession**
of the **gates** of their **enemies**,
and in your **descendants** all the nations of the **earth**
   shall find **blessing**—
all **this** because you **obeyed** my **command**."

[Shorter: Genesis 22:1–2, 9a, 10–13, 15–18]

when he answers, ironically, that God will provide the sacrifice. While we know a ram waits in the brambles, Abraham thinks only of Isaac.
   The details that follow are shocking. Almost robotically, Abraham binds his son and places him on the altar of sacrifice. Let your tone suggest the immense (but unseen) effort it took to force his hands to prepare the altar and arrange the wood. The emotional strain increases as you describe him placing the boy "on top of the wood." When you relate how Abraham took the knife "to slaughter his son,"

remember that he believed he was really going to do it. That riveting moment should cause every heart to stop. Pause before God's voice intervenes so the fearful image can make its impact.
   "But" is like a heavenly hand reaching out and catching Abraham's wrist just in time. At first urgent and authoritative, God's voice eventually mellows into tenderness and compassion. Relate the incident with the ram quickly and with great relief, especially the comment that it was offered "in place of his son."

The closing section reveals the true meaning of this story. God does not desire the taking of human life, but the *giving* of one's whole self in the kind of unflinching obedience demonstrated by Abraham. The words of the Lord's messenger are spoken in praise. With strength and conviction, speak of the abundant and enduring blessings that will rain down not only on Abraham, but on all who imitate his example of unwavering trust.

READING III | Stories of ancestors play a significant role in the life

Don't fear the repetitions in this text and have confidence in the power of this story to move your listeners. Be eager to tell it to people eager to hear it again. Begin with the strong voice of God.

The sacred writer sees God behind all things, even Pharaoh's obstinacy.

"Pharaoh . . . army . . . chariots . . . charioteers"—this will become a much repeated refrain. Use all of the words each time it recurs.

The "column of cloud" and the "angel" are both manifestations of God's presence and protection. The action intensifies. Build suspense.

Slow your pace to suggest the passage of time over the long night. Pause after "all night long."

Speak with renewed vigor. Visualize what you describe.

READING III   Exodus 14:15—15:1

A reading from the Book of Exodus

The LORD said to Moses, "Why are you crying out to me?
Tell the Israelites to go forward.
And you, lift up your staff and, with hand outstretched
     over the sea,
     split the sea in two,
     that the Israelites may pass through it on dry land.
But I will make the Egyptians so obstinate
     that they will go in after them.
Then I will receive glory through Pharaoh and all his army,
     his chariots and charioteers.
The Egyptians shall know that I am the LORD,
     when I receive glory through Pharaoh
     and his chariots and charioteers."

The angel of God, who had been leading Israel's camp,
     now moved and went around behind them.
The column of cloud also, leaving the front,
     took up its place behind them,
     so that it came between the camp of the Egyptians
     and that of Israel.
But the cloud now became dark, and thus the night passed
     without the rival camps coming any closer together
     all night long.
Then Moses stretched out his hand over the sea,
     and the LORD swept the sea
     with a strong east wind throughout the night
     and so turned it into dry land.

of a people: they foster identity, encourage and inspire, and focus the future. This is such a story. Understanding that this is *our* story, and telling it with the zeal of an eyewitness, brings energy and variety to it. Then the patterns and repetitions take on a ritual dimension, and the telling, rather than boring or redundant, becomes a communal experience that draws everyone into the circle of remembrance.

This is the story of Israel's great deliverance, their Exodus from slavery to freedom led, not just by Moses, but by God who intervenes on behalf of the people and becomes their strong right arm, their protector and their shield. All the details in the story are subordinate to that fact. It is God who leads and shows the way, God who has ordained the safety and deliverance of Israel.

Reluctantly, Pharaoh had acceded to Moses' demand to release the Israelites. But soon afterward, Pharaoh regretted his decision and assembled a vast army to bring them back. Suddenly endangered, the Israelites panic and blame Moses for risking their lives and their futures. As Moses attempts to silence their tongues and their fears, the Lord intervenes, ordering him to act decisively and be the leader he was called to be. God makes it clear he will intervene on their behalf, but it is in order to "receive glory through Pharaoh and his army." Israel's deliverance will be a sign of God's sovereign power. The author of Exodus sees the divine hand even in Pharaoh's obstinance; all things work together to achieve the divine plan; all things point to God as creator and sustainer of the chosen people.

Each year we proclaim this text because the events narrated here not only

Convey the wonder of this marvelous sight.

When the **water** was thus **divided**,
   the **Israelites** marched into the **midst** of the sea on **dry** land,
    with the water like a **wall** to their **right** and to their **left**.

The Egyptians **followed** in **pursuit**;
   all Pharaoh's **horses** and **chariots** and **charioteers**
     went after them
   right into the **midst** of the sea.

Quicken your pace here. As narrator, shake your head (figuratively) at the foolishness of the Egyptian's tactics.

In the **night** watch just before **dawn**
   the LORD **cast** through the column of the fiery cloud
   upon the Egyptian force a **glance** that threw it into a **panic**;
   and he so **clogged** their chariot wheels
   that they could hardly **drive**.

Aware that it was *God* who saved, speak slowly and quietly.

With **that** the Egyptians sounded the **retreat** before Israel,
   because the LORD was fighting for them **against** the Egyptians.

Then the LORD told **Moses**, "**Stretch** out your hand over the **sea**,
   that the water may flow **back** upon the Egyptians,
   upon their **chariots** and their **charioteers**."

God's justice is uncompromising. Don't hold back in narrating the awful consequences for the Egyptians. "Dawn" is the moment of liberation.

So Moses **stretched** out his hand over the **sea**,
   and at **dawn** the sea flowed **back** to its normal **depth**.
The Egyptians were **fleeing** head **on** toward the sea,
   when the LORD **hurled** them into its midst.
As the water flowed **back**,

Narrate these lines without any hint of vindictiveness.

   it **covered** the **chariots** and the **charioteers**
     of Pharaoh's whole **army**
   which had **followed** the Israelites into the **sea**.
Not a single **one** of them escaped.
But the **Israelites** had marched on dry **land**

Your voice fills with gratitude, relief, and not a little pride.

   through the **midst** of the sea,
    with the water like a **wall** to their **right** and to their **left**.
Thus the LORD **saved** Israel on that day
   from the **power** of the **Egyptians**.

---

bring salvation to Israel, they foreshadow our own deliverance in Christ's Passover from death to life, and symbolize our salvation in the waters of Baptism. The more convincingly you relate these events, the better this text can speak of our own movement from slavery to freedom.

    Through "angel" and "cloud," both manifestations of God's presence, the Lord leads the people. But at night, when the shining cloud's light would have benefited the Egyptians, it becomes "dark," preventing the Egyptians from advancing on Israel. After this strategic activity comes darkness and waiting "all night long." Suddenly,

Moses takes action. Note the strong rhythm of the lines that describe wind and sea and the recurring "s" sounds that suggest both driving wind and raging storm. The force of the wind splits the sea. With utter conviction and a hint of vindication, marvel at the walls of water through which the people march on "*dry* land."

    Egypt follows in vain. Your tone betrays the futility of their action as you narrate how the Egyptians lose their heads and their lives by foolishly pursuing "right into the midst of the sea." Begin speaking of the "night watch" in hushed tones, but

quickly build volume and intensity as the Egyptians "panic" and sound "the retreat."

    We might wonder at the severity of the destruction visited upon Pharaoh's army. But scripture never shies from relating actions with consequences. Here, Pharaoh's obstinacy seals the fate of his army. Soberly, but without rancor or vindictiveness, speak of their total destruction. Divine justice is uncompromising: "Not a single" Egyptian escapes. No gloating, but no apologies either. The story doesn't dwell on Egypt's destruction but quickly reiterates the wonder of Israel's

God's power inspires a reverential fear among the Israelites. Speak in hushed tones.

The joy of this song must ring in your voice and show on your face.

When Israel **saw** the Egyptians lying **dead** on the **seashore**
and beheld the great **power** that the LORD
had shown **against** the Egyptians,
they **feared** the LORD and **believed** in him
and in his **servant Moses**.

Then **Moses** and the **Israelites** sang this **song** to the LORD:
I will **sing** to the LORD, for he is **gloriously triumphant**;
horse and **chariot** he has **cast** into the **sea**.

READING IV   Isaiah 54:5–14

"Husband" and "Maker" are meant to express tenderness and compassion. Persuade us that God can love us this much. The sense of the sentence is that the one who is now your husband is God, your Creator.

Speak the line "like a wife forsaken . . ." briskly, and increase the intensity of "a wife married . . . ."

Contrast the *regret* of "For a brief moment . . ." with the *joy* of "but with great tenderness." The four lines that follow restate the same idea. Maintain the energy and conviction throughout.

"Redeemer" is a joyful title suggesting compassion, not authority.

A reading from the Book of the Prophet Isaiah

The One who has become your **husband** is your **Maker**;
his name is the LORD of **hosts**;
your **redeemer** is the **Holy** One of **Israel**,
called **God** of all the **earth**.
The LORD calls you **back**,
like a wife **forsaken** and grieved in **spirit**,
a wife married in **youth** and then cast **off**,
says your God.
For a brief **moment** I **abandoned** you,
but with great **tenderness** I will take you **back**.
In an outburst of **wrath**, for a **moment**
I **hid** my **face** from you;
but with enduring **love** I take **pity** on you,
says the LORD, your **redeemer**.

rescue through the miraculous corridor of water. In amazement, tell again how God led them to safety "on dry land." Then, with gratitude, announce God's favors and wonders! Finally, with reverent awe tell how the people "feared" "and believed." Hushed awe suddenly turns to jubilant song. Let the joyous gratitude of those who sang become your joy, too, as you invite *all* to delight in God's saving power.

READING IV   This text is a *mood* reading whose imagery and tone express, in very human terms, the depths and dimensions of God's love for his people. With dramatic metaphors, Isaiah announces Israel's deliverance from slavery and exile, and her restoration in the promised land. The humiliation of the past is over, a new day dawns bringing promise of peace and prosperity. Isaiah's poetry describes what God has in store for the chosen people when they return to Jerusalem, which, though languishing in decay and desolation, soon will be restored to its former glory.

Although some scripture conveys God's transcendence and distance from us, other passages, like this one, ascribe very human ways to God. Here Isaiah portrays God as a husband, not a newlywed in the thrall of first love, but a middle-aged lover old enough to know betrayal, yet young enough to forgive and love with renewed passion. In this reading, God is the husband and Israel is the estranged wife. Speaking in the first person, God addresses Israel, talking of temporary anger, unconditional forgiveness, and tender love. Let your tone match the sincerity of Isaiah's poetry. Such effusive language can't be delivered without feeling. Persuade us that

The exile is compared to Noah's flood. God is saying, "As I swore then, so I swear now never to punish you again."

These words represent the excess of divine love. Don't hold back here.

Here, God speaks directly to Jerusalem. Speak lovingly, as if embracing one with whom you are reconciling.
carnelians = kahr-NEEL-yuhnz

Carnelians are reddish quartz and carbuncles are smooth, round deep red garnets.

God is making a promise. Speak with reassuring strength and conviction. Make sure it's clear when you finish this line that you've concluded the reading.

This is for me like the days of **Noah**,
   when I **swore** that the **waters** of Noah
   should never **again deluge** the earth;
so I have sworn not to be **angry** with you,
   or to **rebuke** you.
Though the **mountains** leave their **place**
   and the **hills** be **shaken**,
my **love** shall never **leave** you
   nor my covenant of **peace** be **shaken**,
   says the LORD, who has **mercy** on you.
O **afflicted** one, **storm-battered** and **unconsoled**,
   I lay your **pavements** in **carnelians**,
   and your **foundations** in **sapphires**;
I will make your **battlements** of **rubies**,
   your gates of **carbuncles**,
   and all your **walls** of precious **stones**.
All your **children** shall be taught by the LORD,
   and **great** shall be the **peace** of your children.
In **justice** shall you be **established**,
   far from the fear of **oppression**,
   where **destruction** cannot come **near** you.

READING V   Isaiah 55:1–11

A reading from the Book of the Prophet Isaiah

Thus says the LORD:
All you who are **thirsty**,
   come to the **water**!

Despite the imperatives, the tone is magnanimous—like inviting hungry, homeless children to a feast.

God loves us, longs for us, like a husband loves a wife; that God can forgive like some rare and special spouses forgive their partner's infidelity. If your listeners don't hear that, they won't have heard this reading. The various emotions are all here. First there is the initial anger: "For a brief moment I abandoned you . . . ," then a forgiveness that's arresting: "but with tenderness I will take you back." Ironically, expressing such great love requires controlled delivery; don't exaggerate, but be sure your listeners catch the depth of feeling expressed here.

In an earlier age, God was severe with humanity. The story of Noah recalls both God's uncompromising justice and God's deep mercy. After the devastating flood, God promised never again to destroy the earth. Now, says the Lord, I will never again be angry with you or reject you. That's a promise you must speak with such conviction that all who hear will know even their own infidelity won't nullify it.

In the final section of the text, God speaks directly to the city of Jerusalem. The words are tender and consoling, ("O afflicted . . .") assuring Jerusalem that

she will be restored to her original grandeur. Deliver the lines as if to a person who needs reassurance that they are truly pardoned. God promises to restore the people like a worker rebuilds a fallen city, but using sapphires and rubies instead of bricks. The needs of her children will be satisfied and all their fears relieved.

This Easter liturgy invites us to see in Israel's return from exile and slavery every Christian's deliverance from the bondage of sin through Christ's death and Resurrection. All tonight's texts speak of hope, renewal, and salvation. As you proclaim, convey the passion that characterizes a God who

Ignore the comma after the word "come."

Ask the questions sincerely, as if expecting an answer.

To be nourished, it is necessary to *heed* and *listen* to the Lord. Speak those words not as commands but as calls to conversion. "That you may have life" is the heart of God's promise. Speak more slowly here.

"Him" refers to David. The nation will be restored.

Renew your energy here. Imagine those you are trying to persuade getting up to leave. Your words must stop and hold them.

This is not a condemnation, but an earnest call for conversion.

This section explains why God can be so "generous in forgiving": God's plans are not our plans; God's methods not our methods. Speak slowly, with great dignity.

You who have no **money**,
    come, receive **grain** and **eat**;
come, without **paying** and without **cost**,
    drink **wine** and **milk**!
Why spend your **money** for what is not **bread**,
    your **wages** for what **fails** to **satisfy**?
Heed me, and you shall eat **well**,
    you shall **delight** in rich fare.
Come to me **heedfully**,
    listen, that you may have **life**.
I will **renew** with you the everlasting **covenant**,
    the **benefits** assured to **David**.
As I made him a **witness** to the peoples,
    a **leader** and commander of **nations**,
so shall you **summon** a nation you knew **not**,
    and nations that knew you not shall **run** to you,
because of the LORD, your **God**,
    the **Holy** One of Israel, who has **glorified** you.

Seek the LORD while he may be **found**,
    call him while he is **near**.
Let the **scoundrel** forsake his **way**,
    and the **wicked** man his **thoughts**;
let him turn to the LORD for **mercy**;
    to our **God**, who is **generous** in **forgiving**.
For **my** thoughts are not **your** thoughts,
    nor are **your** ways **my** ways, says the LORD.
As high as the **heavens** are above the **earth**,
    so high are **my** ways above **your** ways
    and **my** thoughts above **your** thoughts.

offers precious stones as signs of solid and enduring divine love.

READING V   We are born hungry, physically and spiritually. Saint Augustine confessed to God, "My soul will not be at rest until it rests in you." More recently, a song proclaimed, "Everybody's got a hungry heart." Much of our lives is spent seeking food that does not satisfy, settling for drink that numbs the senses but does not calm the soul. Through the prophet Isaiah, God reminds us that the richest, most nourishing food, the drink that delights, are found only at one table.

God addresses us directly in this passage: "All you who are thirsty, come! . . . delight in rich fare!" Imagine God as host, wearing an apron, inviting those who have spent "wages" (and their lives) on "what fails to satisfy."

Isaiah wrote as the time of the Exile was drawing to an end. He announces God's promise of new life with all the "benefits assured to David." God made a covenant with David, which even the infidelity that brought exile upon the people could not nullify. The covenant will be renewed and the nation restored, says the Lord. But the people must repent, their hearts must be new minted, their faithless ways left behind in the land of exile. God is urgent and insistent, pleading with the people to forsake their wrongdoing. God's words are persuasive and full of urgency: Do it now, God says, before it's too late! No one is unworthy; no one will be turned away. God's mercy will embrace even the "scoundrel" and the "wicked"; for our God is "generous in forgiving," whose

This is an important teaching about the word of God: it accomplishes what it sets out to do! Go slowly. This is a long comparison. Just as rain and snow don't evaporate and return to the sky till after they have watered the earth, helping seed to grow and yielding bread for the hungry, the word that goes forth from my mouth does not return without having accomplished the purpose for which it was sent. Speak with conviction and authority.

For just as from the **heavens**
    the **rain** and **snow** come down
and do not **return** there
    till they have **watered** the earth,
    making it **fertile** and **fruitful**,
giving **seed** to the one who **sows**
    and **bread** to the one who **eats**,
so shall my **word** be
    that goes **forth** from my **mouth**;
my word shall not **return** to me **void**,
    but shall do my **will**,
    achieving the end for which I **sent** it.

READING VI Baruch 3:9–15, 32—4:4

Baruch = buh-ROOK

This is exhortation motivated by love.

The five lines following "How is it . . . ?" ask the question "Do you know why?" The answer comes in the sixth line.

Here is the answer. "I'll *tell* you why!" should be the tone of your proclamation, but love is still the motive.

A reading from the Book of the Prophet Baruch

Hear, O Israel, the **commandments** of **life**:
    listen, and know **prudence**!
How **is** it, Israel,
    that you are in the **land** of your **foes**,
    grown **old** in a **foreign** land,
defiled with the **dead**,
    accounted with those **destined** for the **netherworld**?
You have **forsaken** the fountain of **wisdom**!
    Had you **walked** in the way of **God**,
    you would have **dwelt** in enduring **peace**.

"thoughts" and "ways" are as different from ours as the earth is from the heavens.

    This final section calls us to take on the heart of a child, for as long as children remain innocent and open, a parent's word is reality. God calls for that childlike trust: The word that goes forth from my mouth will not return void. Embracing that notion involves trust, a leap into the darkness convinced that a net of mercy waits below. God's words actualize what they express. God says it and it is! (Remember tonight's First Reading?) God urges us to hear these offers of life and renewal not as things

hoped for but as things assured. So speak confidently, trusting the truth of what you say. In tonight's liturgy, as in every liturgy, God's promise of rich fare is fulfilled beyond all expectation at the table of the Eucharist.

READING VI Before Baruch speaks of wisdom, he mentions the "commandments." That link is integral to the argument of this entire text. Couched in gorgeous poetry, Baruch makes a simple point: wisdom is found by embracing the law of the Lord. Forsaking the law plunges

one into darkness and death. By abandoning God's law, Israel has incurred the penalty of exile in Babylon, "the land of [her] foes." The path back to grace is wisdom herself. Wisdom is personified as a woman, but more significantly, wisdom is identified with the law, "the book of the precepts of God," that is, the commandments given by God as a gift.

    In scripture, law is not a burden, but a benefit; following the law pleases God, but also saves us from (self) destruction. Israel repeatedly forgot this bedrock conviction, and her disregard of the law imperiled

Here you announce the better way: follow it and find peace! You are cajoling, exhorting, wanting to spur a change in behavior. There is a lilting cadence in these lines. Don't rush them. "Days" and "peace" can be sustained.

A dramatic shift in mood occurs here. This is a poetic song of praise to Wisdom.

"The One" refers to the omnipotent God. You are retelling the story of Creation. Utilize a faster, joyous tempo.

"Dismisses light" is an order for the sun to go down. "Calls it" refers to the sunrise. Maintain high energy here.

Let your voice ring with joy at God's goodness on "Such is our God!".

A new beat begins here; speak in a more sober tone. In the phrase "Given her . . ." "her" refers to understanding and knowledge. "Jacob" and "Israel" represent the whole people.

"She has appeared on earth" refers to wisdom, now personified as the book of the precepts, the law.

Contrast those who "live" and those who "die." Pause before the next line.

Imagine yourself saying, "Oh, my dear child, turn and receive."

Learn where **prudence** is,
    where **strength**, where **understanding**;
that you may know **also**
    where are length of **days**, and **life**,
    where light of the **eyes**, and **peace**.
Who has **found** the place of **wisdom**,
    who has **entered** into her **treasuries**?

The One who knows all **things** knows **her**;
    he has **probed** her by his **knowledge**—
the One who established the **earth** for all **time**,
    and **filled** it with four-footed **beasts**;
he who **dismisses** the light, and it **departs**,
    calls it, and it **obeys** him **trembling**;
before whom the **stars** at their posts
    shine and **rejoice**;
when he **calls** them, they answer, "Here we **are**!"
    shining with **joy** for their **Maker**.
Such is our **God**;
    no **other** is to be **compared** to him:
he has traced out the whole way of **understanding**,
    and has given her to **Jacob**, his **servant**,
    to **Israel**, his beloved **son**.

Since then she has **appeared** on earth,
    and **moved** among people.
She is the **book** of the **precepts** of **God**,
    the **law** that endures **forever**;
all who **cling** to her will **live**,
    but those will **die** who **forsake** her.
Turn, O Jacob, and **receive** her:
    walk by her **light** toward **splendor**.

temple, monarchy, and nation. Baruch's poetry, filled with rich imagery and intentional repetition, implores Israel to return to the Lord by taking up the book of the law and storing it, not on a shelf, but in their hearts. Christian faith has always seen Jesus as the embodiment of wisdom, the true teacher of what pleases God. He, too, pointed to the commandments as the path to life and discipleship. Baruch's powerful words are less reprimand and much reflections of God's love.

Good parents also point out the advantages of right behavior. They give

hope that one can change, that help is always available. Baruch has the instincts of a good parent. He follows his exhortation to "Learn," with a song of praise to the God who is our only hope of finding the wisdom we need.

The questions "Who has found?" and "Who has entered?" are really declarations that God is the answer to all our questions. It is God who has found wisdom. Ask the questions with an energy that signals you can't wait to answer them yourself. With joy and a quickened tempo describe this God who "established the

earth" and "filled it," whom the sun and the stars obey gladly. The luminous stars model the character of your proclamation: "shining with joy for [your] maker."

The final section focuses on the personification of wisdom as the book of the law that has been given to Jacob (the Hebrew people) and still is present on the earth. Plead, as he does, that we "receive her (and) walk by her light." By teaching us what pleases God, the law gives us reason to rejoice and to pronounce ourselves "Blessed."

"Glory" refers to the law, while "privileges" refer to knowing and observing the law. You are saying, "Don't throw away the riches you've been given." End on a note of joy and gratitude.

Give not your **glory** to **another**,
   your **privileges** to an **alien** race.
Blessed are we, O Israel;
   for what **pleases** God is **known** to us!

READING VII   Ezekiel 36:16–17a, 18–28

A reading from the Book of the Prophet Ezekiel

The **word** of the LORD came to me, saying:
   Son of **man**, when the house of **Israel** lived in their **land**,
      they **defiled** it by their **conduct** and **deeds**.
Therefore I poured out my **fury** upon them
   because of the **blood** that they poured out on the **ground**,
      and because they **defiled** it with **idols**.
I **scattered** them among the **nations**,
   dispersing them over **foreign** lands;
      according to their **conduct** and **deeds** I judged them.
But when they came among the nations **wherever** they came,
   they served to **profane** my holy name,
      because it was said of them: "**These** are the people of the LORD,
   yet they had to **leave** their **land**."
So I have **relented** because of my holy **name**
   which the house of Israel **profaned**
      among the **nations** where they **came**.
Therefore **say** to the house of Israel:
Thus says the Lord **GOD**:
   Not for **your** sakes do I act, house of Israel,
      but for the sake of my holy **name**,
   which you **profaned** among the nations to which you **came**.

"Their land" is Israel. Ezekiel's tone is blunt. Don't dilute the anger. "Fury," "scattered," "dispersing," "judged," and "profane" are strong words that convey God's wrath. Let them work.

"Because of the blood . . ." refers to idol worship.

The Exile is God's punishment for Israel's infidelity.

But the punishment "backfired" because it gave God a bad name.

Speak this taunt in the voice of the foreigners.

Pause at the start of this new beat. Frustrated, God reluctantly adopts a new approach. Note that "profaned among the nations" is repeated three times.

God must restore his "good name."

READING VII Once again, the biblical writer gives God human qualities we don't normally associate with the Lord. For their idolatrous ways, for the blood they sacrificed to idols, Israel was punished—dispersed to foreign lands. But that just punishment is casting God in a negative light. The foreigners among whom Israel was dispersed are questioning God's fidelity to the covenant. "These are the people of the Lord," they taunt, "yet they had to leave their land." Such talk is an embarrassment. The foreign nations interpret the punishment as rejection;

worse, as God's abandonment of the covenant with Israel. They don't recognize this as the action of a loving parent correcting errant behavior. So God decides, for the sake "of my holy name," to relent and start anew with these stubborn children.

Eventually, this reading gets to a place of tender love. But on the way, we hear a divine voice that's full of righteous anger. Save for the first line, it is God who speaks throughout the reading. But here, God's voice contrasts with the voice we heard in the Fifth Reading, where he beckoned anxiously and tenderly. This night's readings

comprise a mosaic of which this text is an important piece. It presents a God capable of righteous anger over the nation's infidelity. Find the words—"Fury," "scattered," "dispersing," "judged," "profane"—that convey that wrath.

Halfway through the text, God orders the prophet to announce a shift in policy. "I have relented," God says. But we sense ambivalence. Three times God says the holy name was "profaned among the nations." The repetitions suggest frustration and reluctance to show mercy. Therefore, God says, "Not for *your* sakes" will I act, but to

God's anger slowly yields to mercy and love. Speak these lines as a promise.

The tone becomes more reassuring and loving here.

God will purify the people. This is an important image of Baptism for tonight's liturgy.

Make eye contact here. This is a classic and memorable line. Speak slowly and sincerely.

Imagine saying this to a child whom you love in order to ensure the child's success and prosperity. "You shall be my people, and I will be your God" should be proclaimed like a spouse vowing fidelity.

I will prove the **holiness** of my great name,
    profaned among the **nations**,
      in whose **midst** you have profaned it.
Thus the nations shall **know** that I am the LORD,
    says the Lord **GOD**,
      when in their sight I prove my **holiness** through **you**.
For I will take you **away** from among the nations,
    gather you from all the foreign **lands**,
      and bring you **back** to your **own** land.
I will sprinkle **clean water** upon you
    to **cleanse** you from all your **impurities**,
      and from all your **idols** I will cleanse you.
I will give you a **new** heart and place a new **spirit** within you,
    taking from your bodies your **stony** hearts
      and giving you **natural** hearts.
I will put my **spirit** within you and make you live by my **statutes**,
    careful to observe my **decrees**.
You shall **live** in the land I gave your **fathers**;
    you shall be my **people**, and **I** will be your **God**.

restore my reputation. I will correct the incorrect impression that I failed to be Israel's God and protector.

But soon we sense that God's mercy and love will trump the call of justice. God promises to purify the people and give them new hearts made of flesh, not stone. Mercy triumphs, after all. We knew it would. By the time we hear the tender "you will be my people and I will be your God" we know God has not only saved his "name," but his people, who now will be empowered to keep God's statutes back home "in the land [of their] fathers."

EPISTLE In this foundational text, Paul establishes our identity: we are those who in Baptism have died with Christ and who now live in the "newness of life" that his Resurrection makes possible. Those who will be baptized at the Vigil have been made keenly aware of the transformation the waters of Baptism will effect in their lives. But Paul's words also speak to each of us who come this night to renew our baptismal promises. Baptism is a once in a lifetime initiation' but transformation into the likeness of Christ takes a lifetime. So Paul

asks, "Are you not aware . . . ?" that the death of Baptism initiated you into a new life in Christ? Your old self died and was buried with Christ. That's good news, because the Resurrection follows for us as it did for Christ. But there's also a difference: while our risen life has been *initiated* here on earth, it won't be *fully* realized till after death. In the meantime, we continue to struggle with sin and all its consequences. However, Paul reminds us that we no longer need to be slaves to sin. Today, most of all, we claim the freedom

EPISTLE   Romans 6:3–11

A reading from the Letter of Saint Paul to the Romans

Brothers and sisters:
Are you **unaware** that we who were **baptized** into Christ **Jesus**
    were baptized into his **death**?
We were indeed **buried** with him through baptism into **death**,
    so that, just as Christ was **raised** from the dead
    by the glory of the **Father**,
    we **too** might live in **newness** of **life**.

For if we have grown into **union** with him through a **death**
    like his,
    we shall also be **united** with him in the **resurrection**.
We know that our **old** self was **crucified** with him,
    so that our **sinful** body might be done **away** with,
    that we might no longer be in **slavery** to sin.
For a **dead** person has been **absolved** from sin.
If, then, we have **died** with Christ,
    we believe that we shall also **live** with him.
We know that **Christ**, **raised** from the dead, dies no **more**;
    death no longer has **power** over him.
As to his **death**, he died to sin **once** and for **all**;
    as to his **life**, he lives for **God**.
Consequently, you **too** must think of yourselves
    as being **dead** to **sin**
    and **living** for **God** in Christ **Jesus**.

Paul's literary device is a rhetorical question. Let it sound like a question. Make eye contact with the assembly and speak as directly as Paul writes.

Work to make Paul's point explicit. What happened to Christ will happen to us. He died and was buried, then rose. We die and are buried in Baptism, and we, too, will rise to new life.

Paul develops his idea here. We were made one with Christ by sharing a death like his (Baptism); so we also will be made one with him by experiencing Resurrection. Speak "We know" with conviction and good eye contact.

Don't let this sound redundant. Sustain your energy. Remember: "Died" and "live" are both spoken with a positive attitude.

"We know" means we are convinced!

"Dies no more . . . death no longer has power" is the same idea stated twice. The greater stress goes to the second statement.

Balance the words "his death" and "his life."

Make eye contact with the assembly here. We are *dead* to sin, but *alive* in Christ! Announce this joyfully!

(and absolution) into which we were initiated by dying with Christ in Baptism!

Elsewhere, you might contrast the words "death" and "buried" with "raised" and "new life," but not here. Here death and burial don't carry a negative connotation. Paul's point is that death is the *way* to life. Keep your tone hopeful and upbeat as you share Paul's series of balanced ideas: "If we have grown into union with him through a *death* like his, we shall also be united with him in the *resurrection*."

Joyously, Paul announces what "we *know*": that freedom and life are now available to all who believe. Paul's sentences are strong and declarative, presenting several important ideas in quick succession. Christ "dies no more," "Death has no more power over him," "His death was once for all," "he lives for God"!

In the last line, Paul combines instruction and exhortation. Use his words to express your own faith and your gratitude for the new life you've received in Christ. Today, we celebrate Resurrection. The impossible is now woven into the very fabric of our lives!

GOSPEL All of tonight's readings, and the centuries of history they represent, lead to this silent Sunday morning when the early light of dawn shone into an empty tomb. The God of surprises, who parted seas and stopped a dagger's plunge, has saved the best surprise for last: a dead man walks among the living.

Three tired, frightened women, whose names you speak as reverently as you would those of beloved ancestors, are making a sad journey. Mark spends much time setting the scene, and the mood of

A sad and sober mood hangs over the opening of this reading.

Magdalene = MAG-duh-luhn

Mark is precise about the timing of these events.

The task of moving the stone would be impossible for these women.

Mark's emphasis on the size of the stone means the announcement of it being moved should be done with amazement.

They likely would have entered the tomb cautiously; then they are met with the surprise of the "young man."

That the young man needs to tell them not to be "amazed" reveals the depth of the women's reaction.

The young man speaks of "the place" with great reverence.

Note that Peter is singled out from among the disciples. Speak the instruction to "tell" them with joy.

GOSPEL   Mark 16:1–7

A reading from the holy Gospel according to Mark

When the **sabbath** was over,
 Mary **Magdalene**, Mary, the mother of **James**, and **Salome**
 bought **spices** so that they might go and **anoint** him.
Very **early** when the **sun** had risen,
 on the **first** day of the week, they came to the **tomb**.
They were **saying** to one another,
 "Who will roll back the **stone** for us
 from the entrance to the **tomb**?"
When they looked **up**,
 they saw that the stone **had** been rolled back;
 it was very **large**.
On **entering** the tomb they saw a young **man**
 sitting on the right **side**, clothed in a white **robe**,
 and they were utterly **amazed**.
He **said** to them, "Do **not** be **amazed**!
You seek **Jesus** of **Nazareth**, the **crucified**.
He has been **raised**; he is not **here**.
Behold the **place** where they **laid** him.
But **go** and tell his **disciples** and Peter,
 'He is going **before** you to **Galilee**;
 there you will **see** him, as he **told** you.'"

heaviness that surrounds it. The women are loaded down with "spices" and with their heavy hearts. The hour is early, barely light, and fears and sorrow can loom largest in that twilight. They ponder the heaviness of the stone (Mark tells us the stone was very large) and wonder who, if anyone, can roll it back for them. And then without fanfare, they look and see the stone has *already* been rolled back. The women quickly enter and find the "young man." Your tone suggests their sense of alarm. First he exclaims, "Do not be amazed!" and then immediately begins to

soothe with his knowledge of whom they "seek" and why he's not there. For final assurance he points to "the place they laid him," a place the women would consider sacred, for which he shows great respect.

The young man's second task is to commission the women for a ministry of evangelization: "But go and tell . . . ." The young man gives the message the insistent tone and emphasis he hopes the women will use when they relay it to the disciples.

But the young man, it seems, got poor marks for persuasion. The greatest event in human history and the women go off and

say "nothing to anyone"! Scholars tell us Mark's Gospel account originally ended with those words. And perhaps his is the truest rendering; how many of us, given the shock of Easter morning, could understand so quickly and be ready to sing Alleluia? But maybe Mark's is also the most provocative ending. For us believers who already know the song of Resurrection, this stark ending challenges us to imagine the emptiness, shock, and confusion, to ponder the event anew—so as to sing the Alleluia more truly.

EASTER SUNDAY

Lectionary #42

READING I Acts 10:34a, 37–43

A reading from the Acts of the Apostles

Peter proceeded to **speak** and said:
"You know what has **happened** all over **Judea**,
    beginning in **Galilee** after the **baptism**
    that **John** preached,
    how God **anointed** Jesus of **Nazareth**
    with the Holy **Spirit** and **power**.
He went about doing **good**
    and **healing** all those oppressed by the **devil**,
    for **God** was with him.
We are **witnesses** of all that he did
    both in the country of the **Jews** and in **Jerusalem**.
They put him to **death** by hanging him on a **tree**.
This man God **raised** on the **third** day and granted
    that he be **visible**,
    not to **all** the people, but to **us**,
    the witnesses **chosen** by God in **advance**,
    who **ate** and **drank** with him **after** he rose from the dead.
He **commissioned** us to **preach** to the people
    and **testify** that **he** is the one appointed by God
    as **judge** of the **living** and the **dead**.
To him all the **prophets** bear witness,
    that everyone who **believes** in him
    will receive **forgiveness** of **sins** through his **name**."

Except for first six words, the entire reading is spoken in the confident voice of Peter. Remember, Peter is making a public address.

"Spirit" and "power" are important characteristics of Jesus' ministry.

Jesus' healing ministry and his exorcisms are important signs of who he is. Don't rush any of this first paragraph.

Make eye contact with the assembly as you say, "We are witnesses." Peter is saying, "I was there!" There is a personal, intimate quality to the entire text.

Mention of Jesus' Crucifixion is followed immediately by the announcement of his Resurrection. Pause after "tree" and again after "This man." The rest of the paragraph is more upbeat.

Speak "the witnesses chosen by God" with confidence, not pride. This emphasizes Peter's credibility.

Continue with an energetic, earnest tone. "Preach" and "testify" will seem redundant unless you build energy from one to the other.

READING I Impetuous, fumbling, foot-in-the-mouth Peter seems as transformed by the Resurrection as Jesus. Addressing the household of the new convert, Cornelius, Peter speaks with uncharacteristic self-confidence and understanding. His conviction springs from having lived what he describes. All the potential that Jesus saw in Peter has been realized and quickened by the Holy Spirit.

Although he is presenting a basic catechism of early Christian faith, Peter assumes that his hearers are acquainted with Jesus. You can do the same, letting your voice gradually build in intensity as you speak of how he was "anointed" and "went about doing good" and "healing" the oppressed. Peter cites Jesus' baptism through which God "anointed" him with the "Holy Spirit and power." And with his own eyes, Peter witnessed Jesus' self-giving and the healing it produced.

"We are witnesses" is a powerful proclamation both of Peter's authority and of the reliability of what he teaches. He was there; he heard it. This was no small point. It mattered then and it matters now, so give this adequate stress.

Then Peter directly addresses the scandal of the cross. Because he and the apostles were also witnesses to the Resurrection, he can speak of Christ's death without apology. By virtue of that intimacy, not for their eloquence or learning, the apostles were "commissioned" to preach the Gospel. They are grateful, not arrogant. Though part of Peter's message concerns Jesus as judge of the "living and the dead," Peter concludes joyfully by

READING II   Colossians 3:1–4

A reading from the Letter of Saint Paul to the Colossians

Brothers and sisters:
If then you were **raised** with Christ, seek what is **above**,
  where Christ is **seated** at the right hand of **God**.
Think of what is **above**, not of what is on **earth**.
For you have **died**, and your life is **hidden** with Christ in **God**.
When Christ your life **appears**,
  then you **too** will appear with him in **glory**.

Or:

READING II   1 Corinthians 5:6b–8

A reading from the first Letter of Saint Paul to the Corinthians

Brothers and sisters:
Do you not **know** that a little **yeast** leavens **all** the dough?
Clear out the **old** yeast,
  so that you may become a **fresh** batch of dough,
  inasmuch as you are **unleavened**.
For our paschal **lamb**, **Christ**, has been **sacrificed**.
Therefore, let us **celebrate** the feast,
  not with the **old** yeast, the yeast of **malice** and **wickedness**,
  but with the **unleavened** bread of **sincerity** and **truth**.

Colossians = kuh-LOSH-uhnz
This short text requires slow reading.
You will need to concentrate in order to
exhort and convey Paul's enthusiasm,
and still read slowly.

If then you were raised . . ." means
"because you were raised up . . . ."

Paul's tone is firm, but encouraging.

"Appears" refers to the Second Coming.
Speak of it with enthusiasm, for then his
glory will be our glory!

Colossians = kuh-LOSH-uhnz
A short text always requires a slower
reading.

Listeners are expected to know the
answer to Paul's rhetorical question.

You will become a batch of
"unleavened"—that is,
uncorrupted—dough.

Your energy rises on the second "yeast"
clause. Employ *ritardando* (gradually
slowing toward the end) on the words
"of sincerity and truth."

naming Christ as the fulfillment of prophecy, the one through whom forgiveness is offered to "everyone who believes in him!"

READING II COLOSSIANS. Paul is exhorting the Colossians to act as Christians by choosing "what is above" rather than the transitory things of this world. This is a natural result, Paul says, of having been "raised with Christ." Using an if/then construct, Paul links the

two: if you have been raised with him, then you must set your heart on higher realms.

This Easter solemnity reminds us that we who have risen with Christ must live, as best we can, the new life we have been given. In that new life, spiritual realities take precedence over material concerns. Faith requires choices, a *response* to God's generous initiative. For though we have begun to taste the risen life of the kingdom, our experience will remain partial until "Christ [our] life appears." As we

await that fullness, we remain "hidden with Christ." While we wait, according to Paul, our choice is obvious: we make spiritual rather than material things the focus of our lives. Then, when Christ appears (or reappears in the Second Coming) we shall "appear" (or rise) with him in glory, because we have chosen the things above instead of those of earth.

GOSPEL   John 20:1–9

A reading from the holy Gospel according to John

On the **first** day of the **week**,
Mary of **Magdala** came to the **tomb** early in the **morning**,
while it was still **dark**,
and saw the **stone removed** from the tomb.
So she **ran** and went to Simon **Peter**
and to the **other** disciple whom Jesus **loved**, and told them,
"They have taken the **Lord** from the **tomb**,
and we don't know **where** they **put** him."
So **Peter** and the **other** disciple went **out** and came to the **tomb**.
They both **ran**, but the **other** disciple ran **faster** than Peter
and arrived at the tomb **first**;
he **bent** down and saw the **burial** cloths there,
    but did not go **in**.
When Simon **Peter** arrived **after** him,
he went **into** the tomb and saw the **burial** cloths there,
and the cloth that had covered his **head**,
not with the **burial** cloths but rolled up in a **separate** place.
Then the **other** disciple **also** went in,
the one who had arrived at the tomb **first**,
and he **saw** and **believed**.
For they did not yet **understand** the Scripture
that he had to **rise** from the **dead**.

[The Gospel from the Easter Vigil (Mark 16:1–7, p. 152) may be read in place of this Gospel at any time of the day.]

The images are still of death and darkness. Speak of Mary in a way that conveys the mood with which she approached the tomb: weary and greatly saddened.
Magdala = MAG-duh-luh

Proclaim slowly here; the mood is a bit melancholy.

Communicate Mary's obvious distress both as you narrate her seeking out Peter and in her dialogue.

Once again, let your narration convey their frantic and impulsive response; but let Peter and John do the racing, not you.

Peter's arrival brings action back into the scene. He enters, sees, and examines. John's entry into the tomb reintroduces mystery and awe.
"He saw and believed" is John's climactic statement of faith. Pause before speaking, giving John a chance to be touched by the reality of the Resurrection.

1 CORINTHIANS. Paul employs both eucharistic imagery and Passover imagery here to make his point about the moral life. A Jewish custom required every crumb of leavened (yeasted) bread to be swept from the house before Passover to ensure that no trace of the old could corrupt the new. Yeast causes fermentation. For Paul, yeast becomes a symbol of the subtle and menacing spread of "malice and wickedness" within the human heart, and even within the Christian community. (Among the Christians at Corinth, in fact, an individual was spreading doctrinal error.)

Paul urges his readers to exercise the same vigilance in their moral lives that they practice in following dietary laws. They should cast aside anything that, like yeast, might permeate and spoil their spiritual lives. Because Christ has conquered death, we can celebrate. We bring out our best ingredients: the unleavened bread of "sincerity and truth." Christ is the unleavened bread we share at every Eucharist. Through that nourishment, we find strength to resist evil within us and among us. Better still: Feasting on the bread of life enables us to become what we eat!

GOSPEL   John's empty tomb account shares a key similarity with the synoptic accounts: no one saw the moment of Resurrection, but those who witnessed its aftermath were changed.

Lectionary #46

AFTERNOON GOSPEL   Luke 24:13–35

A reading from the holy Gospel according to Luke

That **very** day, the **first** day of the week,
   two of Jesus' **disciples** were going
   to a village seven **miles** from Jerusalem called **Emmaus**,
   and they were **conversing** about all the things
      that had **occurred**.
And it **happened** that while they were **conversing** and **debating**,
   Jesus **himself** drew near and **walked** with them,
   but their **eyes** were **prevented** from **recognizing** him.
He asked them,
   "What are you **discussing** as you walk along?"
They **stopped**, looking **downcast**.
One of them, named **Cleopas**, said to him in **reply**,
   "Are you the **only** visitor to Jerusalem
   who does not **know** of the things
   that have taken **place** there in these days?"
And he replied to them, "What **sort** of things?"
They **said** to him,
   "The things that happened to **Jesus** the **Nazarene**,
   who was a **prophet** mighty in **deed** and **word**
   before **God** and all the **people**,
   how our chief **priests** and **rulers** both handed him over
   to a sentence of **death** and **crucified** him.
But we were hoping that he would be the one to **redeem** Israel;
   and **besides** all this,
   it is now the **third** day since this took place.

The "day" of this occurrence is important.

Emmaus = eh-MAY-us

Note that they are "conversing" and "debating"; they are probing and trying to understand. Let your tone convey the irony of their failure to recognize the very one they're discussing. Jesus is "playing dumb" here.

Cleopas = KLEE-oh-puhs
He responds with annoyance.

Jesus coaxes further. Initially they are a bit annoyed, but soon they are into the story.

Note that it's the "priests" and "rulers" who hand Jesus over.

We can't help but feel sorry for them and their sense of loss.

Magdalene approaches the grave site in the early morning darkness (and in the darkness of her grief). The sight of the stone that had been "removed from the tomb" persuades her that Jesus' body has been stolen. First to respond to her alarm are Peter and John, who race to the tomb. The younger John reaches it first, but does not enter, a sign, some scholars see, of Peter's preeminence in the apostolic brotherhood. (Therefore highlight these lines.) John has looked into the tomb and seen the burial cloths, but not until Peter

arrives do we realize that the carefully "rolled up" cloths negate the stolen body theory, for neither grave robbers nor authorities would take such care.

When "the other disciple," (the young John) finally enters the empty tomb, he believes in the Resurrection, even without seeing the risen Lord, as Magdalene will do shortly. The final sentence might be confusing: if John has just "believed," why are we told they did not yet understand "that he had to rise from the dead"? Often, belief comes in stages. The reality of Resurrection takes time to sink in. So the

closing comment has a joyful, not judgmental tone, for it speaks with present faith about a previous (and not unreasonable) lack of understanding.

Magdalene fails to recognize the risen Lord when she meets him, for Resurrection has transformed him. With a single word, Jesus dispels her blindness and reveals himself. Through her instant response, "Teacher," Mary places herself in the role of disciple. Jesus tells her not to cling to him because he has not yet

Are they dismissing the testimony because it came from women?

They just can't add two and two: the tomb was empty, angels announced his rising, but this does not yet add up to Resurrection.

Jesus' emotion is real: frustration and some sadness.

This is a new beat in the story; don't rush it.

They plead with him to stay!

Slowly narrate this eucharistic scene. Pause after "gave it to them."

Try the line this way: "With that [pause] their eyes were open." Speak with energy and awe.

Some **women** from our group, however, have **astounded** us:
>   they were at the **tomb** early in the **morning**,
>   and did not find his **body**;
>   they came back and reported
>   that they had indeed seen a **vision** of **angels**
>   who announced that he was **alive**.
Then some of those with us **went** to the tomb
>   and found things **just** as the women had **described**,
>   but **him** they did not **see**."
And he said to them, "Oh, how **foolish** you are!
How **slow** of heart to believe all that the **prophets** spoke!
Was it not **necessary** that the Christ should **suffer** these things
>   and enter into his **glory**?"
Then beginning with **Moses** and all the **prophets**,
>   he **interpreted** to them what **referred** to him
>   in all the **Scriptures**.
As they approached the **village** to which they were **going**,
>   he gave the impression that he was going on **farther**.
But they **urged** him, "**Stay** with us,
>   for it is nearly **evening** and the day is almost **over**."
So he went in to **stay** with them.
And it **happened** that, while he was with them at **table**,
>   he took **bread**, said the **blessing**,
>   **broke** it, and **gave** it to them.
With **that** their eyes were **opened** and they **recognized** him,
>   but he **vanished** from their **sight**.

ascended to the Father. In Luke's account, Christ's Resurrection, Ascension (glorification before the Father), and the coming of the Holy Spirit (Pentecost) are separated in time. But here they occur on the same Easter Sunday. By the time Jesus appears to the apostles the evening of that day, he is glorified and can impart the Spirit. So his "Ascension" must occur after this encounter with Mary. The message he asks her to deliver to his "brothers" is vital. By his death, Resurrection, Ascension, and glorification, Jesus can impart the Spirit to the disciples, and the Spirit will make them children of God. Mary goes, announcing that she has "*seen* the Lord."

AFTERNOON GOSPEL Downcast and discouraged, these two disciples journey home, leaving behind the events of the Passion, though still clinging to some shreds of the hope they had pinned on Jesus. Though they speak of him, they fail to recognize him when he approaches. Jesus feigns ignorance and coaxes them into telling him his own story. In their response, they speak of a mighty prophet, of betrayal, and of dreams now dashed, dreams that he was the messiah. Yet, by also mentioning rumors of angels dressed in white and talking of an empty tomb, they reveal the smoldering coals of hope that await the wind of the Spirit to reignite them and set them blazing once again. Jesus marvels at their lack of faith, their ignorance, their inability to see in the very story they've just told the outline of the One who stands before them. In response to their narration, Jesus says, "How foolish you are!" How

The pacing quickens here, but keep it natural and realistic.

Remember this is a story. Tell it throughout as if for the first time, with enthusiasm and suspense.

Speak these lines with great reverence and awareness of their significance. Use *ritardando* (gradual slowing toward the end) on the words "in the breaking of the bread."

Then they **said** to each other,
  "Were not our **hearts burning** within us
  while he **spoke** to us on the way and opened the **Scriptures**
    to us?"
So they set out at **once** and returned to **Jerusalem**
  where they found gathered **together**
  the **eleven** and those with them who were saying,
  "The Lord has **truly** been **raised** and has appeared to **Simon**!"
Then the **two** recounted
  what had taken **place** on the way
  and how he was made **known** to them in the **breaking** of **bread**.

could they have experienced and seen and heard so much and still not understand?

So Jesus plays the rabbi once again. He walks with them, opening up and explaining the scriptures to them. At their destination, they coax him inside, and he's soon sitting at their table. He takes, blesses, and breaks the bread, and suddenly their eyes are open, and he departs from their midst. Any thinking person would have said, "Where'd he go?" But the

disciples are still so filled with the presence of Jesus that they fail to comment on his departure. With hearts now blazing, they realize their whole journey to Emmaus had been blessed with his presence. And they know they'll never again be without it, for Christ had not only appeared to them at the table; he had been with them throughout the day, despite their inability to notice. That awareness propels them back to Jerusalem where they proclaim what the disciples know already. You'd be

hard-pressed to find, in all of scripture, a more important ecclesiological line than the one that ends this text: they knew him "in the breaking of the bread."

2ND SUNDAY OF EASTER   DIVINE MERCY SUNDAY

Lectionary #44

READING I   Acts 4:32–35

A short reading always calls for slow reading.

Don't share this with a matter-of-fact tone; make sure your listeners understand how remarkable it was that the community enjoyed such unanimity.

Your tone says, "Hard as it may be to believe . . . ."

Here your tone suggests, "Even harder to believe but true . . . ."

Speak with conviction, joy, and admiration for these heroic ancestors in faith.

A reading from the Acts of the Apostles

The community of **believers** was of one **heart** and **mind**,
    and **no one** claimed that any of his **possessions** was his **own**,
    but they had everything in **common**.
With great **power** the apostles bore **witness**
    to the **resurrection** of the Lord **Jesus**,
    and great **favor** was accorded them **all**.
There was no **needy** person among them,
    for those who owned **property** or **houses** would **sell** them,
    bring the **proceeds** of the sale,
    and put them at the feet of the **apostles**,
    and they were distributed to **each** according to **need**.

READING II   1 John 5:1–6

This is the first of six consecutive weeks that we read from this letter of John.

Note the salutation.

Here is the central idea; proclaim it boldly.

A reading from the first Letter of Saint John

Beloved:
Everyone who **believes** that Jesus is the **Christ** is **begotten**
    by **God**,
    and everyone who loves the **Father**
    loves **also** the one **begotten** by him.

READING I   Beginning moments are often tinged with special grace. We call them honeymoons, and married or not we all have them now and then—in new jobs, new friendships, or romantic relationships. Even presidents enjoy them during their initial days in office. Mistakes are more easily excused, hurts are more easily forgotten, and most anything seems possible during those heady times when all is new and fraught with possibility. Luke describes the honeymoon period of the new "community of believers" formed after the Ascension of Jesus. He's genuinely excited about those early days when "all for one" was a way of life. The apostles were among them then, the very men who had eaten and laughed and walked and slept under the stars with Jesus. "What exciting times!" we muse now. How energizing to be a believer then, when miracles were commonplace and when your faith might cost your life!

This passage is not a history lesson; it's a beacon shining through the ages, illuminating the possibilities of the Christian life. Heroism, idealism, and selflessness are all possible in that beacon's bright light. To our more troubled times it proclaims boldly: Yes, the same Spirit who empowered the first Christian community can make of ours a fellowship that is "of one heart and mind." Speak with energy, enthusiasm, and joy of these ancestors; speak as if you knew them and want to brag about them. Speak not just to brag, but to call us to that same radical and joyous living of our faith that enabled them to lay their goods (and their lives!) at the feet of the apostles (and their Lord). Their lifestyle was a miracle, a work of purest

Love and obedience are equated: you can obey without loving, but you can't love without obeying.

Two ideas are shared here: 1) keeping the commandments is not burdensome and 2) those born of God conquer the world.

This sentence asks and answers its own question. Pause briefly after "the world."

Note the repetition of "water and blood." Water signifies Jesus' baptism; blood, his death.

Be sure your proclamation has also testified to Christ.

In this way we **know** that we love the **children** of God
 when we love **God** and obey his **commandments**.
For the love of God is **this**,
 that we **keep** his **commandments**.
And his commandments are not **burdensome**,
 for whoever is begotten by God **conquers** the **world**.
And the **victory** that conquers the world is our **faith**.
Who indeed is the **victor** over the world
 but the one who **believes** that **Jesus** is the Son of **God**?

This is the one who came through **water** and **blood**, Jesus **Christ**,
 not by water **alone**, but by **water** and **blood**.
The **Spirit** is the one that **testifies**,
 and the **Spirit** is **truth**.

This rich text requires rapid mood shifts and character definition, plus strong emotional involvement. The narrator is not uninvolved, but a concerned and proselytizing teacher whose goal is the building up of the reader's faith.

Don't let your listeners miss the details: first day of the week; locked doors; fear of the Jews.

Jesus tempers their rejoicing with another "Peace . . . ." His agenda is to commission, not celebrate.

Take plenty of time relating this critical moment of empowerment.

GOSPEL   John 20:19–31

A reading from the holy Gospel according to John

On the evening of that **first** day of the week,
 when the doors were **locked**, where the **disciples** were,
 for **fear** of the Jews,
 Jesus came and stood in their **midst**
 and said to them, "**Peace** be with you."
When he had **said** this, he showed them his **hands** and his **side**.
The disciples **rejoiced** when they saw the Lord.
Jesus said to them **again**, "**Peace** be with you.
As the **Father** has sent me, so **I** send **you**."
And when he had said this, he **breathed** on them and said to them,
 "**Receive** the Holy **Spirit**.

---

grace. On this Second Sunday of Easter Time, when we remember and celebrate Divine Mercy, can we hope for anything less than miracles?

READING II Imagine you're scaling a building with a sectional ladder just long enough to reach the first floor landing. There you find the next section of the ladder that, after you attach it, takes you to the second landing where another ladder section is waiting to advance you to the next landing, and so forth. Today's letter from John works the

same way. Each sentence relies on the one before it and sets up the one after it. Like ladder sections that must overlap to achieve strength, meaning that some rungs on the new section repeat the work of rungs on the section before, these sentences repeat information from the previous sentence before advancing the thought with new information.

The ladder analogy should tell you two things: build carefully and proceed slowly. The opening sentence is the first ladder section on which the rest is built. It's the most important idea and it ought to

be stated boldly: faith consists in accepting Jesus for who he is—the divine Son of God. And our faith in Christ is proven by our willingness to "keep his commandments." A brief discussion follows—"his commandments are not burdensome"—and then another peak: "Whoever is begotten by God . . . is our faith."

John tells us that the true conquerors of the world are those who believe that Jesus is truly what Christian faith says he is, God's Son. There's no compromising that truth. It not only names Jesus' identity, it gives us ours. He is the one who was

Whose **sins** you **forgive** are **forgiven** them,
   and whose sins you **retain** are **retained**."

The mood shifts with the new scene and the pace quickens.

Thomas, called **Didymus**, one of the **Twelve**,
   was not **with** them when Jesus came.
So the **other** disciples said to him, "We have **seen** the **Lord**."
But **he** said to them,
   "Unless I **see** the mark of the **nails** in his **hands**

Make the dialogue real and animated. Thomas is strong-willed.

   and put my **finger** into the nailmarks
   and put my **hand** into his **side**, I will not **believe**."

The narrator knows the story, so the tone should suggest his inside knowledge.

Now a week **later** his disciples were again inside
   and Thomas **was** with them.
Jesus **came**, although the doors were **locked**,
   and stood in their **midst** and said, "**Peace** be with you."
Then he said to **Thomas**,

Jesus is as strong-willed as Thomas here.

   "Put your **finger** here and see my **hands**,
   and bring your **hand** and put it into my **side**,
   and do not be **unbelieving**, but **believe**."

Thomas' declaration is wholly sincere.

Thomas **answered** and said to him, "My **Lord** and my **God**!"
Jesus said to **him**, "Have you come to **believe**
     because you have **seen** me?

Put your emphasis on extolling believers, not chiding Thomas.

Blessed are those who have **not** seen and have **believed**."

This summary statement is meant to strengthen faith and is directed at the assembly, so maintain good eye contact.

Now Jesus did many **other** signs in the presence of his **disciples**
   that are not **written** in this book.
But **these** are written that you may come to **believe**
   that **Jesus** is the **Christ**, the Son of **God**,
   and that **through** this belief you may have **life** in his **name**.

---

baptized ("water") by his cousin John and who willingly gave his life ("blood") for all. The "Spirit" *testifies* to that. Today with your words, as each day with your life, you must also.

GOSPEL   Jesus invades the apostles' safe house (and their anxiety) and announces, "Peace be with you." That's a recurring theme in the post-Resurrection accounts, and Jesus repeats it here. Their anxiety turns to joy when they see the Lord. Immediately, Jesus commissions them and imparts his Holy Spirit,

then gives them the power to forgive sins—three separate actions that each require from you a distinctive delivery.

The episode with Thomas gives this text its appealing, human quality. Can we disdain his uncertainty? Deprived of the encounter granted the others, Thomas is understandably skeptical. What's compelling about him is the clarity and boldness of his conditions: "Unless I see the mark . . . ." Jesus does not disappoint. A week later, aware of Thomas's doubt and the conditions set, Jesus returns, repeating the greeting of peace. He doesn't let

Thomas off easily, but invites him to publicly satisfy his doubts. Thomas is overwhelmed and responds with a powerful assent of faith. Now Jesus chides him and extols those who, unlike the doubter, will believe without seeing. Be sure to maintain good eye contact with the assembly on the "Blessed are . . . " line. Sustain that eye contact during the final lines. They are addressed to all future believers to bolster their faith and to ensure that, through that faith, they might live forever.

3RD SUNDAY OF EASTER

Lectionary #47

READING I   Acts 3:13–15, 17–19

Peter has become bold and authoritative. He's just worked a miracle, so the audience is enraptured.

The listing of Israel's great ancestors must be done with reverence.

Jesus was glorified through his death, Resurrection, and Ascension.

These titles he gives Jesus are usually reserved for God. He does not shy from "telling it like it is."

Having made his case, he now can soften it with understanding for their "ignorance." That his suffering was foretold, is more evidence that Jesus was the promised Messiah.

Let this be Peter's (and your) heartfelt exhortation to come to Christ.

A reading from the Acts of the Apostles

Peter said to the **people**:
"The God of **Abraham**,
    the God of **Isaac**, and the God of **Jacob**,
    the God of our **fathers**, has **glorified** his servant **Jesus**,
    whom **you** handed over and **denied** in Pilate's **presence**
    when he had decided to **release** him.
You **denied** the **Holy** and **Righteous** One
    and asked that a **murderer** be released to you.
The author of **life** you put to **death**,
    but God **raised** him from the dead; of this we are **witnesses**.
Now I **know**, brothers,
    that you acted out of **ignorance**, just as your **leaders** did;
    but God has thus brought to **fulfillment**
    what he had announced **beforehand**
    through the mouth of all the **prophets**,
    that his **Christ** would **suffer**.
Repent, therefore, and be **converted**,
    that your **sins** may be wiped **away**."

READING I   Peter, newly emboldened and comfortable in the role Christ had prophesied for him, addresses the people so directly, so honestly and earnestly that what might otherwise seem harsh, antagonistic language becomes instead a cord that draws them into a circle of reconciliation. In our view, Peter is an elder statesman who speaks with divine authority, but to his listeners he was the leader of a new sect making outlandish claims about its founder. And yet the people listen. He has claimed the attention of the crowd not only by asserting that the God of their ancestors has "glorified" Jesus, but by a miracle of healing that has amazed the crowd. They must hear this miracle worker, even if they don't especially like what he's saying.

They also listen because Peter's tone, though not his words, is conciliatory. About the past, he pulls no punches: "you handed over" God's servant Jesus even though Pilate "had decided to release him;" you "denied the Holy and Righteous One" and preferred a murderer. You killed the "Author of life." He says all that and still has an audience. Apparently, the over-tone of forgiveness is evident long before Peter mentions the possibility of sins being "wiped away." His compelling message is: You so missed the mark, and yet God's mercy still enfolds you!

In the second paragraph Peter presents mitigating factors: "ignorance" and fulfillment of prophecy. Confidently, Peter offers the next step: "repent!" There's urgency and paternal love in that exhortation (Is he remembering the cock crow?) So generous an offer of forgiveness could only come from one who experienced it first hand. Like Peter—or, perhaps *you*.

READING II   1 John 2:1–5a

A reading from the first Letter of Saint John

My **children**, I am **writing** this to you
  so that you may not commit **sin**.
But if anyone **does** sin, we have an **Advocate** with the Father,
  Jesus **Christ** the **righteous** one.
He is **expiation** for our sins,
  and not for **our** sins **only** but for those of the whole **world**.
The way we may be **sure** that we know him is to **keep**
  his **commandments**.
Those who say, "I **know** him," but do **not** keep
  his commandments
  are **liars**, and the **truth** is not **in** them.
But whoever **keeps** his word,
  the love of God is truly **perfected** in him.

GOSPEL   Luke 24:35–48

A reading from the holy Gospel according to Luke

The two disciples **recounted** what had taken **place** on the way,
  and how Jesus was made **known** to them
  in the **breaking** of **bread**.

While they were still **speaking** about this,
  he **stood** in their **midst** and said to them,
  "**Peace** be with you."

This is the second of six consecutive weeks we read from John's letter.

The greeting sets the tone. Make and sustain eye contact with the assembly and, with great care, explain the reason *for writing.*

We all know that avoiding sin completely is impossible, so here is hope for all who sin.

The word "know" requires special care for it suggests an intimate, not a passing kind of knowing.

Speak this truth without restraint. John makes the point twice: they are "liars" and they are void of "truth."

Pause before the last sentence, and then gently and lovingly announce this good and hopeful news.

These disciples speak with hearts still burning from Emmaus.

Jesus' greeting of peace is calm, but authoritative.

READING II   John expresses clearly how he feels about those to whom he pens his letter: they are his spiritual children—children for whom he cares with pastoral love and devotion. When a relationship is based on love and mutual respect, you can speak about hard things without fear of alienation.

The hard thing about which John writes is "sin." I am trying to keep you from sinning, he says. But sin we do, and Jesus is the remedy, not only for our own sins, but for those of "the whole world." There is a conversational quality here—the tone of a grandparent imparting advice to a cherished grandchild.

But even grandparents can chide and exhort. Now that the conversation is flowing and defensiveness is suspended, John goes further. When we accept Christ's gift of forgiveness, we enter an intimate relationship with him that is witnessed by the way we live our lives. In scripture "knowing" implies intimacy. Therefore, to say we "know" Christ, that is, to claim we are "intimate" with him, without living the way he asks us, is a charade—a lie, in fact. John is unafraid to use such strong language because he speaks out of love and is trying to steer us clear of danger. Proclaim with confidence, trusting the truth of what you say. The last sentence reassures us that your words are not judging or condemning, but calling us to an ideal we can attain.

GOSPEL   Often someone expresses the need to see miracles, some unmistakable sign, in order to believe. Then, when you point to one, they say, "That's no miracle!" Hearing claims of the Resurrection, most of the disciples

The disciples' panic contrasts with Jesus' greeting.

But they were **startled** and **terrified**
⠀⠀⠀and thought that they were seeing a **ghost**.
Then he **said** to them, "Why are you **troubled**?
And why do **questions** arise in your hearts?
Look at my **hands** and my **feet**, that it is I **myself**.
Touch me and **see**, because a **ghost** does not have **flesh** and **bones**
⠀⠀⠀as you can see I have."

There is an undercurrent in Jesus' dialogue that suggests these disciples should know better.

And as he **said** this,
⠀⠀⠀he **showed** them his hands and his feet.
While they were still incredulous for **joy** and were **amazed**,
⠀⠀⠀he asked them, "Have you anything here to **eat**?"

Besides proving he is not a ghost, this detail conveys Jesus' practical, caring nature.

They gave him a piece of baked **fish**;
⠀⠀⠀he took it and **ate** it in **front** of them.

The tone shifts for this closing teaching. Jesus is rabbi once again. His tone suggests they should have these "words that I spoke to you" inscribed on their hearts. Don't rush the items "written of the Christ." The operative words are: "suffer," "rise," "repentance," "preached," and "nations." Establish eye contact with the assembly before the final line.

He said to them,
⠀⠀⠀"These are my **words** that I **spoke** to you while I was still
⠀⠀⠀⠀⠀**with** you,
⠀⠀⠀that everything **written** about me in the law of **Moses**
⠀⠀⠀and in the **prophets** and **psalms** must be **fulfilled**."
Then he opened their **minds** to understand the **Scriptures**.
And he said to them,
⠀⠀⠀"Thus it is **written** that the Christ would **suffer**
⠀⠀⠀and rise from the **dead** on the third **day**
⠀⠀⠀and that **repentance**, for the forgiveness of **sins**,
⠀⠀⠀would be preached in his **name**
⠀⠀⠀to all the **nations**, beginning from **Jerusalem**.
You are **witnesses** of these things."

insisted on proof—seeing Jesus, touching his hands and side. So Jesus appears and what happens? Panic, fright, doubts, troubled hearts, and talk of seeing a ghost. Even when they touch his hands and feet they remain "incredulous," forcing Jesus to consume a fish to convince them he's real.

⠀⠀⠀In these first Sundays of Easter Time, we read of post-Resurrection appearances whose original intent was to bolster faith in the risen Christ. Today's reading opens with the excitement of the two disciples

who had recognized Jesus in the "breaking of the bread." But despite that testimony, panic strikes when Jesus suddenly appears. Jesus tries to reason, speaking loudly to be heard over their panicked outcries. Perhaps there's the same frustration in his voice now that he earlier expressed on the road to Emmaus: "Oh, how foolish you are . . . How slow of heart to believe . . . !" (After all, two of those present were the privileged travelers to Emmaus!). Is there reluctance in Jesus' offer to eat the fish, to insist he's no magician playing with smoke and mirrors?

Once their fears are quelled, Jesus recalls the words he had spoken before his death. He seems to suggest that they should have remembered those words, that they should cling to them and preserve them for the future. Then, as with Cleopas and friend, he opens their minds to the scriptures. Jesus teaches, reminding them that his death and Resurrection fulfilled scripture. Now the evidence they've *seen* must enable them to become bold witnesses of the Resurrection for those of us who believe but have *not* seen.

4TH SUNDAY OF EASTER

Lectionary #50

READING I   Acts: 4:8–12

A reading from the Acts of the Apostles

Don't gloss over the influence of the Holy Spirit.

His bold attitude suggests: "If we have to explain, then, by gosh, we will!"

Increase volume and intensity on "then all of you . . . ."

Build energy from the phrase "whom you crucified" to "whom God raised from the dead."

Obviously there is vindication in this line, but don't betray a superior attitude.

The final sentence is the heart of Christian evangelism: No one else— no one—but Jesus can save.

Peter, filled with the Holy **Spirit**, said:
  "**Leaders** of the people and **elders**:
  If we are being **examined** today
  about a good **deed** done to a **cripple**,
  namely, by what **means** he was saved,
  then all of **you** and all the people of **Israel** should know
  that it was in the name of Jesus **Christ** the **Nazorean**
  whom you **crucified**, whom God **raised** from the **dead**;
  in **his** name this man stands before you **healed**.
He is *the stone **rejected** by you, the **builders**,
  which has become the **cornerstone**.*
There is no **salvation** through anyone **else**,
  nor is there any other **name** under **heaven**
  given to the human **race** by which we are to be **saved**."

READING I The fear and self-interest that formerly afflicted Peter are long gone. Now, assuming a prophetic mantle, he speaks boldly in the name of Jesus. Peter and John are under arrest for healing a cripple and teaching about Jesus, and yet, in the grip of the Holy Spirit, Peter launches into this bold and unapologetic speech. If *you* were under arrest for doing a "good deed" that manifested the power of God and suddenly felt the fire of the Spirit burning within you, might you not become bold and fearless? Peter is recovering from much personal history: abandoning Jesus in the garden, his threefold denial, the fearful waiting in the upper room. What a relief to be done with all that! What freedom comes from a willingness to risk everything for Jesus!

Peter stands before hostile "leaders" and "elders" but uses the opportunity to proselytize. This amazing miracle of healing has occurred precisely because of the man you crucified, he insists. His faith is not philosophical, but based on concrete realities like the empty tomb and a walking cripple. His confidence growing, he speaks of "the name" with great and gentle reverence. Convince the leaders that "the stone rejected" by them has been thrown back into their lives. Then, without malice and with a real desire to give even these leaders the good news of Jesus, tell them that *no* other name "under heaven" can save.

READING II This passage is also proclaimed on All Saints Day. Read that commentary for additional perspectives. On that day when we celebrate

This is the third of six consecutive Sundays we read from John's first letter.

Eye contact with the assembly is essential. John's tone is direct and intimate. Don't let your tone contradict that.

You are naming our identity as God's children. Let your smile support that assertion.

Proclaim a bit faster as you critique the world's blindness.

Read slowly about our current and future states.

To give this line proper emphasis, it requires *ritardando* (gradual slowing till the end).

READING II   1 John 3:1–2

A reading from the first Letter of Saint John

Beloved:
See what **love** the Father has bestowed on us
    that we may be called the **children** of **God**.
Yet so we **are**.
The **reason** the world does not **know** us
    is that it did not know **him**.
Beloved, we are God's children **now**;
    what we **shall** be has not yet been **revealed**.
We **do** know that when it **is** revealed we shall be **like** him,
    for we shall **see** him as he **is**.

Eye contact with the assembly is essential for this entire reading.

Don't deliver the text as if it were oratory; instead go for the intimacy of a private conversation with friends.

The judgment on the "hired man" is harsh.

GOSPEL   John 10:11–18

A reading from the holy Gospel according to John

Jesus said:
    "I am the **good shepherd**.
A **good** shepherd lays down his **life** for the sheep.
A **hired** man, who is **not** a shepherd
    and whose **sheep** are not his **own**,
    sees a **wolf** coming and **leaves** the sheep and runs **away**,
    and the wolf **catches** and **scatters** them.
This is because he works for **pay** and has no **concern**
    for the sheep.

our faith heroes, John's words give us hope that one day we will *all* be saints. But in light of today's First Reading and of the dangerous situation in which the disciples found themselves in the early days after the Resurrection, we sense a more sober message: "the world does not know us"! Christian tradition held that John had known imprisonment and exile for his beliefs. The world's hostility is nothing new. Yet his message makes it possible to live in a hostile world. Forget what the world says or doesn't see, he tells us. The

greater danger is *our* not seeing what "we are" and what God has done for us!

A short passage always requires slow reading, and John's name at the top often means "slow and tender." The greeting, "beloved," signals intimate and *intense* communication. John works hard to convey his message. Right now, in the midst of whatever trials or fears or setbacks we experience, he says, *right now* we belong to God. That's excellent news! And later, even better news: We shall see God and we shall be *like* God. You have few words with which to make an impact; so today,

more than ever, your face, intensity, and your desire to communicate will be the medium that is also the message.

GOSPEL Here, the Good Shepherd discourse serves as a covert attack on the Pharisees who are the unreliable and self-serving hired hands of Jesus' analogy. Jesus distinguishes himself from those he considers false leaders. The false ones don't recognize his voice and so refuse to follow him, but those open to the kingdom, like the blind man and the apostles, do recognize his voice.

Here, Jesus defines what constitutes the goodness of the shepherd: he *knows* and is *known*.

"Other sheep" may refer to Gentiles or other Christians not in harmony with John's community.
Convey the conviction that this must and will be so.
These lines are neither boasting nor argumentative.

Let your tone suggest that Jesus is saying more about his love for us than anything about himself.

I am the **good** shepherd,
  and I know **mine** and mine know **me**,
    just as the **Father** knows **me** and I know the **Father**;
    and I will lay down my **life** for the sheep.
I have **other** sheep that do not **belong** to this fold.
These **also** I must lead, and they will **hear** my voice,
    and there will be **one** flock, **one shepherd**.
This is **why** the Father loves me,
  because I **lay** down my **life** in order to take it **up** again.
No one **takes** it from me, but I **lay** it down on my **own**.
I have **power** to lay it down, and power to take it **up** again.
This **command** I have received from my **Father**."

A stage director helping an actor play Jesus might invite the actors playing the apostles into a tight circle and place Jesus in the center. He might ask that actor to speak his dialogue while moving from man to man, looking into the eyes of one, grasping the shoulder of another, cradling the face of a third in his hands as he spoke with his own face only inches away. The hushed tones such physical proximity would elicit might appropriately convey the laying-down-his-life kind of love Jesus professes for his friends.

Your tone and eye contact should manifest for us the same love Jesus had for his friends. This discourse could easily sound like the progressive reasoning of courtroom debate: I do this, the hired hand does that; my motives are these, his are those, and so forth. That would be inappropriate. There's a single-mindedness and a rhythm here that climaxes in Christ's assertion that "I will lay down my life for the sheep." See him in that circle of friends above, longing to enlarge it with the sheep that "do not belong to this fold." He speaks about them with urgency: "These also I *must lead*."

In the closing lines we learn the meaning of discipleship as demonstrated in Jesus' own life: "The Father loves me because I lay down my life." Once again, we hear that love equals obedience to the will of God. The freedom with which Jesus offers himself is both radical and unfamiliar to the sheep, so he must help them understand it. Jesus is who he is, the Good Shepherd, precisely because he *freely* lays down his life. Why must they (and we) understand this? Because if they don't, they won't understand how beloved they are.

5TH SUNDAY OF EASTER

Lectionary #53

READING I Acts 9:26–31

A reading from the Acts of the Apostles

When **Saul** arrived in **Jerusalem** he tried to join the **disciples**,
   but they were all **afraid** of him,
   not **believing** that he was a disciple.
Then **Barnabas** took charge of him and **brought** him
      to the **apostles**,
   and he **reported** to them how he had **seen** the **Lord**,
   and that he had **spoken** to him,
   and how in **Damascus** he had spoken out **boldly** in the name
      of **Jesus**.
He moved about **freely** with them in Jerusalem,
   and spoke out **boldly** in the name of the **Lord**.
He also **spoke** and **debated** with the **Hellenists**,
   but they tried to **kill** him.
And when the brothers **learned** of this,
   they took him down to **Caesarea**
   and sent him on his way to **Tarsus**.

The church throughout all **Judea**, **Galilee**, and **Samaria**
was at **peace**.
It was being built **up** and walked in the fear of the **Lord**,
   and with the **consolation** of the Holy **Spirit** it grew in **numbers**.

Let your tone convey an understanding of Paul's situation and his motives.

Barnabas = BAHR-nuh-buhs
The tone that introduces Barnabas should suggest he was an ally who made things better.
Give this narration the feel of dialogue spoken by Barnabas.
Damascus = duh-MAS-kuhs

Don't be too upbeat here, or the news of their effort to kill him will seem humorous.
Hellenists are Greek-speaking Jews.

The tone shifts here to one of fraternal concern.
Caesarea = sez-uh-REE-uh
Tarsus = TAHR-suhs
Judea = joo-DEE-uh
Galilee = GAL-ih-lee
Samaria = suh-MAYR-ee-uh
This is a deep-down peace that's not subject to circumstances. Stress the role of the Holy Spirit.

READING I This reading from Acts seems more historical than theological, that is until you peer beneath the surface. Under the facts of who arrived where and how he was treated, broods the Holy Spirit, changing hearts and growing the number of believers. Saul's transformation into Paul is remarkable—and wrought by a miracle. But the Jerusalem community knew his reputation, so their suspicion is to be expected. Who would think that instead of persecuting Christians the future Paul would become one? A former enemy can't become a trusted friend overnight; fear and disbelief are sooner served than the bread of hospitality. So Saul needs introductions and explanations. Barnabas obliges. Knowing Saul's history and the fears it engenders, he lobbies on Saul's behalf and convinces the apostles of Saul's conversion.

Once accepted, Saul quickly proves his sincerity, speaking "boldly" about Jesus. Oddly, the response of the "Hellenists" is stated so matter-of-factly that it creates a comic effect. Don't fall into that trap. The tension-filled tone you employ in speaking of how he debated with them will alert us that their response was hostile. But as you tell of the brothers' efforts to escort him quickly and safely out of town, your tone shifts to fraternal concern.

We've just heard of efforts to kill Saul, yet everywhere, we're told, the Church "was at peace." The peace of which Luke writes is internal, the kind that prevails despite external circumstances. It was a peace of the heart, the place where "fear of the Lord" is born and where the "consolation" of the Spirit is experienced.

READING II   1 John 3:18–24

This is the fourth of six consecutive weeks we read from John's first letter. The opening salutation and the blunt message call for blunt delivery.

Eye contact with the assembly and sincerity of tone will be key to your delivery.

"In whatever our hearts condemn" means "No matter what our hearts, or consciences, may charge us with."
"Beloved" sets the tone of this sentence. John is trying to dispel self-doubt.

As if speaking to one (beloved) member of the assembly, speak these lines with sincerity and authority.

It is the gift of the Spirit that enables us to stand confident before the Lord.

A reading from the first Letter of Saint John

Children, let us **love** not in **word** or **speech**
    but in **deed** and **truth**.

Now **this** is how we shall know that we belong to the **truth**
    and reassure our **hearts** before him
    in whatever our hearts **condemn**,
        for God is **greater** than our hearts and knows **everything**.
Beloved, if our **hearts** do not condemn us,
    we have **confidence** in God
    and **receive** from him whatever we **ask**,
        because we keep his **commandments** and do what **pleases** him.
And his commandment is **this**:
    we should **believe** in the name of his **Son**, Jesus **Christ**,
    and **love** one another just as he **commanded** us.
Those who **keep** his commandments **remain** in him,
        and **he** in **them**,
    and the way we **know** that he remains in us
    is from the **Spirit** he gave us.

READING II Blessed Pope John XXIII said "The heart follows the mind almost as often as the mind follows the heart." He understood that often our hearts don't *feel* what our minds *know*, but sometimes, if we cling to what we know, the feeling follows. When we know something is good for us but don't *feel* it, we don't just quit the job or throw away the medicine; we keep believing until reason overwhelms the heart. After telling us not to be "all talk and no action," John informs us, with profound intimacy, that when we live a life of love in action we can be sure, that

no matter what guilt our "hearts condemn" us of, in fact, we do abide in God. God's knowledge of us (God "knows everything") overwhelms our self-doubting hearts.

"Beloved" continues John's tone of paternal encouragement. Sometimes it's those who try the hardest who most severely question their goodness and God's closeness. John wants to dispel self-doubt and insists that if our hearts cannot condemn us, we can be confident and bold before the Lord, who is pleased with our obedience.

John reminds us that fidelity to God consists in believing that Jesus is God's Son and in following his commandments. The tone of the final lines is didactic, but John speaks as if to only one "beloved" individual. He tells us that discipleship is not lonely or fraught with fear. When we keep the commandments God is with us, and God's Spirit guarantees it. It will be the tone of your delivery, more than the words, that persuades your assembly this message is meant for them.

GOSPEL   John 15:1–8

A reading from the holy Gospel according to John

Jesus said to his **disciples**:
   "I am the **true vine**, and my **Father** is the vine **grower**.
He takes away every **branch** in me that does not bear **fruit**,
   and every one that **does** he **prunes** so that it bears **more** fruit.
You are **already** pruned because of the **word** that I spoke to you.
Remain in me, as **I** remain in **you**.
Just as a **branch** cannot bear fruit on its **own**
      unless it remains on the **vine**,
   so neither can **you** unless you remain in **me**.
I am the **vine**, **you** are the **branches**.
Whoever **remains** in me and I in **him** will bear much **fruit**,
   because **without** me you can do **nothing**.
Anyone who does **not** remain in me
   will be **thrown** out like a **branch** and **wither**;
   people will **gather** them and throw them into a **fire**
   and they will be **burned**.
If you **remain** in me and my **words** remain in **you**,
   ask for whatever you **want** and it will be **done** for you.
By **this** is my Father **glorified**,
   that you bear much **fruit** and become my **disciples**."

This text seems simple, but the repetitions could make it a blur if the tempo is too fast or the images rushed. Read slowly and deliberately.

This line reassures the disciples of their right relationship with God.

Here we have an analogy that speaks of the need to stay rooted in Christ.

Just as Jesus is "vine" to the Father's "grower," so he is "vine" to our "branches."

A serious tone of warning is needed for these lines. Pay special attention to the words "wither," "gather," "throw," "fire," and "burned."

The tone changes to joyful encouragement.

Be sure to end with sustained eye contact with the assembly.

GOSPEL   We resort to poetry when the mind alone can't apprehend a thought, when our senses are needed to help us see and hear and smell a slippery concept that eludes our feeble brains. Jesus knows that images give shape and sound and fragrance to the radical ideas he came to share. And so he wraps his thoughts in images of vines and branches, of fruit, and fire, and decay.

Writers write in thought units, and so readers must share one unit at a time. Frequently sentences contain more than a single thought unit, so good readers must use the voice to distinguish one from another. In today's text, almost every line introduces a new thought. This doesn't mean you pause at the end of each line, but it does mean you look for and lift out the new information each line offers.

The poetry of this text speaks of the union between Jesus and his disciples: they are one plant, each living in and through the other. A branch can't yield fruit "unless it remains on the vine," and a vine has no fruit without its branches. Though the imagery is agrarian, it is not entirely unfamiliar, even if the particulars are vague. There is praise here—"You are already pruned," but caution also, "He takes away every branch . . . that does not bear fruit." Those who do not abide in Christ are tossed out "like a branch and wither," and "they will be burned." These negative images are given as warnings and require a corresponding tone. In the final sentences Jesus returns to the theme of oneness, informing his disciples (and us) of the blessings and benefits that union brings. The closing sentence rings with joy, a joy in which we share when as disciples we bear "much fruit."

6TH SUNDAY OF EASTER

Lectionary #56

READING I Acts 10:25–26, 34–35, 44–48

A reading from the Acts of the Apostles

When **Peter entered**, **Cornelius met** him
 and, falling at his **feet**, paid him **homage**.
Peter, however, **raised** him up, saying,
 "**Get** up. I myself am **also** a human **being**."
Then Peter proceeded to **speak** and said,
 "In **truth**, I see that God shows no **partiality**.
Rather, in **every** nation whoever **fears** him and acts **uprightly**
 is **acceptable** to him."

While Peter was still **speaking** these things,
 the Holy **Spirit** fell upon all who were **listening** to the word.
The **circumcised** believers who had accompanied Peter
 were **astounded** that the gift of the Holy Spirit
 should have been **poured** out on the Gentiles **also**,
 for they could hear them speaking in **tongues**
  and glorifying **God**.
Then Peter **responded**,
 "Can anyone withhold the **water** for **baptizing** these people,
 who have received the Holy **Spirit** even as **we** have?"
He **ordered** them to be baptized in the name of Jesus **Christ**.

Cornelius is clearly awed by Peter.
Cornelius = kohr-NEEL-yuhs

There is no hint of reproach here, only Peter's humility.

Peter acknowledges that even the uncircumcised can become members of Christ's body, the Church. In this, he is yielding to the position held by Saint Paul.

The pace quickens here. There is excitement as they witness the manifestation of the Spirit.

"The circumcised believers" means "the Jewish believers."
Gentiles = JEN-tĭls

There is a sense here that this is hardly believable!

Regaining composure, Peter takes charge and makes his solemn pronouncement. Pause briefly at the end of his question.

READING I Even the best-intentioned person can sometimes misinterpret the will of God. And sometimes God acts decisively to correct our misinterpretations. Two unlikely companions are brought together in this seminal event in the life of the Church: Peter—elder, man of God, Jew; and Cornelius—centurion, devout and God-fearing, Gentile. They have been drawn together by divine intervention (each has had a vision) and neither knows exactly why (read the preceding verses in Acts to find out). Cornelius greets Peter as if he were an angel who has just stepped out of his vision. Peter responds with warm humility, sensing immediately this Roman is no ordinary Gentile.

The meaning of his vision—in which he was instructed to eat foods considered unclean—suddenly dawns on Peter. God does not play favorites; even Gentiles are "acceptable to him." Peter regrets his earlier decision to deny membership in the Church to non-Jews. His voice betrays the realization that his bias led him into error.

In the midst of his realization, an amazing occurrence takes place: uninvited and unexpected, the Spirit descends "upon all who were listening," surprising everyone in the room—including the Gentiles who suddenly find themselves speaking in tongues. God demonstrates once again that his ways are not our ways, leaving the "circumcised believers" looking around in amazement, for these Gentiles have clearly received the gift of the Spirit without first being baptized.

Peter's slowness in perceiving the truth doesn't prevent him from plucking the opportunity it offers. Turning to his companions, he asks rhetorically a question whose answer these events have made too

This is the fifth of six consecutive weeks we read from this first letter of John.

Choose the person in your life you could most comfortably address so openly, and fix that person's face in your mind's eye as you begin. Of course, such a short text requires careful pacing.

Speak lovingly even of those who do not know love.

You are speaking gratefully of Christ's death and Resurrection.

This is poetry, not a courtroom argument. Let it swell with appropriate emotion.

READING II   1 John 4:7–10

A reading from the first Letter of Saint John

Beloved, let us **love** one another,
  because **love** is of **God**;
  everyone who **loves** is **begotten** by God and **knows** God.
Whoever is **without** love does **not** know God, for **God** is **love**.
In **this** way the love of God was **revealed** to us:
  God sent his only **Son** into the world
  so that we might have **life** through him.
In **this** is love:
  not that **we** have loved **God**, but that **he** loved **us**
  and sent his **Son** as expiation for our **sins**.

plain. Then, in his rightful role as leader, he gives the order that they be baptized in the name of Jesus.

READING II Few texts are as inspiring or as simply profound as this passage. Like a classic piece of music or a classic line of poetry, we don't tire of these words. There is such striking truth, such simple, yet arresting theology here, that the words catch and hold us each time we hear them: God is love. Your assembly has heard that before; today help them to feel it.

If there's a difficulty, it's with the earnestness and directness of John's style. "Beloved"—even in our families we sometimes find it difficult to speak so lovingly. But John's words require us to look our listeners squarely in the eye, and convince them these words are meant for them. John reminds us that God first loved us and that God's love for us calls us to love one another. Further, we can see God's love every time we look at the cross and remember the price Christ paid for the "expiation of our sins."

John's equating of love with knowledge of God is remarkable: Those who do not love do not know God—simple, straightforward, and shocking. The concluding declaration that God took the initiative and taught us love by sending "his only Son" furnishes the most compelling motivation for the first line of this reading—John's imperative to "love one another." But don't proclaim it as the summation of a logical argument. Consider it the last verse of a love song, sung with joy and gratitude that can't be faked and that becomes contagious.

GOSPEL   John 15:9–17

A reading from the holy Gospel according to John

Jesus said to his **disciples**:
"As the **Father** loves **me**, so I also love **you**.
Remain in my love.
If you **keep** my **commandments**, you **will** remain in my love,
    just as **I** have kept my **Father's** commandments
    and remain in **his** love.

"I have **told** you this so that my **joy** may be in you
    and your joy might be **complete**.
This is my commandment: **love** one **another** as **I** love **you**.
No one has greater love than **this**,
    to lay down one's **life** for one's **friends**.
You are my friends if you do what **I command** you.
I no longer call you **slaves**,
    because a slave does not **know** what his master is **doing**.
I have called you **friends**,
    because I have told you **everything** I have heard
        from my **Father**.
It was not **you** who chose **me**, but **I** who chose **you**
    and **appointed** you to go and bear **fruit** that will **remain**,
    so that **whatever** you ask the Father in my **name**
        he may **give** you.
This I **command** you: **love** one **another**."

Jesus grounds his love for the apostles, and his command that we love one another, in the divine love of Father and Son. The entire text is spoken in the voice of Jesus.

Establish eye contact with the assembly as you exhort them to love and to keep the commandment.

Imagine speaking these words to a special person in your life who needs the assurance of your love.

Here again is the challenging part of Jesus' message. Look at the assembly and don't hold back.

There's a theological sense to "friends" that should not be lost. Jesus doesn't mean people with whom he socializes.

God is always the initiator. But from that initiative comes the responsibility to bear good fruit.

Speak the final directive with the love it commands.

GOSPEL   If the greeting card industry made a card out of this Gospel, they'd bring in an editor with sharp scissors. Into the wastebasket would go the references to "commands" and "commandments," "lay[ing] down one's life," and "bear[ing] fruit." What survived would be Jesus' references to love, joy, and friendship. The wastebasket might get more than the card.

Jesus is less saccharine, for he mixes challenge with his divinely earnest protestations of love: "keep my commandments . . . love one another . . . lay down [your] life . . . go and bear fruit . . . do what I command you . . . *love* one another." While there is intimacy that must not be diluted, there are also these expectations and clear commands. Jesus can demand so much because he loves so much. He asks no more than he's already given or is about to give. This is a Last Supper discourse, remember, and Jesus knows what lies ahead. Speak Christ's great love for his friends as if he were addressing one disciple at a time. In scripture Moses, Elisha, and David were called "servants" or "slaves" of the Lord. Only Abraham was called a "friend of God." Jesus gives the apostles a title reserved till then for just one person. It's a special moment for this group that your tone should reverence.

As in the Second Reading where we heard of God's initiative, Jesus speaks of *choosing* us, and he says it's a choice with a purpose. Through the ages (and through you) Jesus' voice comes to your church today 1) to encourage his "friends" *there* to bear much fruit; 2) to convince them of his love; and 3) to request—no, to "command"—that they "love one another"!

ASCENSION OF THE LORD

Lectionary #58

READING I   Acts 1:1–11

A reading from the beginning of the Acts of the Apostles

This document has shaped our faith and deserves our greatest respect and finest reading.

Theophilus = thee-AWF-uh-luhs

For Luke, this is a story of the Holy Spirit guiding the new community and spreading the good news of Jesus. So the two references to the Spirit in the text must be highlighted.

All of these details are important, so don't rush. The "forty days" was a sacred period of time shared by Jesus and his disciples.

Speak these lines in the persona of Jesus.

Of course, they should know better, but the question is sincere.

In the **first** book, Theophilus,
  I dealt with all that Jesus **did** and **taught**
  until the day he was taken **up**,
  after giving **instructions** through the Holy **Spirit**
  to the **apostles** whom he had **chosen**.
He presented himself **alive** to them
  by many **proofs** after he had **suffered**,
  appearing to them during **forty** days
  and **speaking** about the kingdom of **God**.
While **meeting** with them,
  he enjoined them not to depart from **Jerusalem**,
  but to **wait** for "the promise of the **Father**
  about which you have heard me **speak**;
  for **John** baptized with **water**,
  but in a few days **you** will be baptized with the Holy **Spirit**."

When they had gathered **together** they asked him,
  "**Lord**, are you at **this** time going to restore
    the **kingdom** to Israel?"
He **answered** them, "It is not for **you** to know the **times**
    or **seasons**
  that the Father has established by his own **authority**.

READING I   Is this reading about a con-clusion or an inaugural moment? In fact, the Ascension is both. Jesus had to conclude his earthly ministry and ascend to the Father in order for the gift of the Spirit to be imparted to the Church he left behind. Luke's narrative is all about taking seriously Jesus' injunc-tions to be his "witnesses . . . to the ends of the earth." By the time of Luke's writing, the Christian community had abandoned the notion that Christ would return in glory during their lifetime. They got busy with the work at hand—claiming their Baptism in the Spirit and spreading the Gospel throughout the world.

Luke addresses the Acts of the Apostles to Theophilus, which could be the name of a given individual or, as some scholars suspect, a reference to anyone who "loves God," for Theophilus means God (*theo*-) lover (-*philus*). Luke's tone is subdued, polished, and professional, but he becomes more storyteller than reporter as he relates the interaction between the dis-ciples and the risen Jesus. Pause after "he enjoined them not to depart" and speak all of what follows in the persona of Jesus try-ing to infect the apostles with hope for the future he knows awaits them. The apostles respond with a sincere question that betrays their lack of understanding. They expect a "yes" from Jesus, still unaware that he did not come to establish an earthly kingdom. Jesus responds patiently, still the teacher, trying yet again to help them understand. He promises the Spirit, not the hidden knowledge they requested. Infuse your reading with confidence in their abil-ity to carry on in Jesus' name.

Instead of special knowledge, Jesus promises the Spirit. The words are meant to reassure and inspire. This prophecy continues being fulfilled even to this day.

You are narrating a sacred and awe-inspiring moment. Sustain the mood of the previous line on "While they were . . . ." Break the mood on "Suddenly. . . ."

Galilee = GAL-ih-lee

The exhortation of the "two [angelic] men" reinforces the "Let's get to it!" feel of this passage. The word "return" suggests the need to be ever ready.

But you will receive **power** when the Holy **Spirit** comes upon you,
  and you will be my **witnesses** in **Jerusalem**,
    throughout **Judea** and **Samaria**,
    and to the **ends** of the **earth**."
When he had **said** this, as they were **looking** on,
  he was **lifted** up, and a cloud **took** him from their **sight**.
While they were looking **intently** at the **sky** as he was **going**,
  suddenly two **men** dressed in white **garments**
    stood **beside** them.
They said, "Men of **Galilee**,
  why are you **standing** there looking at the **sky**?
This **Jesus** who has been taken **up** from you into **heaven**
  will **return** in the same way as you have seen him
    going into heaven."

Ephesians = ee-FEE-zhuhnz

Remember that you are reciting a prayer. Speak it earnestly.

You are praying that we know three things: hope, riches, power. Let your energy climb as you move from the first item to the last.

God exalts us in the same way he first exalted Christ. You are praising Christ with these words.

READING II   Ephesians 1:17–23

A reading from the Letter of Saint Paul to the Ephesians

Brothers and sisters:
May the **God** of our Lord Jesus **Christ**, the Father of **glory**,
  give you a Spirit of **wisdom** and **revelation**
  resulting in **knowledge** of him.
May the eyes of your **hearts** be **enlightened**,
  that you may know what is the **hope** that belongs to his call,
  what are the riches of **glory**
    in his **inheritance** among the holy **ones**,
  and what is the surpassing **greatness** of his **power**
    for us who **believe**,
  in accord with the **exercise** of his great **might**,

Follow Jesus' exhortation with a fast-paced narration: "When he had said this . . . "; but then, stop abruptly and become an apostle watching the scene—telling us, slowly, how Jesus was "lifted up" before your eyes. To suggest the sudden appearance of the two men in white who jolted the apostles from their reverie, increase your volume and tempo when you introduce them. Their tone is strong and energetic, not saccharine or scolding. "This Jesus . . . will return," they say. In the meantime, there's work to be done. So let's get to it! The angels said that to the apostles; you say it to the rest of us.

READING II **EPHESIANS 1. This text is a marvelous piece of oratory. The rhythmic and ebullient sound of these words carries a large portion of the meaning of the passage. The author's ideas are complex and important.**

Notice that in terms of form, the text moves from greeting, to prayer, to hymn of praise. The prayer is both theological and pastoral. Using a Trinitarian formula, he prays for "wisdom" and "revelation."

Expressing tremendous good will for his readers, the author prays that they see with their hearts what their eyes fail to see: the "riches of glory . . . [the] inheritance" that belongs to all "who believe" in Christ. The second of this lesson's three sentences extols the risen Christ who now reigns at God's right hand, wearing the mantle of glory he received when he ascended to heaven. There, he reigns over every rank of angel and over every creature for all eternity. Because the sentence is long and unwieldy, move through the

which he worked in **Christ**,
raising him from the **dead**
and **seating** him at his right **hand** in the **heavens**,
far **above** every **principality**, **authority**, **power**, and **dominion**,
and every **name** that is **named**
not only in **this** age but **also** in the one to **come**.
And he put all **things** beneath his **feet**
and gave him as **head** over all things to the **church**,
which is his **body**,
the **fullness** of the one who fills **all** things in every **way**.

Or:

"Principality," "authority," "power," and "dominion" are four distinct ranks of angels. Don't run them together.

Christ is Lord of heaven and earth. The phrase "head of the church" is not used in this sentence, but that is what is being said, so read carefully to convey that idea. Speak joyfully of our identity as Jesus' body.

READING II   Ephesians 4:1–13

A reading from the Letter of Saint Paul to the Ephesians

Brothers and sisters,
I, a **prisoner** for the **Lord**,
  urge you to **live** in a manner worthy of the **call**
    you have received,
  with all **humility** and **gentleness**, with **patience**,
  bearing with one another through **love**,
  striving to preserve the **unity** of the spirit
  through the bond of **peace**:
  one body and **one** Spirit,
  as you were also **called** to the one **hope** of your call;
  one **Lord**, one **faith**, one **baptism**;
  one **God** and Father of **all**,
  who is **over** all and **through** all and **in** all.

Ephesians = ee-FEE-zhuhnz

Note Paul's immediate reference to his imprisonment. The word "urge" tells you the tone of what follows.

This litany must not be rushed. It is a familiar mantra that blesses those who speak and those who hear it. Heed all the commas and the words marked for stress.

reading phrase by phrase, building one thought on the next.

The third sentence heralds Jesus as head of his body the Church. Pray this text as you might pray a blessing over your own children or closest friends. Let your intensity increase as you compare what God can do for us with what God has done for Christ. When describing the glory that was given to Christ, help us feel that we, too, are destined for glory! The last sentence climaxes the reading. Look to all parts of your assembly as you earnestly proclaim

that we, the Church, are Christ's body, always filled with his presence and love.

EPHESIANS 4. In Christ, God fashioned a new chosen people called to transform the world into the likeness of Christ. But because we still live in the midst of the world, a world often hostile to the ways of God's kingdom, we are easily distracted and divided; we fall victim to many temptations, among which the foremost, it seems, is the inclination to go our own ways and do our own thing. Hence, the spirited plea for unity we hear in this elegant text. Through the gift of the Spirit we have been

made one; we belong to no one but Christ; we are given but one route to eternal salvation: Baptism, that initiates into Christ.

That is the Christian conviction. Christ is one and we are his body, therefore we are one in him. And we are drawn together by the generous use of the various gifts Christ has given to the members of the body: gifts given and used for the common good. Paul quotes Psalm 68: "He ascended on high . . . he gave gifts to men" and makes Christ the triumphant hero of the psalm who lavishes gifts on his followers. Indeed, by virtue of his death, Resurrection,

Each of us shares according to the gift received from Christ.

But **grace** was given to **each** of us
   according to the measure of Christ's **gift**.
Therefore, it says:
   *He **ascended** on high and took prisoners **captive**;*
   *he gave **gifts** to men.*
What does "he **ascended**" mean except that he also **descended**
   into the **lower** regions of the **earth**?
The one who **descended** is also the one who **ascended**
   far above all the **heavens**,
   that he might **fill** all things.

Christ is our champion who ascended on high and now rains down gifts upon us.

It is the same Christ who came from God to become human who has returned to God and intercedes for us.

And he gave some as **apostles**, others as **prophets**,
   others as **evangelists**, others as **pastors** and **teachers**,
   to equip the holy ones for the work of **ministry**,
   for **building** up the body of **Christ**,
   until we all attain to the **unity** of faith
   and **knowledge** of the Son of God, to mature **manhood**,
   to the extent of the full **stature** of **Christ**.

"Evangelists" refers to missionaries, not Gospel writers. "Pastors and teachers" are those who lead congregations.

[Shorter: Ephesians 4:1–7, 11–13]

Our full maturity will be manifested when we are visibly united in Christ.

and Ascension, Christ reigns victorious above all creatures and is the wellspring of all the Church's spiritual gifts.

Paul begins by alluding to his imprisonment, using his status as added incentive for his readers to heed his words and live in harmony. Nothing less is worthy of our calling and our Baptism, he says. His litany, "one Lord, one faith, one baptism; one God and father of all" rhythmically and elegantly reinforces the message. The same Lord who descended from heaven to share our flesh has now ascended to the heavens, and from there he dispenses his

gifts to the members of his body, the Church. Some are "apostles," some "prophets" or "evangelists," some "pastors and teachers." We each have a role to play, but it is only together that we manifest the fullness of Christ, as we "mature" by becoming one in Christ, our Lord.

GOSPEL | Here is the surprising structure of this Gospel: Now you see him, now you . . . still see him. Jesus appears to the disciples, is "taken up into heaven," but then we're told that somehow he still "worked with them."

This is not really the story of a farewell, but of an unbroken relationship that transcends time and space. Jesus is as present at the end of this episode as at the beginning, and in equally marvelous ways. His sudden and miraculous appearance among the disciples is matched by the "signs" that Jesus works with them after the Ascension. Instead of sadness and letting go, there is hope and promise.

However, there is a melancholy tone in the declaration that while the Good News will be proclaimed to "all creation," some "will be saved" and, sadly, some will

GOSPEL Mark 16:15–20

This reading begins abruptly, so begin more slowly than usual.

A reading from the holy Gospel according to Mark

Jesus said to his **disciples**:
  "Go into the **whole world**
  and proclaim the **gospel** to every **creature**.
Whoever believes and is **baptized** will be **saved**;
  whoever does **not** believe will be **condemned**.

Don't shy from the stark contrast in the fate of those who do and don't believe.

These **signs** will accompany those who **believe**:
  in my **name** they will drive out **demons**,
  they will speak new **languages**.

Let there be joy in your enumeration of the signs manifest in the lives of believers.

They will pick up **serpents** with their **hands**,
  and if they drink any **deadly** thing, it will not **harm** them.
They will lay hands on the **sick**, and they will **recover**."

This is the most significant of the items enumerated. Pause before starting the next section.

Speak less in an awed tone and more like this was the necessary prerequisite for the disciples to assume their proper roles.

So **then** the Lord **Jesus**, after he **spoke** to them,
  was **taken** up into **heaven**
  and took his seat at the right hand of **God**.
But they went **forth** and preached **everywhere**,
  while the Lord **worked** with them
  and **confirmed** the word through accompanying **signs**.

Once again, "signs" are mentioned (and stressed).

not. In the verses immediately preceding today's selection, Jesus rebukes the disciples for failing to believe those who had seen him after he had been raised (Mary Magdalene and the disciples walking to Emmaus). It is on that note that Jesus begins his exhortation to go forth and "proclaim the gospel." Even their flabby faith didn't disqualify the disciples from carrying out the mission of Jesus. He will be with them to help them, and no demon or natural obstacle will impede them. Some of the early Church Fathers interpreted the

"signs" that would accompany faithful believers in spiritual, metaphoric ways—the poison of false doctrine, the serpents of evil intent or evil works—for as Gregory the Great observed in his interpretation of this passage, "Holy Church does every day in spirit what then the Apostles did in body."

The repetition of "they will . . ." creates a pattern that builds momentum and deepens the impact of the lines. Be deliberate in your use of the refrain. The break in the pattern just before the final "they will lay hands . . . and they will recover" appropriately throws focus to that, most

important, final promise. Build your intensity and rate through the first four promises, then slow your delivery and visualize the hand of a caring minister (yours?) on the head of an ailing believer.

"So then" shifts the mood and scene, but not up to where Jesus is taken "into heaven," but outward where Jesus goes forth disguised, as on the Emmaus road, to continue the work of the kingdom and to "confirm" the message of salvation—only now his disguise has him looking remarkably like you and me.

7TH SUNDAY OF EASTER

Lectionary #60

READING I — Acts 1:15–17, 20a, 20c–26

A reading from the Acts of the Apostles

> Read carefully to establish the scene and speak of Peter and "the brothers" with reverence. Establish eye contact immediately.
> Peter's tone should reveal his confident authority over the community of believers.

Peter stood up in the midst of the **brothers**
  —there was a group of about one hundred and twenty persons
  in the one **place**—.
He said, "My **brothers**,
  the **Scripture** had to be **fulfilled**
  which the Holy **Spirit** spoke **beforehand**
  through the mouth of **David**, concerning **Judas**,
  who was the **guide** for those who **arrested** Jesus.
He was numbered **among** us
  and was allotted a **share** in this ministry.

> There is no little regret in this mention of Judas' squandered "ministry."

> The citing of scripture suggests the necessary next step.

"For it is written in the Book of **Psalms**:
  *May **another** take his **office**.*

"Therefore, it is **necessary** that one of the men
  who **accompanied** us the **whole** time
  the Lord Jesus **came** and went **among** us,
  beginning from the baptism of **John**
  until the **day** on which he was taken **up** from us,
  become with us a **witness** to his **resurrection**."
So they proposed **two**, **Judas** called **Barsabbas**,
  who was also known as **Justus**, and **Matthias**.

> "The whole time" means from the Baptism in the Jordan until his Ascension.

> Your tone suggests that these are both fine candidates.
> Barsabbas = bahr-SAH-buhs;
> Justus = JUS-tuhs;
> Matthias = muh-THĪ-uhs

READING I Jesus is gone and the band of twelve, reduced to eleven, must now direct the course of the movement born in the wake of his Ascension. What to do? Where to start? Since Jesus had initiated a new Israel, and since Israel had twelve tribes, what's needed first is to return the number of elders to a full complement of twelve.

Peter rises in the assembly, his role as leader readily acknowledged, reviews the events that removed Judas from their number, and suggests what the next step might be. Give Peter a confident, authoritative voice, the kind that would inspire a small band of believers to feel they've been left in good hands. He quotes scripture that mandates that "another take his place," then stipulates the criteria by which the replacement for Judas will be sought. Stress the importance of it being someone who knew and walked with Jesus from the beginning of his ministry, and someone who was witness to the Resurrection. For Peter, witnessing the Resurrection is an essential aspect of the apostolic ministry.

Name the nominees with respect for the upright, holy men they must have been (note, the "loser" gets the bigger mention). "Then they prayed . . . ." Pause to let that simple phrase sink in. The prayer is most sincere, for they leave the choice entirely to God through the casting of "lots," so pray it slowly and earnestly. With the prayer and the closing narration, create suspense about the outcome, then speak the name "Matthias" with a clear sense that a good and holy man was chosen to complete the ranks of the apostolic brotherhood.

Pray this prayer sincerely. It's an important matter.

Don't rush the announcement of the new apostle.

Then they **prayed**,
  "**You**, Lord, who know the hearts of **all**,
  show which **one** of these two you have **chosen**
  to take the **place** in this apostolic ministry
  from which Judas turned **away** to go to his **own** place."
Then they gave **lots** to them, and the lot fell upon **Matthias**,
  and he was **counted** with the eleven **apostles**.

READING II   1 John 4:11–16

This is the last of six Sundays that we read from the first letter of John.
Immediately establish eye contact with the assembly.

Don't let this sound like a technical point; it comes from the heart: When we love, we see God.

These lines offer comfort and reassurance. Remember, "we" includes you.

Don't just state this; invite the assembly to agree with you.

Don't rush here. Though ideas are repeated, the repetition makes an impact.

You should deliver this final sentence from memory, without looking down.

A reading from the first Letter of Saint John

Beloved, if **God** so loved **us**,
  we **also** must love one **another**.
No one has ever **seen** God.
Yet, if we **love** one another, God **remains** in us,
  and his love is brought to **perfection** in us.

This is how we **know** that we remain in **him** and he in **us**,
  that he has given us of his **Spirit**.
Moreover, we have **seen** and **testify**
  that the **Father** sent his **Son** as **savior** of the world.
Whoever **acknowledges** that Jesus is the **Son** of God,
  God remains in **him** and he in **God**.
We have come to **know** and to **believe** in the love God **has** for us.

God is **love**, and whoever **remains** in love
  remains in **God** and God in **him**.

READING II This portion of John's letter continues the message we've read in earlier sections: our love for one another flows from our faith in Jesus as God's Son and imitates the example of God's unconditional love for us. The only difference here is the melody that provides the setting for John's words.

The best popular songs contain a "hook," a line or phrase so catchy that it hooks you because you can't forget it. The hook of a song becomes our favorite part, so we wait for it; we can always identify the hook because it's usually the only part

of a song people remember well enough to sing. John's hook is the last sentence of this passage: "God is love . . . ." Many can quote the words verbatim because they are familiar and beloved words. But have we really heard the rest of the passage? Today let's make sure the entire "song" gets heard, not just the hook.

State energetically that when we "love one another" God becomes so present among us that it is the same as seeing God. Then assure the assembly that the "Spirit" guarantees that we can remain one with God. Notice that you use the

plural "we" throughout the text, thus including yourself in everything you say. Reflect on the depth of your own conviction that "the Father sent his Son as savior of the world" so you can proclaim that boldly. Speak "Whoever acknowledges" not as a statement but as a *request* for that acknowledgement in the hearts of all your listeners.

When something is undeniably true, we don't need to shout it. Like waters that run deep, deep truths make little noise, so speak the last lines softly. But it's essential that your face broadcast clearly that

GOSPEL   John 17:11b–19

A reading from the holy Gospel according to John

Lifting up his eyes to **heaven**, Jesus **prayed**, saying:
   "Holy **Father**, keep them in your **name** that you have **given** me,
      so that they may be **one** just as **we** are one.
When I was **with** them I **protected** them in your name that you
         gave me,
      and I **guarded** them, and none of them was **lost**
      except the son of **destruction**,
      in order that the Scripture might be **fulfilled**.
But now I am **coming** to you.
I **speak** this in the world
      so that they may share my joy **completely**.
I gave them your **word**, and the world **hated** them,
      because they do not **belong** to the world
      any more than **I** belong to the world.
I do not ask that you take them **out** of the world
      but that you **keep** them from the **evil** one.
They do not belong to the world
      any more than **I** belong to the world.
Consecrate them in the **truth**. Your **word** is truth.
As you sent **me** into the world,
      so I sent **them** into the world.
And I **consecrate** myself for them,
      so that they **also** may be consecrated in **truth**."

Jesus typically prays looking up to heaven and addressing God as Father. Raise your eyes up and out as well.

Jesus is insistent about how carefully he cared for his disciples and protected them from harm. The mention of Judas is resigned and unemotional.

Energy builds as Jesus anticipates his departure from his friends.

Although these ideas are stated twice, don't rush them either time; in fact, speak with greater urgency on the second iteration.

"Consecrate them" means to "make them holy."

Stress the parallel between the mission God gave to Jesus and the one Jesus gives to his disciples.

"love" is a place worth remaining because there, and only there, will God be found.

GOSPEL   This passage consists entirely of a prayer of Jesus, a prayer for his disciples and for us. Here is a sterling example of intimate conversation with God. Don't tell us *about* Jesus' prayer, *pray* it and let the assembly be the disciples in whose presence you pray. Jesus is speaking to God, not teaching the disciples, so even declarative statements like "they do not belong to the world" are void of didactic tone. Jesus'

voice is soft and full of concern for these friends from whom he will soon be parted. Eye contact with the assembly is unnecessary today; instead look upward, over their heads as you speak the prayer.

Jesus prays that the disciples be protected by the "name" of God, that God "keep them" in himself. He also prays that the disciples' unity duplicate that between Father and Son, and he recalls his care for them so that "none of them was lost." Now he will be leaving these friends and he worries that they will suffer at the hands of "the world" and "the evil one." While he

longs for them to share his "joy" he knows that hardships are inevitable. A rush of thoughts and feelings seems to flood upon Jesus as he prays. You've experienced the difficulties and divisions about which Jesus prays, so speak of them as sincerely as you might in your own prayer to God.

"So then" shifts the mood and scene, to where Jesus goes forth disguised, as on the Emmaus road, to continue the work of the kingdom and to "confirm" the message of salvation—only now his disguise has him looking remarkably like you and me.

PENTECOST: VIGIL

Lectionary #62

A reading from the Book of Genesis

Genesis = JEN-uh-sis

As narrator, you know this innocent age is lost.

Shinar = SHĪ-nahr

Speak with the arrogance that motivates their defiance.
bitumen = bih-TYOO-m*n

Their plan is in direct defiance of God's order to "fill the earth." They plan to enhance their own reputation without any help from God.

This is a new scene. Immediately suggest the disapproval with which God views the city and tower.

God is not being vindictive, but protecting humanity from itself.

This might be the reply if an ancient child asked, "Why do people speak different languages?"

The whole **world** spoke the same **language**,
     using the same **words**.
While the people were **migrating** in the **east**,
     they came upon a **valley** in the land of **Shinar** and **settled** there.
They **said** to one another,
     "**Come**, let us mold **bricks** and **harden** them with **fire**."
They used bricks for **stone**, and bitumen for **mortar**.
Then they said, "**Come**, let us build ourselves a **city**
     and a **tower** with its top in the **sky**,
     and so make a **name** for ourselves;
     otherwise we shall be **scattered** all over the **earth**."

The LORD came down to **see** the city and the **tower**
     that the people had built.
Then the LORD said: "If **now**, while they are **one** people,
     all speaking the **same** language,
     they have started to do **this**,
     nothing will **later** stop them from doing
          whatever they **presume** to do.
Let us then go **down** there and **confuse** their language,
     so that one will not **understand** what another **says**."
Thus the LORD **scattered** them from **there** all over the **earth**,
     and they **stopped** building the city.

Today options are given for the readings. Contact your parish staff to learn which readings will be used.

READING I   **GENESIS.** The solemnity of Pentecost celebrates the undoing of the grave error we see beginning in this passage: the alienation of nation from nation. This narrative climaxes a string of "sin stories" that the Genesis author used to illustrate the spread of sin and its deadly consequences. We've already seen that sin alienates people from God (Adam and Eve are expelled from the Garden and from one another; Cain kills his brother Abel). Here we see the effects go even further, alienating nation from nation. (Suddenly people speak different languages and can't understand each other. Misunderstandings doubtless will follow, leading surely to conflict and war.) The Spirit of Pentecost will reverse this situation, making alien peoples miraculously able to understand one another. But tonight is the vigil, so we await that miracle.

Lay the groundwork for the marvel of Pentecost by building clear images of human pride that seeks to "make a name" for itself, and of misguided human efforts to be like the gods. That underlying sinful motivation won't be apparent to your listeners unless you create a tension between the *narrator* who reports this event of final alienation and the Babel *builders* who arrogantly undertake their project, blind to its potential consequences. The narrator speaks with nostalgia of the "good old days" when "the whole world spoke the same language." But a haughty tone infects lines like "a tower . . . in the sky" and "make a name for ourselves," suggesting the builders' intent to thwart God's

Speak with conviction that what God has accomplished is just.

That is why it was called **Babel**,
　because there the Lord **confused** the speech of all the **world**.
It was from that **place** that he **scattered** them all over the **earth**.

Or:

Exodus = EK-suh-duhs
The opening narration must intimate the extraordinary nature of Moses' ascent up the mountain: he is about to meet his God.
Let your tone convey, without apology, the "scandal" of God's special love for Israel.

READING I　Exodus 19:3–8a, 16–20b

A reading from the Book of Exodus

Moses went up the **mountain** to **God**.
Then the Lord **called** to him and said,
　"**Thus** shall you say to the house of **Jacob**;
　tell the Israelites:
　You have seen for **yourselves** how I treated the **Egyptians**
　and how I **bore** you up on **eagle** wings
　and **brought** you here to **myself**.
Therefore, if you **hearken** to my voice and **keep** my **covenant**,
　you shall be my **special possession**,
　dearer to me than all **other** people,
　though **all** the earth is **mine**.
You shall be to me a **kingdom** of **priests**, a holy **nation**.
That is what you must tell the **Israelites**."
So Moses **went** and **summoned** the elders of the people.
When he **set** before them
　all that the Lord had **ordered** him to tell them,
　the people all answered **together**,
　"**Everything** the Lord has **said**, we will **do**."

Stress the conditions God sets: "hearken," "keep."

"Kingdom of priests" refers to the nation as a whole. Among the nations, Israel is as special as are the priests among the people.

This is a solemn yet joyful statement of assent to God's conditions.

directive that they "be scattered" and fill the earth.

　The Lord responds to this affront with surprisingly human reasoning and emotions. Don't be afraid of letting God sound human, but avoid a vindictive tone. God acts for the good of humanity, like a parent chastising a presumptuous child. Deliver the closing sentences slowly, with a tone of regret, summarizing what happened to the world as a result of human pride: people were "scattered" and took refuge behind walls from which they would eventually throw stones at one another.

EXODUS. The events in this fascinating reading precede one of the most pivotal moments in salvation history. Amidst thunder and lightening, heavy clouds and trumpet blasts, God will soon give the commandments and seal a covenant with Israel that will establish them as God's chosen people. This face-to-face encounter is the prelude to the moment when God delivers the commandments to Israel, through their surrogate, Moses.

　We must imagine Moses scaling the mountain with awe and trembling, for ancients believed that no one saw the face of God and lived. Here, awe means wonder and overwhelming reverence. So, from the opening narration, suggest that Moses' ascent is no ordinary climb. Although awesome, God is comfortingly tender, recounting Israel's deliverance from slavery with incredible intimacy: God brings Israel not to the mountain, but "to *myself*," the covenant is "*my* covenant," Israel is God's "*special* possession," and the nation is "holy," a "kingdom of priests." Boldly and without apology, God expresses divine preference for this one nation over all the nations of the earth. But note the condition: "*if*"

Describe the great theophany (manifestation of God's powerful presence) with a sense of awe, but skip the melodrama.

Fire and smoke are common manifestations of God. Wind and fire imagery dominate both here and in the Pentecost story.

"Trumpet" is a likely metaphor for a strong, driving wind.

Speak this line slowly. There is great suspense here.

On the morning of the **third** day
    there were peals of **thunder** and **lightning**,
    and a heavy **cloud** over the mountain,
    and a very loud **trumpet** blast,
    so that all the people in the camp **trembled**.
But **Moses** led the people **out** of the camp to meet **God**,
    and they **stationed** themselves at the **foot** of the mountain.
Mount **Sinai** was all wrapped in **smoke**,
    for the LORD came down upon it in **fire**.
The smoke **rose** from it as though from a **furnace**,
    and the whole mountain trembled **violently**.
The **trumpet** blast grew **louder** and **louder**,
        while Moses was **speaking**,
    and God **answering** him with **thunder**.

When the LORD came **down** to the top of Mount Sinai,
    he **summoned** Moses to the **top** of the mountain.

Or:

READING I   Ezekiel 37:1–14

A reading from the Book of the Prophet Ezekiel

The hand of the LORD came upon me,
    and he **led** me out in the **spirit** of the LORD
    and **set** me in the center of the **plain**,
    which was now **filled** with **bones**.
He made me **walk** among the **bones** in every **direction**
    so that I saw how **many** they were on the surface of the plain.

Ezekiel = ee-ZEE-kee-uhl
To enhance rather than slight the unique features of this text (the refrain-like repetitions and the extraordinary visions), you will need extra preparation time. Practice until you are comfortable with and enjoying the rich imagery and the poetic flow of the language.
Ezekiel finds himself transported into the midst of this scene of devastation.

you keep my covenant, *then* you'll be mine. God's tender love, as relayed to the people by Moses, evokes heartfelt assent: "*Everything . . . we will do!*"

   In the second paragraph we find the dramatic fireworks we associate with this event. As in the Pentecost narrative, wind and fire dominate here, together with thunder and lightening and the ever-louder trumpet blast. As Moses and Israel approach God to transact the covenant, the atmospheric display fills them with trembling. With balance and proper nuance, enjoy recounting this awesome encounter.

The final line, a paragon of suspense, should insinuate that the real excitement waits at "the top of the mountain."

   EZEKIEL. It may take time to get comfortable with the unusual characteristics of this text. The refrains and repetitions, not to mention Ezekiel's extraordinary vision, are unlike anything we encounter in contemporary prose. Let that awareness excite you, for you have an opportunity to proclaim an iconic text that swells with musical language and stunning imagery.

   Some events can shake a nation to its core. Consider the Civil War in American

history. For ancient Israel, the Exile was a disorienting trauma that tested its faith. God calls on Ezekiel to prophesy in the midst of the Exile when the people have lost heart after the destruction of Jerusalem and its temple. The profound shock of these events robbed the nation of all hope. As a gesture of mercy and healing, God grants Ezekiel this vision of the dry bones, challenging despair with an image of hope and restoration. But Ezekiel is not easily roused. God makes him linger among the bones to absorb the utter devastation they represent, and he gets the

His despondency should be apparent in
your tone.

prophesy = PROF-uh-sī
God *orders* Ezekiel to prophesy.
Speak these words with authority.

Don't overdramatize these events; they
should have an air of reality. Achieve that
with a lively rate; too slow a pace will
make the lines burdensome. Throughout,
tone and energy are more important than
specific words.

prophesying = PROF-uh-sī-ing

These repetitions, like the repeated
phrases of a song, add beauty to the text
and etch its message in our memories.
Don't treat them like redundancies to be
gotten around as quickly as possible.

Only when they receive God's spirit do
the bones come alive.

How **dry** they were!
He **asked** me:
  Son of man, can these **bones** come to **life**?
I answered, "Lord GOD, you **alone** know that."
Then he said to me:
  Prophesy over these bones, and **say** to them:
  Dry **bones**, hear the word of the LORD!
Thus says the Lord GOD to these bones:
  See! I will bring **spirit** into you, that you may come to **life**.
I will put **sinews** upon you, make **flesh** grow over you,
  cover you with **skin**, and put **spirit** in you
  so that you may come to **life** and know that **I** am the LORD.
I, Ezekiel, **prophesied** as I had been **told**,
  and even as I was **prophesying** I heard a **noise**;
  it was a **rattling** as the bones came **together**, **bone** joining bone.
I saw the **sinews** and the **flesh** come upon them,
  and the **skin** cover them, but there was no **spirit** in them.
Then the LORD said to me:
  Prophesy to the **spirit**, **prophesy**, son of man,
  and **say** to the spirit: Thus says the Lord **GOD**:
  From the four winds **come**, O spirit,
  and **breathe** into these **slain** that they may come to **life**.
I prophesied as he **told** me, and the spirit **came** into them;
  they came **alive** and stood **upright**, a vast **army**.
Then he said to me:
  Son of **man**, these bones are the whole **house** of **Israel**.
They have been saying,
  "Our bones are **dried up**,
  our **hope** is **lost**, and we are cut **off**."

point. In response to God's question, "Can these bones come to life?", Ezekiel can muster only an unenthusiastic, "You alone know that," which deepens the despair.

Clearly, no human effort can reverse this situation. So God takes charge, ordering Ezekiel to *speak* God's Spirit into the bones and promising restoration that no human heart could conceive. A spellbinding scene unfolds. Notice the interplay between God's commands and Ezekiel's compliance. God orders boldly; at first, Ezekiel complies tentatively, but then marvels at the dramatic results his words

induce. The miracle unfolds in stages. Amid the roar of wind and rattling bones, flesh, sinews, and skin appear on the bare bones, "but there was no spirit in them."

Your energy and momentum must grow continually, but don't cheapen the beauty of the vision by over-dramatizing what requires an air of reality. The marvelous imagery of this text was for Israel a promise of Exile's end and of the future restoration of nation and temple. While God may chastise, he will never abandon the chosen people nor revoke the covenant. The Spirit that restores these bones

will later descend at Pentecost and guide the Church throughout its history. The certainty of "I have promised and I will do it" is vital in your proclamation. Experience these amazing events through Ezekiel's eyes and describe them with his sense of wonder, paying attention to Pentecost words like: "spirit," "life," and "breath."

JOEL. Joel is a prophet and prophets do hard work. So must those who proclaim their words. Many words are marked for stress in the passage. Though you may choose other words to emphasize, you'll still need great energy to communicate

This promise should arouse hope in the listener.

The fulfillment of the promise will prove God's sovereignty.

The covenant will not be abandoned!

The final line contains two strong declarations: "I have promised" and "I will do it." Don't run them together.

Therefore, **prophesy** and say to them: **Thus** says the Lord GOD:
O my **people**, I will open your **graves**
and have you **rise** from them,
and bring you **back** to the land of **Israel**.
Then you shall **know** that I am the LORD,
when I **open** your graves and have you **rise** from them,
O my **people**!
I will put my **spirit** in you that you may **live**,
and I will **settle** you upon your **land**;
thus you shall **know** that I am the LORD.
I have **promised**, and I will **do** it, says the LORD.

Or:

Joel = JOH-*l
This text forms the basis of much of Peter's Pentecost sermon (Acts 2:17–21).

prophesy = PROF-uh-sī
Stress the variety of those who will receive the Spirit.

This is unexpected: "Even upon the servants." Stress these words appropriately.

There is a more sober mood here. The images are not terrifying, but awe-inspiring.

READING I   Joel 3:1–5

A reading from the Book of the Prophet Joel

Thus says the LORD:
I will pour out my **spirit** upon all **flesh**.
Your **sons** and **daughters** shall **prophesy**,
   your **old** men shall dream **dreams**,
   your **young** men shall see **visions**;
even upon the **servants** and the **handmaids**,
   in those **days**, I will pour out my **spirit**.
And I will work **wonders** in the **heavens** and on the **earth**,
   blood, **fire**, and columns of **smoke**;

Joel's message. A plague of locusts had devastated Israel, which Joel interpreted as God's judgment against the people's lukewarm faith. He called for repentance and the people responded with genuine sorrow, so God has already promised to restore the land.

But now, God promises even greater blessings. With tremendous urgency, as if the message must be shared before it's too late, God's voice speaks throughout. God's added blessings are threefold, each signaled by a divine declaration.

The first is, "I will pour out my spirit . . . ." In a religious tradition that believed the Spirit could only be imparted to a select few, Joel/God announces a bountiful outpouring of the spirit upon sons and daughters, old men and young, even servants and handmaids. The spirit even makes servants the equals of their masters. Speak these lines with the joy and generosity that pervades them.

The second declaration is "I will work wonders . . . ." The vivid and powerful images of "blood, fire, and columns of smoke," of a darkened sun and a bloody moon, all on that "great and terrible day," should fill us more with awe than terror. You announce remarkable events that are, in fact, a blessing that prepares us for the coming of the Lord. They are "terrible" not in the sense of awful but *awesome*; like the birth of a child that can be frightening and painful, but ultimately glorious.

The final declaration is, "everyone shall be rescued . . . ." A significant pause after "terrible day" allows a transition to the message of comfort that follows. All who call on God's name will be safe. But not all will be saved, for Mount Zion will

"Great" and "terrible" characterize the mood of the entire reading.

Those who call on God need not fear the "terrible day" of the Lord.

"Zion" and "Jerusalem" are much beloved images that combine with "remnant" and "survivors" to create a sense of joyful hope.

the **sun** will be turned to **darkness**,
    and the **moon** to **blood**,
at the coming of the **day** of the LORD,
    the **great** and **terrible** day.
Then everyone shall be **rescued**
    who calls on the **name** of the LORD;
for on Mount **Zion** there shall be a **remnant**,
    as the LORD has **said**,
and in **Jerusalem survivors**
    whom the LORD shall **call**.

READING II   Romans 8:22–27

A reading from the Letter of Saint Paul to the Romans

Brothers and sisters:
We **know** that all **creation** is **groaning** in **labor** pains
        even until **now**;
    and not only **that**, but we **ourselves**,
    who have the **firstfruits** of the **Spirit**,
    we **also** groan within ourselves
    as we wait for **adoption**, the **redemption** of our **bodies**.
For in **hope** we were **saved**.
Now hope that **sees** is **not** hope.
For who **hopes** for what one **sees**?
But if we hope for what we do **not** see, we wait with **endurance**.

"Labor pains" is unexpected. Don't rush past the image.

While we have already tasted life in the Spirit, we long for the fullness only the kingdom can offer.

There is a lively, colloquial feel to Paul's logic. He is not arguing like a lawyer, but as a believer sharing faith. Recalling your own longing for what you cannot see—health of loved ones, a just society, inner peace—call us to yearn patiently for what eyes fail to perceive.

---

harbor not everyone, but only a "remnant." Offer assurance with that promise that some will hear and heed the call of the Lord and find in his arms a place of refuge.

READING II   Because all things are from God and of God, we, and all Creation, long for the full-flowering of the kingdom. Like us, all Creation bears the consequences of sin, and like us, it will enjoy the rewards of redemption and future glory. With the rest of Creation we "groan" as if experiencing the pangs of childbirth because our full adoption as

God's children is not yet realized. This longing and groaning that has characterized generations of faithful believers will at last be resolved through the indwelling of God's Spirit. Even now, though not as wholly as in the kingdom, we receive the Spirit as the "firstfruits," a foretaste of the fullness that is to come. Our "faith" alone guarantees liberation from the bondage of sin and enables us to wait in hope. Paul defines hope as expecting what we cannot see, and because we believe without seeing, we develop "endurance."

If we trust, we will find that God provides for everything, even our inadequacy in prayer. We may wonder why our prayers often seem to go unanswered. Paul helps us understand: "We do not know how to pray as we ought." But the Spirit comes to our aid, praying within us "with inexpressible groanings" that communicate our deepest yearnings to God. Paul ends assuring us that God, "who searches hearts," fully comprehends the Spirit's prayers for us. With confidence, convince the assembly that, unlike us, the Spirit prays only according to God's perfect will.

The Spirit even prays within us when we don't know how to pray.

God, who searches hearts, understands our spirit-led prayers better than we do. Offer that assurance to your assembly with confidence and don't rush past this beautiful image.

In the **same** way, the Spirit **too** comes to the aid of our **weakness**;
  for we do not know **how** to **pray** as we **ought**,
  but the Spirit **himself** intercedes with inexpressible **groanings**.
And the one who searches **hearts**
  knows what is the **intention** of the Spirit,
  because he **intercedes** for the holy ones
  according to God's **will**.

GOSPEL   John 7:37–39

A reading from the holy Gospel according to John

On the **last** and **greatest** day of the **feast**,
  Jesus stood up and **exclaimed**,
  "Let anyone who **thirsts** come to **me** and **drink**.
As Scripture says:
  *Rivers of **living** water will flow from **within** him*
    *who **believes** in me."*

He said this in reference to the **Spirit**
  that those who came to **believe** in him were to **receive**.
There was, of course, no Spirit **yet**,
  because **Jesus** had not yet been **glorified**.

Suggest that he rose and spoke with great vigor. Make eye contact as you speak, "Let anyone . . . ."

"From within him" is one of those rare instances when you should stress the preposition.

Although this sounds parenthetical, sustain the energy. It's important.

Jesus' glorification was his death, Resurrection, and Ascension.

The Feast of Tabernacles was both a commemoration of Israel's wanderings in the desert and a celebration of the harvest. For seven days water was carried into the city from the Pool of Siloam to remind the people of the water from the rock in the desert and to symbolize hope of Messianic deliverance. Jesus speaks these words on the eighth day.

GOSPEL   Fully aware that his enemies are plotting to kill him, Jesus nonetheless stands in the midst of the harvest festival and makes a bold proclamation. Few New Testament narratives are written in the screenplay style of this brief text. With the festival at its climax, Jesus commands the attention of friend and foe alike. He knows many in the crowd will grasp at any word they can use against him, and still he daringly proclaims himself the source of living water, water that will issue from him in the form of God's Spirit. In the midst of prayer and

great rejoicing, Jesus offers himself as the source of even greater joy. Come to me and drink, he says, and you yourselves will become "rivers of living water." With that image of inexhaustible abundance, Jesus assures us that the gift of the spirit he imparts will end our spiritual wanderings and sate even our deepest thirst.

  Scholars disagree whether Christ or the believer is the source of "living water," but clearly Jesus is alluding to the wisdom of the Spirit that he will pass on to those who believe in him. By stressing "rivers of living water" rather than "him" you will

highlight this central image of the passage. In John, imparting the Spirit must await Jesus' glorification, which is accomplished through his death, Resurrection, and Ascension. That's the meaning of the final sentence: the Spirit is not yet given because Jesus has not yet ascended to the Father. So brief a text requires a slower pace, lest you finish before your listeners have fully tuned in. Read in a familiar tone, as if taking the assembly into your confidence, sharing special information, and inviting them to be among those who "come to [him] and drink."

PENTECOST: DAY

Lectionary #63

READING I   Acts 2:1–11

A reading from the Acts of the Apostles

When the time for **Pentecost** was **fulfilled**,
    they were all in one place **together**.
And **suddenly** there came from the **sky**
    a noise like a **strong** driving **wind**,
    and it **filled** the entire **house** in which they were.
Then there appeared to them **tongues** as of **fire**,
    which **parted** and came to **rest** on each **one** of them.
And they were all **filled** with the **Holy Spirit**
    and began to speak in different **tongues**,
    as the Spirit **enabled** them to **proclaim**.

Now there were **devout** Jews from every **nation** under heaven
    staying in Jerusalem.
At this **sound**, they gathered in a large **crowd**,
    but they were **confused**
    because **each** one heard them **speaking** in his own **language**.
They were **astounded**, and in **amazement** they asked,
    "Are not all these people who are speaking **Galileans**?
Then how does **each** of us hear them in his **native** language?
We are **Parthians**, **Medes**, and **Elamites**,
    inhabitants of **Mesopotamia**, **Judea** and **Cappadocia**,

---

The opening is subdued, lacking any hint of the impending fireworks.

Distinguish the three moments as the "Tongues of fire" appear, part, and rest on each one. Renew your energy on "And they were filled."

Drop your energy level for the narration about the devout Jews. Then raise it again on "At the sound . . . ."

"Astounded . . . amazement" suggest how to narrate this section.

Name each nation carefully, not because each is individually important, but because together they express the universality of the Christian message.

Galileans = gal-ih-LEE-uhnz
Parthians = PAHR-thee-uhnz
Medes = meedz
Elamites = EE-luh-mīts
Mesopotamia = mes-uh-poh-TAY-mee-uh
Judea = joo-DEE-uh
Cappadocia = cap-uh-DOH-shee-uh

Today options are given for the readings. Contact your parish staff to learn which readings will be used.

READING I The opening sentence offers no hint of the excitement that will follow. Here, "Pentecost" refers to the Jewish harvest festival, not the Christian solemnity we celebrate today. "Suddenly" breaks the calm and introduces the spectacular: "Strong, driving wind" automatically signals Spirit, and the rushing, compelling energy it generates dramatically manifests the new

moment in salvation history that God is here initiating. "Tongues as of fire" also hints at divinity, reminding us of Sinai, where similar fireworks accompanied the inauguration of the old covenant. The new covenant, sealed in Christ's blood, is inaugurated here. "They were all filled . . ." announces the dramatic power of God's Spirit. Speak slower here to stress and absorb the impact of God's intervention, then announce the results as manifested in the apostles' sudden ability to speak in different languages.

"Jews from every nation" hear (and we assume will carry forth) the good news of salvation. Each proper name deserves attention, not because each is individually important, but because together they anticipate the universality of Christ's Church. The words "astounded" and "amazement" are textual clues regarding proclamation. But don't over-dramatize. Instead, recall a time when you experienced God's presence in some special way and let that memory color your delivery. Keep in mind that the crowd is suddenly able to understand the apostles, not each

Pontus = PON-thus
Phrygia =FRIJ-ee-uh
Pamphylia = pam-FIL-ee-uh
Libya = LIB-ee-uh
Cyrene = sī-REE-nee
Cretans = KREE-tuhns

Final line summarizes the amazement that builds throughout the listing of nations. Distinguish the two ideas found here: "in our own tongues" and "mighty deeds of God."

Don't let Paul's logic and balanced structure cause you to miss the emotional structure of the text. Paul loves the Corinthians and desires harmony among them. Recall the need for harmony in your own world—whether local or global—and perhaps you'll find a proper balance between logic and passion.

Don't stress the repetitions of "different"; instead, stress "service," "Lord," "workings," and "God."

This line concludes and summarizes the first section.

Speak the body analogy carefully and slowly. Paul says much with few words. Stress the contrasts. Note the suggestions for when to stress the word "one." The oneness of the body is maintained with the glue of the Spirit: "Jews or Greeks, slaves or free" reinforces that idea, saying no matter how large or diverse the community, it remains one body in the spirit.

Pontus and **Asia**, **Phrygia** and **Pamphylia**,
Egypt and the districts of **Libya** near **Cyrene**,
as well as travelers from **Rome**,
both **Jews** and **converts** to Judaism, **Cretans** and **Arabs**,
yet we hear them **speaking** in our own **tongues**
of the mighty **acts** of **God**."

READING II 1 Corinthians 12:3b–7, 12–13

A reading from the first Letter of Saint Paul to the Corinthians

Brothers and sisters:
No one can say, "**Jesus** is **Lord**," except by the Holy **Spirit**.

There are different **kinds** of spiritual **gifts** but the same **Spirit**;
    there are different forms of **service** but the same **Lord**;
    there are different **workings** but the same **God**
    who produces **all** of them in **everyone**.
To **each** individual the **manifestation** of the Spirit
    is given for some **benefit**.

As a body is **one** though it has many **parts**,
    and **all** the parts of the body, though **many**, are **one** body,
    so also **Christ**.
For in **one** Spirit we were all **baptized** into **one body**,
    whether **Jews** or **Greeks**, **slaves** or **free** persons,
    and we were all given to **drink** of one **Spirit**.

Or:

---

other. Pentecost's miracle doesn't end tensions and divisions between nations; it opens the hearts of many to the good news of salvation so that the Gospel might become the leaven that eventually draws all people into the oneness of Christ.

READING II **1 CORINTHIANS.** In Paul's bold, uncompromising words, we see that even the Spirit does not erase tension and division within a community. Paul's readers are Christians splintered by the very reality that should be their source of unity, the Holy Spirit. The

gifts of the Spirit had rained down upon them but, instead of rejoicing at each others good fortune, they started comparing what they received to what others got and, like selfish siblings, they bragged or pouted accordingly. Because the Corinthians had fallen into jealousy, Paul reminds them that while they have *different* gifts, they share a *common* Spirit.

Gifts are given to individuals, but to be exercised as forms of "*service*" for the good of all. Even the impulse to acknowledge Jesus as Lord comes from God's Spirit—not the false spirits of pagan experience, as

some believed. So, he argues, all of you who worship Jesus as Lord are heeding the prompting of the *same* Spirit. Knowing we *share* the one Spirit should make it easier to accept disparities in the distribution of the other gifts given to the community.

Paul says the Body of Christ works the same way as the human body: we can't rank the importance of the various parts, because the body functions well only when all the parts work in harmony. Some perform one service and others a different task, but it is the same Spirit who enables each to contribute to the whole.

READING II   Galatians 5:16–25

A reading from the Letter of Saint Paul to the Galatians

The opening declaration must ring with authority and with conviction that what you command is possible.

Brothers and sisters, **live** by the **Spirit**
    and you will certainly not **gratify** the desire of the **flesh**.

Your tone is not judgmental, but reveals an understanding of the difficulty of the struggle between spirit and flesh, of the painful frustration of not being *able* to do what we *want* to do.

For the **flesh** has desires **against** the Spirit,
    and the **Spirit** against the **flesh**;
    these are **opposed** to each other,
    so that you may not **do** what you **want**.

Another line that needs to be spoken with conviction.

But if you are guided by the **Spirit**, you are not under the **law**.

Don't read this list with finger-wagging, but with a clear sense that these things bring death and can only end badly.

Now the works of the flesh are **obvious**:
    immorality, **impurity**, **lust**, **idolatry**,
    sorcery, **hatreds**, **rivalry**, **jealousy**,
    outbursts of **fury**, acts of **selfishness**,
    dissensions, **factions**, occasions of **envy**,
    drinking bouts, **orgies**, and the like.

Remember, Paul's warning is done out of love for his readers. Imagine speaking the words to a beloved child.

I **warn** you, as I warned you **before**,
    that those who **do** such things will not **inherit** the kingdom
        of **God**.

"In contrast" tells you to proclaim this list with a different tone. Don't rush the list; let it ring with life and hope.

In **contrast**, the **fruit** of the Spirit is **love**, **joy**, **peace**,
    patience, **kindness**, **generosity**,
    faithfulness, **gentleness**, **self-control**.
Against **such** there **is** no law.

This very serious line should be delivered with sustained eye contact. End on a note of joyful hope.

Now those who belong to Christ **Jesus** have **crucified** their flesh
    with its **passions** and **desires**.
If we **live** in the Spirit, let us also **follow** the Spirit.

Focusing on gifts requires a focus on forgiveness: in order for the body to run smoothly, its members must be willing to forgive the inevitable hurts they inflict on one another—even hurts that result from the exercise of God-given gifts.

GALATIANS. Paul reminds us that we live each day with an inner tension that sometimes may flare into open warfare. Human life is comprised of spirit and flesh, but oftentimes one aspect rages against the other, for the desires of the flesh clash with the desires of the spirit. In stark terms, that's the human condition, Paul says. But he goes further: though the battle rages, we do not fight alone. We have the gift of the Spirit who leads and guides us, who frees us from the bondage of the flesh law and enables us to yield to the prompting of the spirit. Though Paul's tone tends toward stern and threatening, there is a strong underpinning of joy and love. He warns in order to protect us, because he understands the danger of yielding to the flesh and its many allurements, here starkly enumerated. Paul's listing of the "works of the flesh," though sobering, would be downright demoralizing were it not balanced by his listing of the "fruit of the Spirit."

Paul's goal must become yours—to persuade that yielding to the spirit is possible, that those who "*live* in the Spirit" can also "follow the Spirit." In plain terms, Paul has drawn the contours of the Christian life: a constant effort to forsake those things that lead to death (lust, hatreds, jealousy, factions, envy) balanced by an even greater effort to embrace the things that lead to life (love, patience, generosity, self-control). Your tone should draw clearly the opposing sides in this

In John, Jesus' Resurrection, Ascension, and conferral of the Spirit all occur on one day. For further commentary, see Gospel of the Second Sunday of Easter.

Pause before the greeting of peace.

John says he showed his "hands and his side," which in this Gospel was "pierced." Luke speaks of his "hands and feet."

Put your stress on "Lord," not "saw," because they rejoiced not at the sight but at the *certainty* that it was Jesus.

Now that they perceive, Jesus offers peace a second time.

"Breathed" sounds like it means.

Today Jesus' formula points more to initiation through baptismal faith than to penance.

GOSPEL   John 20:19–33

A reading from the holy Gospel according to John

On the evening of that **first** day of the week,
 when the doors were **locked**, where the **disciples** were,
 for fear of the **Jews**,
 Jesus came and **stood** in their midst
 and said to them, "**Peace** be with you."
When he had **said** this, he showed them his **hands** and his **side**.
The disciples **rejoiced** when they saw the Lord.
Jesus said to them **again**, "**Peace** be with you.
As the **Father** has sent **me**, so **I** send **you**."
And when he had said this, he **breathed** on them
 and said to them,
 "**Receive** the Holy **Spirit**.
Whose sins you **forgive** are **forgiven** them,
 and whose sins you **retain** are **retained**."

Or:

---

struggle: rather than disapproval, name the works of the flesh with an understanding of the very real destruction they bring into one's life. Conversely, name the fruit of the Spirit with conviction that these comprise the path to life, and nothing else.

| GOSPEL | **JOHN 20.** The opening sentence of this brief passage |

is packed with significant information: on the first day of the week (Resurrection day), with the disciples hiding fearfully behind locked doors, Jesus unexpectedly and miraculously comes to them and offers

"peace." By reading deliberately and not rushing, you can help your assembly hear all the information the evangelist has crammed into that sentence. Jesus' first offer of peace is given to calm them, but the disciples don't respond immediately. So Jesus shows his hands and side, and finally they rejoice. Note, however, that they rejoiced not at the sight but at the certainty that it was the Lord. It takes the evidence of his Passion and death to persuade his closest friends that the one before them is the Lord. Even on this great solemnity, the Gospel reminds us that we walk

under the shadow of the cross, that victory was won at great cost.

In the midst of their rejoicing, Jesus repeats his peace greeting, perhaps suggesting that peace is the most necessary virtue in the Christian life. He comforts as he commissions the disciples. In speaking "As the Father has sent me" he makes them apostles ("those sent"), but by imparting the Holy Spirit he is also giving them the assurance that they will be able to carry out their mission as Jesus himself accomplished his. John condenses Pentecost into a single phrase: "He breathed on them

Read this complex sentence slowly. To get the sense of it, start with the main clause: "He will testify to me," and then follow with the three subordinate clauses: "When . . . ," "whom . . . ," "the Spirit . . . ." Then practice it as given.

Be sure to stress the word "also."

Make eye contact with the assembly before beginning this section.

The Spirit speaks not on his own, but on behalf of the Father and the Son. The Trinity is one and undivided.

There is no boasting here, but a declaration that in Christ we see God, and the Spirit comes to reveal God in Christ.

GOSPEL   John 15:26–27; 16:12–15

A reading from the holy Gospel according to John

Jesus said to his **disciples**:
  "When the **Advocate** comes whom I will **send** you
      from the **Father**,
   the Spirit of **truth** that **proceeds** from the Father,
   he will **testify** to me.
And you **also** testify,
   because you have **been** with me from the **beginning**.

"I have much **more** to tell you, but you cannot **bear** it now.
But when he **comes**, the Spirit of **truth**,
   he will **guide** you to **all** truth.
He will not speak on his **own**,
   but he will speak what he **hears**,
   and will **declare** to you the things that are **coming**.
He will **glorify** me,
   because he will take from what is **mine** and **declare** it to you.
Everything that the Father **has** is mine;
   for this **reason** I told you that he will take from what is **mine**
      and declare it to **you**."

and said . . . Receive." In that line, we hear echoes of Creation, when God imparted life with the divine breath. Here, Jesus breathes new life into his disciples, life in the Spirit, empowering them to carry on his mission of healing and reconciling.

JOHN 15. Today's solemnity celebrates Jesus' promise, in this part of the Last Supper discourse, that the Father will send an "Advocate," the Holy Spirit. The Spirit will "testify" to Jesus and the truth he has spoken. He will empower the disciples to bear witness to Jesus, testifying to all they have witnessed from the beginning

of his ministry. The Spirit will be the ongoing assurance of the risen Christ's presence in his body, the Church. But, above all, the Advocate will be a teacher, helping Jesus' followers fully comprehend the meaning of all Jesus said and did in his earthly ministry. That is the meaning of "He will . . . declare to you the things that are coming." Those words are not a promise that the "Spirit of Truth" will provide a glimpse of future events, but a guarantee that, through the Spirit, the disciples will be able to correctly interpret what has already happened.

Jesus' ministry of teaching is not complete, for he has more to "tell" them that they cannot yet bear. It will be for the Spirit to guide Jesus' followers into the fullness of truth. Throughout this text we see the workings of the communion of divine persons in the Trinity. The Spirit is the gift of Jesus sent by the Father. He declares only what is given him to share, and what he shares from the Father belongs to Jesus. We cannot focus on one person of the Trinity without seeing all three.

MOST HOLY TRINITY

Lectionary #165

READING I   Deuteronomy 4:32–34, 39–40

A reading from the Book of Deuteronomy

Establish who is speaking, then pose the questions as much to your assembly as Moses did to his.

Moses said to the **people**:
    "**Ask** now of the days of **old**, **before** your time,
    ever since God created **man** upon the earth;
    ask from **one** end of the sky to the **other**:
    Did anything so great ever happen **before**?
Was it ever **heard** of?

To be effective, these rhetorical questions need to beg for an answer.

Did a people ever hear the voice of **God**
    speaking from the midst of **fire**, as **you** did, and **live**?

Be aware of Moses' allusions: God's voice on Sinai, choosing Israel as his special people, deliverance from Egypt by means of ten plagues, and the destruction of the Egyptian army.

Or did **any** god venture to go and take a **nation** for **himself**
    from the midst of **another** nation,
    by **testings**, by **signs** and **wonders**, by **war**,
    with strong **hand** and outstretched **arm**, and by great **terrors**,
    all of which the LORD, your **God**,
    did for **you** in **Egypt** before your very **eyes**?

Although delivered with energy and heightened tempo, you mustn't run together the specifics of Moses' list.

This is why you must now **know**,
    and **fix** in your heart, that the LORD is **God**
    in the heavens **above** and on earth **below**,
    and that there is no **other**.

The mood of Moses' homily shifts here. Slow your tempo and focus on compassion and gratitude as motives for obedience.

You must keep his **statutes** and **commandments** that I **enjoin**
        on you today,
    that **you** and your children **after** you may **prosper**,
    and that you may have long **life** on the land
    which the LORD, your **God**, is **giving** you **forever**."

Here is what is at stake: prosperity, even life itself, depend on fidelity to God's law.

READING I   A fine orator is someone with a good memory who knows a people's history and can evoke it with passion. Anyone making a speech about momentous events in our own time would do well to imitate Moses: "Did anything so great ever happen before? Was it ever heard of?" The Jewish people are sometimes called the "People of the Book" because their faith (and ours) is so rooted in memory, the memory of God's saving actions as told in the books of the Bible. We need those books because human memory is feeble. Even after astonishing events, excitement wanes and the recently impossible becomes the taken for granted. Moses fights that human tendency to forget. With great oratorical skill he shares his profound awareness of the marvels God worked for Israel in an effort to awaken their drowsy memories and fuel in them the sense of awe that burns in him.

You take on the same task as Moses: to inspire, awaken, and fill your listeners with awe. Moses is blunt: "Ask," he says, I dare you, "ASK! Survey all of history and see if anything like what our God has done was ever done before." Soon, he's on a roll, hurling question after question. Of course they are rhetorical, but each projects an implied, "Well, I'm waiting!" The last and longest question is tricky; so slow down, but simultaneously build intensity, making each phrase a finger jab in the face of your forgetful neighbors.

Suddenly Moses' tone shifts: no more finger pointing; instead, he seems to extend his arms in a plea for fidelity to the God who has shown such love. In light of that love, the injunction to "keep his statutes" is more appeal than command. Moses then establishes a cause-effect relationship:

READING II   Romans 8:14–17

A reading from the Letter of Saint Paul to the Romans

Brothers and sisters:
Those who are led by the **Spirit** of God are **sons** of God.
For you did not receive a spirit of **slavery** to fall back into **fear**,
     but you received a Spirit of **adoption**,
          through whom we cry, "**Abba, Father!**"
The Spirit himself bears **witness** with **our** spirit
     that we are **children** of God,
     and if **children**, then **heirs**,
     heirs of **God** and **joint** heirs with **Christ**,
     if only we **suffer** with him
     so that we may also be **glorified** with him.

Declare the opening sentence, and then pause before continuing with the ensuing explanation.

Speak in a solicitous tone, as if explaining to a loved one an obvious point they failed to understand.

On this Trinity Sunday, references to the Spirit deserve extra emphasis. Highlight Paul's logic: if we are "children," then we are also "heirs."

The last two lines contain two distinct ideas: if we are willing to "suffer" we will also be "glorified." Lift out both ideas.

keep the commandants, *then* your children will prosper. So much depends on our fidelity—prosperity, long life, land—that living our commitment is hardly an option. With love-motivated urgency, call us to that faithfulness.

READING II This brief and fluid passage joyfully proclaims great news: "we are children of God." With a convincing tone and sustained eye contact, urge us to live like we believe that! Baptism doesn't initiate us into timidity

and shyness. On the contrary, it gives us permission to call the great God "Abba," "Father," Daddy!

Paul's words speak of our very identity: we are not merely members of some religion, we are children of God. God's own Spirit bears witness to that great truth. God is our father and therefore we are "children" and "heirs" in the same way Christ is "son" and "heir." Proclaim this news with conviction and joy.

This new status is bestowed on us through God's goodness, not our merit. Only one thing is needed, a willingness to

"suffer" with Christ. So briefly stated as it is, one might almost think that Paul was slipping this point in to avoid notice; but that is not Paul's style. That truth is so second nature to Paul, it is so much a part of his lived experience, that he doesn't need to beat a drum when he says it. Baptism initiates us into Christ's death so that we might also (and here's why we proclaim with a smile instead of a frown) "be glorified with him!"

GOSPEL   Matthew 28:16–20

A reading from the holy Gospel according to Matthew

The **eleven** disciples went to **Galilee**,
　　to the **mountain** to which Jesus had **ordered** them.
When they all **saw** him, they **worshiped**, but they **doubted**.
Then Jesus **approached** and **said** to them,
　　"All power in **heaven** and on **earth** has been **given** to me.
Go, therefore, and make **disciples** of all **nations**,
　　baptizing them in the name of the **Father**,
　　and of the **Son**, and of the Holy **Spirit**,
　　teaching them to **observe** all that I have **commanded** you.
And **behold**, I am **with** you **always**, until the **end** of the **age**."

There are three important pieces of information here: "eleven," "Galilee," and "mountain."

Contrast their "worship" and their "doubt." Jesus first establishes his universal authority, then commissions them for their mission.
Jesus gives them specific tasks: go, make, baptize, and teach.

Let the final promise bring the kind of assurance to your assembly that Jesus wished to impart to his disciples.

GOSPEL | The Trinitarian formula that ends this reading is the apparent reason this text was selected for today's solemnity. But there is more here than a Trinitarian formula. That *eleven* disciples made their way up the mountain immediately conjures the painful memory of Judas' desertion. "Galilee," and the "mountain" site, arouse expectations that this will be a time of revelation—for that is the role these sites often play in scripture. Read slowly to allow those nuances to surface. You are narrating an awe-filled moment in the lives of the disciples, who fall on their faces to worship, though some are still plagued with doubts. The Greek text uses the same verb Matthew uses earlier to speak of Peter's "little faith."

Jesus responds with assurance and final instruction. His tone is all strength and confidence, qualities he'd like to bestow on this timid group. Having declared universal authority, Jesus shifts focus to their responsibilities: Go, make, baptize, teach. This is Jesus, friend and counselor, encouraging with each word of command, inviting them into closer intimacy by living out the ministry he entrusts to them. Baptizing "in the name" of someone signifies belonging to that person, so speak the baptismal formula as the offer of life and love that it is.

Jesus has an advantage over every friend who has ever left loved ones; he can assure them of his abiding presence after he's gone. Let your words and eyes reach out to your assembly to offer that assurance.

MOST HOLY BODY AND BLOOD OF CHRIST

Lectionary #168

READING I   Exodus 24:3–8

A reading from the Book of Exodus

When **Moses** came to the **people**
   and related all the **words** and **ordinances** of the LORD,
   they all answered with one **voice**,
   "We will do **everything** that the LORD has **told** us."
Moses then wrote **down** all the words of the LORD and,
   rising **early** the next day,
   he erected at the **foot** of the mountain an **altar**
   and twelve **pillars** for the twelve tribes of **Israel**.
Then, having sent certain young men of the Israelites
   to offer **holocausts** and sacrifice young **bulls**
   as **peace** offerings to the LORD,
   Moses took half of the **blood** and put it in large **bowls**;
   the **other** half he splashed on the **altar**.
Taking the book of the **covenant**, he read it **aloud** to the people,
   who answered, "All that the LORD has **said**,
     we will **heed** and **do**."
Then he took the **blood** and **sprinkled** it on the people, saying,
   "This is the blood of the **covenant**
   that the LORD has **made** with you
   in accordance with all these **words** of his."

Be sure you stress what it is the people are agreeing to "do."

Speak the line with enthusiasm and gratitude, not reluctance.

Allow a sense of mounting suspense to fill these lines.

Speak in a slower pace here. We are unfamiliar with such graphic rituals; don't gloss over the details. The "altar" symbolizes God; sprinkling symbolizes union.

The people are promising obedience to God's law in every phase of their lives.

The use of blood is even more graphic here. Speak with awareness of the gravity of this unique ritual that binds God and Israel forever.

READING I This text narrates an extremely significant event in the life of Israel: at Sinai, with Moses as mediator, God fashions a covenant with these former slaves, who begin to glimpse the meaning of being God's chosen people. It's an encounter between divinity and humanity that's told in an almost matter-of-fact manner, so your tone must suggest the exalted nature of this unique moment. A sense of expectancy fuses with the solemnity of a sacred ritual to create a profoundly moving experience of the intimate bond forged between God and Israel.

Suggest a growing sense of expectancy in the way you narrate the interaction between Moses and people. "All the words and ordinances" refers not only to the Ten Commandments, but also to laws regarding every aspect of social and religious life. God requires an all-encompassing commitment and the Israelites respond with unanimous assent, awaiting the next step in the process. Moses immediately takes action: he writes down the words of the Lord, erects an altar, and sends young men to offer holocausts. Speak of those activities with a mounting sense of expectancy and urgency that finally peaks in the arrestingly graphic outpouring of blood.

Don't shy from this vivid image. In scripture, blood is a source and sign of life; here it becomes a symbol of the union between God and the people. Embrace the word with vigor each time it recurs, making sure it is heard, for it provides a link to today's Gospel. Blood suggests new life, hope, and reconciliation as well as the unbreakable bond God establishes with Israel.

You must read slowly and lead your listeners, as if by the hand, through this complex passage. Pay special attention to the words marked for stress and be sure to highlight the contrasts.

Jesus intercedes in heaven directly before the Father, offering his own blood, not that of sacrificial animals.

Stress the logic of this argument. Animal sacrifice brought legal purification, but besides purification, the blood of Christ offers new life and access to the living God. Speak with joyful conviction.

See the commentary regarding this sentence. "A death . . ." refers to Jesus' death. Pause after "taken place." The words "for deliverance from transgressions under the first covenant" comprise a single thought. Although complex, this sentence announces good news.

READING II   Hebrews 9:11–15

A reading from the Letter to the Hebrews

Brothers and sisters:
When **Christ** came as **high** priest
　　of the **good** things that have come to **be**,
　　passing through the **greater** and more **perfect** tabernacle
　　not made by **hands**, that is, not belonging to **this** creation,
　　he entered **once** for **all** into the **sanctuary**,
　　not with the blood of **goats** and **calves**
　　but with his **own** blood, thus obtaining **eternal** redemption.
For if the blood of **goats** and **bulls**
　　and the sprinkling of a heifer's **ashes**
　　can **sanctify** those who are **defiled**
　　so that their flesh is **cleansed**,
　　how much **more** will the blood of **Christ**,
　　who through the eternal Spirit offered himself **unblemished**
　　　　to God,
　　cleanse our **consciences** from dead **works**
　　to **worship** the living **God**.

For this reason **he** is mediator of a **new** covenant:
　　since a **death** has taken place for deliverance
　　from **transgressions** under the **first** covenant,
　　those who are **called** may receive the **promised**
　　　　eternal inheritance.

With sincerity and love, speak the people's second promise of obedience more slowly than in the first sentence. The sound of their words should reflect humility before the generous love of God. Moses' final comment seals the newly formed union, and the blood he sprinkles is the enduring sign that God and people will forever belong to one another.

READING II The blood sacrifices of today's First Reading set a context for this passage. It's a difficult text, but understanding will aid your proclamation. Christ is high priest of the spiritual blessings ("the good things that have come to be") that were only foreshadowed in the Old Testament rites. As high priest, he now intercedes for us—not in the human-made temple of Jerusalem, but in the "greater and more perfect tabernacle" of heaven, which is not of human origin.

Although Christ entered heaven with a blood sacrifice, it was not the annually repeatable sacrifice of "goats and calves," but the once-for-always sacrifice of himself through which he achieved "eternal [not temporary] redemption." The lines that follow are pure logic: "if the blood of goats . . . can sanctify . . . how much more will the blood of Christ!" Although he reasons like a lawyer, the author shares the passion of a believer. That passion is best communicated with eye contact, and a tone that says *you* believe every word you speak.

The final sentence is again a bit abstruse. The verses following this passage clarify the legal point the author is

GOSPEL   Mark 14:12–16, 22–26

A reading from the holy Gospel according to Mark

On the **first** day of the Feast of Unleavened **Bread**,
    when they **sacrificed** the Passover **lamb**,
    Jesus' **disciples** said to him,
    "**Where** do you want us to go
    and **prepare** for you to eat the **Passover**?"
He sent two of his **disciples** and said to them,
    "Go into the **city** and a **man** will meet you,
    carrying a jar of **water**.
Follow him.
Wherever he **enters**, say to the **master** of the house,
    'The **Teacher** says, "Where is my **guest** room
    where I may eat the **Passover** with my **disciples**?"'
Then he will show you a large upper **room** furnished and **ready**.
Make the preparations for us **there**."
The disciples then went off, **entered** the city,
    and found it **just** as he had **told** them;
    and they **prepared** the **Passover**.

While they were **eating**,
    he took **bread**, said the **blessing**,
    broke it, **gave** it to them, and said,
    "**Take** it; this is my **body**."
Then he took a **cup**, gave **thanks**, and **gave** it to them,
    and they all **drank** from it.

Don't rush these details, for they set the context. And don't gloss over the reference to the sacrificial lamb, which serves as a clear type of Jesus.

Jesus speaks these instructions with confidence.

Suggest the surprise or incredulity they must have experienced at finding Jesus' words fulfilled so completely.

The scene changes abruptly. Slow your pace and speak the words as if for the first time.

making: one can only receive an "inheritance" once the writer of a will has died. Here the author says, "Since a death [Jesus' death] has *taken* place for [in order to make possible] deliverance from transgressions [committed] under the first covenant, those who are called [us!] may [now] *receive* the promised eternal inheritance." More simply: Jesus had to die in order for us to receive the inheritance he willed us. He did die. So, now we can claim the inheritance: forgiveness and eternal life. And in dying, Jesus mediated a

new covenant between us and God—a covenant that replaces the old one.

GOSPEL   (Refer also to comments on this passage contained in the Palm Sunday Passion commentary.) We might wonder about the value of the long prelude that precedes the "body and blood" in this passage. Before we arrive at the meal, we hear many details regarding where and who and how that may seem superfluous to today's solemnity. But look again. The first is hardly wasted verbiage when you consider that Jesus' response

to the disciples' inquiry reveals he has thought about and carefully prepared for this event. His prescient knowledge surrounds the whole affair with a sense of mystery and majesty.

The implications of the forethought Jesus has given this final gathering with his chosen twelve are clear: this will be no ordinary meal; something memorable is likely to happen. This supper, then, requires our full attention, respect, and reverence. The disciples may have embarked on their mission to find the "guest room" with a

Establish eye contact here.

Contrast the words "shall not drink" with "drink it new."

He **said** to them,
"This is my **blood** of the **covenant**,
which will be **shed** for **many**.
Amen, I say to you,
I shall not drink **again** the fruit of the vine
until the day when I drink it **new** in the kingdom of **God**."
Then, after singing a **hymn**,
they went out to the **Mount** of **Olives**.

sense of expectancy that was surely reinforced by the accurate fulfillment of Jesus' prophecy. Doubtless those disciples entered the upper room with anticipation and hope, though surely they could not anticipate the nature of the revelation they would experience there.

Suddenly, the text places us in the midst of the meal, and immediately we know it is, indeed, no ordinary dinner. "This is my body . . . this is my blood" are nothing less than shocking words. Earlier in his ministry, many had walked away from Jesus for intimations such as these. Yes,

these words are revolutionary, but they are also the intimate words of a dear friend spoken as last will and testament to those dearest and closest to him. Your delivery of the action words "took," "blessing," "broke," and "gave" will establish the intimacy. Jesus' focus is not on his imminent death, but on his friends. He offers them and us a means of remaining connected with him after he's gone, a means they don't fully understand, nor realize they need. Speak Jesus' words simply, slowly, and softly. And deliver his solemn assurance that he will not "drink again" until

the coming of the kingdom in a subdued tone, letting your *expression* convey the emotional fervor as well as your voice.

Although not stated, the "hymn" sung at the end of the meal was actually a set of thanksgiving songs (Psalms 114–118). Although seemingly an afterthought, the final sentence becomes significant because it communicates the attitude that should characterize our own response to the gift of Christ's body and blood: joyful praise.

11TH SUNDAY IN ORDINARY TIME

Lectionary #92

READING I   Ezekiel 17:22–24

A reading from the Book of the Prophet Ezekiel

"Crest of the cedar" refers to the House of David; "tender shoot" refers to a new leader God will raise up.

The second iteration of "mountain" requires higher energy (though not volume) than the first.

These lines should sound like a song of celebration.

This image speaks of divine shelter and protection.

Here is a regal pronouncement. Highlight the contrasts ("low"/"high" and "green"/"withered") in these lines.

In the phrase "So will I do," stress all of the words.

Thus says the Lord **GOD**:
  I, **too**, will take from the **crest** of the cedar,
    from its topmost branches tear off a **tender** shoot,
  and **plant** it on a **high** and lofty **mountain**;
    on the mountain heights of **Israel** I will plant it.
  It shall put forth **branches** and bear **fruit**,
    and become a majestic **cedar**.
  Birds of every kind shall **dwell** beneath it,
    every winged thing in the shade of its **boughs**.
  And all the trees of the field shall **know**
    that **I**, the **LORD**,
  bring **low** the **high** tree,
    lift **high** the **lowly** tree,
  wither up the **green** tree,
    and make the **withered** tree **bloom**.
  As I, the **LORD**, have **spoken**, so will I **do**.

READING I Today we hear God asserting his sovereignty in no uncertain terms. In the lines preceding this poetry, Ezekiel delivers God's rebuff to King Zedekiah, who had angered God by breaking a covenant and refusing to cooperate with his plan. God will eventually restore Israel under a faithful king of his choosing, and that is what you will proclaim. The tone of the closing line "As I . . . have spoken, so will I do" pervades the entire passage. God, author of life, sovereign lord of all the universe, says, "Watch what I will do; see the life I will generate; wait for the wonders I will work!"

Let divine confidence ring in your voice as you announce God's decision to take from "the crest of the cedar" (a symbol of the royal line of David) "a tender shoot" that God will nurse into a majestic tree. This promise of restoration for the exiled nation, of renewal under a messianic King from David's own line, should be spoken with gentle confidence, suggesting the tender care with which God handles the fragile "shoot." Ezekiel paints vivid images of the utopia God is readying for the people. In joyful strains, he sings of the tree that will grow from the shoot and of the "birds of every kind" its ample branches will accommodate.

Having seen the marvels God has accomplished, "All the trees . . ." (the nations of the earth), "shall know" that God is Lord. God announces this as a statement of fact, not as a boast. With sure authority God says, Know that I can "bring low" or "lift high," and even "make the withered tree bloom." The regal power of those lines sets the stage for the final assertion that as God says, so will God do.

READING II   2 Corinthians 5:6–10

A reading from the second Letter of Saint Paul to the Corinthians

"Confident" sets the tone for the reading. Stress both "body" and "Lord."

"We walk by faith . . ." is one of the great truths of Christianity.

We seek to please him in order to be with him forever.

This is a sobering thought: We will all be judged according to our actions. Speak with authority.

Brothers and sisters:
We are **always courageous**,
   although we know that while we are at home in the **body**
   we are **away** from the **Lord**,
   for we walk by **faith**, not by **sight**.
Yet we are **courageous**,
   and we would rather **leave** the body and go home to the **Lord**.
Therefore, we aspire to **please** him,
   whether we are at **home** or **away**.
For we must all **appear** before the **judgment** seat of **Christ**,
   so that each may receive **recompense**,
   according to what he **did** in the **body**, whether **good** or **evil**.

READING II   Paul speaks of a confidence that defies logic, a confidence sustained by "faith," not by "sight." In worldly terms, that's nonsense. Only what can be seen (at least with scientific instruments) and measured is real. All else is wishful thinking. But for Paul, faith provides as solid a foundation as concrete. It takes faith, he tells us, to walk through a life that feels like an exile from our true "home." Our home, he tells us, is "with the Lord"; anything this side of heaven is far from ideal and often painful. Yet we endure this life and strive to "please him" by all

we do, for one day we will have to "appear before the judgment seat of Christ" where we will all be judged according to how we lived "in the body."

Paul's confidence mustn't sound like overconfidence or arrogance. Remember, it is born of faith, not ego. Reassure us that though the life we see is fraught with distress, there is an unseen homeland that awaits us in Christ. Paul urges us to make the best of our earthly life, for we'll ultimately be judged on how we lived it. As you argue his point, contrast "at home" and "away" and emphasize "please him."

Our recompense, he insists, will be based not on the gifts with which we entered the world, but on what we've accomplished with them by the time we leave it.

GOSPEL   Parables do much work and save much effort; they are marvels of pedagogy. No wonder Jesus had recourse to them on so many occasions. Because they are cast in everyday language and utilize everyday imagery, they open windows into mysteries. Amazingly, though these use agricultural images, they communicate even to the modern reader.

GOSPEL   Mark 4:26–34

A reading from the holy Gospel according to Mark

Engagingly assume the persona of a
storyteller, not a teacher.

Jesus said to the **crowds**:
"**This** is how it is with the kingdom of **God**;
it is as if a man were to scatter **seed** on the land

Be aware of the passage of time.

and would **sleep** and **rise night** and **day**
and through it **all** the seed would **sprout** and **grow**,
he knows not **how**.
Of its own **accord** the land yields **fruit**,

The farmer can do no more than wait
and trust.

first the **blade**, then the **ear**, then the full **grain** in the ear.
And when the grain is **ripe**, he wields the **sickle** at once,

Quicken the pace and employ a joyful
tone.

for the **harvest** has come."

He said,
"To what shall we **compare** the kingdom of God,

He's "reaching" for another image.

or what **parable** can we use for it?
It is like a **mustard** seed that, when it is **sown** in the ground,

And here it is!

is the **smallest** of all the seeds on the earth.
But once it is **sown**, it **springs** up and becomes the **largest**
of plants
and puts forth large **branches**,

The tree (kingdom) provides comfort
and safety.

so that the **birds** of the sky can dwell in its **shade**."
With many such **parables**

The parables help the crowd to
understand.

he spoke the **word** to them as they were able to **understand** it.
Without parables he did not **speak** to them,

Yet he only offers explanations to his
disciples.

but to his own **disciples** he explained **everything** in **private**.

The first parable, which appears only in Mark's Gospel account, makes the point that the harvest develops on its own, independent of the sower's efforts. So, too, the kingdom. Mysteriously, it develops quietly and often unnoticed, but with an irresistible power. This story comforts all who fear they aren't able to do enough to advance the kingdom, so proclaim in an upbeat, encouraging tone.

Because the passage of time required for the development of the seed into ripe wheat is a key component of the analogy Jesus draws, you must not rush the telling.

"Night and day" spans several months, and by the time the sprouting "seed" meets the "sickle," an entire season has passed. With tone, emphasis, and pacing you can convey a sense of the passage of time. Your tone also conveys trust, the confident knowledge that the crop is developing as it should.

But we sense that maybe some of Jesus' listeners didn't get it. Perhaps he sees question marks on people's faces that prompt him, like any good teacher, to reach for another image. He may be improvising here. Pause briefly, as if to think, after

"What parable will we use . . . ," then let your face announce, "I have it!" and continue at a faster pace with the mustard seed parable. It's a short (one sentence) and familiar analogy, but you can speak each phrase with excited energy, pausing between phrases as if the images were coming piecemeal to Jesus' mind as he teaches. The final sentence should make us wonder: Why did Jesus explain his parables only to the disciples and not the crowd? Perhaps you can use the homily to explain.

NATIVITY OF SAINT JOHN THE BAPTIST: VIGIL

Lectionary #586

READING I Jeremiah 1:4–10

Jeremiah = jahr-uh-MĪ-uh

The reading opens in Jeremiah's narrative voice, followed by the voice of God.

In order to evoke Jeremiah's overwhelmed reaction, let the voice of God ring with authority and majesty that resolves into compassion on "a prophet to the nations."

Jeremiah's response is full of innocence and insecurity. It is a plea for help, not a rejection of the mission given to him.

Here God's voice needs to reassure. The words are stark and phrased as imperatives, but underneath we must hear the encouragement of a loving father.

Narrate this scene in the voice of Jeremiah, retelling it with the awe of the original moment.

God's final words to Jeremiah assign the boy his mission. The words signal a future of turmoil and danger, so in a confident tone suggest the absolute necessity of what Jeremiah will do on God's behalf.

A reading from the Book of the Prophet Jeremiah

In the days of King **Josiah**, the word of the LORD **came** to me,
    saying:

Before I **formed** you in the **womb** I **knew** you,
    before you were **born** I **dedicated** you,
    a **prophet** to the **nations** I **appointed** you.

"Ah, Lord **GOD!**" I said,
    "I know not how to **speak**; I am too **young**."
But the LORD **answered** me,
    Say **not**, "I am too **young**."
    To whomever I **send** you, you shall **go**;
    whatever I **command** you, you shall **speak**.
Have no fear before them,
    because I am with you to **deliver** you, says the LORD.

Then the LORD extended his **hand** and touched my **mouth**, saying,

See, I place my **words** in your mouth!
    This day I **set** you
        over **nations** and over **kingdoms**,
    to root **up** and to tear **down**,
        to **destroy** and to **demolish**,
        to **build** and to **plant**.

Today options are given for the readings. Contact your parish staff to learn which readings will be used.

READING I In this beautiful text that chronicles the divine call of Jeremiah to his prophetic ministry, what stands out most is God's selection of Jeremiah while he was still growing within his mother's womb. God holds nothing back in expressing divine favor for Jeremiah: I knew you and I loved you; I chose and dedicated you to my service;

I appointed you as my voice to the nations. Such hyperbole prompted some of the early Fathers to speculate that God had freed Jeremiah from original sin before his birth. This text is chosen for this solemnity because its words can be so closely identified with another divinely favored figure, also chosen from the womb to become God's spokesperson.

Jeremiah fears that his youth will handicap his ministry, but the Lord dismisses that concern: You will go where

I send you and do what I command. Have no fear, for you are not alone. "I am with you," says the Lord. There is both compassion and power in those lines; both the sentiments of a general and of a parent sending a young man to his destiny with words of encouragement and of love.

The divine touch of the young man's lips is an extraordinary moment. Isaiah's were touched with a burning ember held by an angel, but here it is God's own hand that places prophetic words into Jeremiah's mouth. His mission will not be easy. He is sent to nations and kingdoms, but his word

READING II   1 Peter 1:8–12

A reading from the first Letter of Saint Peter

Beloved:
Although you have not **seen** Jesus Christ you **love** him;
even though you do not see him **now** yet **believe** in him,
you **rejoice** with an **indescribable** and **glorious** joy,
as you attain the **goal** of your faith, the **salvation** of your **souls**.

Concerning this salvation,
prophets who prophesied about the **grace** that was to be yours
searched and **investigated** it,
investigating the **time** and **circumstances**
that the Spirit of Christ **within** them **indicated**
when he testified in **advance**
to the **sufferings** destined for **Christ**
and the **glories** to **follow** them.
It was **revealed** to them that they were serving not **themselves**
but **you**
with regard to the things that have now been **announced**
to you
by those who preached the Good **News** to you
through the Holy **Spirit** sent from **heaven**,
things into which **angels longed** to look.

Speak these words directly to your assembly; they are as true today as they were 2,000 years ago.

You are not stating facts, but encouraging and affirming your listeners.

This is a deeply felt joy, not superficial frivolity. Speak of it with an almost hushed intensity.

Speak slowly, almost word by word. You are telling us how much more fortunate we are than even the prophets, for we see and know what they longed for but never saw.

The Holy Spirit gave the prophets knowledge of Christ's future sufferings and of his Resurrection.

The ministry of the prophets was not to benefit them but those who would later come to know and serve Christ.

The Spirit at work in the prophets is also at work in all those who proclaim the good news of salvation (including you).

will not be welcome, least of all to his own people. He is commissioned to an unpopular role that will encompass rooting up and tearing down, destroying and demolishing, as well as building and planting. And for his fidelity to God's commands, Jeremiah is rewarded with attacks from family members, beatings and imprisonment, opposition from false prophets, threats of murder, and solitary confinement in a muddy pit. No wonder God builds him up at the start of his ministry.

READING II This text is not as difficult as it might appear at first glance. Begin with the last line that speaks of "things into which angels longed to look." That line establishes the context of this reading: we who know Christ are more privileged than the prophets who prophesied his coming; more privileged, in fact, than the angels in heaven. How can this be? It is because we, yes, we—not just the Twelve who walked and ate with Christ—but we who have not seen or known him in the flesh, we partake in an "indescribable and glorious joy" because through the

mercy of God demonstrated in the life of Jesus, we are able to attain the only goal that really matters: eternal salvation.

The prophets of old tried to understand this salvation that is now ours: they "searched and investigated it," and they prophesied about the suffering of the future messiah and the "glories" that would follow those sufferings. But, of course, they were denied specific knowledge of "time and circumstances" regarding the messiah's entry into human history—knowledge we are privileged to share.

The only names that need stand out are Zechariah (zek-uh-RĪ-uh) and Elizabeth.

More important than the historical information is that they are "righteous" and why.

Slow down for these details that set the scene for the heavenly visitor.

These are atmospheric details, helpful for setting the scene, but not of primary importance. Keep the pace brisk.

Slow down at the mention of the angel, but don't over-dramatize Zechariah's "fear."

Let the content of the salutation guide your delivery: the angel is trying to quell fear, so speak in an authoritative but reassuring manner.

Since John is the focus of this solemnity, don't rush these details about his future ministry; give special stress to his being filled with the Holy Spirit.

GOSPEL Luke 1:5–17

A reading from the holy Gospel according to Luke

In the days of **Herod**, King of **Judea**,
    there was a priest named **Zechariah**
    of the priestly division of **Abijah**;
    his **wife** was from the daughters of **Aaron**,
    and her name was **Elizabeth**.
Both were **righteous** in the eyes of God,
    observing all the **commandments**
    and **ordinances** of the Lord **blamelessly**.
But they had no **child**, because Elizabeth was **barren**
    and both were **advanced** in years.
Once when he was serving
    as priest in his division's **turn** before God,
    according to the practice of the priestly **service**,
    he was chosen by **lot**
    to enter the **sanctuary** of the Lord to burn **incense**.
Then, when the whole **assembly** of the people
        was praying **outside**
    at the hour of the **incense** offering,
    the **angel** of the **Lord** appeared to him,
    standing at the right of the altar of **incense**.
Zechariah was **troubled** by what he saw, and **fear** came upon him.
But the angel **said** to him, "Do not be **afraid**, Zechariah,
    because your **prayer** has been **heard**.
Your wife **Elizabeth** will bear you a **son**,
    and you shall name him **John**.
And you will have **joy** and **gladness**,
    and many will **rejoice** at his birth,
    for he will be **great** in the sight of the Lord.

The same Spirit who was at work in the ancient prophets also inspired the apostles to preach "the good news" of salvation. The prophets realized that the prophetic insight given to them was not given for their own benefit, but for the benefit of those who would later believe in Christ. Such were the first recipients of this letter from Peter; such, too, are those who will gather in your church to hear this letter proclaimed anew.

Within a culture where a barren womb was a sure sign of sin and God's displeasure, we are introduced to a childless couple and told both that they were righteous in God's eyes and the reasons why: they observed God's law "blamelessly." And not only is the couple childless, but they are advanced in age. In biblical terms, the stage is fully set for a divine intervention.

We are not disappointed, for as this elderly man takes his turn ministering within the Jerusalem temple, grace breaks in the form of an angel who so overwhelms

him that he is filled with fear. The details surrounding the angelic visitation add great texture to the scene—Zechariah is within the sacred sanctuary; the "whole assembly" is gathered outside in prayer; incense rises, carrying the people's prayers to heaven, and suddenly the angel appears. Encounters with divinity are always fearful moments in scripture and this one is no different, for Zechariah is immediately "troubled" and filled with fear. The angel addresses Zechariah with

Continue the description of his ministry and influence with energy and joy.

Contrast "disobedient" with "righteous."

Those listening to your proclamation are such "a people."

John will drink neither **wine** nor strong **drink**.
He will be filled with the Holy **Spirit**
    even from his mother's **womb**,
      and he will turn many of the children of **Israel**
      to the Lord their **God**.
He will go **before** him in the spirit and power of **Elijah**
    to turn their hearts toward their **children**
    and the **disobedient** to the understanding of the **righteous**,
    to **prepare** a people **fit** for the **Lord**."

a familiar Old Testament phrase typically used to soothe the fears of someone experiencing a heavenly visitation—the same phrase Jesus will later employ throughout his ministry: "Do not be afraid."

The angel continues with details: Elizabeth will bear a son who will be named John. He will emulate Samson and Samuel by forsaking "wine" or "strong drink," a sign that John will be set apart to serve the Lord in the way of the Nazirites of the Old Testament, who vowed to live

ascetic lifestyles. But the truly significant information follows in the announcement that John will be "filled with the Holy Spirit" while still in his mother's womb—amply demonstrated when the developing child leaps in Elizabeth's womb at the sound of Mary's voice. The description of John's future ministry is exalted and inspiring, and the mention of Elijah brings to our minds the fierce and charismatic prophet whose coming would precede the "great and terrible day of the Lord" (Malachi 3:23). The price John will eventually pay for the privilege of serving God is

not hinted here. Instead, we are told he will turn many to the Lord; open hearts and reconcile, inspire obedience and righteousness. All of which will add up to preparing a people for the Lord. In the mission outlined here for John, we can detect the ministerial agenda of anyone who seeks to serve the Gospel of Jesus Christ.

NATIVITY OF SAINT JOHN THE BAPTIST: DAY

Lectionary #587

READING I   Isaiah 49:1–6

A reading from the Book of the Prophet Isaiah

The opening words signal an exalted tone. Don't rush.

Hear me, O coastlands,
  listen, O distant peoples.
The **LORD** called me from **birth**,
  from my mother's **womb** he gave me my **name**.

When an idea is stated twice, the second iteration requires more energy or intensity.

He made of me a sharp-edged **sword**
  and **concealed** me in the shadow of his **arm**.

Maintain a brisk tempo; the specifics are not as important as the exuberant tone.

He made me a polished **arrow**,
  in his quiver he **hid** me.

Use a slower pace for this line; let the sound be more reflective and intimate.

You are my **servant**, he said to me,
  Israel, through whom I show my **glory**.

Though I thought I had toiled in **vain**,
  and for **nothing**, **uselessly**, spent my **strength**,
yet my **reward** is with the **LORD**,
  my **recompense** is with my **God**.

The joyful tone of these two lines contrasts with that of the two lines that precede them.

For now the LORD has **spoken**
  who formed me as his **servant** from the **womb**,

Start this stanza briskly, and then slow down as you announce the restoration of "Jacob" and "Israel."

that **Jacob** may be brought **back** to him
  and **Israel gathered** to him;
and I am made **glorious** in the sight of the **LORD**,
  and my **God** is now my **strength**!

READING I   Prophets enjoyed a special relationship with God. Sent often to proclaim an unpopular message, met usually with resistance, and undoubtedly assaulted by self-doubts, prophets could only persevere in their ministry if they possessed in the depths of their being a profound conviction of God's love and guidance in their role in the life of the nation. Here Isaiah speaks from that profundity and conviction. In poetic rhythms, the prophet rejoices in his mission, recognizing that through him God is unfolding the divine plan for Israel.

This is one of Isaiah's four "Songs of the Servant of the Lord" and its words are buoyant and full of hope. The prophet thought his work was done in vain, but now he perceives the "reward" and "recompense" that come from the hands of God. In all he says, the prophet refers back to God's initiative in choosing him from his mother's womb and setting him apart for this special work. Relish the poetry that calls him a "two-edged sword" and tells us he was hidden within God's "quiver."

The third stanza identifies the servant with Israel herself; his virtues represent-ing what is best in the nation. There is no prideful boasting in the assertion that "I am made glorious"; it is all gratitude and praise. The joy and enthusiasm of the text builds to the climactic announcement of the last verse: the prophet's ministry will not be limited to the restoration of Israel. God's love and mercy is so boundless that the prophet's light will shine among all the nations and God's salvation will extend to all people. Slow down to make that point so all who listen will understand they are among those touched by that light and mercy.

It is too **little**, he says, for you to be my **servant**,
　to **raise** up the tribes of **Jacob**,
　and **restore** the survivors of **Israel**;
I will make you a **light** to the **nations**,
　that my **salvation** may reach to the **ends** of the **earth**.

"It is too little" means "It is not enough!" God is telling Isaiah that his mission will be greater than he realizes: besides the people of Israel, Isaiah's message will go to the "ends of the earth"!

READING II　Acts 13:22–26

A reading from the Acts of the Apostles

In those days, **Paul** said:
"God raised up **David** as **king**;
　of him God **testified**,
　*I have found **David**, son of **Jesse**, a man after my own **heart**;*
　*he will **carry** out my every **wish**.*
From this man's **descendants** God, according to his **promise**,
　has brought to Israel a **savior**, **Jesus**.
John **heralded** his coming by proclaiming a baptism
　of **repentance**
　to all the people of **Israel**;
　and as John was **completing** his course, he would say,
　'What do you suppose that I **am**? I am not **he**.
Behold, one is coming **after** me;
　I am not **worthy** to unfasten the **sandals** of his feet.'

"My **brothers**, **sons** of the family of **Abraham**,
　and those **others** among you who are **God-fearing**,
　to **us** this word of **salvation** has been sent."

Remember, Paul is preaching and his goal is to win over hearts to Jesus.

Speak of David with great respect.

The connection of Jesus to David is very important. Stress it.

Since John is the focus of this day, pause before and after speaking his name.

Speak John's dialogue with strength, as if addressing a crowd.

John's tone is more reflective here.

This is the climax of the reading; it is summary and proclamation: God has sent salvation to *us*.

READING II Paul figures prominently in the Acts of the Apostles. Here we learn about how, in the midst of a missionary journey, he is invited to speak during a Sabbath service in the local synagogue. Paul begins his oration by reviewing the history of God's saving intervention in the life of Israel—delivering them from slavery, guiding them through the desert, gifting them with the Promised Land, guiding them through the leadership of judges and, later, kings, including Israel's greatest monarch, David. This David God loved with a special love for he was "a man after

[God'] own heart" who would carry out his every wish. It is from this very special ancestor that God raised up Israel's messiah, Jesus. And it is this Jesus whom John the Baptist heralded through his ministry of Baptism.

Because John himself was such a remarkable person, filled with the Holy Spirit from his mother's womb, many sought him out in the hope he was the long awaited Messiah. He must have tired of saying, "I am not he." But he never tired of proclaiming the truth God gave him to speak, and for that he paid the ultimate

price. Here we hear one of his most famous statements: "I am not worthy to unfasten the sandals of his feet." (Another is like it: "He must increase, I must decrease.") Paul cites John's confession to declare the fulfillment of God's promise of a savior. "To us," he says, "this word of salvation has been sent." Recall that he is preaching in a synagogue, and you will intuit the conviction, intensity, and most of all the *purpose* of that line. Speak it as Paul would have: to persuade your listeners that God has been supremely generous in sending to us the incarnation of his mercy—Jesus, the Savior.

GOSPEL   Luke 1:57–66, 80

A reading from the holy Gospel according to Luke

The joy of a birth announcement echoes in these lines.

When the time arrived for **Elizabeth** to have her **child**
she gave birth to a **son**.
Her neighbors and relatives **heard**
that the Lord had shown his great **mercy** toward her,
and they **rejoiced** with her.

The details of circumcision and naming are important; read slowly and let the dialogue give this the feel of a family story.

When they came on the **eighth** day to **circumcise** the child,
they were going to call him **Zechariah** after his **father**,
but his **mother** said in reply,
"**No**. He will be called **John**."
But they answered her,
"There is **no one** among your **relatives** who has this name."

Perhaps they are a bit annoyed with Elizabeth.

So they made **signs**, asking his **father** what **he** wished him
to be called.

Zechariah's decision is definitive.

He asked for a **tablet** and wrote, "**John** is his name,"
and all were **amazed**.

Relate these details with pleasure and wonder.

Immediately his mouth was **opened**, his tongue **freed**,
and he **spoke** blessing **God**.

Here, too, the attitude is one of awe, of knowing they have been visited by God.

Then **fear** came upon all their neighbors,
and all these matters were discussed
throughout the hill country of **Judea**.

This question is asked with admiration.

All who **heard** these things took them to **heart**, saying,
"**What**, then, will this child **be**?"
For **surely** the hand of the **Lord** was with him.

Most of John's life is told in these three lines.

The child **grew** and became **strong** in **spirit**,
and he was in the **desert** until the day
of his **manifestation** to Israel.

GOSPEL   "Fear came upon them . . . and they wondered what will this child be?" He was born to aged parents after an angelic visitation during which his father was struck dumb. No wonder they speculated and feared, but their fear was more akin to awe than dread. The in-breaking of grace is always a shock, and sometimes intimidating. God's ways are not our ways and when God comes close, as happened here, the natural reaction is wonder.

Luke's chief purpose in relating the account of John's circumcision is to stress that this starstruck child is a true Israelite, made one of the Chosen People by means of the divinely ordained sign of the covenant. The birth of John will soon be followed by the birth of Jesus, and in both narratives the Jewish identity of the child is clearly established. Something radically new will issue from these events, but Luke wants to assure his readers that the new has deep roots in the old. So the circumcision of John is very important. Important, too, is the name chosen for the child.

Elizabeth takes the initiative, asserting the boy is to be called John. The relatives prefer his father's name, though tradition would have dictated the grandfather's name be given. Zechariah's confirmation of the name John, and the sudden return of his voice signal fulfillment of the message given by the angel in the temple. The lines that end the text are as stark and impressive as John's reputation: he grew strong in the spirit and lived in anonymity until God focused the searing light of prophecy upon him.

13TH SUNDAY IN ORDINARY TIME

Lectionary #98

READING I   Wisdom 1:13–15, 2:23–24

Suffering and death raise hard questions for people; aware that those questions may be rumbling through the minds of some of your listeners, approach the ambo with a quiet serenity.

Declare this truth with utter conviction. Philippians 2:6–11 also praises Christ who, "though he was in the form of God, did not regard equality with God something to be grasped . . . [but] emptied himself" to take on human flesh.

A slow pace and good eye contact will peak your effectiveness.

Here is an echo of Genesis, reminding us we were destined, like God, to live forever.

Here is the true culprit and, sadly, some fall into his clutches. Even as you speak this sober truth, remember that Christ has forever won victory over sin, death, and Satan.

A reading from the Book of Wisdom

God did not make **death**,
    nor does he **rejoice** in the **destruction** of the **living**.
For he fashioned all things that they might have **being**;
    and the **creatures** of the world are **wholesome**,
and there is not a **destructive** drug among them
    nor any domain of the **netherworld** on earth,
        for **justice** is **undying**.
For God **formed** man to be **imperishable**;
    the **image** of his own **nature** he made him.
But by the envy of the **devil**, death entered the world,
    and they who **belong** to his company **experience** it.

READING I The presence of evil in the world, best represented by death, has always been a source of much puzzlement. Did God create it to punish humankind for original disobedience and ongoing sinfulness? The Wisdom of God answers plainly: "God did *not* make death." It was never the divine will to bring corruption into the world, says this elegant text. Rather, God's unfailing intent is life, wholesome, energizing, generative life. The Gospel will revisit the theme of death and illness, human realities that touch everyone. In biblical times, illness was sometimes seen as directly inflicted by God. But the author of Wisdom says that cannot be so. All of God's creation is good. Echoing Genesis, the text reminds us we are made in God's own image, created "to be imperishable."

While striving to absolve God of guilt for the "destruction" that surrounds us, realize you may be addressing many who are struggling with the very question of whether or not to blame God for the pain that has invaded their lives. Some of them you may know personally, so speak in a persuasive but non-threatening manner.

Reverence and delight characterize your attitude toward the "creatures of the world" fashioned by God in the beginning and among which "there is no a destructive drug." The text restates the opening theme: God is not the author of death but of eternal life, but then the reading pivots on the word "But" and turns suddenly foreboding. Speaking of death in spiritual as well as physical terms, the author attests that it was Satan's "envy" that concocted the bitter pill of death, and those who belong to him must swallow it!

Corinthians = kohr-IN-thee-uhnz

The opening tone is upbeat and encouraging.

Paul is saying: You know what Christ did for you: try to imitate his generosity.

Here he equivocates a bit saying: Helping others shouldn't impoverish you; equality is the goal.

Paul's logic is clear: Help others now, and they may help you later.

Paul is alluding to the collection of manna during Israel's wandering in the wilderness during which no one had too much and no one had too little.

READING II   2 Corinthians 8:7, 9, 13–15

A reading from the second Letter of Saint Paul to the Corinthians

Brothers and sisters:
As you excel in every **respect**, in **faith**, **discourse**,
    knowledge, all **earnestness**, and in the **love** we have for you,
    may you excel in **this** gracious act **also**.

For you know the gracious **act** of our Lord Jesus **Christ**,
    that though he was **rich**, for **your** sake he became **poor**,
    so that by his **poverty you** might become rich.
Not that others should have **relief** while you are **burdened**,
    but that as a matter of **equality**
    your **abundance** at the present time
        should supply their **needs**,
    so that **their** abundance may also supply **your** needs,
    that there may be **equality**.
As it is written:
    *Whoever had **much** did not have **more**,*
        *and whoever had **little** did not have **less**.*

GOSPEL   Mark 5:21–43

A reading from the holy Gospel according to Mark

When **Jesus** had crossed again in the boat to the other **side**,
    a large **crowd** gathered around him, and he stayed close
        to the **sea**.
One of the synagogue **officials**, named **Jairus**, came forward.

Begin with upbeat energy. Jesus clings to the shore to avoid being overrun by the crowd.

Let your tone suggest the unusual nature of his initiative.

READING II The first sentence ends with an ambiguous term that makes Paul's point difficult to grasp. The "gracious act" of which he speaks is actually a collection he is asking them to take up on behalf of the Christian community in Jerusalem. To inspire their generosity, he first acknowledges how they excel in all other arenas—their faith and speech, their knowledge and earnestness—they even excel in winning Paul's affection! If you can shine in all these other areas, he says, then strive also to excel in charity. He then urges them to imitate the preexistent

Christ who willingly emptied himself to become one like us.

To make his point, Paul uses a literary device called *chiasmus*, which reverses the word order in two otherwise parallel phrases: Jesus, though he was *rich* (his preexistence with God) made himself *poor* (his earthly life and death), so that you might become rich (salvation) by his poverty (his human life and death). Even in the midst of a financial appeal, Paul lavishes his readers with rich theology. He then continues his plea with more mundane logic: Helping others should not make you

"burdened," for there is balance in God's plan: your surplus, he says, may relieve others' need now, but later, perhaps their surplus will relieve yours.

In the desert, Paul suggests finally, God assured equitable distribution of the miraculous manna, for no matter the effort they exerted, each family had only enough for their daily needs. The quote with which Paul closes could be paraphrased as follows: those who "gathered much had no *excess*" while those who "gathered little had no *lack*." The moral? Imitate the generosity of God and no one will be lacking.

He speaks as a parent, not an "official."

Seeing him he fell at his **feet** and pleaded **earnestly** with him,
　　saying,
　"My **daughter** is at the point of **death**.
Please, come lay your **hands** on her
　　that she may get **well** and **live**."
He went **off** with him,
　　and a large **crowd** followed him and **pressed** upon him.

Here is a sudden and unnatural shift in the scene. Make the shift evident and detail her woes convincingly.

There was a **woman** afflicted with **hemorrhages** for twelve **years**.
She had suffered **greatly** at the hands of many **doctors**
　　and had spent all that she **had**.
Yet she was not **helped** but only grew **worse**.
She had heard about **Jesus** and came up behind him in the crowd
　　and **touched** his **cloak**.

Her line reveals both desperation and hope.

She said, "If I but **touch** his **clothes**, I shall be **cured**."
Immediately her flow of blood dried **up**.
She felt in her body that she was **healed** of her affliction.

Don't rush this detail: Jesus *knows*, despite the disciples' skepticism.

Jesus, aware at once that **power** had gone out from him,
　　turned around in the crowd and asked, "**Who** has touched
　　　my **clothes**?"
But his **disciples** said to Jesus,
　"You see how the crowd is **pressing** upon you,
　　and **yet** you ask, 'Who **touched** me?'"
And he looked around to **see** who had done it.

Narrate from the woman's point of view—her "fear and trembling."

The **woman**, realizing what had **happened** to her,
　　approached in **fear** and **trembling**.

Perhaps the "whole truth" includes opening her heart to his forgiveness.

She **fell** down before Jesus and **told** him the whole **truth**.
He said to her, "**Daughter**, your **faith** has **saved** you.
Go in **peace** and be **cured** of your affliction."

GOSPEL An insider approaches the ultimate outsider because he has a need. Desperation can break down walls, and Jairus is desperate. Though he risks his reputation, he doesn't hesitate to approach Jesus. "Earnestly" he pleads that his sick daughter be made well "and live," for the child teeters on the edge of death. Jesus readily assents and as they go, the crowd envelops them.

The second paragraph opens like the sound-bite of a television news-magazine show. "Twelve years . . . suffered greatly" . . . spent all that she had . . . [and] only grew worse!" Deliberately, the woman makes her way to Jesus and, grateful for the camouflage of the crowd, she gingerly reaches out "to touch his clothes." Like Jairus, she intuits the need for physical touch to effect a healing. In her we see the impossible faith of one who, despite twelve years of dead ends, musters enough hope for one more try.

Immediately, her body tells her the touch was efficacious. But Jesus steals the moment from her as he wheels round and asks a question his disciples find so foolish. What do you mean; everybody's touching you, they say. But Jesus seeks out the woman and the scene unfolds with great poignancy. With "fear and trembling" the woman draws near to Jesus and, like Jairus, falls at his feet and risks confessing what she did. This courage is even greater than the boldness that impelled her to touch him, for she risks punishment or even a reversal of her healing. With unexpected tenderness, Jesus attributes to her faith the healing of her body and her spirit.

Suddenly, the scene earlier put on hold retakes center stage. With brutal

Jesus' tone is both strong and compassionate.

While he was still **speaking**,
  people from the synagogue official's **house** arrived and said,
    "Your daughter has **died**; why **trouble** the teacher any **longer**?"
Disregarding the message that was reported,
  Jesus said to the synagogue official,
    "Do not be **afraid**; just have **faith**."

Their lack of sensitivity is appalling.

He did not allow anyone to **accompany** him inside
  except **Peter**, **James**, and **John**, the **brother** of James.
When they **arrived** at the house of the synagogue official,
  he caught sight of a **commotion**,
  people **weeping** and wailing **loudly**.

Jesus immediately jumps in to counter the terror they've placed in Jairus' heart.

So he went **in** and said to them,
  "**Why** this commotion and **weeping**?
The child is not **dead** but **asleep**."
And they **ridiculed** him.
Then he put them all **out**.

Jesus is undiplomatic with these hired mourners.

He took along the child's **father** and **mother**
  and those who were **with** him
  and entered the room where the **child** was.

In the New Testament, death is often equated with sleep.

Read slowly and reveal the poignancy of this intimate scene.

Speak the translation of *Talitha koum* in the same gentle manner as the rest of the scene.

He took the child by the **hand** and said to her, "*Talitha koum*,"
  which means, "Little **girl**, I say to you, **arise**!"
The girl, a child of **twelve**, arose **immediately**
  and walked **around**.
At that they were utterly **astounded**.

Contrast the astonishment of the family with Jesus' directive that they feed the child.

He gave strict **orders** that no one should **know** this
  and said that she should be given something to **eat**.

[Shorter: Mark 5:21–24, 35b–43]

bluntness Jairus is told his daughter is dead and is urged to stop troubling the teacher. Jesus ignores these messengers and focuses on Jairus, telling him to abandon fear and cling to faith.

As if needing to focus his energies for the task at hand, Jesus first forbids anyone but his closest intimates to follow him, and then dismisses the entourage of mourners he discovers at the home. The words "commotion" and "weeping and wailing loudly" suggest the distasteful din the mourners were creating. Jesus reacts harshly to

their hired antics, so the mourners retaliate with "ridicule." But Jesus won't endure it and sends them out the door.

The First Reading explored the mystery of sickness and death. Though not God's doing, still those evils lurk around us, bringing darkness where there should be light. This Gospel narrative stands against all that. It tells us there is a power greater than death, a light no darkness can dispel; and his name is Jesus. The final scene begins with tender imagery: taking the girl's parents, Jesus slowly enters the child's room, reaches for her hand, and

softly speaks a gentle command. Parents and disciples cluster round, timid, confused, expectant. Jesus is self-assured and as soon as he speaks, the spell is broken. "Immediately" the girl rises and walks. Jesus wipes no tears nor waits for their applause. His only response to the family's astonishment is an admonition to silence, and an order to get on to more important matters: giving her "something to eat."

14TH SUNDAY IN ORDINARY TIME

Lectionary #101

READING I   Ezekiel 2:2–5

Ezekiel = ee-ZEEK-ee-uhl

Prophets were never welcome for they shook things up and spoke God's truth—a message seldom appreciated by those who know they've strayed. Prophets also warn of the consequences of infidelity, and that will be Ezekiel's mission.

Speak with intensity from the start, with special attention to the "spirit."

God's voice bears an uncompromising tone.

Although these words are hard, they also reveal God's love and concern for the people's conversion of heart.

The parenthetical phrase ("for they are a rebellious house") requires an uptick of energy.

Don't rush this elegant line. It is the main point of the entire text. Warn them anyway, God says, then, at least they will know a "prophet"—my spokesperson, my living appeal for reform, my visible sign of love and fidelity, my self in human guise, has been among them! The line should make us wonder if we have recognized the prophets among us.

A reading from the Book of the Prophet Ezekiel

As the LORD **spoke** to me, the **spirit** entered into me
    and set me on my **feet**,
    and I heard the one who was **speaking** say to me:
Son of **man**, I am sending you to the **Israelites**,
    rebels who have **rebelled** against me;
    they and their ancestors have **revolted** against me
        to this very **day**.
Hard of face and **obstinate** of heart
    are they to whom I am **sending** you.
But you shall **say** to them: Thus says the LORD **God**!
And whether they **heed** or **resist**—
    for they are a **rebellious** house—
    they shall **know** that a **prophet** has been **among** them.

READING I | One of scripture's classic lines graces this text, making a direct link with today's Gospel story. Jesus' prophetic ministry is not accepted or recognized by his neighbors, and he goes away amazed. God's word to Ezekiel steels him for such a possibility. We hear no divine imperative here, only a characterization of the Israelites to whom the prophet is sent. They are "rebels . . . hard of face and obstinate of heart." A priest called to prophesy in the land of exile,

Ezekiel will bring an unwelcome message to his fellow exiles, and the first piece of bad news will be that the city of Jerusalem, believed to be sacred and unassailable, will in fact be crushed.

Upon hearing the divine call, God's "spirit" enters Ezekiel, that is, he is filled with God's life-giving power that enables the prophet to hear and internalize God's message and empowers him to carry out his mission. All we know is the mission won't be easy, for as we are told several times, the people are rebellious! But go he

must and whether the people heed him or reject him, they shall know (and here is that classic line) "that a prophet has been among them."

READING II | Soon after his conversion, Paul was graced with mystical visions through which he acquired his intimate knowledge of Jesus, despite never having known him in the flesh. Here he acknowledges that in addition to the great privilege of that mystical knowledge,

Corinthians = kohr-IN-thee-uhnz

To counter his opponents, Paul bolstered his credibility with talk of his special "revelations." Here he qualifies and presents bluntly the flip side of his special privilege.

Paul is explaining here. Although trying to be humble, he can't resist naming the "abundance" of the revelations.

Paul's triple request echoes Jesus' threefold prayer in the garden.

These words from Jesus are like a soothing balm for Paul.

Paul is a willing student who readily masters the perverse wisdom of the God of reversals.

Paul wears these afflictions like medals on his chest.

The news that all doesn't depend on us is comforting (especially for those of us who proclaim the word).

READING II 2 Corinthians 12:7–10

A reading from the second Letter of Saint Paul to the Corinthians

Brothers and sisters:
That I, **Paul**, might not become too **elated**,
    because of the abundance of the **revelations**,
    a **thorn** in the **flesh** was given to me, an angel of **Satan**,
    to **beat** me, to **keep** me from being too elated.
Three **times** I **begged** the Lord about this, that it might **leave** me,
    but he said to me, "My **grace** is **sufficient** for you,
    for **power** is made **perfect** in **weakness**."
I will rather boast most **gladly** of my **weaknesses**,
    in order that the power of **Christ** may **dwell** with me.
Therefore, I am **content** with **weaknesses**, **insults**,
    hardships, **persecutions** and **constraints**,
    for the sake of **Christ**;
    for when I am **weak**, then I am **strong**.

he was also given something to restore a sense of balance in his soul. Great privilege can lead to self-aggrandizement and God made sure to shield Paul from that fate. The "thorn in the flesh" of which he speaks has puzzled commentators for 2,000 years. There has been much speculation about the exact nature of that affliction—a physical or psychological malady, a temptation, a human opponent, perhaps—but no one knows. Obviously it was a burden,

for "three times" Paul asks God to remove it. God's response skirts the issue and reveals a truth that Paul and we are called to live each and every day: "My grace is sufficient for you."

Yet more profound truth is contained in these few lines, and that truth is this: "Power is made perfect in weakness . . . when I am weak, then I am strong." It's one of those ironic and mystifying truths so characteristic of Christianity. We can even "boast" of weakness, for weakness can

clear the heart, making room for the "power of Christ." We can even laugh in the face of trials; we can swallow "insults" and endure "hardships" because the less there is of us in us, the more room there is for Christ. That's why weakness is our strength.

GOSPEL Even then, familiarity poisoned one's possibilities: He's just a carpenter, they say. We know his family; they live right here with us. His

GOSPEL   Mark 6:1–6

In this event, Jesus discovers that the least receptive to his gifts are the very people whose lives had been the playground and the classrooms of his youth.

Begin with a festive tone; Jesus' return home brings a large crowd to the synagogue.

The mood turns sinister as rivalry and resentment begin to surface. Each question grows bolder and angrier.

His family recently tried to spirit him away, fearing he'd gone mad (Mark 3:21). Perhaps, he shares this familiar proverb about prophets for their benefit. The words themselves are powerful, so you need not over-dramatize them.

We might assume anger here, imagining Jesus kicking dust from his feet as he leaves town. But he must have had profound sadness, too, and perhaps he goes forth not only to teach, but also to forget.

A reading from the holy Gospel according to Mark

Jesus departed from there and came to his **native** place,
    accompanied by his **disciples**.
When the **sabbath** came he began to **teach** in the synagogue,
    and many who **heard** him were **astonished**.
They said, "**Where** did this man **get** all this?
What kind of **wisdom** has been given him?
What mighty **deeds** are wrought by his **hands**!
Is he not the **carpenter**, the son of **Mary**,
    and the brother of **James** and **Joses** and **Judas** and **Simon**?
And are not his **sisters** here with us?"
And they took **offense** at him.
Jesus said to them,
    "A **prophet** is not without **honor** except in his **native** place
    and among his own **kin** and in his own **house**."
So he was not **able** to perform any mighty **deed** there,
    apart from **curing** a few **sick** people by laying his **hands**
        on them.
He was **amazed** at their lack of **faith**.

mother is our neighbor. How insulting that he should pretend to be so much more than he is! They *truly* "took offense at him."

But go back to the start: he taught and they were "astonished." They buzz and tremble with infectious excitement. Where "did he get all this . . . . What wisdom . . . . What mighty deeds!" An amazing contrast within the span of several lines; but the reason for the dramatic shift becomes apparent. Jesus experiences the effects of

the darkness that penetrates the human heart whenever jealousy comes knocking. With biting precision, Gore Vidal has described the dark beast of envy: "It is not enough to succeed," he said. "Others must fail . . . . Every time a friend succeeds, I die a little." It seems there was much dying in Nazareth that day.

Jesus speaks the famous saying about "a prophet" "in his own house" and then moves on. But it is the final narrative comment, which connects "faith" and "healing," that speaks the greatest truth. Jesus

is "amazed," at their lack of faith, and surely that means saddened and disappointed, too. That he could heal so few that day suggests the role that we play, and that Jesus' ministry illustrated so many times, in the economy of healing and salvation: in the spirit and in life, little, if anything, can happen without faith.

15TH SUNDAY IN ORDINARY TIME

Lectionary #104

READING I   Amos 7:12–15

Amos = AY-m*s

Amaziah = am-uh-ZĪ-uh

Political rivalry and personal jealousy color Amaziah's words: What right does this self-appointed, uneducated country bumpkin have to come stirring things up.

He practically spits out the word "visionary."

Amaziah insinuates Amos' prophesying is his "occupation" instead of his "ministry."

True prophets never volunteer; Amos insists he was conscripted.

He wears his lowly origins as a badge of honor.

Speak the divine command with authority and strength.

A reading from the Book of the Prophet Amos

Amaziah, priest of **Bethel**, said to **Amos**,
   "**Off** with you, visionary, **flee** to the land of **Judah**!
There earn your bread by **prophesying**,
   but never **again** prophesy in **Bethel**;
   for it is the king's **sanctuary** and a **royal** temple."
Amos **answered** Amaziah, "**I** was no **prophet**,
   nor have I belonged to a **company** of prophets;
   I was a **shepherd** and a dresser of **sycamores**.
The **LORD** took me from following the flock, and **said** to me,
   Go, **prophesy** to my people **Israel**."

READING II   Ephesians 1:3–14

Ephesians = ee-FEE-zhuhnz

This is the first of seven consecutive weeks that we read from Ephesians.

This is not a progressive reasoning text, but a song of praise.

Make an extra effort to establish eye contact with individual faces as you name the attributes that identify those chosen, blessed, and marked with the Holy Spirit.

A reading from the Letter of Saint Paul to the Ephesians

Blessed be the God and **Father** of our Lord Jesus **Christ**,
   who has **blessed** us in Christ
   with every spiritual **blessing** in the **heavens**,
   as he **chose** us in him, before the **foundation** of the **world**,
   tó be **holy** and without **blemish** before him.

READING I   Prophets often pay dearly for the prophetic office they receive. Amos was no different. He preached in the northern kingdom during prosperous times, but still the needy were neglected, worship was little more than insincere posturing, and immorality was common. Even the trials God permitted to touch the lives of the people didn't change hearts or turn lives back to God. So God calls Amos from his life as a shepherd and "dresser of sycamores" to warn Israel to return to the moral and religious demands of the covenant. He rails against the false spirituality that marked so much of the worship at Bethel, a prominent religious center of the northern kingdom. His fiery oratory made Amos unpopular, but he sealed his fate when he prophesied that Bethel itself would be overthrown, the monarchy would fall, and the people led away into exile.

   That bold declaration roused the hostility of the powerful elite who rose up against him, culminating in what we read in today's text. Here, Amaziah, the high priest of Bethel, banishes Amos from the sanctuary. This is the *king's* sanctuary and the royal temple, he scoffs. Go off to Judah (the southern kingdom) and earn your keep there through your prophetic babbling. Amos is eager to dissociate himself from the disreputable prophets of Bethel, so vehemently asserts that he doesn't belong to any of the "professional" bands of prophets. Reluctantly he left his fields and pastures only because the Lord God commanded: "Go, prophesy."

READING II   Primarily, scripture doesn't tell us what to do, but who we are. Today's text exemplifies this

These next three sentences enumerate God's good deeds at a slower pace. The sentences are long and comprised of many phrases, so use your inflection to distinguish one thought from another.

In **love** he destined us for **adoption** to himself
    through Jesus **Christ**,
  in accord with the **favor** of his **will**,
  for the **praise** of the glory of his **grace**
  that he **granted** us in the **beloved**.
In him we have **redemption** by his **blood**,
  the **forgiveness** of **transgressions**,
  in accord with the **riches** of his grace that he **lavished** upon us.
In all **wisdom** and **insight**, he has made known to us
  the **mystery** of his will in accord with his **favor**
  that he set **forth** in him as a **plan** for the fullness of **times**,
  to sum up **all** things in **Christ**, in **heaven** and on **earth**.

You can hardly believe God could do so much for us.

Let your own gratitude at knowing Christ sound in these lines.

In this paragraph, "we" refers to Jewish Christians.

In **him** we were also **chosen**,
  destined in accord with the **purpose** of the One
  who **accomplishes** all things according to the **intention**
    of his **will**,
  so that we might exist for the **praise** of his **glory**,
  we who first **hoped** in Christ.
In him you **also**, who have **heard** the word of truth,
  the **gospel** of your salvation, and have **believed** in him,
  were **sealed** with the promised Holy **Spirit**,
  which is the first **installment** of our **inheritance**
  toward **redemption** as God's **possession**, to the **praise**
    of his **glory**.

"You also . . ." refers to the Gentile believers in Christ.

Address the assembly as you would a beloved family member who needs reassurance.

[Shorter: Ephesians 1:3–10]

dictum. Look at what it tells us about ourselves: we are blessed, chosen, made for holiness, destined for adoption, redeemed, forgiven of sins, informed of God's will, destined to live for God's glory, sealed with the Holy Spirit, and God's possession. The text is a song of praise, and its words flow quickly, phrase upon phrase. So, mindful that you are proclaiming a hymn, use the rhythmic flow and the images to create a portrait of the Christian believer and of the God who calls us to faith.

Your proclamation must ring with enthusiasm and gratitude because God

"chose us," predestined us, in fact, to be adopted children. Caring for us is God's great "pleasure;" ours is to respond with praise. In these complex sentences, move carefully from phrase to phrase.

The last paragraph presents an expanded vision of Church, which has grown from a *local*, to *global* community," incorporating *all* into Christ's body. The words "We" in the first sentence and "you" in the second refer respectively to Jews and Gentiles. What was first extended to God's Chosen People, now is extended to "you [Gentiles] also" because

you've accepted the "gospel." That acceptance "sealed" you with the Holy Spirit and put your name, as it were, in the family will. Now, like the Jews, you share in the "inheritance" of which the Spirit is the "first installment." Throughout, the tone is reassuring, as if telling an estranged family member they have not been left out of the family's benefits or affection.

GOSPEL | Some argue it's easier to *do* the will of God than to *know* it. If only we could ask: Tell me what to do and give me the tools I need, and I'll

GOSPEL   Mark 6:7–13

A reading from the holy Gospel according to Mark

Jesus summoned the **Twelve** and began to send them out
  two by **two**
  and gave them **authority** over unclean **spirits.**
He **instructed** them to take **nothing** for the journey
  but a **walking** stick—
  no **food,** no **sack,** no **money** in their belts.
They **were,** however, to wear **sandals**
  but **not** a second **tunic.**
He said to them,
  "Wherever you enter a **house, stay** there until you **leave.**
Whatever place does not **welcome** you or **listen** to you,
  leave there and shake the **dust** off your feet
  in testimony **against** them."
So they **went** off and preached **repentance.**
The **Twelve** drove out many **demons,**
  and they **anointed** with oil many who were **sick**
    and **cured** them.

Speak of "the Twelve" with familiarity and affection.

Take a slight pause after "instructed them" and then begin the list of instructions.

Stress each item of Jesus' list, for the continued emphasis will drive home the point that their ministry will not be sustained by any earthly goods.

This section has a more intimate feel; Jesus is anticipating the resistance they will inevitably encounter and steels them for it.
Pause before this final section. Note two aspects of their ministry: repentance and dismissing demons. Let your tone signal the success that accompanied their mission.

get to work. Give me my marching orders— just make them clear—and I'll be off. Such simplicity, though comforting, clearly is not the way of Jesus. Working for the kingdom is essentially a matter of radical trust in God. Mark's account permits the use of "walking stick" and "sandals"—not granted in Matthew and Luke—but all else must come from the bounty of God. What Jesus does give the apostles is "authority" and the directive to use it to teach and expel "unclean spirits."

Be ready to act at a moment's notice, says Jesus. Don't be weighed down or dis- tracted by what you think are essentials; the only necessity is to entrust yourself to the mercy of God. This is not the barking of a drill sergeant, but directives that amount to survival training. Share them with the compassion that inspired them. Jesus is forming them more than teaching them, preparing them to be his representatives, to model what essential kingdom living really means. If disciples are to become configured to Christ, then they must imitate

the Son of Man who has no place to lay his head.

Jesus sends "the twelve," not "the seventy-two," making his tone intimate and solicitous with these privileged friends. With them, he is both frank ("Wherever you enter a house, stay there"—that is, don't shop around for the nicest home or offend your host by opting for an upgrade down the street) and fiercely loyal ("what- ever place does not welcome you . . . shake the dust off your feet"). Mark reports the ministry of the twelve with joy and a sense of pure amazement.

16TH SUNDAY IN ORDINARY TIME

Lectionary #107

READING I Jeremiah 23:1–6

Jeremiah = jayr-uh-MĪ-uh

Jeremiah's anger is impassioned, like the parent of a victimized child.

The shepherds, charged to gather and protect, have instead "scattered [God's] sheep and driven them away."

God's tone asks: How could you have squandered the responsibility I entrusted to you?

The shepherds have permitted chaos, so God asserts control.

A reading from the Book of the Prophet Jeremiah

Woe to the **shepherds**
   who **mislead** and **scatter** the flock of my pasture,
   says the LORD.
Therefore, **thus** says the LORD, the God of **Israel**,
   against the shepherds who shepherd my **people**:
   You have **scattered** my sheep and **driven** them away.
You have not **cared** for them,
   but **I** will take care to **punish** your evil deeds.
I **myself** will gather the **remnant** of my flock
   from all the lands to which I have **driven** them
   and bring them back to their **meadow**;
   there they shall **increase** and **multiply**.
I will appoint **shepherds** for them who **will** shepherd them
   so that they need no longer **fear** and **tremble**;
   and none shall be **missing**, says the LORD.

God speaks of restoration. We hear the determination of a mighty monarch proclaiming boldly from his seat of power.

"And none shall be missing . . ." introduces the more pastoral tone found in the poetic oracle of the final paragraph.

   Behold, the days are **coming**, says the LORD,
      when I will raise up a righteous **shoot** to David;
   as **king** he shall reign and govern **wisely**,
      he shall do what is **just** and **right** in the land.
   In his days **Judah** shall be **saved**,
      Israel shall dwell in **security**.
   This is the **name** they give him:
      "The LORD our **justice**."

God describes how differently the ideal future king will rule. The words embrace and comfort. Speak "the Lord . . ." as if it were the name of one who can bring the dead back to life.

READING I Warning and comfort, the twin aspects of the prophet's mission, are both clearly manifested here. The warning is first and it is blunt, searing, and terrifying for anyone who shares the privilege and burden of pastoring. As in government, a system of checks and balances marks the socio-religious economy of Israel. While kings and priests rule and lead, the prophets offer God's perspective on that leadership and, as we hear today, the judgment is often critical and harsh. False prophets, priests, and kings are all indicted here. Priests and prophets have abandoned their true ministry and failed to teach the people the true demands of the covenant and the right practice of religion. Worse even than the fact that the false prophets are themselves immoral, they have deluded evildoers into thinking God will bless them. Jeremiah is a true prophet and so his fate is to reveal to these charlatans the inevitable and dire consequences of sin.

   But the text is less fury than promise. "I will take care . . ." expresses God's determination to re-establish order from the chaos the shepherds have created. God will bring true shepherds and these will serve the "remnant" God will gather from the lands of dispersion. But an even greater promise follows: from the stump of David's royal line God will raise a "righteous shoot" who will rule wisely and incarnate God's justice. His name plays with the name of the reigning and ineffectual King Zedekiah whose ironic name is "The Lord is Justice." But God's choice, the future messiah, will embody integrity and be called "our justice."

Ephesians = ee-FEE-zhunz

Proceed slowly and carefully. The core message is simple: by shedding his blood for us, Christ made all people one.

In addition to the central point, the author adds: Jesus broke down the religious "dividing wall" that kept apart Jews (who were "near") and Gentiles (who were "far off") by abolishing "the [Mosaic] law with its commandments and legal claims." Jesus thereby made us *one* people ("one new person") who, through the "one Spirit," have "access . . . to the Father."

Speak like this is news worth hearing and tell your listeners they have been transformed from those who were "far" to those who are "near"!

Through repetition, the last lines ensure the main point is understood. Although it's been said already, speak now as if you were Jesus drawing listeners to your bosom where the "Spirit" waits to open the door to the "Father."

READING II Ephesians 2:13–18

A reading from the Letter of Saint Paul to the Ephesians

Brothers and sisters:
In Christ **Jesus** you who once were far **off**
    have become **near** by the **blood** of Christ.

For he is our **peace**, he who made both **one**
    and broke down the dividing wall of **enmity**, through his **flesh**,
    abolishing the law with its commandments and **legal** claims,
    that he might create in himself **one new person** in place
        of the **two**,
    thus establishing **peace**,
    and might **reconcile** both with **God**,
    in one **body**, through the **cross**,
    putting that enmity to **death** by it.
He came and preached **peace** to you who were far **off**
    and peace to those who were **near**,
    for through him we **both** have access in one **Spirit**
        to the **Father**.

READING II The salvation brought by Christ is meant not only for God's chosen people, but for all people. Even the Old Testament prophets pointed to God's intent for universal salvation. Guided by the Mosaic Law and by privileged knowledge of the one, true God, the people of Israel anticipated from ancient days the promised messiah. Now, Gentiles who were once far removed from these truths have been brought "near by the blood of Christ." It was always God's intent that salvation would be universally available; now, in Christ, the grace of salvation is, in fact, available to all, without consideration of race, gender, or even adherence to the Law of the old covenant.

Christ came as the embodiment of "peace," breaking down divisions and reconciling factions so we might become "one new person"—or better, one new humanity, rather than two. In his body, through his willing sacrifice, Christ reconciled Jews and non-Jew to God, the Father. The "enmity" that previously divided us was crucified with Christ on the cross. His death and Resurrection were a living sermon on peace for both Jew and Gentile. Christ preached less in word than in deed, and his sacrifice has given all who seek him equal access through the Spirit to our almighty and loving Father.

GOSPEL It's one of the most poignant lines in scripture and, unfortunately it proclaims bad news: "They were like sheep without a shepherd." But tragic as it was, it will never be true again. No matter how faithless those

GOSPEL   Mark 6:30–34

A reading from the holy Gospel according to Mark

The **apostles** gathered together with **Jesus**
  and reported all they had **done** and **taught**.
He **said** to them,
  "Come away by **yourselves** to a **deserted** place
    and **rest** a while."
People were coming and going in great **numbers**,
  and they had no opportunity even to **eat**.
So they went off in the **boat** by themselves to a **deserted** place.
People **saw** them leaving and many came to **know** about it.
They **hastened** there on **foot** from all the towns
  and arrived at the place **before** them.

When he **disembarked** and saw the vast **crowd**,
  his heart was moved with **pity** for them,
  for they were like **sheep** without a **shepherd**;
  and he began to **teach** them **many** things.

Jesus wants to hear the disciples' tales of preaching and healing. Their energy infects this introduction.

The narrator explains Jesus' desire for quiet, private time but also simultaneously reveals annoyance with the crowd's insensitivity to Jesus' personal needs. So speak of how the crowd "hastened" on foot not with the people's eagerness, but with disapproval of their thoughtlessness. Jesus' effort to escape the crowd fails, adding greater poignancy to his generous response to them. Pause slightly after "saw the vast crowd."

For obvious reasons, this line needs slow delivery and extra stress. Pause before announcing his decision to "teach them."

who accept the mantle of Christ, no matter how scandalous or even immoral their lives, there will always be a faithful Shepherd who will not mislead, who will not abandon the truth, who will never desert the flock. The eternal shepherd has come; the teacher of truth will be always with his people. This is a straightforward text whose final lines connect it with today's First Reading. That single line proclaims the lesson of this day: Human shepherds can fail us, as we in these recent years know. Whether the priest of Bethel, or Judas, or anyone from a long succession of leaders who have squandered the privilege and responsibility given them, the result is the same: God's flock suffers, and the heart of Jesus stirs with pity.

It was meant to be an intimate scene between teacher and disciples: Jesus wants to hear the report of their missionary journeys, so the passage opens with the eager energy of the twelve who can't wait to tell Jesus all they've experienced. But the (perhaps insensitive) crowd foils their effort to get away in private. When Jesus sees them, that is, when he sees their *need*, he responds in love.

We who know him from a distance still rely on the reluctance to say "no" this crowd expected. Their need calls forth from him what he does best—generously subordinate his needs so he can minister to the needs of others.

17TH SUNDAY IN ORDINARY TIME

Lectionary #110

READING I   2 Kings 4:42–44

So short a reading requires a slower pace lest your reading end before the assembly has fully focused.

Baal-shalishah = BAH-ahl-shahl-ih-SHAH

Elisha = ee-LĪ-shuh

Highlight both the number of loaves and the number of people to be fed.

Both times he speaks this line, Elisha's tone is authoritative and strong.

He feels foolish in even trying.

Deliver this line with simple confidence rather than too much emphasis.

A reading from the second Book of Kings

A man came from **Baal-shalishah** bringing to **Elisha**,
   the man of **God**,
   twenty **barley** loaves made from the **firstfruits**,
   and fresh **grain** in the **ear**.
Elisha said, "Give it to the **people** to **eat**."
But his servant **objected**,
   "How can I set this before a **hundred** people?"
Elisha **insisted**, "Give it to the **people** to eat."
For thus says the LORD,
   'They shall **eat** and there shall be some left **over**.'"
And when they had **eaten**, there **was** some left over,
   as the LORD had **said**.

READING I   In a chapter that chronicles many wonders worked at the hands of the prophet Elisha, we also find this brief story of how little food was made sufficient for many. Of course, we read this text today because of its close link with the Gospel story of the multiplication of the loaves and fish. In both accounts the extravagant generosity of God confronts and challenges our inability to trust that God could be so good.

The man from Baal-shalishah brings "twenty" loaves made from the "firstfruits," as well as fresh grain. The firstfruits of the harvest were often shared with God's prophets by pious Israelites. But in doing so, this simple man cannot anticipate the order he will receive to set his donation before all the people. Despite the man's doubt, Elisha patiently repeats his instruction, explaining that it will not only be enough but will exceed the people's need. That God's word was, indeed,

fulfilled is shared simply and without fanfare. The message is also simple: everyday, not just when we see wonders, human life is sustained because of human generosity linked to God's abundant mercy.

READING II   Although brief, this text is rich. Paul is imprisoned, so his usual urgency is heightened by his circumstances. He exhorts the community to

Ephesians = ee-FEE-zhuhnz

This is the third of seven consecutive weeks we read from Ephesians.

That Paul is imprisoned is an important aspect of his communication. The word "urge" tells you how to proclaim.

Imagine urging a couple threatening to divorce with these words from Paul.

In naming the seven "unities," don't stress the word "one," but the nouns instead.

This line provides a rare opportunity to legitimately stress prepositions. It is a joyful declaration of God's sovereignty and God's infusion in all of life. Don't rush.

READING II   Ephesians 4:1–6

A reading from the Letter of Saint Paul to the Ephesians

Brothers and sisters:
I, a **prisoner** for the Lord,
    urge you to live in a manner **worthy** of the call
        you have received,
    with all **humility** and **gentleness**, with **patience**,
    bearing with one another through **love**,
    striving to preserve the **unity** of the spirit through the bond
        of **peace**:
    one **body** and one **Spirit**,
    as you were also **called** to the one **hope** of your call;
    one **Lord**, one **faith**, one **baptism**;
    one **God** and **Father** of **all**,
    who is **over** all and **through** all and **in** all.

Mention of the "signs" is significant. They not only manifested Christ's divine power, but also opened people's hearts to the Gospel.

The story begins as an intimate tale about Jesus and his disciples.

The proximity of the feast of Passover signifies the connection Jesus makes between the feast and his saving work.

GOSPEL   John 6:1–15

A reading from the holy Gospel according to John

Jesus went across the Sea of **Galilee**.
A large **crowd** followed him,
    because they saw the **signs** he was performing on the **sick**.
Jesus went up on the **mountain**,
    and there he sat down with his **disciples**.
The Jewish feast of **Passover** was near.
When Jesus raised his **eyes**
    and saw that a large **crowd** was coming to him,

resist the pull of the world and the tendency to fracture. Persevere in "unity," he exhorts and be rooted in the "peace" of the Spirit. Peace and unity are to be the hallmarks of Christian life and the route to this goal are the virtues of "humility, gentleness and patience." Note that the entire passage comprises but a single sentence, and it is a sentence in which every word matters, so none can be neglected or rushed over.

Once he has made his call for peace and oneness, Paul enumerates the seven centers of Christian unity: one body, one faith, one hope, one Lord, one faith, one Baptism, and one God of us all. The temptation will be to read the list as one might read the ingredients needed for a casserole. But even if you avoid that trap, you must be sure to give variety to your pacing and to the placement of stress, so this sounds not like a lifeless list but like the joyous expression of faith it is meant to be. The imprisoned Paul writes not to multiply words but to bolster faith and remind us that God permeates all of life.

GOSPEL Much in this narrative mitigates against the usual reading of this story as an example of divinely activated human generosity. The miracle, it's often asserted, rests in the sharing Jesus inspires, for the crowd already has more than enough for everyone, if only they would share. In that scenario, humans are the true agents of abundance; Jesus only provided the inspiration. Some may choose that course for their homily, but surely that is not the narrative we are given.

Jesus is a bit ingenuous; though he wants to care for the crowd, he already knows what he will do.

Philip's response must ring with authentic alarm.

What intuition impels Andrew to bring forth this boy who has so little?

All of these details add to the effectiveness of the story. Be sure not to gloss over the eucharistic allusions in this section.

Even in the abundance of the kingdom there is room for practicality.

Contrast the number of leftover baskets with the original number of loaves.

This sign, like so many of Jesus' other miracles, inspires faith.

The people's awe wells up into a coronation frenzy, but the ending is melancholic, suggesting the inevitable loneliness of one who gives people not what they want, but what they need.

he said to **Philip**,
"Where can we buy enough **food** for them to eat?"
He said this to **test** him,
because he himself **knew** what he was going to do.
Philip **answered** him,
"Two hundred days' **wages** worth of food would not
be enough
for each of them to have a **little**."
One of his disciples,
Andrew, the brother of Simon **Peter**, said to him,
"There is a **boy** here who has five **barley** loaves and two **fish**;
but what good are **these** for so **many**?"
Jesus said, "Have the people **recline**."
Now there was a great deal of **grass** in that place.
So the men **reclined**, about five **thousand** in number.
Then Jesus **took** the loaves, gave **thanks**,
and **distributed** them to those who were reclining,
and also as much of the **fish** as they **wanted**.
When they had had their **fill**, he said to his disciples,
"Gather the fragments left **over**,
so that nothing will be **wasted**."
So they **collected** them,
and filled **twelve** wicker **baskets** with fragments
from the five barley loaves
that had been **more** than they could **eat**.
When the people **saw** the sign he had done, they said,
"This is truly the **Prophet**, the one who is to come
into the **world**."
Since Jesus **knew** that they were going to come and carry him **off**
to make him **king**,
he **withdrew** again to the mountain **alone**.

Told in all four Gospel accounts, in John the miracle of multiplication substitutes for the Last Supper narrative, providing a look at John's eucharistic theology. The pattern of this event follows that of Jesus' last meal with his friends: he takes, gives thanks, and gives. In the Eucharist, the human contributions of bread and wine don't compare with the activity of the Spirit, who transforms those elements into the very body and blood of Christ. Here on the hillside, then, the boy's contribution of loaves and fish in no way approximates the abundance that God produces. At face value, this story says only God can create abundance. We contribute but a small amount—some loaves and fish—but God must do the rest. Yes, our contribution matters and is needed, whether it's bread and wine or loaves and fish, or some other act of generosity; but alone our share will not create abundance. That part comes only from God.

18TH SUNDAY IN ORDINARY TIME

Lectionary #113

READING I Exodus 16:2–4, 12–15

A reading from the Book of Exodus

Immediately the tone of "grumbling" is established.

The whole Israelite **community grumbled** against **Moses**
> and **Aaron**.
The Israelites **said** to them,

This is not a prayer, but rather a whining complaint.

"Would that we had **died** at the LORD's hand in the land
> of **Egypt**,
as we sat by our **fleshpots** and ate our fill of **bread**!

They long for the physical comforts of life in Egypt in place of desert risks.

But you had to lead us into this **desert**
> to make the whole community die of **famine**!"

The mood switches instantly. God's tone is patient, though guarded.

Then the **LORD** said to Moses,
"I will now rain down **bread** from **heaven** for you.
Each **day** the people are to go out and gather their daily **portion**;
> thus will I **test** them,
> to see whether they **follow** my instructions or **not**.

"I have heard . . ." suggests a divine willingness to indulge the people's peevishness.

"I have **heard** the grumbling of the Israelites.
Tell them: In the evening **twilight** you shall eat **flesh**,
> and in the **morning** you shall have your fill of **bread**,
> so that you may **know** that I, the LORD, am your **God**."

Let God's voice echo with weighty authority.

In the **evening quail** came up and **covered** the camp.
In the **morning** a **dew** lay all about the camp,
> and when the dew **evaporated**, there on the **surface** of the desert
> were fine **flakes** like **hoarfrost** on the ground.

Describe the appearance of the quail and manna with the wonder and gratitude of a believer who recognizes in these events the saving hand of God.

READING I Despite witnessing the parting of the Red Sea and their miraculous deliverance from slavery, still the people grumble, and even long for the subservience from which God had freed them. In Egypt, they whine, at least they had full stomachs. Now hunger has them yearning for the "fleshpots," or metal cauldrons, in which wealthy Egyptians boiled meat. No longer hero and deliverer, Moses is instead indicted for leading them to starve in the desert. This makes for an exciting proclamation.

Almost as remarkable as the people's whining is God's indulgence of these capricious pilgrims. Without a word from Moses, God promises to rain "bread from heaven" for the people. But note that God plans to "test" the people's obedience. The verses deleted from this portion tell how the Israelites failed in trust and in compliance, ignoring God's instructions about how much and when to gather manna. And still God shows mercy. In today's Gospel Jesus alludes to the miraculous manna, clarifying that its source was not Moses, but God the Father. God's patience and

compassion are abundantly demonstrated in the promise of evening quail and morning manna. Speak of these miraculous occurrences with the faith of a descendant looking back and marveling at God's provident care of these unruly ancestors. Let your tone convey the wonder of seeing want turn to plenty and the impossible become reality. In response to the people's query, Moses speaks a multi-layered line that says, Are you too blind to see that what lies before you is the answer to your prayers?

On **seeing** it, the Israelites asked one another, "What **is** this?"
for they did not **know** what it was.
But **Moses** told them,
"This is the **bread** that the LORD has given you to **eat**."

Moses both names the miracle and tells the people to recognize it.

A reading from the Letter of Saint Paul to the Ephesians

Brothers and sisters:
I declare and **testify** in the Lord
that you must no **longer** live as the **Gentiles** do,
in the **futility** of their minds;
that is **not** how you learned **Christ**,
assuming that you have **heard** of him and were **taught** in him,
as **truth** is in **Jesus**,
that you should put **away** the **old** self of your **former** way of life,
corrupted through deceitful **desires**,
and be **renewed** in the spirit of your **minds**,
and put on the **new** self,
created in **God's** way in **righteousness** and **holiness** of **truth**.

This is the fourth of seven consecutive weeks we read from Ephesians.

The urgency and conviction of the opening phrase sets the tone for the entire reading. Note also the imperative "you must no longer . . . ".

The comparison is not intended as a harangue against Gentiles but as a way of calling believers to their true identity.

Don't rush the imagery of clothing oneself with "new self" given in Baptism.

Throughout, the mood is hopeful: we can embrace the holiness of God.

GOSPEL   John 6:24–35

A reading from the holy Gospel according to John

When the **crowd** saw that neither **Jesus** nor his **disciples**
were there,
they **themselves** got into boats
and came to Capernaum **looking** for Jesus.

This crowd turned their heads and Jesus slipped away. Start with their urgency and confusion, which increases when they finally find Jesus. Jesus arrived where he is by walking on water and the crowd wonders how he got there.

READING II Paul constantly heralded the new life that comes with incorporation into Christ: In Christ, we have already begun to live the resurrected life that won't be fully ours until the kingdom. But though we have only a foretaste in this life, still incorporation into Christ's Resurrection is enough to completely change us. So the author can confidently "declare and testify" that knowledge of Christ, assuming we have "heard of him" and were "taught" his truth, means we can no longer live as the unthinking Gentiles who, ignorant of the

Gospel, have hardened their hearts and abandoned themselves to immorality.

In the two verses deleted from this portion, the author of Ephesians laments the darkness that clouds the hearts and minds of Gentiles. But that is not you, he says; that is not "how you learned Christ!" You have the benefit of the light of the Gospel. It exhorts you to abandon your old self, which was "corrupted" by the desires of the flesh. You were "renewed" by "putting on" the new self you received at Baptism. This image of putting on the "new self" like a piece of clothing is powerful.

At our Baptism, we received a baptismal garment that represents our new self. Our new self, the author tells us, is "created in God's way"; it manifests our likeness to God, who is "righteousness and . . . truth."

GOSPEL Today's pericope begins the Bread of Life passage that will continue for three Sundays. It won't end well. Scandalized by what sounds like blasphemy or lunacy, many disciples will abandon Jesus because of this discourse, which takes place soon after the miraculous feeding of the multitude. The crowd

In their question about his arrival, we can almost hear them wonder, "Did we miss a miracle?"

Jesus chides them, yet yearns for them to recognize him for who he truly is. His tone invites their dialogue because he wants them to discover the bread that doesn't perish.

The crowd follows his lead, but again becomes myopic, insisting on miracles and proofs. They are not evil, only disappointingly human in their need to see Jesus conjure manna from the air in a miraculous display that would top their ancestors.

Calmly, and eager to communicate, Jesus teaches them. Like the woman at the well, these people are literalists who think Jesus will satisfy their physical hunger. Speak like a caring teacher: Jesus' patience is not spent here.

Finally, because nothing else will do it, Jesus speaks bluntly. Like the thirst of the Samaritan woman, their hunger will only be sated when they find their home in Jesus.

And when they **found** him across the **sea** they said to him,
    "**Rabbi**, when did you **get** here?"
Jesus **answered** them and said,
    "Amen, amen, I **say** to you,
    you are looking for me **not** because you saw **signs**
    but because you ate the **loaves** and were **filled**.
Do not work for food that **perishes**
    but for the food that **endures** for eternal **life**,
    which the Son of **Man** will give you.
For on **him** the Father, **God**, has set his **seal**."
So they **said** to him,
    "What can we do to **accomplish** the works of God?"
Jesus answered and **said** to them,
    "**This** is the work of God, that you **believe** in the one he sent."
So they said to him,
    "What **sign** can you do, that we may **see** and **believe** in you?
What can you **do**?
Our ancestors ate **manna** in the desert, as it is written:
    He gave them bread from **heaven** *to eat.*"
So Jesus said to them,
    "Amen, amen, I **say** to you,
    it was not **Moses** who gave the bread from heaven;
    my **Father** gives you the **true** bread from heaven.
For the bread of **God** is that which comes down from **heaven**
    and gives **life** to the world."

So they said to him,
    "**Sir**, **give** us this bread **always**."
Jesus said to them,
    "**I** am the bread of **life**;
    whoever comes to **me** will never **hunger**,
        and whoever **believes** in me will never **thirst**."

has tracked Jesus to the synagogue of Capernaum. With searing insight, Jesus challenges their motives. In John, Jesus' signs were meant to inspire conversion. Those privileged to witness these signs should have seen in Jesus a divine companion who satisfy the deepest cravings of their souls. But this crowd seeks nothing more than another helping of miraculous bread from the wonder-worker. Jesus urges them to seek instead food for the soul that leads to "eternal life."

The crowd eagerly responds to this suggestion, asking that he show them how to acquire this food; but then things quickly turn. Jesus' simple answer is: believe in me. But their simpler retort is "What will you do to *make* us believe?" Clearly, not all in the crowd had witnessed the miracle, but had surely heard of it, and have come in hopes of some similar marvel here. They even make a suggestion: How about something like "the manna in the desert" that fed our ancestors? Jesus quickly takes up their reference and develops it into one of his most important but hardest teachings. After clarifying that the Israelites were fed not by Moses but by God, he begins to equate himself with the bread that "comes down from heaven" and gives "life to the world." Again misunderstanding, the practical-minded crowd asks him for this heavenly bread. In words both disappointing and deeply troubling, Jesus stuns the crowd with the solemn pronouncement that he is this bread that doesn't perish but endures for eternal life. The offer of bread that will sate all hunger, of one who can slake all thirst must be appealing to the crowd. But their enthusiasm won't last for long.

19TH SUNDAY IN ORDINARY TIME

Lectionary #116

READING I   1 Kings 19:4–8

A reading from the first Book of Kings

Elijah went a day's journey into the **desert**,
    until he came to a broom tree and **sat** beneath it.
He **prayed** for **death** saying:
    "This is **enough**, O LORD!
Take my **life**, for I am no better than my **fathers**."
He lay down and fell **asleep** under the broom tree,
    but then an **angel** touched him and ordered him to **get** up
        and **eat**.
Elijah **looked** and there at his head was a **hearth** cake
    and a jug of **water**.
After he ate and drank, he lay **down** again,
    but the angel of the LORD came back a **second** time,
    touched him, and ordered,
        "**Get** up and **eat**, else the journey will be too **long** for you!"
He **got** up, **ate**, and **drank**;
    then **strengthened** by that food,
    he walked forty **days** and forty **nights**
        to the mountain of **God**, **Horeb**.

Elijah = ee-LĪ-juh

He's not going on vacation: what drives Elijah is depression, anger, and fatigue.

He's had enough! All his good effort brings only trial and danger, and it seems so unfair!

God immediately takes the initiative to revive Elijah's body and spirit.

Elijah has not yet fully responded to God's initiative.

God's angel is persistent; he now *orders* Elijah to comply.

Read the last lines slowly, for they suggest a major transformation. Like the wandering Israelites, he is led to the mountain where Moses received the commandments.

READING I This episode follows one of the most dramatic and bloody events in the Old Testament. As the only true prophet in Israel, Elijah comes against the 450 false prophets of Baal (the god of Queen Jezebel) and challenges them to a showdown: both sides will sacrifice a young bull and then ask Baal and the Lord to send down fire to consume them; the one who "answers with fire" is truly God. Elijah taunts his opponents whose offering remains unburned while his is devoured in a great conflagration. Following this victory, Elijah has the false prophets put to death—every one of them. Upon hearing this, Jezebel, wife of Ahab, judged more evil than all the kings before him, threatens to slay Elijah in the same way he slew the prophets. Fearing for his life, Elijah flees, taking with him neither companion nor supplies, and openly laments his fate in a moment of sheer desperation. Despite God's dramatic intervention in the contest against the false prophets, Elijah won't turn to God for help and begs, instead, for death. His daring and successful work, it seems, has backfired. He is depressed, frustrated, and angry, feeling he deserves better than this.

But God cuts short this indulgence in self-pity. An angel awakens Elijah, offering him bread and water. He takes some sustenance, but refuses to be roused by this sign of divine compassion and care. So the angel wakes him again and orders him to fortify himself for his unfinished work. The few words that follow suggest a major change in the prophet. He is not only strengthened in body, but revived in spirit. Like his wandering ancestors who trav-

Ephesians = ee-FEE-zhuhnz

This is the fifth of seven consecutive weeks that we read from Ephesians.

This opening line must be delivered with great deliberateness. You are saying, "Don't drive away the Spirit who is your path to salvation."

Each offense is different; so don't run them together. Shift your tone for the contrasting list of Gospel values.

Pause and establish eye contact before beginning these final lines. You are calling your listeners to sacrifice their resentments and divisions in imitation of Christ's self-giving love.

READING II   Ephesians 4:30—5:2

A reading from the Letter of Saint Paul to the Ephesians

Brothers and sisters:
Do not **grieve** the Holy Spirit of **God**,
　with which you were **sealed** for the day of **redemption**.
All **bitterness**, **fury**, **anger**, **shouting**, and **reviling**
　must be **removed** from you, along with all **malice**.
And be **kind** to one another, **compassionate**,
　forgiving one another as God has forgiven **you** in **Christ**.

So be imitators of **God**, as beloved **children**, and live in **love**,
　as Christ **loved** us and handed himself **over** for us
　as a sacrificial **offering** to God for a fragrant **aroma**.

eled 40 years, Elijah journeys 40 days to Horeb, the mount of the covenant.

READING II The Spirit is Christ's gift—the Advocate who makes plain all that Christ taught and who empowers us to live according to Christ's gospel of love. We say the Church was born on Pentecost, the day the Spirit descended on the orphaned disciples. It is that Spirit who sustains the Church and who, when invited into the hearts of individual believers, provides the gifts to enable us to live like Christ. And when we live like Christ,

we manifest the *fruit* of the Spirit in our lives. Aware of the central role the Spirit plays in Christian life, the author uses human categories to warn us that our behavior can inhibit the flow of grace and even "grieve" the Holy Spirit. He's not saying the Spirit may pack up and leave us, but alerting us to a hardness of heart that can stifle the Spirit to such a degree that we start bearing *rotten* fruit. These admonitions are intended for believers who should know better but who, nonetheless, succumb to everyday temptations that can have dire consequences.

The listing of sinful behavior alludes to real problems within the Christian community and within individual hearts. Don't rush the list, but let each item add weight to the millstone these offenses hang around our necks. In contrast, you also share a list of what leads to life: kindness, compassion, and forgiveness. Perhaps a reflection on the effects of bitterness and anger in your own life will add conviction to the call to be "imitators of God" that concludes the reading.

GOSPEL John 6:41–51

A reading from the holy Gospel according to John

Emphasize the word "murmured" each time it occurs.

The strength of Jesus' assertion helps provoke their hostile response. How can this familiar face be the bearer of divine truth?!

Jesus scolds, and then recovering his patience he begins to teach. These strong statements about himself reveal Jesus' confidence and inner strength, and should be spoken with those qualities. Give the quoted scripture a distinctive tone.

This aside is spoken lest the crowd misunderstand. He's saying: Only the one who is from God has seen the Father; believe that and you'll live forever.

Jesus' tone softens as he asserts his readiness to be food for them.

Jesus offers himself knowing his listeners may reject him. Speak slowly and with authority, like a doctor offering advice you know is true but aware the patient may refuse it.

The Jews **murmured** about Jesus because he said,
  "I am the **bread** that came down from **heaven**,"
  and they said,
  "Is this not **Jesus**, the son of **Joseph**?
Do we not know his **father** and **mother**?
Then **how** can he say,
  'I have come down from **heaven**'?"
Jesus **answered** and said to them,
  "Stop **murmuring** among yourselves.
No one can come to me unless the **Father** who **sent** me **draw** him,
  and I will **raise** him on the last **day**.
It is written in the **prophets**:
  They shall all be taught by **God**.
Everyone who **listens** to my Father and **learns** from him
    comes to me.
Not that anyone has **seen** the Father
  except the one who is **from** God;
  he has seen the Father.
Amen, amen, I **say** to you,
  whoever **believes** has eternal **life**.
I am the **bread** of life.
Your ancestors ate the **manna** in the desert, but they **died**;
  this is the bread that comes down from heaven
  so that one may **eat** it and **not** die.
I am the **living** bread that came down from heaven;
  whoever eats **this** bread will live **forever**;
  and the bread that I will **give** is my **flesh** for the **life**
    of the **world**."

GOSPEL Jesus often orders the disciples to refrain from revealing his true nature or sharing information that might cause controversy. Here, it is Jesus who shocks and speaks in ways that will eventually lead many to desert him. In earlier parts of John, the term "bread of life" expresses God's revelation through Jesus. But now the term takes on a more eucharistic character and becomes increasingly controversial. In this text we hear echoes of last week's First Reading in which the Israelites "grumbled" in the desert. As the forebears grumbled against

the Father, so these now grumble against the Son. It is the same kind of fruitless and faithless moaning Moses endured. Again, the familiar-prophet syndrome undermines Jesus' credibility, for his listeners take offense that this son of Joseph speaks so scandalously.

Jesus' admonition to stop their murmuring is not so much an order to stop denigrating him, as it is a command to start believing the truth he shares. Anyone who is open to God's prompting will be drawn to me, he says. God teaches, but we must listen; and if we hear the Father, then we

will seek out the Son. Alluding to the bread that fed the chosen people in the desert, Jesus says that the manna—like the bread he so recently multiplied—was earthly food that could sustain only for a time. The bread that he will give, however, being the true bread of heaven, will bring eternal life to those who receive it. That final verse where he speaks not of "this . . . bread," but asserts "I am the . . . bread" clarifies the eucharistic nature of this discourse. He is not alluding broadly to God's revelation but speaking specifically of his very flesh.

ASSUMPTION OF THE BLESSED VIRGIN MARY: VIGIL

Lectionary #621

READING I 1 Chronicles 15:3–4, 15–16; 16:1–2

Chronicles = KRAH-nih-k*ls

Someone bringing to your town the Declaration of Independence, Liberty Bell, and Statue of Liberty might cause the kind of awed excitement reported here.
Narrate the description of David's preparations with a tone of expectant joy.

Name the musical instruments and other details slowly, suggesting that no expense was spared!

Speak of the enshrinement with reverence, as if speaking of the arrival of a powerful and awe-inspiring person.

Anticipation climaxes with the Ark's arrival. Lift out the word "blessed."

A reading from the first Book of Chronicles

David assembled all **Israel** in **Jerusalem** to bring the **ark**
    of the LORD
  to the **place** that he had **prepared** for it.
David **also** called together the sons of **Aaron** and the **Levites**.

The **Levites** bore the ark of God on their **shoulders** with **poles**,
  as **Moses** had **ordained** according to the **word** of the LORD.

David commanded the **chiefs** of the **Levites**
  to appoint their **kinsmen** as **chanters**,
  to play on musical **instruments**, **harps**, **lyres**, and **cymbals**,
  to make a loud **sound** of **rejoicing**.

They **brought** in the ark of God and set it within the **tent**
  which David had **pitched** for it.
Then they offered up **burnt** offerings and **peace** offerings to God.
When David had **finished** offering up the burnt offerings
    and peace offerings,
  he **blessed** the people in the **name** of the LORD.

READING I The Ark of the Covenant held Israel's most sacred possessions—the tablets of the law and remnants of the manna God provided in the wilderness. The great reverence accorded here to the Ark bespeaks not only the importance of the objects it held, but also Israel's awareness of God's special love for them, which God demonstrated by raining down bread from heaven and instructing them through the law. With great ceremony and liturgical splendor, King David has the Ark brought into the tent he had especially erected to house it. The ceremony is lush with music, song, and royal procession. Adhering to the instructions set out by Moses, the Ark is enshrined in a place of honor where it will remind the people of God's holy presence and be a source of blessing.

Christianity's most sacred vessel is Mary who carried within her womb not divine symbols or gifts, but God's own son. We call Mary the Ark of the New Covenant. As the means of the Incarnation, she bore within her body not words etched in stone, but the living Word of God.

READING II A classic line of biblical literature graces this brief text: "Where, O death, is your victory" Where . . . your sting?" Using the progressive reasoning of a lawyer, Paul assembles a poetic paean declaring the death of death and the victory of grace.

When the mortal and passing becomes lasting and immortal, then God's word first proclaimed by Hosea will be fulfilled: Death will be swallowed up in victory! Death is the gravest consequence of sin, subjecting our bodies to the corruption and stink of the grave. But Christ promises life

Corinthians = kohr-IN-thee-uhnz
A short reading always requires a slower proclamation.

The opening line is like a gradually building trumpet blast of good news. Don't mispronounce the word "immortality."

Emboldened with courage to confront death (like a cornered kid in a playground who's suddenly joined by *both* his older brothers) you say (loud enough for death to hear you), "Hey, death, where's your victory, huh? O death [perhaps a whispered taunt, this time] where is your sting?"

The taunt is over; these final lines explain the reason for confronting this formidable foe so boldly: Christ is our victory!

READING II   1 Corinthians 15:54b–57

A reading from the first Letter of Saint Paul to the Corinthians

Brothers and sisters:
When that which is **mortal** clothes itself with **immortality**,
    then the **word** that is **written** shall come **about**:

> *Death is swallowed up in **victory**.*
> *Where, O death, is your **victory**?*
> *Where, O death, is your **sting**?*

The **sting** of death is **sin**,
    and the **power** of sin is the **law**.
But thanks be to **God** who gives us the **victory**
    through our **Lord** Jesus **Christ**.

GOSPEL   Luke 11:27–28

A reading from the holy Gospel according to Luke

While **Jesus** was **speaking**,
    a **woman** from the **crowd called** out and said to him,
    "Blessed is the **womb** that **carried** you
    and the **breasts** at which you **nursed**."
He replied,
    "**Rather, blessed** are those
    who **hear** the word of **God** and **observe** it."

Don't rush or you'll risk finishing before your assembly has fully focused.

To be heard in the crowd, the woman had to speak slowly and distinctly. Likely, she speaks from experience of bearing and nursing her own children.

Jesus had driven out a demon and some feared he did it by Satan's power. The woman affirms he is a man of God.

Jesus shows no disrespect for Mary, but announces the greater privilege: hearing God's word and obeying it. Mary was the exemplar of such discipleship!

beyond the grave and Mary, his mother, is the first, after him, to taste the victory of bodily Resurrection promised to all who die in Christ.

With imagery borrowed from Hosea, Paul reasons elegantly that the poison that causes death (its "sting") is "sin." But Jesus *conquered* sin, whose power comes from the law. No longer subject to the law, we are also no longer subject to sin and death. Death's sting is lost, its power finally broken. Paul mocks death boldly, because this victory is not won by human effort, but by the unassailable power of our Lord Jesus Christ.

GOSPEL This shortest of the Gospel accounts in the Lectionary names both the lesser and the greater focus of this solemnity. The lesser focus is Mary, the mother of Jesus, who "carried" him in her womb and nursed him at her breast. But, just as Jesus did, today's liturgy points beyond Mary to an even greater focus: those who hear the word of God and keep it. Jesus knows his mother's glory and her victory are completely bound in his, and therefore assured. He needn't take the time to praise her or to fret over her fate. But about his followers he worries. Their welfare is his chief concern and their success his greatest reason for celebration. From his own lips we know that we are "blessed."

ASSUMPTION OF THE BLESSED VIRGIN MARY: DAY

Lectionary #622

READING I   Revelation 11:19a; 12:1–6a, 10ab

A reading from the Book of Revelation

God's **temple** in heaven was **opened**,
    and the **ark** of his **covenant** could be seen in the temple.

A great **sign** appeared in the sky, a **woman** clothed with the **sun**,
    with the **moon** under her **feet**,
    and on her **head** a **crown** of twelve **stars**.
She was with **child** and **wailed** aloud in **pain** as she **labored**
        to give **birth**.
Then **another** sign appeared in the sky;
    it was a huge red **dragon**, with seven **heads** and ten **horns**,
    and on its heads were seven **diadems**.
Its **tail** swept away a third of the **stars** in the sky
    and **hurled** them down to the **earth**.
Then the dragon **stood** before the woman about to give **birth**,
    to **devour** her child when she gave birth.
She gave birth to a **son**, a **male** child,
    destined to **rule** all the **nations** with an iron **rod**.

Remember, you are recounting a mystical vision, not something that happened at the grocery. Speak of temple and ark with great reverence.

Although this reading is awesome and dramatic, you must avoid a melodramatic tone as you narrate these surprising and striking events. The key is to speak with sincerity and belief.

A sudden mood shift occurs here: the stately woman is actually in painful labor.

The mood shifts again, this time it turns threatening (but again, don't become melodramatic).

Pause and then slowly announce the dragon's murderous intentions.

READING I   Today's First Reading is rich with imagery that can be variously applied to the nation of Israel, the church of Christ, and to Mary, who as mother of the Messiah, becomes the meeting place of the Old and the New Testaments. The church calls Mary the Ark of the New Covenant, because—unlike the original ark that merely *represented* God's presence—Mary bore that presence within her womb when she conceived Jesus, the incarnate Son of God. Eve, the primordial mother of all humankind, is also evoked in these lines. By choosing this text, the Church places Mary at the intersection of all these themes: through her, the Old Testament is fulfilled and the New Covenant initiated; in her, as the new Eve, a new Creation is initiated through Christ, who—again through her—becomes the new Adam.

Most of that will not be apparent to your listeners as you proclaim; it will be for the homilist to make those connections. What you must do is render the text in an exalted and dignified manner that suggests the depths that are here to be mined. Most of us have no experience of this kind of vision. But you must share it in a way that helps us experience it as the lofty and awe-inspiring revelation John was given. God's temple in heaven opens, revealing the holy *ark*. Suddenly, an even greater sign appears: a woman wearing the sun as a garment while she stands upon the moon, her splendor augmented by the crown of stars that adorns her head. But immediately this grand image dissolves into the sight of a mother laboring to give birth, wailing in pain.

If there were theme music behind the text, it would suddenly turn tense and

Speak of the child with strength and dignity, suggesting he has nothing to fear from the threatening beast.

Don't rush these lines. Suggest the protective care of God for the Church, here symbolized by the "woman."

Pause, and then begin the narration. The declaration should resound with power and hope.

Take a slight pause after the salutation, then boldly declare the great truth of Christ's Resurrection that presages ours.

Although Paul's tone is logical and well reasoned, let the good news of what he says also shine through. Yes, a man caused death, but a man also brought life; in Adam we all die, but in Christ we live!

Here, too, there is an undercurrent of hope and joy. Although there is a proper order, the good news is that we will get our turn.

"Those who belong to Christ" have believed in him and lived in such a way as to come to resemble him.

Her child was caught up to **God** and his **throne**.
The woman herself **fled** into the **desert**
  where she had a **place** prepared by **God**.

Then I heard a loud **voice** in heaven say:
  "Now have **salvation** and **power** come,
    and the **Kingdom** of our **God**
    and the **authority** of his **Anointed** One."

READING II   1 Corinthians 15:20–27

A reading from the first Letter of Saint Paul to the Corinthians

Brothers and sisters:
Christ has been **raised** from the **dead**,
  the **firstfruits** of those who have fallen **asleep**.
For since **death** came through **man**,
  the **resurrection** of the dead came **also** through man.
For just as in **Adam** all **die**,
  so too in **Christ** shall all be brought to **life**,
  but **each** one in proper **order**:
  Christ the **firstfruits**;
  then, at his **coming**, those who **belong** to Christ;

threatening as the "dragon" with many heads and horns takes the sky and with its tail snuffs out one-third of its stars! Then a confrontation: the dragon stands ready to devour the woman's child as soon as it is born. Pause there to transition to the calmer mood that follows and announce the birth of the "male child" whose destiny will eclipse the dragon and encompass all the nations of the earth. Announce with joy and relief that the child was swept up into heaven; then, without anxiety, speak of the woman fleeing to the safe place prepared for her by God.

The vision ends as dramatically as it began—you can almost hear trumpet blasts precede the final declaration. After a pause, speak the "then I heard . . ." narration and then continue right into the regal final lines that herald the coming of God's kingdom and of "his Anointed One."

READING II The commentary for today's First Reading discusses how Mary is the Eve of the new covenant who births the new Man, Jesus the Christ. Here, Paul draws a very deliberate comparison between the old Adam and Jesus, the new Adam who ushers in the new covenant and redeems the world. With clear progressive reasoning, Paul argues that as sin and death entered the world through the "man" Adam, so life and Resurrection came through a "man" who is like Adam in all things but sin. Adam's sin made us all subject to death, but Christ's perfect obedience to God's will, his sinlessness, brings life to all.

Paul asserts a proper order in this new Creation. The first to experience this coming to life or Resurrection is Christ himself. But later, when he returns at the end of

then comes the **end**,
   when he hands over the **Kingdom** to his God and **Father**,
   when he has **destroyed** every **sovereignty**
   and every **authority** and **power**.
For he must **reign** until he has put all his **enemies** under his **feet**.
The **last** enemy to be destroyed is **death**,
   for "he subjected **everything** under his **feet**."

End on a note of regal power. Christ will reign forever and over all things, including the great enemy—death.

GOSPEL   Luke 1:39–56

A reading from the holy Gospel according to Luke

Mary set **out**
   and traveled to the **hill** country in **haste**
   to a town of **Judah**,
   where she entered the house of **Zechariah**
   and greeted **Elizabeth**.
When Elizabeth **heard** Mary's greeting,
   the infant **leaped** in her **womb**,
   and **Elizabeth**, **filled** with the Holy **Spirit**,
cried out in a loud **voice** and said,
   "**Blessed** are you among **women**,
   and blessed is the **fruit** of your **womb**.

It is her faith in the angel's message that impels Mary's haste.

Pause before announcing Elizabeth's greeting. She sees more than her young cousin standing before her. Suggest that with a tone of reverence and admiration.

That the "infant leaped" and that Elizabeth was "filled with the Holy Spirit" are both significant details.

Don't recite the blessing as in the Hail Mary, but as a spontaneous exclamation.

time, all who "belong to Christ" will also experience Resurrection from the dead. The other sequence Paul names is the vanquishing of the forces that have resisted the unfolding of God's kingdom. The "end" when Christ hands over the kingdom to God the Father will come only after he has first destroyed all those foes. The lesser enemies ("every sovereignty . . . authority and power") will be overcome first; then the greatest enemy will be vanquished—death itself. And the place of death's defeat will be the place where it has reigned since the dawn of humanity—our human bodies.

That is why today's solemnity is so important: our belief in Mary's Assumption is also our assurance that we, too, will be delivered from the destruction of our bodies that results from sin. Christ promised to prepare a place for us so that "where [he] is, [we] might be also" (John 14:3). Mary stands as his pledge that that promise will be fulfilled. Whether Mary first died and then was assumed physically into heaven or whether she transitioned from earthly life to eternal life without undergoing death is not defined by Church dogma.

What is unmistakably clear is that Mary was taken up into heaven both in body and in soul and she now lives the resurrected life that Jesus first experienced, and that each of us hope to be granted following the Last Judgment.

GOSPEL   In Luke we read the story and hear the song that remind us why Mary was destined for the unique distinction we celebrate today: "all generation will call me blessed . . . the Almighty has done great things for me . . . ." Scripture constantly presents

Don't ignore Elizabeth's naming Jesus "Lord."

What is said of Mary can be said of all believers who hear this Gospel today.

The canticle stands apart from the rest of the text. Pause before beginning and sustain a fairly brisk and joyful tempo.

Although she is called "blessed," Mary identifies herself as a lowly "servant."

"Fear" of the Lord is a venerable biblical notion that should be highlighted.

The God of the Bible, even the New Testament, is not one-dimensional: besides mercy and love, there is also strength and justice.

These reversals are typical of the kingdom of God. Give them proper stress.

The song ends on a note of enduring gratitude.

Pause before reading this coda that tells us Mary stayed until the birth of John.

And how does this **happen** to me,
　that the mother of my **Lord** should come to **me**?
For at the moment the sound of your **greeting** reached my **ears**,
　the **infant** in my womb leaped for **joy**.
Blessed are you who **believed**
　that what was **spoken** to you by the Lord
　would be **fulfilled**."

And Mary said:

"My **soul** proclaims the **greatness** of the Lord;
　my spirit **rejoices** in God my **Savior**
　for he has looked with **favor** on his lowly **servant**.
From this day all **generations** will call me **blessed**:
　the Almighty has done **great** things for me
　and **holy** is his **Name**.
He has **mercy** on those who **fear** him
　in **every** generation.
He has shown the **strength** of his arm,
　and has **scattered** the proud in their **conceit**.
He has cast down the **mighty** from their **thrones**,
　and has **lifted** up the **lowly**.
He has filled the **hungry** with **good** things,
　and the **rich** he has sent away **empty**.
He has come to the **help** of his servant **Israel**
　for he has **remembered** his promise of **mercy**,
　the promise he made to our **fathers**,
　to **Abraham** and his children for **ever**."

Mary **remained** with her about three **months**
　and then **returned** to her **home**.

figures whose lives are interrupted and upended by God; Mary and Elizabeth are but two in a long and illustrious line. Having received the angel's announcement, Mary hastens to the side of her cousin whose unexpected pregnancy is the sign that confirms Gabriel's promise. Both women, kindred by more than blood, are vessels of grace and conduits of love. In her Spirit-led greeting, Elizabeth not only names Mary and the child she bears as "blessed," but she also becomes the first to identify Jesus as "Lord."

Unlike Zechariah, who doubted the angel, Mary comes in expectant faith to assist her aged cousin in her pregnancy. Mary also "rejoices" in the grace God has bestowed on her, knowing "generations" will follow Elizabeth's lead in calling her "blessed." It is for that faith that Elizabeth (and Luke!) extols her. She has not held back, but has trusted and surrendered, becoming the first and ideal disciple. The song Luke gives her to sing expresses the longings of generations of faithful Israelites; it rejoices in God's goodness, acknowledges God's favor upon the lowly,

and names the amazing reversals that characterize the kingdom—the mighty are cast down and the lowly lifted up, the rich go away empty while the hungry are fed, and so on.

Narrate the visitation story with Elizabeth's joy, suggesting the strength the women derived from each other's company. Mary's canticle contains several powerful and important images that, while proclaimed briskly, should not be rushed. It is in this song that we find our own spiritual communion with these two women.

20TH SUNDAY IN ORDINARY TIME

Lectionary #119

READING I   Proverbs 9:1–6

The personification of Wisdom will take some listeners by surprise, so begin slowly and share each image with a tone of joyful gratitude.

"Her house" refers to the world; "seven columns" is an ancient notion of how the earth and sky were supported.

There is a mood shift here: the festive meal is prepared, now Wisdom must hurry to gather guests at her table.

"Simple" does not mean simple-minded, but guileless and pure of heart. The humble and sincere are welcome in Wisdom's home.

Because Folly also stands in her doorway inviting the simple to taste her poisonous sweets, Wisdom must entreat earnestly so those passing by are not seduced by "foolishness." Our lives depend on heeding this advice.

A reading from the Book of Proverbs

> **Wisdom** has built her **house**,
>   she has set up her seven **columns**;
> she has dressed her **meat**, mixed her **wine**,
>   **yes**, she has spread her **table**.
> She has sent out her **maidens**; she **calls**
>   from the **heights** out over the **city**:
> "Let whoever is **simple** turn in **here**";
>   to the one who lacks **understanding**, she says,
> "**Come**, eat of my **food**,
>   and drink of the **wine** I have mixed!
> **Forsake** foolishness that you may **live**;
>   **advance** in the way of **understanding**."

READING I   In the verses that follow today's selection (9:13–18) we meet Folly, Wisdom's foil, who, like her more prudent counterpart, also invites passersby to feast on sweet and pleasing fare. But Folly's table is not set with nourishing food; though tantalizing, her meal consists of "junk food" that's grown in the soil of selfish desire, and it only leads to death. Wisdom, on the other hand, does not offer the shortcuts of deceit and self-indulgence that Folly serves those foolish enough to take a seat at her table. Wisdom's fare is virtue and divine truth; those who dine with her will "live" and "advance in . . . understanding."

This kind of anthropomorphism is not unusual in scripture and here the biblical writer utilizes it to emphasize two key ideas. First is God's initiative in calling us to dine on nutritious food that sustains us. God's love is so great that it reaches out to us, calls us from "the heights out over the city," inviting us to come and dine. That God is presented as Lady Wisdom, who has labored to prepare a splendid meal makes the divine initiative all the more appealing.

The second point is as important, but more subtly presented than the first. Our freedom to choose is a great responsibility that ultimately determines whether we live or die. We can choose to dine with Wisdom and take in the "understanding" she offers, or we can enter Folly's banquet hall, seeking the self-indulgence she serves. The latter leads to death, but the former leads to the heavenly banquet, of which Eucharist is a foretaste, where we will dine forever among those "simple" enough to answer Wisdom's call.

Ephesians = ee-FEE-zhunz

Without racing, strive for a pace that suggests a sense of urgency about what you share.

The sentences are long, but the ideas are simple. First you caution ("Watch carefully") then you admonish ("live not as foolish persons"); finally you motivate ("[Make] the most of the opportunity). Paul's tone is strong, for he knows the dangers of these vices.

After telling them what *not* to do, Paul presents ideal behavior.

As you proclaim, your smile and joyous attitude can model the gratitude that Paul says should characterize Christian life.

READING II   Ephesians 5:15–20

A reading from the Letter of Saint Paul to the Ephesians

Brothers and sisters:
Watch **carefully** how you **live**,
    not as **foolish** persons but as **wise**,
    making the **most** of the opportunity,
    because the days are **evil**.
Therefore, do not continue in **ignorance**,
    but try to **understand** what is the will of the **Lord**.
And do not get **drunk** on wine, in which lies **debauchery**,
    but be **filled** with the **Spirit**,
    addressing one another in **psalms** and **hymns**
        and spiritual **songs**,
    singing and **playing** to the Lord in your **hearts**,
    giving thanks **always** and for **everything**
    in the name of our Lord Jesus **Christ** to God the **Father**.

READING II   Rarely is there such consonance between the First and Second Readings. The themes of wisdom and foolishness announced in the first reading are echoed in this short text from Paul who, just like the author of Proverbs, warns us about the dangers of being "foolish" and the advantages of being "wise." "Ignorance" and "debauchery" are the food of the foolish; the poisonous fare that Lady Wisdom's antagonist, Folly, serves her diners. Paul warns his readers to avoid such poison. Throughout this chapter, Paul is exhorting the Ephesians to be imitators

of God and so he names the behaviors that are godlike and those that are not. As always, his motive is the welfare of his spiritual children whose conversion he won with more than two years of effort.

Paul doesn't refrain from giving orders and speaking bluntly: Don't be "foolish" but be wise, he says; understand God's will, don't get drunk, and don't sink into debauchery. Instead, he says with great eagerness, let yourselves be filled with God's Spirit and let the Spirit inflame you so that you burst into song! Let song be your greeting and your prayer, let it echo in

your hearts and rise to the heavens. He is urging the Church to imitate the heavenly choirs in giving endless praise to God. Paul doesn't hesitate to ask what to us might seem impossible: at all times and in every situation, he says, yes even the hard and painful situations, give thanks to God the Father through Jesus Christ, our Lord!

GOSPEL   Today's text from Proverbs introduced the notion of food that truly satisfies. Christian faith sees the feast to which Lady Wisdom invites us as fulfilled in the Eucharist

GOSPEL John 6:51–58

A reading from the holy Gospel according to John

Jesus said to the **crowds**:
  "**I** am the living **bread** that came down from **heaven**;
  whoever **eats** this bread will live **forever**;
  and the bread that **I** will give
  is my **flesh** for the life of the **world**."

The Jews **quarreled** among themselves, saying,
  "How can this man give us his **flesh** to eat?"
Jesus **said** to them,
  "Amen, amen, I **say** to you,
  unless you **eat** the flesh of the Son of **Man** and drink his **blood**,
  you do not have **life** within you.
Whoever **eats** my **flesh** and **drinks** my **blood**
  has **eternal** life,
  and I will **raise** him on the last **day**.
For my **flesh** is true **food**,
  and my **blood** is true **drink**.
Whoever **eats** my flesh and **drinks** my blood
  remains in me and **I** in **him**.
Just as the living **Father** sent **me**
  and I have life **because** of the Father,
  so also the one who **feeds** on me
  will have life **because** of me.
This is the bread that came down from **heaven**.
Unlike your **ancestors** who ate and still **died**,
  whoever eats **this** bread will live **forever**."

Knowing that these words will cause controversy, Jesus does not hold back.

Obviously, not all are put off by Jesus' comments.

Jesus' phrasing underscores the import of what he says.

Jesus links reception of his body and blood with eternal salvation.

We hear echoes here of the text from the book of Proverbs.

Don't rush this analogy of Jesus deriving life from the Father and the believer deriving life from Jesus.

Jesus is the new manna, but the life he gives will last forever.

---

through which we are nourished by Christ's own body and blood. Though it has roots in ancient thought, everything Jesus says (and Catholics believe) about Eucharist defies logic. No wonder the people ask, "How can this man give us his flesh to eat?" It was not unheard of in the pagan world that devotees would somehow share in divinity by consuming their god. But these Jews are no pagans and for them Jesus' words are either blasphemy or insanity.

Jesus must have known his words would stir up controversy, yet he risks the crowd's contempt for the sake of the truth. Enduring their skepticism and scorn, he forcefully pronounces the revolutionary truth that he is "true food," the manna of the new covenant.

The crowd's dispute signals that not all are unbelievers, or there would be no argument. Jesus makes consuming his body and blood a necessity for attaining eternal life. Only those who feast at his table will be raised "up on the last day." Jesus' listeners cannot possibly anticipate his self-sacrifice on the cross, nor the eucharistic meal that will make that sacrifice sacramentally present for those who gather round the table to remember. Yet Jesus drives the point home all the more forcefully, saying his body and blood are true food and drink and that he becomes one with those who eat his flesh and drink his blood. Just as Jesus derives life from the Father who sent him, so the believer derives life from feeding on the bread of life. And the bread Jesus offers, unlike the manna of their ancestors, will not simply sustain them for a day or a season, but for all time.

21ST SUNDAY IN ORDINARY TIME

Lectionary #122

READING I Joshua 24:1–2a, 15–17, 18b

Joshua = JOSH-oo-uh

Let the narration suggest the weighty significance of this gathering.

Shechem = SHEK-uhm

A reading from the Book of Joshua

Joshua gathered together all the tribes of **Israel** at **Shechem**,
  summoning their **elders**, their **leaders**,
  their **judges**, and their **officers**.
When they stood in **ranks** before God,
  Joshua **addressed** all the people:
  "If it does not **please** you to serve the LORD,
  decide today whom you **will** serve,
  the gods your **fathers** served beyond the River
  or the gods of the **Amorites** in whose **country**
    you are now dwelling.
As for **me** and my **household**, we will serve the LORD."

Don't let there be rancor in Joshua's voice, but a direct and serious challenge.

But the **people** answered,
  "Far be it from us to forsake the LORD
  for the service of **other** gods.
For it was the LORD, our **God**,
  who brought **us** and our **fathers** up out of the land of **Egypt**,
  out of a state of **slavery**.
He performed those great **miracles** before our very **eyes**
  and **protected** us along our entire **journey**
  and among the **peoples** through whom we passed.
Therefore we **also** will serve the LORD, for he is our **God**."

Pause before this important declaration. Let it be your own affirmation of fidelity to God.

Let the tone of the narration signal the people's eagerness to serve the Lord.

Recount this history with gratitude and pride, and a bit of awe at the God who made it all possible.

These are eyewitness affirmations, not a reporter's second-hand telling.
Pause, and then make the declaration simply and sincerely.

READING I In today's First Reading and Gospel, a great leader confronts his followers with a momentous decision. Jesus will ask the disciples if they, too, will abandon him; here, Joshua asks the Israelites to decide who will rule the nation and their hearts—the Lord, or the false gods of their ancestors and neighbors. The responses of the Israelite tribes and of the apostles are hauntingly similar, for both acknowledge there is no other choice but to remain faithful to the one who first called them.

In the verse that follows today's text from Joshua, the great leader reminds his people that following the law of the Lord will not be easy, therefore they must be ready to resist the lures of the pagan world that surrounds them. The people know how easily they can stray, as they readily abandoned the Lord during the desert wanderings, surrendering themselves to a golden calf. So Joshua's question is blunt and clear: If you won't serve the Lord, then decide whom you *will* serve! He concludes his address with one of scripture's classic lines that, without melodrama, you must

deliver with the dignity, confidence, and faith that it expresses.

Unlike the panicked time in the desert when they seemingly developed amnesia and forgot all the Lord had done to deliver them from the hands of the Egyptians, the people now recall the mighty deeds of the Lord and, with gratitude and appropriate fear of the Lord, they swear to serve God faithfully.

READING II Ephesians 5:21–32

A reading from the Letter of Saint Paul to the Ephesians

Brothers and sisters:
Be **subordinate** to one another out of **reverence** for **Christ**.
Wives should be subordinate to their **husbands** as to the **Lord**.
For the husband is **head** of his wife
    just as **Christ** is head of the **church**,
    he himself the **savior** of the body.
As the **church** is subordinate to **Christ**,
    so **wives** should be subordinate to their husbands
        in **everything**.
Husbands, **love** your wives,
    even as **Christ** loved the **church**
    and handed himself **over** for her to **sanctify** her,
    cleansing her by the bath of **water** with the **word**,
    that he might present to himself the church in **splendor**,
    without **spot** or **wrinkle** or **any** such thing,
    that she might be **holy** and without **blemish**.
So also husbands should **love** their wives as their own **bodies**.
He who loves his **wife** loves **himself**.
For no one **hates** his own **flesh**
    but rather **nourishes** and **cherishes** it,
    even as **Christ** does the **church**,
    because we are **members** of his body.
*For this reason a man shall **leave** his father and his mother*
        *and be joined to his **wife**,*
    *and the **two** shall become **one** flesh.*
This is a great **mystery**,
    but I speak in reference to **Christ** and the **church**.

[Shorter: Ephesians 5:2a, 25–32]

Ephesians = ee-FEE-zhuhnz
This is the last of seven consecutive weeks that we read from Ephesians.

This is the most important line of the text. Paul asks everyone to "be subordinate" not because of anyone's superiority, but "out of reverence for Christ."

Put your emphasis on the need to imitate the Church's love of Christ. Paul adds the obligation of Christian love to the cultural expectations of his day.

This is a call to selfless service.

Pause after the word "husbands" to survey the assembly, and then boldly declare their responsibilities toward their wives.

"Cleansing her by the bath" is a baptismal allusion.

Throughout, we hear of Christ's willingness to sacrifice for the sake of his bride.

When they care for each other, husband and wife are also caring for themselves, and when they do, they manifest the love of Christ for the Church.

Slow your delivery so the quote from Genesis is made more apparent.

This has been a teaching text; this last line presents that reality with prayerful humility.

READING II Paul's letter to the Ephesians is his great treatise on the Church, so it is fitting that even in speaking about marital relationships he utilizes the analogy of Christ's relationship with his bride, the Church. The opening line sets the tone, for there Paul calls for the mutual submission of one to another. All that follows must be heard in that context—none is greater than the other, for all are members of Christ's body, the Church. No real or imagined notion of superiority has a place within the Christian community. Women are called to submit to their husbands in the same life-affirming way that the Church submits to Christ. The subordination of the Church to Christ never demeans its members, but results always in the affirmation of our innate dignity.

Paul spends far more time tutoring husbands who bear the great responsibility of loving their wives as Christ loves his Church. Such love is never self-indulgent, but always self-sacrificing, for Christ gave his life for the Church. The seven lines of this long sentence all make one point: Christ's love for the Church is manifest in his effort to cleanse and "sanctify" her, to remove every "spot" and "blemish" so she will be "holy" and splendid in his sight. That willingness to extend oneself for the love of the other is the model of spousal love Paul gleans from Christ.

But Paul goes even further: a man's love for his wife must at least equal his love of himself; he must nourish and cherish her as he nourishes himself and as Christ nourishes the Church. Finally, Paul alludes to Genesis, reminding us that man and woman become "one flesh" in marriage—a great mystery that somehow expresses the relationship between Christ and his bride.

GOSPEL John 6:60–69

A reading from the holy Gospel according to John

The narrator's tone hints at the anger and frustration of the disciples.

Many of Jesus' **disciples** who were **listening** said,
    "This saying is **hard**; who can **accept** it?"
Since Jesus **knew** that his disciples were murmuring about this,
    he said to them, "Does this **shock** you?

Jesus is not intimidated by their complaining. His question suggests: If you think this is hard, just wait!

What if you were to see the Son of Man **ascending**
    to where he was **before**?
It is the **spirit** that gives **life**,
    while the **flesh** is of no **avail**.

Jesus is playing the teacher here; his energy is high and motivated by love.

The words I have spoken to you are **Spirit** and **life**.
But there are **some** of you who do not **believe**."

These words are spoken by a sympathetic narrator.

Jesus knew from the **beginning** the ones who would **not** believe
    and the one who would **betray** him.
And he said,
    "For this **reason** I have told you that no one can **come** to me
    unless it is **granted** him by my **Father**."

Narrate the departure of his disciples with a tone that suggests the hostile attitude that caused them to break away.

As a **result** of this,
    many of his disciples returned to their **former** way of life
    and no longer **accompanied** him.

Pause, as if to survey the faithful minority that remains, and then speak Jesus' question.

Jesus then said to the **Twelve**, "Do you **also** want to leave?"
Simon **Peter** answered him, "**Master**, to **whom** shall we go?

Pause again, then give Peter his moment of glory. One can imagine a humble, open armed gesture as he asks, "To whom shall we go?"

You have the words of eternal **life**.
We have come to **believe**
    and are **convinced** that you are the **Holy** One of **God**."

GOSPEL Skepticism about Jesus' teaching has reached the ranks of his disciples. Before it was the crowd that was scandalized by his claims that they must eat his body and drink his blood, but now even those close to him are "murmuring." The Greek word rendered here as "hard" doesn't mean Jesus' teaching is hard to *understand* but to *accept*.

In response, Jesus seems to warn them that there will be even greater challenges to their faith than this teaching about him being true food. The only way Jesus can "ascend to where he was before" is by means of the cross and that will be a greater scandal and stumbling block than any of his teachings. Ironically, in light of his insistence that one must eat his flesh to attain eternal life, Jesus now asserts that only the "spirit . . . gives life," while the flesh "is of no avail." But he is not speaking here of his own eucharistic flesh; rather, he is likely contrasting the things that are born of human motives and desires with those that are prompted by God's spirit.

There is a note of sadness in Jesus' acknowledgment that, although he is the source of "spirit and life," some among these close followers simply do not believe in him. The narrator's parenthetical aside reveals a sense of resignation, but Jesus' statement that faith is God-given suggests none of us is fully master of our own fate. The break between Jesus and "many of his disciples" is clearly final, for many return to their former lives. Jesus then turns to the twelve and asks the frank but painful question. It is Peter who takes the lead making a bold declaration of faith and revealing a depth of insight only the Spirit could give.

22ND SUNDAY IN ORDINARY TIME

Lectionary #125

READING I   Deuteronomy 4:1–2, 6–8

A reading from the Book of Deuteronomy

Always make sure your listeners know who the speaker is.

You are proclaiming a text written in a lofty and inspiring oratorical style. Don't let it sound like mundane advice. Picture Moses, in full authority, proclaiming before the people this profound exhortation.

This divine law is a source of life, and it cannot be tampered with.

A loving parent might share similar advice with a child going off to school or a career in a new city.

Speak this line in the voice of the admiring nations.

This is as true now for us as it was then for them.

Here, as throughout, the goal is to encourage and persuade.

Moses said to the **people**:
  "**Now**, Israel, hear the **statutes** and **decrees**
    which I am **teaching** you to **observe**,
    that you may **live**, and may enter in and take **possession**
      of the land
    which the LORD, the God of your **fathers**, is **giving** you.
In your **observance** of the commandments of the LORD,
      your God,
    which I **enjoin** upon you,
    you shall not **add** to what I command you nor **subtract** from it.
Observe them **carefully**,
    for thus will you give evidence
    of your **wisdom** and **intelligence** to the nations,
    who will **hear** of all these statutes and say,
      'This great **nation** is truly a **wise** and **intelligent** people.'
For what great nation **is** there
    that has gods so **close** to it as the LORD, our God, is to **us**
    whenever we **call** upon him?
Or what great nation has **statutes** and **decrees**
    that are as **just** as this whole law
    which I am setting before you **today**?"

READING I   The book of Deuteronomy is presented as Moses' last will and testament, his parting wisdom to the people he has led for many years, as he prepares for his own death. Though most of the its material is also found elsewhere in the Old Testament, Deuteronomy's rhetorical style and its profound spirituality are so distinctive that it held a unique place in Israel's religious consciousness. The verses omitted from this text and those that follow it urge Israel to remember God's great deeds on their

behalf, the miracles they have seen with their own eyes. Remembering God's favor and passing on that memory to all subsequent generations is an essential part of Israelite spirituality, and Moses makes love, remembrance, and handing on of the law part of that essence.

Moses speaks of the law as gift, a sign of God's enduring care of the people. Law is never a burden in Israelite spirituality. Instead, it is a sign of Israel's special status, of the divine favor that distinguishes her from all the nations. The law manifests divine wisdom shared with

human beings; but even more, it manifests the intimate relationship between God and Israel. Moses impresses on the people the absolute necessity of adhering to the law: taking possession of the promised land— even their very lives—depend on it. The sacred law can neither be amplified nor diminished, for it came from the hand of God. Cut from the eloquent oratory that is the book of Deuteronomy, this text is part of Moses' effort to ensure the physical and spiritual future of the people he has led and loved for so long.

READING II James 1:17–18, 21b–22, 27

Note the superlative form in the greeting. Joy and gratitude immediately characterize the tone of this reading.

This line means there is no variation in God, nor shadowing over of God's light because God never changes.

We are the "firstfruits" traditionally offered as a sacrifice to God.

Such a direct admonition must be delivered with clarity and conviction.

James is saying, "Don't delude yourselves into thinking it is enough to *hear* the word!" Speak the line with authority.

Utilize a slower pace and a tone of sincerity and compassion, though not lacking in authority.

A reading from the Letter of Saint James

Dearest **brothers** and **sisters**:
All **good giving** and every perfect **gift** is from **above**,
    coming down from the Father of **lights**,
    with whom there is no **alteration** or shadow caused by **change**.
He **willed** to give us birth by the word of **truth**
    that we may be a kind of **firstfruits** of his creatures.

Humbly **welcome** the word that has been **planted** in you
    and is able to **save** your **souls**.

Be **doers** of the word and not **hearers** only, **deluding** yourselves.

Religion that is **pure** and **undefiled** before God and the Father
    is **this**:
    to care for **orphans** and **widows** in their affliction
    and to keep oneself **unstained** by the world.

GOSPEL Mark 7:1–8, 14–15, 21–23

The details in the opening narration give necessary information; so don't rush past them.

This interesting aside can be delivered at a more rapid pace. Note that what is enumerated here constitutes the "tradition of the elders," not the law of God.

A reading from the holy Gospel according to Mark

When the **Pharisees** with some **scribes** who had come
    from **Jerusalem**
    gathered around **Jesus**,
    they **observed** that some of his **disciples** ate their meals
    with **unclean**, that is, **unwashed**, hands.
—For the **Pharisees** and, in fact, **all** Jews,
    do not **eat** without **carefully** washing their hands,
    keeping the **tradition** of the **elders**.

READING II The unchangeable God in whom "there is no alteration or shadow caused by change" is the source of the good gifts that flow daily into our lives. (Yes, you've heard a variation of the opening line in the music of *Godspell*.) God reigns over the lights of the heavens that daily wax and wane, but unlike them God's light never diminishes. It is a steady and reliable source of guidance. But God's greatest gift to us is our "birth by the word of truth," that is, the new life we received by embracing the Gospel of Christ. The

Gospel makes us the "firstfruits" of God's new Creation and, when it takes root, it can "save [our] souls." There is joyous energy in these lines that should be evident in your proclamation.

James' insistence on coupling *doing* with *believing* is part of the reason Martin Luther called the Letter of James "that book of straw!" For James, faith alone is not enough, for "faith of itself, if it does not have works, is dead" (James 2:17). So he calls us to be "doers," living an authentic faith that recognizes the needs of the "widow" and "orphan" and that responds

with action. This is likely the only time the word "religion" appears in the New Testament, and James is adamant that it be authentic. What makes it "pure and undefiled" is compassionate and concrete love of one another.

GOSPEL Because Jesus loved God's law, because he was so well acquainted with its true demands, its call for compassion toward the lowly and the outcast—the widow and orphans of today's reading from James—he rails

And on coming from the **marketplace**
    they do not eat without **purifying** themselves.
And there are many **other** things that they have
    traditionally observed,
    the purification of **cups** and **jugs** and **kettles** and **beds.**—
So the Pharisees and scribes **questioned** him,
    "Why do your disciples not **follow** the tradition of the **elders**
    but instead eat a meal with **unclean** hands?"
He responded,
    "**Well** did Isaiah prophesy about you **hypocrites**,
        as it is written:
    *This people honors me with their **lips**,*
        *but their **hearts** are **far** from me;*
    *in **vain** do they worship me,*
        *teaching as doctrines **human** precepts.*
You disregard **God's** commandment
    but cling to **human** tradition."
He summoned the crowd **again** and said to them,
    "**Hear** me, **all** of you, and **understand**.
Nothing that enters one from **outside** can **defile** that person;
    but the things that come out from **within** are what **defile**.

"From **within** people, from their **hearts**,
    come **evil** thoughts, **unchastity**, **theft**, **murder**,
    adultery, **greed**, **malice**, **deceit**,
    licentiousness, envy, blasphemy, arrogance, folly.
All these **evils** come from **within** and they **defile**."

Assume the judgmental tone of the questioners.

Jesus' ire is immediately aroused. He quotes Isaiah with great purpose.

Stress the human origin of the "precepts" in question.

Here, Jesus addresses the crowd, not the leaders. His tone, though strong and authoritative, lacks a harsh or judgmental edge.

Jesus' intensity increases in order to drive home this important teaching. Don't rush the list of evils, and speak them with a realization of how embedded they are in our own experience.

The final line is an exclamation point on the entire reading.

---

against those who distort God's law and, worse, replace it with human decrees that lack the authority, integrity, and heart of God's commandments. His disciples are under attack for violating the unwritten, human laws that were the scribes and Pharisees' special purview. Jesus doesn't hold back in his denunciation of the hypocritical stance from which these religious leaders operate. The omitted verses in today's pericope point to the glaring hypocrisy of allowing children to set aside their resources "for God" in order to deny them to

their own parents. For such abuses Jesus cites the harsh words of Isaiah that condemn the people for abandoning the spirit of the law in favor of human encrustations.

Basically nullifying the law regarding clean and unclean food, Jesus declares a new teaching and he states it boldly: Only what comes from inside a person can defile, not the food they take in from outside, which passes through them into the latrine. Though the call of the Gospel is to a person, Jesus, more than to a moral system, moral instruction is not absent in Jesus' teaching, and here we get a good

dose. The list of heart-born evils is rather long and should not be rushed. Each item hits home with any sincere listener. "Folly" may seem a strange bedfellow among the other, seemingly more egregious, sins. But here it does not refer to a lack of good sense, but to actions so foolish as to be tragic and criminal. Because corruption is possible, we must be clear about what things truly "defile."

23RD SUNDAY IN ORDINARY TIME

Lectionary #128

READING I   Isaiah 35:4–7a

A reading from the Book of the Prophet Isaiah

Thus says the LORD:
  Say to those whose hearts are **frightened**:
    Be **strong**, fear **not**!
  Here is your **God**,
    he comes with **vindication**;
  with divine **recompense**
    he comes to **save** you.
Then will the eyes of the blind be **opened**,
    the **ears** of the deaf be **cleared**;
then will the lame **leap** like a stag,
    then the tongue of the mute will **sing**.
Streams will burst forth in the **desert**,
    and **rivers** in the **steppe**.
The **burning** sands will become **pools**,
    and the **thirsty** ground, **springs** of **water**.

Isaiah = ī-ZAY-uh

It is the Lord who speaks and God's words are strong imperatives. A double imperative like this requires greater energy on the second utterance.

Here you announce the reason for abandoning fear: God comes with vindication.

Pause after "save you." A new beat begins here, full of joyous good news.

Pause slightly after "mute will sing." Then another new beat follows, announcing nature's transformation.

READING I Isaiah is Israel's greatest prophet and his oracles are unparalleled in beauty and influence. This brief text is but a morsel of the rich feast that is Isaiah's poetry. Though originally written to bolster Israel's courage in the face of threats from a hostile neighbor, the text announces today, as well as in any previous age, the abundance of hope and miraculous intervention that comes at the hands of our mighty and merciful God. In today's Gospel we will see Jesus give these prophetic words literal life when he opens the ears of a deaf man.

The text's opening lines speak hope and encouragement to those racked with fear. We need not be anticipating a foreign attack to be in fear's grip, so address these lines to the array of fears believers bring with them every Sunday morning. The strong language speaks of God coming to settle the score ("with vindication") and bring ominous payback ("divine recompense")!

All of life will respond to God's coming in power, and miracles will abound: the blind and deaf will be healed; the lame will leap and the mute will sing. Even nature will be transformed! In these lines, God's power is not a source of just retribution, but a font of new life. Dry and desolate places will bud with life as springs and pools burst forth in response to God's merciful reign.

READING II James is asking believers to go against their natural instincts. In so many ways, the Gospel of Jesus Christ reverses expectations and defies our usual categories. If a statesman or a prelate, a celebrity or business leader

READING II   James 2:1–5

A reading from the Letter of Saint James

My brothers and sisters, show no **partiality**
   as you adhere to the **faith** in our glorious Lord Jesus **Christ**.
For if a man with gold **rings** and fine clothes
   comes into your assembly,
   and a **poor** person in **shabby** clothes **also** comes in,
   and you pay **attention** to the one wearing the **fine** clothes
   and say, "Sit **here**, please,"
   while you say to the **poor** one, "Stand **there**,"
     or "Sit at my **feet**,"
   have you not made **distinctions** among yourselves
   and become **judges** with evil **designs**?

Listen, my beloved brothers and sisters.
Did not God choose those who are **poor** in the world
   to be rich in **faith** and heirs of the **kingdom**
   that he **promised** to those who **love** him?

This is the second of five consecutive weeks we read from the letter of James. From the start, let your delivery be direct and unassuming.

Respect the folksy style of this writing. Don't exaggerate, but also don't underplay the interesting contrasts and dialogue.

Your tone signals that the answers to these two rhetorical questions are obvious.

Those who are listening are among the "poor" who have been made "rich in faith."

---

of note enters a room, eyes go in their direction and people scramble to accommodate and please. James is not condemning that behavior, but he is calling for a radical realignment of how we see things. In God's kingdom, he says, all are worthy of "royal treatment," not just dignitaries or the well off. The letter of James abounds in earthy images and examples like the one we find here. Similar to how Jesus taught, James gets to the point, using clear illustrations to teach his lesson.

Your tone, therefore, should match the folksy manner of the writing. This is not lofty or elegant prose, but practical, everyday speech that says if you start playing favorites or judging people not by their hearts but by their pocketbooks, you have betrayed the Gospel. You don't want to overdo the presentation of James' illustrative scene, but it contains contrasts in both description and dialogue that give his illustration a fun and lively energy. The word "listen" that begins the last sentence signals a very simple and direct style. James writes in more of an oral than literary

style, so speak as you would in a debate with friends in which you make a point that is both obvious and revolutionary.

GOSPEL   Even in Gentile territory, where the people's faith evokes a manifestation of his divine power, Jesus proclaims the Good News in word and deed. The healing story is very straightforward and we've seen it before: a man in need is brought by those who love him to the one who can "lay his hand on him" and make a difference. Jesus doesn't

Speak with familiarity of these ancient places.
 	
Tyre = tīr
 	
Decapolis = dih-KAP-uh-lis
 	
There are four pieces of information here: the people 1) brought and 2) begged, and the man was 3) deaf and had 4) a speech impediment.
 	
Note that Jesus "took him off" and "away from the crowd." The repetition is significant.
 	
These graphic details must not be rushed. The physicality is fascinating and important.
 	
There are three events named here: 1) his ears were opened, 2) his impediment was removed, and 3) he spoke plainly.
 	
Share this detail with delight.
 	
Jesus fulfills Isaiah's prophecy, making the blind to see and the lame to walk.
	GOSPEL Mark 7:31–37
	
	A reading from the holy Gospel according to Mark
	
	Again Jesus left the district of **Tyre**
	   and went by way of **Sidon** to the Sea of **Galilee**,
	   into the district of the **Decapolis**.
	And people brought to him a **deaf** man
	      who had a **speech** impediment
	   and **begged** him to lay his **hand** on him.
	He took him off by **himself** away from the **crowd**.
	He put his **finger** into the man's **ears**
	   and, **spitting**, touched his **tongue**;
	   then he looked up to **heaven** and **groaned**, and said to him,
	   "Ephphatha!"—that is, "Be **opened**!"—
	And **immediately** the man's ears were **opened**,
	   his **speech** impediment was **removed**,
	   and he spoke **plainly**.
	He ordered them not to tell **anyone**.
	But the more he ordered them **not** to,
	   the more they **proclaimed** it.
	They were exceedingly **astonished** and they said,
	   "He has done **all** things **well**.
	He makes the deaf **hear** and the mute **speak**."

hesitate and leads the man away from the crowd. Through Mark's details, we recognize some special aspects of this healing miracle. Not only is the man taken off alone, but Jesus first places his fingers in the man's ears and then commingles his saliva with the man's by directly touching the man's tongue. Jesus then looks up to heaven and groans before speaking the command "Ephphatha!"

So much physical detail gives this healing a unique quality. We are not dealing with metaphor, but with two very real men, one in need and the other so open, so aware, so full of love that it spills out and takes concrete form. The "form" may seem uncouth and invasive—he put his fingers in the man's ears and touched his tongue—yet the effect is one of astounding presence and care. Jesus is not performing for the crowd—or he would not have taken the man aside in private—but manifesting the love of God. As God incarnate, he shows that love in an incarnational way—physically, through intimacy and touch, through sound and spoken word. Though Jesus orders them not to speak of the mir-

acle, the people sense in him the dawn of the time of salvation spoken of by the prophets. Even if they were stones they would have to announce "He has done all things well!"

24TH SUNDAY IN ORDINARY TIME

Lectionary #131

READING I   Isaiah 50:4c–9a

A reading from the Book of the Prophet Isaiah

The Lord **GOD** opens my **ear** that I may **hear**;
and I have not **rebelled**,
 have not turned **back**.
I gave my **back** to those who **beat** me,
 my **cheeks** to those who plucked my **beard**;
my **face** I did not **shield**
 from **buffets** and **spitting**.

The Lord **GOD** is my **help**,
 therefore I am not **disgraced**;
I have set my face like **flint**,
 knowing that I shall **not** be put to **shame**.
He is **near** who upholds my **right**;
 if anyone wishes to **oppose** me,
 let us appear **together**.
Who **disputes** my right?
 Let that man **confront** me.
See, the Lord **GOD** is my help;
 who will prove me **wrong**?

Isaiah = ĭ-ZAY-uh

The Servant immediately acknowledges God's presence in the midst of his suffering.

Your delivery should match the short and clipped structure of the phrases.

These are words of gratitude, not anger. Make good use of the colorful language: "Plucked," "buffets," "spitting."

This is the heart of the message: God is ever at the side of the Servant, shielding him from shame.

The final sentences contain the confrontational daring of a youth who has secretly taken karate lessons. After throwing out a challenge that no one accepts, you say that no one dares because "God is my help." Then you ask if anyone can "prove" that isn't true.

READING I Each year, we proclaim the first four verses of this text on Palm Sunday in a context that closely identifies the speaker, Isaiah's Suffering Servant, with the suffering Christ who endures the Passion for our salvation. We proclaim it today because it paints a picture of the Messiah that corresponds perfectly with the destiny of the Son of Man Jesus announces in the Gospel. There, Jesus speaks openly of the necessity of his suffering with clear implications about its redemptive power. Since

suffering surrounds us, we must face its enduring mystery.

The bedrock Christian conviction regarding suffering is that we do not suffer alone, for God is always with us in the midst of our trials. The Servant understands that and therefore willingly submits to whatever God allows, neither rebelling nor turning away. The spotlight is not focused on the Servant's personal strength, but on the God-given courage and determination that sustained him through his torment. God is the rock of strength that enables the Servant to "set [his] face like

flint" and to trust he "shall not be put to shame." Those are not boastful words, but a confession that for the God who "is near" nothing is impossible. There is a satisfying boldness, even challenge, in the final lines. The Servant is not a victim, woeful and bereft, but a believer, full of the confidence (Who will prove me wrong?) and hope (God is my help!) that makes it possible to confront even the greatest challenge.

READING II   James 2:14–18

A reading from the Letter of Saint James

What **good** is it, my brothers and sisters,
  if someone says he has **faith** but does not have **works**?
Can that faith **save** him?
If a brother or sister has **nothing** to **wear**
  and has no **food** for the day,
  and one of you says to them,
  "Go in **peace**, keep **warm**, and eat **well**,"
  but you do not **give** them the **necessities** of the **body**,
  what **good** is it?
So also **faith** of **itself**,
  if it does not have **works**, is **dead**.

Indeed someone might say,
  "**You** have faith and **I** have works."
Demonstrate your faith to me **without** works,
  and **I** will demonstrate my faith to you **from** my works.

We might want to call those who don't live their faith "hypocrites," but James calls them "brothers and sisters."

The answers to the rhetorical questions are made obvious by your tone.

Employ a conversational tone, as if debating with a friend.

This character is "clueless," not evil.

This is James' very serious point. Be sure to highlight it.

His suggested response has the flavor of folksy and animated banter between friends. You challenge the other without hostility: I can prove my faith through my works; can *you* prove your faith *without* any works?

READING II   The letter of James is often at the heart of debates between those who argue that faith alone is sufficient for salvation and those who say faith without works is lifeless posturing. James argues convincingly for both and his approach is very straightforward and intuitive. The implied answer to his rhetorical second question is clearly, No, because it follows that faith calls us to certain behavior as well as certain convictions; without the necessary behavior, the convictions are hollow. What is obvious to him was not (and still is not) obvious to all,

so he does not call anyone a hypocrite. Hypocrisy is a knowing disregard for what we understand to be true. James seeks to impart understanding to those who lack it, so he addresses his readers as "brothers and sisters" because, truth be told, even those of us in the know can be guilty of the inconsistency he names so starkly and so cleverly.

James invents an exaggerated character whose dialogue is almost comic in its clueless insensitivity. Though out of touch, the character is not sinister; he/she demonstrates a blindness that has likely afflicted

most of us. James' strong assertion that this person's faith is "dead" is meant to help us avoid the grave mistake of not putting faith into action. Though some think James contradicts Paul's teaching on salvation by faith, he is most likely countering the argument of extremists who used Paul's teaching as justification for picking and choosing the kind of behavior that characterized Christian life. James concludes with a challenge: Show me how your faith exists apart from works and I will show you how my works demonstrate my faith. It's an earlier version of the oft quoted

Mark tells the story in three acts: 1) Jesus and disciples in friendly conversation regarding notions of his identity—climaxed by Peter's confession, 2) serious teaching about Jesus' inevitable suffering and repudiation of Peter's narrow vision, and 3) teaching the crowd about the cost of discipleship.

Pay careful attention to the atmosphere and pace of each "act."

Imagine Jesus in an intimate setting with the disciples when he asks what people are saying about him.

Speak the replies as if by different disciples trying to top each other naming the amazing rumors that are afloat.

Peter's reply is spontaneous, not a profound statement of faith. Only Jesus' order to keep silent suggests the true import of their exchange.

Jesus teaches openly about the Passion without being heavy or didactic.

Peter is disappointed. We can almost hear him say, "How could you say such things?"

Speak the rebuke softly, as if Jesus wants the disciples to hear the reprimand but without humiliating Peter. Jesus is frustrated at Peter's lack of understanding.

Jesus speaks this hard saying with an insistent but hopeful attitude. Don't rush the line, for it conveys the truth the disciples (and we) have found so hard to embrace.

GOSPEL   Mark 8:27–35

A reading from the holy Gospel according to Mark

Jesus and his **disciples** set out
    for the villages of **Caesarea Philippi**.
Along the way he **asked** his disciples,
    "**Who** do people say that I **am**?"
They said in reply,
    "John the **Baptist**, others **Elijah**,
    still others one of the **prophets**."
And he asked them,
    "But who do **you** say that I am?"
Peter said to him in reply,
    "You are the **Christ**."
Then he **warned** them not to tell **anyone** about him.

He began to **teach** them
    that the Son of Man must **suffer** greatly
    and be **rejected** by the **elders**, the chief **priests**, and the **scribes**,
    and be **killed**, and **rise** after three **days**.
He spoke this **openly**.
Then **Peter** took him aside and began to **rebuke** him.
At this he turned around and, looking at his **disciples**,
    rebuked Peter and said, "Get **behind** me, **Satan**.
You are thinking not as **God** does, but as human **beings** do."

He summoned the **crowd** with his disciples and **said** to them,
    "Whoever wishes to come **after** me must **deny** himself,
    take up his **cross**, and **follow** me.
For whoever wishes to **save** his life will **lose** it,
    but whoever **loses** his life for **my** sake
    and that of the **gospel** will **save** it."

---

question we hear today: "If you were put on trial for being a Christian, would there be enough evidence to convict you?"

GOSPEL   Progress and backsliding mark the spiritual life. We either move forward or we lose ground; there is no standing still. This episode from Mark's account presents that truth through the lives of Peter and the disciples. Jesus asks them the key question: Who do others, and who do you say that I am? They offer all the popular opinions and then Peter nails it: "You are the Christ." This

question is central because Christianity is a commitment to a person who is the Son of God. The commandments, the beatitudes, and the golden rule are merely our way of living out our conviction that Jesus is who we say he is and that he won our salvation through the blood of the cross.

After Peter glimpses and names Jesus' true identity, Jesus elaborates on what it means to be "the Christ," naming the suffering, rejection, and even death that will be his destiny. But Peter isn't ready to go that far. He got the right answer, but he could not yet see all of its implications—

like a child who sees his father in uniform, but won't or can't yet face the possibility that soldiers die and don't come back. Jesus speaks so freely of his impending fate that Peter pulls him aside to chastise him for such demoralizing talk. But it's Peter who gets rebuked. You're a tempter, Jesus tells him; you see what you want to see, not what God is showing you. So Jesus turns to the crowd and shares with them the profound truth of the Gospel: Whoever wishes to save his life must lose it; whoever would be a disciple must carry a cross, and Jesus will be the first to do it.

25TH SUNDAY IN ORDINARY TIME

Lectionary #134

READING I   Wisdom 2:12, 17–20

To prepare to proclaim this text and to better understand the context of this passage, read all of chapters 1 and 2 of the Book of Wisdom.

From the point of view of the wicked, these plots are crucial for survival, so read not like an "evil" person, but like anyone who is desperate to achieve what they perceive as an important and necessary goal.

They make excuses for their evil intentions and won't admit their corrupt motives even to themselves.

The level of wickedness intensifies; somehow, they feel justified in their scheming.

The level of self-delusion reaches its climax here. Be sure the evil intentions of those speaking are apparent—"God will take care of him" must not sound like an expression of concern for the just one.

A reading from the Book of Wisdom

The **wicked** say:
Let us beset the **just** one, because he is **obnoxious** to us;
    he sets himself **against** our doings,
reproaches us for transgressions of the law
    and charges us with **violations** of our training.
Let us **see** whether his words be **true**;
    let us find out what will **happen** to him.
For if the just one be the son of **God**, God will **defend** him
    and **deliver** him from the hand of his **foes**.
With **revilement** and **torture** let us put the just one to the **test**
    that we may have **proof** of his **gentleness**
    and **try** his **patience**.
Let us **condemn** him to a **shameful** death;
    for according to his own **words**, **God** will take **care** of him.

READING I God is not responsible for evil in the world, says the first chapter of the Book of Wisdom, evildoers are! Rather than loving justice, the wicked seek only their own gratification. Life is short, they say, so let's eat, drink, and do whatever it takes—tell any lie, distort any truth, climb over any do-gooder, even condemn them to death—to be merry and enjoy the pleasures of the earth! But this text from chapter two does more than place responsibility for evil squarely on the shoulders of selfish humanity. It presents sinister plotting that often has been seen as a direct prophecy of the scheming that led to the Passion of Christ. Clearly, the liturgy makes a connection between the plots of the evildoers in Wisdom and the fate Jesus announces for himself in today's Gospel.

The level of rancor among the evildoers is shocking. Like workers who shun a colleague who sets the bar too high and works so hard that he makes them look bad, these schemers willfully plot against "the just one," simply because he makes their lives inconvenient. His very presence is an indictment of their self-serving behavior; his goodness exposes their evil. Ego often seeks refuge in the humiliation of others, so they justify their plans by telling themselves that if he is as good as he seems, God will protect him. They will employ all their resources—"revilement and torture"—to see how good the just one really is. Even death is not off limits. The righteous and innocent Jesus, suffered the same fate for the same reasons at the hands of his enemies.

READING II James 3:16—4:3

A reading from the Letter of Saint James

Beloved:
Where **jealousy** and selfish **ambition** exist,
there is **disorder** and every foul **practice**.
But the **wisdom** from above is first of all **pure**,
then **peaceable**, **gentle**, **compliant**,
full of **mercy** and good **fruits**,
without **inconstancy** or **insincerity**.
And the fruit of righteousness is sown in **peace**
for those who **cultivate** peace.

Where do the **wars**
and where do the **conflicts** among you **come** from?
Is it not from your **passions**
that make war within your **members**?
You **covet** but do not **possess**.
You **kill** and **envy** but you cannot **obtain**;
you **fight** and wage **war**.
You do not **possess** because you do not **ask**.
You **ask** but do not **receive**,
because you ask **wrongly**, to spend it on your **passions**.

Let the grave harm done by "jealousy" and "ambition" be apparent in your tone.

"But" signals a contrast: move slowly through this list of positive qualities, as if it were a prayer that these attributes come to fully describe your community.

The tone turns again to instruction and concern for the welfare of the community.

The New Revised Standard Version translation of the Bible renders these verses as, "You want something and do not have it; so you commit murder. And you covet something and cannot obtain it; so you engage in disputes and conflicts."
Don't end on a harsh note, but instead make this final line a prayer that those listening learn to pray as they ought.

READING II The author of James is concerned about his readers' ethical behavior, so, like the Wisdom literature of the Old Testament, he constructs a work that consists of many proverbs and exhortations endorsing right conduct. He has already spoken of the need to put faith into action and warned of the dangers of an unbridled tongue. Now, he addresses the inevitable dissensions—fueled by "jealousy" and "ambition"—that arise within and threaten the life even of communities of faith. Having debunked the earthly wisdom that leads to "disorder" and "foul practice," James lists the attributes of heavenly wisdom. Emphasize the negative tone of the opening sentence so the contrast will keep this positive list from sounding like an impossible, pie-in-the-sky catalogue of virtues.

James' practical wisdom sees and tells it like it is. The conflicts we experience among us, he says, come from within ourselves, from the passions and cravings that war within us. We desire what we cannot have and the frustration leads us to vile and sinful behavior like fights, wars, and even murder. These grave problems are exacerbated by our inability to pray as we ought, for either we fail to pray at all or we pray, but not for God's will but for ours to be done, so we can indulge our selfish pleasures. James' words might seem unusually harsh and condemning, but remember, it is not enjoyment that's being condemned, but the selfish attitude that puts our pleasure ahead of the legitimate needs of others.

GOSPEL Mark 9:30–37

A reading from the holy Gospel according to Mark

Jesus and his **disciples left** from there and began a **journey**
    through **Galilee**,
  but he did not wish anyone to **know** about it.
He was **teaching** his disciples and **telling** them,
  "The Son of **Man** is to be handed **over** to men
  and they will **kill** him,
  and **three** days after his **death** the Son of Man will **rise**."
But they did not **understand** the saying,
  and they were afraid to **question** him.

They came to **Capernaum** and, once inside the **house**,
  he began to **ask** them,
  "What were you **arguing** about on the way?"
But they remained **silent**.
They had been **discussing** among themselves on the way
  who was the **greatest**.
Then he **sat** down, called the **Twelve**, and **said** to them,
  "If anyone wishes to be **first**,
  he shall be the **last** of all and the **servant** of all."
Taking a **child**, he placed it in their midst,
  and putting his **arms** around it, he said to them,
  "Whoever receives one **child** such as this in my **name**,
    receives **me**;
  and whoever receives **me**,
  receives not **me** but the One who **sent** me."

Jesus and his disciples have just descended the mountain of Transfiguration.
Jesus predicts his Passion three times in Mark's Gospel account and each time he meets with a disappointing response.
Begin quietly to suggest Jesus didn't want anyone to know his whereabouts. Jesus is teaching the disciples—a clue to the tone of the entire passage—about his Passion, so speak slowly and significantly.
The disciples receive the prediction with confusion and fear, shown by their failure to understand and their fear of questioning him.
Jesus knows full well what they had been discussing.
Their silence speaks of their embarrassment.

Jesus teaches this lesson because they clearly need it.

There is gentle intimacy in the description of Jesus embracing the child.
The disciples don't realize it, but the child represents them: whoever welcomes a servant like them welcomes Jesus and whoever welcomes Jesus welcomes God. With those closing words, Jesus encircles the disciples (and us) within his warm embrace.

GOSPEL Just prior to this Gospel episode, Jesus drives out evil spirits from a mute child and later explains to his disciples that such spirits can only be cast out with prayer. This manifestation of his divine power, and the Transfiguration that preceded it, set the scene for Jesus' prediction of his future suffering. He has acted with a power and authority unavailable to his disciples. He can command demons, so surely he could cast off the enemies who conspire against his life. We sense Jesus is not merely speaking about what will happen to him but about what he will *allow* to happen, about a choice he is willing to make, and this poses a grave problem for his disciples. They don't "understand" this teaching, or perhaps they don't want to. His ability to heal and cast out demons is far more fascinating. That's what they want to participate in (and control, as we see in the verses immediately following this episode), not the suffering he anticipates.

Aware of their fascination with the fireworks aspects of his ministry, Jesus asks bluntly what the disciples were discussing. They won't say, because they know it was inappropriate. So Jesus enacts a parable by taking a child into his arms, demonstrating who will achieve the access and intimacy they are competing for. If you want to draw close to the Son of Man, he says, serve my little ones, the lowly and the poor, and be like them. Earlier, Jesus railed against the "generation" whose lack of faith prevented the disciples from healing the mute child. Here he invites the kind of faith that can work miracles: simple and innocent, uncomplicated and trusting.

26TH SUNDAY IN ORDINARY TIME

Lectionary #137

READING I   Numbers 11:25–29

Remember that it is "the Lord," not some neighbor who comes down to speak with Moses. So, clearly, the opening should sound both solemn and awe-inspiring.

A reading from the Book of Numbers

The LORD came down in the **cloud** and spoke to **Moses**.
Taking some of the **spirit** that was on Moses,
　　the LORD bestowed it on the seventy **elders**;
　　and as the spirit came to **rest** on them, they **prophesied**.

Narrate these details with some amazement, suggesting this is something very unexpected.
Eldad = EL-dad; Medad = MEE-dad

Now **two** men, one named **Eldad** and the other **Medad**,
　　were not in the **gathering** but had been left in the **camp**.
They **too** had been on the list, but had not gone out to the **tent**;
　　yet the **spirit** came to rest on them **also**,
　　and they **prophesied** in the camp.
So, when a young man quickly told **Moses**,
　　"**Eldad and Medad** are **prophesying** in the camp,"
Joshua, son of **Nun**, who from his **youth**
　　had been Moses' **aide**, said,
　　"**Moses**, my lord, **stop** them."

The "young man" shatters the solemn mood with his announcement.
Joshua steps up the tension with his pleas for Moses' intervention.
Joshua = JOSH-oo-uh
Nun = nuhn
Moses' energy matches Joshua's as he tosses off his ingenuous concern, but then he becomes serene and philosophical as he contemplates and prays for an outpouring of God's Holy Spirit.

But Moses answered him,
　　"Are you **jealous** for my sake?
Would that **all** the people of the LORD were **prophets**!
Would that the LORD might bestow his **spirit** on them **all**!"

READING I　This story, told because it so closely parallels today's Gospel episode, presents a not unfamiliar scene: those close to the seat of power, relishing their privileged position, play gatekeeper to ensure that others who are not authorized don't gain access to the coveted power. That's the dynamic in the Gospel where John tries to prevent someone from driving out demons in Jesus' name, and that is the dynamic here where Joshua wants to stop Eldad and Medad from prophesying. In both instances, a subordinate tells his superior that his toes are being stepped on and both times the superior says, "It's not a problem." Subordinates who derive their identity from access to power may find such magnanimity hard to stomach. But this story is less about Joshua's limited vision and about Moses' ability to recognize God's spirit when charismatic gifts suddenly flourish where they were not expected. Moses understands religious authority comes from God and if God chooses to distribute it more widely than anticipated, all that the rest of us can do is rejoice in God's generosity.

In this context, "prophesying" doesn't mean seeing the future but a kind of inspired and spontaneous charismatic utterance that occurred both at the beginning of Old Testament prophecy and within the early New Testament community. The opening sentence describes this type of mystical proclamation taking place in Moses' presence. But when it occurs without Moses, rivalry and accusations of God's spirit being usurped suddenly arise. As Jesus will in the Gospel, Moses rejoices that God's work is being done, no matter

This is the fifth of five consecutive weeks we read from the letter of James.

To prepare to read this text, think of a time you felt righteous anger against some injustice. When you confronted the offending party, chances are your voice was controlled and each word carefully articulated. Sometimes people hear us best when we *don't* raise our voices.

There is no pleasure in speaking these words of judgment; remember, you are trying to open eyes, not close hearts.

Express regret over the impending misery of the unjust rich who will experience decay and destruction as surely as the clothes that have become moth-eaten and the silver that has corroded.

James gives voice to the wages withheld unjustly "from the workers." Speak *for*, not *as*, one of those whose shouts have reached the ears of God, with the passionate intensity of an advocate.

Speak these indictments in a restrained way, letting this evil stand in contrast to "the righteous one" (take a short pause) who offers "no resistance."

READING II James 5:1–6

A reading from the Letter of Saint James

Come now, you **rich**, **weep** and **wail**
    over your impending **miseries**.
Your wealth has **rotted** away,
    your clothes have become **moth-eaten**,
  your gold and silver have **corroded**,
  and that corrosion will be a **testimony** against you;
  it will **devour** your flesh like a **fire**.
You have stored up **treasure** for the last days.
Behold, the wages you **withheld** from the **workers**
  who **harvested** your fields are crying **aloud**;
  and the **cries** of the harvesters
  have reached the ears of the Lord of **hosts**.
You have lived on earth in **luxury** and **pleasure**;
  you have **fattened** your hearts for the day of **slaughter**.
You have **condemned**;
  you have **murdered** the righteous one;
  he offers you no **resistance**.

who the workers. His last line is an earnest prayer for the universal outpouring of God's spirit.

READING II | Without doubt, these words are stark and jarring. James is challenging the rich who have become comfortable in their luxury while the poor wallow in need. Taking the long view, James recognizes the fleeting nature of human life and knows earthly foundations will not last. Wealth, fine clothing, and precious metals will all fade away; they will disappoint us and not sustain us.

Our so-called valuables have no innate worth for they will rot, and corrode, and be eaten by moths.

There can only be two legitimate motives for this kind of blunt and confrontational language: the welfare of the victimized or the welfare of the victimizers themselves. Here, it seems to be both. The author wants the evildoers to be aware of their sin before it's too late, before their excesses "devour [their] flesh like a fire." He mocks them to wake them up, to shake them from their reverie of self-delusion. You have "fattened your hearts," he tells

them, like animals readied for slaughter. The intent is for them to recognize their crimes and to repent.

But the other motive for this writing is the "cries of the harvesters" that have even "reached the ears of the Lord." Such injustice cries out for vengeance. God will not remain unmoved regarding crimes against the innocent poor. Those who oppress them best beware!

GOSPEL | Like in today's First Reading, Jesus deals with overzealous disciples who think they are safeguarding

GOSPEL Mark 9:38–43, 45, 47–48

A reading from the holy Gospel according to Mark

At that time, **John** said to **Jesus**,
  "**Teacher**, we saw someone driving out demons in your **name**,
    and we tried to **prevent** him because he does not **follow** us."
Jesus replied, "Do not **prevent** him.
There is no one who performs a mighty **deed** in my **name**
    who can at the **same** time speak **ill** of me.
For whoever is not **against** us is **for** us.
Anyone who gives you a cup of **water** to drink
    because you belong to **Christ**,
    amen, I say to you, will surely not lose his **reward**.

"Whoever causes one of these **little** ones who **believe** in me
      to **sin**,
    it would be better for him if a great **millstone**
    were put around his **neck**
    and he were **thrown** into the **sea**.
If your **hand** causes you to **sin**, **cut** it off.
It is better for you to enter into life **maimed**
    than with **two** hands to go into **Gehenna**,
    into the unquenchable **fire**.
And if your **foot** causes you to sin, **cut** it off.
It is better for you to enter into life **crippled**
    than with **two** feet to be thrown into **Gehenna**.
And if your **eye** causes you to sin, pluck it out.
Better for you to enter into the kingdom of **God** with **one** eye
    than with **two** eyes to be thrown into **Gehenna**,
    where 'their **worm** does not **die**, and the **fire** is not **quenched**.'"

This dialogue creates the context for all of Jesus' teaching that follows. Don't rush it. John is into an "us/them" mentality that Jesus won't endorse.

Jesus' direction to allow the man to continue is strongly stated.

This classic saying is critical to the text. Speak it with strength and authority.

There is a positive tone to this comment about good deeds being rewarded.

Jesus' instruction turns much more serious here. Perhaps, we hear such warnings too rarely. Let them do their work; they are meant to remind us that all of our decisions have consequences.

The well-crafted rhetoric of this paragraph employs chant-like refrains ("Cut it off . . . pluck"). All three illustrations make a single point.

Speak this entire section moderately fast, using the same inflection for each "if . . . then" construction.

Jesus doesn't intend to be taken literally. He doesn't want a corps of blind and limping followers bearing his name. These metaphors make the point that for salvation, we must remove all obstacles from our path.

---

his authority by forbidding one who is not of their group from exercising power in his name. Two questions immediately arise: what really motivates the disciples' concern and does the "outsider's" use of Jesus' name pose a real problem? In regard to the first, Jesus cautions against the narrow-mindedness and jealousy that hide within the recesses of the heart trying to masquerade as righteous anger. He offers a larger vision summarized in the saying, "Whoever is not against us is for us." The saying also answers the second question: more tolerant than his disciples, Jesus is

not troubled that someone unauthorized takes unexpected initiative. He points to God's generosity in not letting the smallest favor done on behalf of those who work for the kingdom go unrewarded.

    For leaders who are authorized to exercise power, Jesus has disturbing words of warning. Death, he says, is better than causing scandal to one of God's innocent ones. We might ask if he is addressing only those leaders whose great authority gives them great ability to harm and cause scandal, or every parent, teacher, supervisor, and politician who forgets the power

they wield to build or destroy. The almost excessive number of examples he uses reflects the importance that Jesus places on his instruction. He cautions against self-entrapment in a tone that matches the gravity of sin's consequences: "Gehenna." No effort should be spared; no price is too great to pay if it keeps us out of that place of destruction. Your unrestrained proclamation can remind us that our actions have far-ranging consequences.

27TH SUNDAY IN ORDINARY TIME

Lectionary #140

READING I   Genesis 2:18–24

A reading from the Book of Genesis

The LORD God said: "It is not **good** for the man to be **alone**.
I will make a suitable **partner** for him."
So the LORD God **formed** out of the **ground**
    various wild **animals** and various **birds** of the air,
    and he **brought** them to the man
        to see what he would **call** them;
    whatever the man **called** each of them would be its **name**.
The man gave names to all the **cattle**,
    all the **birds** of the **air**, and all wild **animals**;
    but **none** proved to be the suitable **partner** for the man.

So the LORD God cast a deep **sleep** on the man,
    and **while** he was asleep,
    he took out one of his **ribs** and closed up its place with **flesh**.
The LORD God then built up into a **woman** the rib
    that he had **taken** from the man.
When he **brought** her to the man, the man said:
    "**This** one, at last, is **bone** of my **bones**
        and **flesh** of my **flesh**;
    this one shall be called '**woman**,'
        for out of 'her **man**' this one has been **taken**."
That is why a man **leaves** his father and mother
    and clings to his **wife**,
    and the **two** of them become **one flesh**.

Narrate with enthusiasm, as if one of these might become the man's suitable companion.

"Naming" gives the man authority over the creatures that God presents to him.

Make this assertion with authority.

The story resumes with even more energy and brisker pacing, for God is determined to create a worthy partner for the man.
The narration slows again as God presents Eve to Adam. Don't rush Adam's dialogue. He first recognizes and then enthuses about the woman who is of his flesh and bone.
Pause after Adam's dialogue, then perhaps from memory, announce this great teaching about the oneness of husband and wife.

READING I | Today's Genesis text sets the stage for the Gospel in which Jesus will cite its final verse. In a time when Christian assumptions about marriage are much challenged, the words of Genesis remind us of the divine origin of this sacred institution. Having created "man" from the dust of the ground, God uses the same "ground" to fashion him a suitable partner. But none proves fitting. So God sets to work again, putting the man into a "deep sleep," but this time using the man's own rib from which to create

"woman," who is, at last, a suitable partner. Much can be garnered from this story: woman is the equal of man for she is formed from his side as his "partner;" man and woman were divinely created to complete and complement one another; only woman is a suitable partner for man and man for woman and this is why, in the text's most important teaching, the two cling to each other and "become one flesh." God not only approves of the physical union and love between man and woman, but that union and love are God's design for the benefit of the couple and the good of humankind.

Your proclamation must make clear God's concern on behalf of his Creation. Though created here before the rest of God's creatures, human beings are still the summit of God's creation and God cares for them like a parent for a newborn. The reaction of Adam to Eve expresses the realization that he has met his match—in every positive sense of that word: here, at last, is "bone of my bone, flesh of my flesh"—and life of my life, joy of my joy, companion of my soul. The narrator's closing explanation expresses that same exuberance: man

READING II   Hebrews 2:9–11

A reading from the Letter to the Hebrews

Brothers and sisters:
He "for a little **while**" was made "**lower** than the **angels**,"
    that by the **grace** of God he might taste **death** for **everyone**.

For it was **fitting** that he,
    for whom and **through** whom all things **exist**,
    in bringing many children to **glory**,
    should make the **leader** to their salvation **perfect**
        through **suffering**.
He who **consecrates** and those who are **being** consecrated
    all have one **origin**.
Therefore, he is not **ashamed** to call them "**brothers**."

GOSPEL   Mark 10:2–16

A reading from the holy Gospel according to Mark

The **Pharisees** approached **Jesus** and asked,
    "Is it **lawful** for a husband to **divorce** his wife?"
They were **testing** him.
He said to them in reply, "What did **Moses** command you?"
They replied,
    "**Moses** permitted a **husband** to write a bill of **divorce**
    and **dismiss** her."

This is the first of seven consecutive weeks that we read from Hebrews.

Jesus willingly became "lower than the angels" and tasted "death." Hebrews contemplates this astounding love with admiration and gratitude. Your tone explains that Jesus' humanity and suffering are not valid reasons for abandoning the faith.

Read slowly, as if speaking to someone new to Christian faith. The author argues it was fitting for God to perfect Jesus through suffering, for thus he becomes the one who "consecrates" and we those "being consecrated." The tone remains joyous and grateful throughout.

"Suffering" refers to Jesus' Passion.

The "one origin" is God, our Father. Share this great truth with deep appreciation.

Let your tone suggest the ulterior motives of the questioners.

Knowing their intentions, Jesus responds coolly.

There's a bit of arrogance in their over-eager response.

---

and woman are so related and interconnected, so drawn one to the other, that when they come together, they become one flesh.

READING II Hebrews is part of the early Church's effort to understand Christ as both human and divine. The opening alludes to Psalm 8 (quoted in the verses immediately preceding this text) that speaks of humans as made little less than the angels, crowned "with glory and honor," and given authority over all things. The author of Hebrews applies this text to

Jesus who, for "a little while," embraced all the limitations of humanity, except the sinfulness common to us all, in order that he might "taste death for everyone." In any age, faith in Christ is a radical departure from the ways of the world. Even at the time of this letter, the author perceives an erosion of faith among his readers, a danger that came not from external threats of persecution, but from their own inertia—the weakness of their resolve to live the Christian life. Somewhat scandalized by Jesus' humanity and especially his suffering, they have begun to stray.

So the author presents Jesus as the high priest through whom all who follow him are consecrated as he was. Made perfect by his obedience, Jesus now intercedes for us, restores our tepid faith, and brings us to perfection. Jesus became our high priest by becoming one of us. Thus the one who consecrates, Jesus, and those being consecrated, us, share a common origin—God, our Father. Jesus is not ashamed to claim us as his own, because, now and forever, he is our brother.

Jesus' retort is quick and purposeful. He won't let them fool others or themselves with their distortions.

> But Jesus told them,
>   "Because of the **hardness** of your **hearts**
>   he wrote you this commandment.
> But from the beginning of **creation**, *God made them **male*** *and **female***.
> *For this reason a man shall **leave** his father and mother* *and be **joined** to his **wife***,
>   *and the **two** shall become one **flesh***.
> So they are **no longer** two but **one** flesh.
> Therefore what **God** has joined **together**,
>   no human **being** must **separate**."

Quote the text from the book of Genesis in a milder tone, suggesting the beauty of marital union.

> In the **house** the **disciples** again questioned Jesus about this.
> He **said** to them,
>   "Whoever **divorces** his wife and marries **another**
>   commits **adultery** against her;
>   and if **she** divorces her **husband** and **marries** another,
>   **she** commits adultery."

Perhaps somewhat unsettled by Jesus' teaching, the disciples seek clarification.

There is no way to temper the stark nature of this hard teaching.

> And people were bringing **children** to him
>   that he might **touch** them,
>   but the disciples **rebuked** them.
> When Jesus **saw** this he became **indignant** and said to them,
>   "Let the children **come** to me;
>   do not **prevent** them, for the kingdom of **God** belongs
>   to such as **these**.
> Amen, I **say** to you,
>   whoever does not **accept** the kingdom of God like a **child**
>   will not **enter** it."
> Then he **embraced** them and **blessed** them,
>   placing his **hands** on them.

Take a short pause before beginning this new narrative beat.

The disciples' misdirected solicitousness turns this into a tense exchange.

Speak these lines as if to the children themselves.

Take time with this narration, for it describes not only Jesus' love for the children, but for all who embrace the kingdom like a child.

[Shorter: Mark 10:2–12]

GOSPEL Despite the many who loved Jesus, there were always those who sought to entrap him. Today, some sinuous Pharisees, seeking to test him, ask Jesus if a husband can divorce his wife. To demonstrate they have abandoned divine law in favor of human accommodation, he asks what Moses prescribed. They don't hesitate to give the "right" answer, which Jesus immediately shows to be the far from ideal answer. Your stubborn hearts persuaded Moses to permit that modification, he says, but in the beginning God's perfect will was clearly expressed in

Genesis. Since Jesus addresses the crowd as well as the religious leaders, his tone is uplifting rather than scolding, using the poetic words of Genesis to inspire and present marriage as the divine ideal it was meant to be. Only the final injunction, addressed at the leaders—"no human being must separate"—contains a hard edge.

Jesus leaves the harder teaching for the privacy of the house, confiding in the disciples a standard for which the crowd was likely not ready. His words are stark and blunt, tinged with regret.

The disciples' good intentions go awry when they try to become a wall between Jesus and the children. Jesus tops their stern rebukes with his own indignation pointing out that the kingdom belongs only to those with a childlike dependence and trust. From the children Jesus derives energy and hope; by embracing and blessing them, he reveals the deep human connection between the Lord and his little one.

28TH SUNDAY IN ORDINARY TIME

Lectionary #143

READING I   Wisdom 7:7–11

A reading from the Book of Wisdom

I **prayed**, and **prudence** was given me;
　I **pleaded**, and the spirit of **wisdom** came to me.
I **preferred** her to **scepter** and **throne**,
and deemed riches **nothing** in **comparison** with her,
　nor did I liken any priceless **gem** to her;
because all **gold**, in **view** of her, is a little **sand**,
　and **before** her, **silver** is to be accounted **mire**.
Beyond **health** and **comeliness** I loved her,
and I chose to have **her** rather than the **light**,
　because the **splendor** of her never yields to **sleep**.
Yet all good things **together** came to me in her **company**,
　and countless **riches** at her **hands**.

This is a poetic text that must not be rushed, nor delivered like prose.
The language is exalted and intentionally exaggerated. Speak slowly and with the confidence of one whose prayers have been answered. "Pleaded" is an intensification of "prayed."
Be aware that "scepter and throne" refer to authority and power.
"Gold" and "silver" are valuables (let them sound like it) that, compared to Wisdom, come off looking shabby and worthless.
The praise of Wisdom intensifies in the assertion that she is more valuable than one's health and good looks.
In truth, pursuit of Wisdom brings the greatest riches. Speak with upbeat and joyful energy.

READING II   Hebrews 4:12–13

A reading from the Letter to the Hebrews

Brothers and sisters:
Indeed the word of **God** is **living** and **effective**,
　sharper than any two-edged **sword**,
　penetrating even between **soul** and **spirit**, **joints** and **marrow**,
　and able to discern **reflections** and thoughts of the **heart**.

This is the second of seven consecutive weeks that we read from Hebrews.

Read slowly so you don't finish before the assembly has fully focused.

Make eye-contact here.

READING I — In today's Gospel, a young man walks sadly away from Jesus because he has not learned the lesson of this text from Wisdom: none of the world's treasures, nor fame, nor the regard of others, nor even health and beauty approach the value of prudence and wisdom. Nothing in life is to be desired more than knowing and doing the will of God. The rich young man of the Gospel is forever branded for what most of us do everyday—walk away from the demanding God who expects us to view gold as mere "sand" and silver as worthless "mire."

In this brief text you have the opportunity and responsibility to metaphorically smack us upside the head with blunt teaching that easily (but wrongly!) could sound like lovely, gentle poetry. The speaker "prayed" and "pleaded" to be blessed with the "spirit of wisdom." The gift was granted because the desire was so great: I preferred her (that is, "Wisdom") to power and riches, says the author, speaking as King Solomon; to my eyes, he adds, nothing compared with her—not

gold, not silver; nothing! Of course this is poetry, and the device employed is hyperbole. But this is the kind of exaggeration a lover uses to describe a beloved; an overstatement that, in the eyes of the speaker, is absolutely true because their depth of love and conviction makes it true. The final line clarifies the meaning of the text: love of wisdom involves no real sacrifice, for in her company all good things come together; countless and incomparable riches are bestowed on those who seek her above all else. That's a little like moving to the mountains to escape the temptations of

The energy intensifies here. It's bad enough to be "naked," but worse to be "exposed." The second term requires more energy than the first.

Rendering an account can be an intimidating prospect.

No creature is **concealed** from him,
but everything is **naked** and **exposed** to the eyes of him
to whom we must render an **account**.

GOSPEL Mark 10:17–30

A reading from the holy Gospel according to Mark

As **Jesus** was setting out on a **journey**, a man **ran** up,
knelt down before him, and **asked** him,
"Good **teacher**, what must I **do** to inherit eternal **life**?"
Jesus **answered** him, "Why do you call me **good**?
No one is good but God **alone**.
You **know** the **commandments**: *You shall not* **kill**;
you shall not commit **adultery**;
you shall not **steal**;
you shall not bear false **witness**;
you shall not **defraud**;
honor your **father** *and your* **mother**."
He replied and said to him,
"**Teacher**, **all** of these I have observed from my **youth**."
Jesus, looking at him, **loved** him and said to him,
"You are lacking in **one** thing.
Go, **sell** what you have, and give to the **poor**
and you will have treasure in **heaven**; then **come**, **follow** me."
At that statement his face **fell**,
and he went away **sad**, for he had **many** possessions.

The young man comes with haste and sincerity.

Jesus' words are not a reproach, but a teaching.

The commandments are spoken at a brisk pace: they are there to remind and summarize, not to instruct.

Don't let pride color the young man's tone.

Take extra time with this narration as Jesus gazes on this good young man and speaks with calm reserve. Mark's account of this story is less compromising than Matthew's, so don't soften Jesus' call for renunciation of worldly wealth.

The impact of Jesus' words is immediate. Speak "many possessions" with Jesus' awareness of the weighty spiritual burden they so easily become.

the city and discovering you're sitting on a gold mine!

READING II A reading so brief poses special challenges, but one this rich adds extra responsibilities as well. The usual cautions apply: read slowly lest you finish before the assembly has started listening; use the words and pay special attention to word color; pause to let the words sink in before moving on to the next idea. The author of Hebrews was writing to believers who had grown cold in their faith and who were weary of making

the effort required for Christian living. Chances are your assembly has the same needs, so speak these words with the intensity and authority with which they were written.

God's is a word of power; not to be trifled with, not to be ignored. This text is more than a song of praise. It is also a word of warning. The word of God makes a difference, says the author; it achieves God's will and penetrates to the deepest recesses of our being—"between soul and spirit"—and can judge the very "thoughts of the heart." Because God's word is Jesus

himself, the mighty, eternal word who reigns at God's right hand, speak with urgency about letting the word lay bare all that would lay hidden within us. For to him, we must make account for all that we do and all that we are.

GOSPEL It's the last moment of their encounter that lingers in memory—the young man walking away sad because he cannot renounce his great wealth. But the initial moment is also striking: a man of means—not to beg a healing or some other miracle, literally

Jesus looked **around** and said to his **disciples**,
  "How **hard** it is for those who have **wealth**
    to enter the kingdom of **God**!"
The disciples were **amazed** at his words.
So Jesus **again** said to them in reply,
  "**Children**, how **hard** it is to enter the kingdom of **God**!
It is easier for a **camel** to pass through the **eye** of a **needle**
    than for one who is **rich** to enter the kingdom of **God**."
They were exceedingly **astonished** and said among themselves,
  "Then who **can** be saved?"
Jesus **looked** at them and said,
  "For human **beings** it is **impossible**, but not for **God**.
All things are possible for **God**."
Peter began to say to him,
  "We have given up **everything** and followed you."
Jesus said, "**Amen**, I say to you,
    there is no one who has given up **house** or **brothers** or **sisters**
    or **mother** or **father** or **children** or **lands**
    for **my** sake and for the sake of the **gospel**
    who will not receive a hundred times **more** now
      in this **present** age:
houses and **brothers** and **sisters**
and **mothers** and **children** and **lands**,
with **persecutions**, and eternal **life** in the age to **come**."

[Shorter: Mark 10:17–27]

The young man exits in shock, leaving behind the equally shocked disciples. Their amazement is born of the popular notion that wealth equals divine favor.

Read this classic verse slowly and with extra emphasis. Wealth is an illusion; only God provides security in this life and the next.

Their question reveals genuine shock and confusion.

This is another classic verse that must not be rushed.

These words are meant to comfort. Although the words are many and repeated, don't rush the listing. Let the repetition offer assurance of God's mercy and care.

Failing to highlight "with persecutions" would be to miss a major portion of the meaning of this text.

---

runs to Jesus, falls at his feet, and asks what more is required of him. That Jesus "loved him" suggests the young man is sincere in his question and his desire to do more than keep the commandments, which he has observed since childhood. He calls Jesus by the rarely used title "good teacher"; but Jesus deflects it, saying it belongs only to God. Jesus' quick review of the commandments, recited as a summary not as a teaching, is done to establish the basics for justification. The man has

kept them faithfully, we're told, and Jesus looks with love upon one so faithful and pious. But the man seeks perfection, so Jesus tells him what more is needed. This standard is not meant for everyone, but it is meant for the young man. The words nearly stop his heart and he leaves shocked and saddened.

There are two more dramatic beats in this text. The first is Jesus' lament at "how hard it is" for the rich to place the kingdom ahead of their worldly possessions. Jesus' teaching is doubly shocking because it

reverses the popular belief that wealth is a sign of God's favor. The disciples can't hide their astonishment and ask, "Then who can be saved?". The final beat contains Jesus' assurance to Peter and the others that their fidelity and sacrifice won't go unrewarded. But in Mark, even assurance ("a hundred times more now . . . children and lands—*with* persecutions") is given while simultaneously pointing to the cross.

29TH SUNDAY IN ORDINARY TIME

Lectionary #146

READING I   Isaiah 53:10–11

Isaiah = ī-ZAY-uh

A short reading always means a slower proclamation.

You have no introduction with which to ease into the reading, so read this opening with great deliberateness: "The Lord / was *pleased* / to *crush* him / in *infirmity*.

Here are the consequences for the servant of obeying God's will. Speak in a hopeful, peaceful tone.

Here you narrate the consequences both for the Servant and for those who will benefit from his self-sacrifice. The emphasis is on the achievement of God's will and the good fruit it will bear, so the tone remains hopeful.

A reading from the Book of the Prophet Isaiah

The LORD was **pleased**
    to **crush** him in **infirmity**.

If he gives his **life** as an offering for **sin**,
    he shall see his descendants in a **long** life,
    and the **will** of the LORD shall be **accomplished** through him.

Because of his **affliction**
    he shall see the **light** in fullness of **days**;
through his **suffering**, my servant shall justify **many**,
    and their **guilt** he shall **bear**.

READING I This brief text is taken from the fourth of Isaiah's Songs of the Suffering Servant. It describes God's innocent servant who voluntarily takes on the suffering and punishment merited by the sins of his people. Although written long before the coming of Christ, only his life perfectly fulfills this ancient oracle; in today's Gospel we will hear Jesus express the same selflessness that animates this prophecy.

    The Servant is righteous in God's eyes, but embraces both suffering and the scorn of those who look upon him and believe him to be guilty and even spurned by God. God takes no sadistic pleasure in crushing the servant with pain, but delights in the Servant's willingness to suffer on behalf of others, to present himself freely as "an offering for sin." For this remarkable service, this singular self-sacrifice, the Servant will not go unrewarded. He will know the joy of a long life among his descendants and the satisfaction of accomplishing God's holy will. His faithful endurance will bring the light of joy into his life and God's bountiful mercy to the lives of countless others. It's not the heaviness of Good Friday, when we usually hear this text, which characterizes its tone today. "If" and "because" are the operative words that connect his pain with healing and saving consequences for the "many." That's good and joyful news on any day of the year.

READING II A priest is an intermediary between God and God's people. However well and faithfully human priests might serve, their service is always limited by their imperfections and even

A reading from the Letter to the Hebrews

Brothers and sisters:
Since we have a **great** high **priest** who has passed
    through the **heavens**,
    Jesus, the Son of **God**,
    let us hold **fast** to our confession.
For we do not have a high priest
    who is unable to **sympathize** with our **weaknesses**,
    but one who has **similarly** been tested in **every** way,
    yet **without** sin.
So let us confidently **approach** the throne of grace
    to receive **mercy** and to find **grace** for timely **help**.

This is the third of seven consecutive weeks that we read from Hebrews.

Because the passage is brief, read slowly, but don't let your slow pacing stifle the tone of joy and appreciation that infects the text.

You're a cheerleader of sorts, and you cheer for the Christ of the Gospel who came "to serve" and give his life "as a ransom for many."

Assume an explanatory tone making eye contact as you speak.

Here is the climax. Speak with joy and confidence born of your own conviction that God is approachable and merciful.

A reading from the holy Gospel according to Mark

James and **John**, the sons of **Zebedee**, came to **Jesus** and said
    to him,
    "**Teacher**, we want you to **do** for us whatever we **ask** of you."
He replied, "What do you wish me to **do** for you?"
They answered him, "Grant that in your **glory**
    we may sit one at your **right** and the other at your **left**."
Jesus said to them, "You do not **know** what you are **asking**.
Can you drink the cup that **I** drink
    or be **baptized** with the baptism with which **I** am baptized?"

Make sure you take time to clearly identify the players.

This request is unashamedly bold.

Jesus plays along, however, revealing no shock at so brazen a request.

They've clearly rehearsed their request and ask it quickly.

Nonplussed, Jesus asks his own question, to which they respond with too little thought and too much nerve.

sinfulness. But we, brothers and sisters, we have a "great high priest" who transcends the limits of all other intermediaries. He has "passed through the heavens" and taken his rightful place at the right hand of God, and it is from there—in that privileged place that no other can take or even aspire to—from there he intercedes for us that we might receive "mercy" and "grace" in all our times of need.

That would be good news enough, but it gets better. This high priest, so named here and nowhere else in Hebrews, is not an intimidating or unsympathetic figure we might fear to approach. Yes, he is Jesus, the Son of God, and that makes him unique beyond measure. Yes, only we can make the outrageous claim that God's own Son pleads on our behalf. But as different as he is from us, Jesus also knows and understands our weaknesses. Like us, he too was tempted, and not only once at the start of his ministry, but throughout his life, just as we are. The difference, of course, is that though tempted "in every way," he never sinned. The consequences of all this are no less than astounding: we can "confidently" approach "the throne of grace," that is, the throne of God, because Christ, our brother in the flesh and our Lord in eternity, has thrown wide the gates of access to God's merciful love.

GOSPEL   Their audacity is shocking and they've obviously rehearsed it. Without saying what, the Sons of Zebedee ask Jesus to do "whatever [they] ask." Jesus goes along, making them put their request on the table. When they do, he doesn't chide but quickly points

Imagine Jesus looking them square in the eyes and, with a smile and a nod, agreeing that they, indeed, will endure a fate akin to his.

The seriousness of the previous sentence is broken as Jesus informs them that who sits where is not something he can decide. Mention of "the ten" introduces tension and anger. Let your narration suggest the hostile reaction to James and John. Jesus becomes the teacher, instructing them in a patient, peaceful tone.

Try to make this familiar verse ring with freshness. Don't rush it like a memorized line, but like a thought newly sprung in his mind.

As teacher, Jesus' best lesson plan is his own example.

They said to him, "We **can**."

Jesus said to them, "The **cup** that I drink, you **will** drink,
 and with the **baptism** with which **I** am baptized,
  you will be baptized;
 but to sit at my **right** or at my **left** is not mine to **give**
 but is for those for whom it has been **prepared**."

When the **ten** heard this, they became **indignant**
 at James and John.

Jesus **summoned** them and said to them,
 "You know that those who are recognized as **rulers**
  over the Gentiles
 lord it over them,
 and their **great** ones make their authority over them **felt**.

But it shall **not** be so among **you**.

Rather, whoever wishes to be **great** among you
 will be your **servant**;
 whoever wishes to be **first** among you will be the **slave** of all.

For the Son of Man did not come to be **served**
 but to **serve** and to give his **life** as a ransom for **many**."

[Shorter: Mark 10:42–45]

out their naiveté: "You do not know what you are asking," he says. His subsequent questions reveal his awareness that he has hard lessons to teach about suffering and service. Of course James and John think they can endure what lies ahead—they don't yet know what it will be! So they boldly assert their loyalty and request assurance of preeminence and rank in the kingdom. But Jesus will promise only suffering, and the only title he'll bestow is "servant."

Maybe the brothers had Jesus to themselves for a private moment or perhaps they questioned brazenly in front of their brethren; either way they've created a storm Jesus now must calm. He gathers the disciples to himself and begins to teach in a tone that's patient and gentle, for he knows these men will pay with their lives for the privilege of learning at his feet. They all know the social customs and the privileges that come with power: among Gentiles, rulers are served by their subjects. So the next line must have deflated a few egos and sunk a few hearts: "It shall

not be so among you." What follows next is not a scene of poignant melodrama: no violins weep, no trumpets sound in the background. The dialogue between Lord and disciples is ordinary and understated. It's one of those events whose significance is recognized only in hindsight. It's the normal way of things. Such moments just happen; but later we look back and realize they changed our lives.

30TH SUNDAY IN ORDINARY TIME

Lectionary #149

READING I   Jeremiah 31:7–9

A reading from the Book of the Prophet Jeremiah

Thus says the LORD:
Shout with **joy** for Jacob,
   exult at the head of the nations;
   proclaim your **praise** and say:
The LORD has **delivered** his people,
   the **remnant** of Israel.
Behold, I will bring them **back**
   from the land of the **north**;
I will **gather** them from the ends of the **world**,
   with the **blind** and the **lame** in their midst,
the **mothers** and those with **child**;
   they shall **return** as an immense **throng**.
They departed in **tears**,
   but I will **console** them and **guide** them;
I will lead them to brooks of **water**,
   on a **level** road, so that none shall **stumble**.
For I am a **father** to Israel,
   Ephraim is my **first-born**.

Jeremiah = jayr-uh-MĪ-uh

Jacob = JAY-kuhb

Announce boldly that it is the Lord who speaks these promises of healing and hope.

These imperatives are spontaneous and exuberant. You'll need great energy and eye contact.

This exclamation of good news can speak also of our own deliverance from trial and hardship.

Mention of the "blind" helps connect this reading to today's Gospel.

The sorrow of the exile is behind them; now God's guiding hand will wipe away all tears and assure safety and sustenance.

Expectant mothers need much reassurance. With tenderness, God's voice offers it to them and to any of us who are bent or broken.

This last declaration is spoken with authority and tender pride.

Let the closing image of God as "father" and Ephraim as God's "first-born" guide your proclamation of these lines, which are redolent of God's compassionate and solicitous love.

Ephraim = EE-fray-im or EF-r*m

READING I   In reading scripture, there is always a "then" and a "now." First we ask what the text meant "then"—the situation within which it was proclaimed, the historical circumstances the author was addressing. But we proclaim Old Testament scripture in liturgy because it also speaks to us "now," perhaps in a way similar to how it spoke in its original context, or perhaps in a way influenced by the Gospel light by which we read all of scripture.

Jeremiah prophesied before and during the Babylonian exile, sometimes threatening judgment and other times promising mercy and restoration. Today's text falls into the latter category and it overflows with the promise of God's love manifested in an immense throng of God's people returning in joy to the promised land of their birth. "Shout . . . exult . . . proclaim," commands the prophet. God has ended the exile and will restore the nation. From afar her children will gather; both they and many others, comprising an "immense throng." They will return not in tears as they left, but in exuberant joy and praise.

The names "Jacob" (another name for Israel) and "Ephraim" (a son of Joseph who became one of Israel's 12 tribes) both represent the nation as a whole. Like a father, God will clear the way for his people, consoling and guiding them back into the safety of his heart. And that is the "now" of the reading. In every age God, like a parent, cares for his people, ready always and with an ever-open heart to heal and embrace and forgive. You can be sure many in your assembly are in need of the comfort these words promise.

The author reasons gently, guiding us a step at a time to the realization that Jesus is the consummate high priest.

As reader, be like the "priest" described here: patient, aware of your own weaknesses, and humble about the call you have received.

Concentrate on the parallels and contrasts in the author's reasoning: "He is able to deal patiently" with sinners, for he is himself "beset by weakness." He must make sacrifice for "sin offerings for *himself* as well as for the *people*." One does not take "this honor upon *himself*" but only when "called by *God*." Stress the connection to Jesus of all that preceded.

The quotes that end the passage are, respectively, expressions of love and pride. This is the "father" who speaks at the end of the First Reading from Jeremiah and Jesus is the new "Ephraim," who is forever "first-born" and "priest," and brother of us all.

READING II   Hebrews 5:1–6

A reading from the Letter to the Hebrews

Brothers and sisters:
Every **high** priest is taken from among **men**
    and made their **representative** before **God**,
    to offer **gifts** and **sacrifices** for **sins**.
He is able to deal **patiently** with the **ignorant** and **erring**,
    for he **himself** is beset by **weakness**
    and so, for **this** reason, must make sin offerings for **himself**
    as well as for the **people**.
No one takes this honor upon **himself**
    but only when called by **God**,
    just as **Aaron** was.
In the **same** way,
    it was not **Christ** who glorified himself in becoming high priest,
    but rather the one who **said** to him:
    You are my **son***: this day I have* **begotten** *you;*
just as he says in another place:
    You are a priest **forever** *according to the order*
        of **Melchizedek***.*

READING II   The author of Hebrews continues reflecting on the high priesthood of Jesus, comparing and contrasting his role with that of human high priests. Both share a common mission: to represent humanity before God. And both understand human frailty. The high priests of Old Testament tradition had to intercede for their own erring and sinful ways, for they too were beset with weaknesses and sin. Jesus, though sinless, was fully human and thus understands the human struggle with weakness and temptation. Jesus was tempted throughout his life, as we are. Though he never yielded to temptation, the powers of darkness assailed him as much, if not more, than the rest of us. Certainly in the Garden he wrestled with the fear of death. So his human experience qualifies Jesus all the more to serve as our high priest, our representative before God.

As with human candidates for this most important role, Jesus was chosen by God to serve as intermediary. The author cites Psalm 110:4 to assert that Jesus' selection as priest "according to the order of Melchizedek" (King of Salem and the Old Testament's priestly prototype) is divinely ordained. Christ's intercessory role is unique, for he can stand sinless before the throne of God representing, with complete understanding, sinful humanity whose nature he fully shares.

GOSPEL   A blind beggar, the remarkable Bartimaeus, has clearly heard of Jesus, and jumps at the opportunity to make Jesus hear of him. He cries out so boldly that members of the noisy crowd try to silence him. But they

GOSPEL Mark 10:46–52

A reading from the holy Gospel according to Mark

As Jesus was leaving **Jericho** with his **disciples**
    and a sizable **crowd**,
  Bartimaeus, a **blind** man, the son of **Timaeus**,
    sat by the roadside **begging**.
On hearing that it was Jesus of **Nazareth**,
  he began to **cry** out and say,
  "**Jesus**, son of **David**, have **pity** on me."
And many **rebuked** him, telling him to be **silent**.
But he kept calling out all the **more**,
  "Son of **David**, have **pity** on me."
Jesus **stopped** and said, "**Call** him."
So they **called** the blind man, saying to him,
  "Take **courage**; get **up**, **Jesus** is calling you."
He **threw** aside his cloak, **sprang** up, and **came** to Jesus.
Jesus said to him in reply, "What do you want me to **do** for you?"
The blind man replied to him, "**Master**, I want to **see**."
Jesus told him, "**Go** your way; your **faith** has **saved** you."
Immediately he received his **sight**
    and **followed** him on the way.

Jericho = JAYR-ih-koh

The presence of his disciples and the size of the crowd are important details to stress.

Take time with the identification of the blind man.

Without over dramatizing, suggest the loud and insistent effort to get Jesus' attention.

By contrast, mention of the rebukes might be whispered in the hissing tone of the disapproving crowd members.

Take a pause before speaking "Call him."

Now the crowd is solicitous and encouraging.

"Threw," "sprang," and "came" suggest a sudden eruption of activity.

This is a poignant encounter between a believer and his Lord. Jesus and the man share a moment of genuine connection.

The man's response suggests the universal call to discipleship by following Jesus.

fail and he cries out all the more. Once Jesus takes note of him, however, the crowd suddenly becomes his advocate, urging him to "take courage" and "get up," as if they hope that helping Bartimaeus will give them a share in the blessing he will receive. The fickle crowd serves as a foil for the resolute beggar who won't abandon his resolve to be heard.

But Bartimaeus, too, has a flip side. Though he resists the crowd with manly courage, he responds to Jesus in childlike simplicity: "Master, I want to see." Even

his name ("son of Timaeus") seems to be an ironic suggestion of childlike dependency and humility. The blind man is no longer shouting when he makes his request; there's an earnest, intense simplicity that convinces Jesus this man "sees" better than the crowd or even his own disciples.

Unlike other healings where Jesus makes a ritual of spittle and mud, here he merely speaks his healing: "Your faith has saved you." Jesus seems to speak with awareness that the man's faith has already worked an inner healing that Jesus' words

and the physical healing will only manifest. The restoration of this man's sight may well symbolize the insight that will be given later to the disciples. Not till after the Resurrection will they grasp the necessity of Christ's Passion and their need to share in it. But Bartimaeus, as soon as his eyes are opened, recognizes the "way" he must take and, though it leads to Jerusalem and death, he instantly starts to follow Jesus.

ALL SAINTS

Lectionary #667

READING I — Revelation 7:2–4, 9–14

A reading from the Book of Revelation

The vision begins immediately; that means your tone must signal from the start that you are describing an extra-ordinary event.

As you narrate, create the illusion of speed by the excitement you generate, not by actually rushing the words.

"Do not damage . . ." is spoken with an authoritative voice that can command cosmic forces.

Being sealed signifies the protection of the one whose mark you bear. The tone is full of concern.

A new, more expansive vision begins here. "Every nation, race, people, tongue" comprise four distinct images.

The white robes and palm branches signify victory.

The cry of the multitude is a songlike chant of praise.

The "angels" and "elders" join the hymn of praise. "Blessing, glory . . . power, might . . ." (continued on next page) are all distinct images. Don't rush them together. Consider a softer, quieter delivery for this section.

I, **John**, saw another **angel** come up from the East,
    holding the **seal** of the living **God**.
He cried out in a loud **voice** to the four angels
    who were given power to **damage** the **land** and the **sea**,
    "Do **not** damage the **land** or the **sea** or the **trees**
    until we put the **seal** on the **foreheads** of the **servants**
        of our God."
I heard the **number** of those who had been marked with the seal,
    one **hundred** and forty-four **thousand** marked
    from every **tribe** of the children of **Israel**.

After this I had a vision of a great **multitude**,
    which no one could **count**,
    from every **nation**, **race**, **people**, and **tongue**.
They stood before the **throne** and before the **Lamb**,
    wearing white **robes** and holding **palm** branches in their hands.
They cried out in a loud **voice**:

    "**Salvation** comes from our **God**, who is seated on the **throne**,
    and from the **Lamb**."

All the **angels** stood around the throne
    and around the **elders** and the four living **creatures**.

READING I — Today we celebrate the friends of God, those women and men who, throughout the ages, have "lived with the Lord" even while living among us. Their lives have known joy and challenge, failure and success, betrayal and abounding grace. Through it all they desired what Kierkegaard called "the one thing": God.

John's vision describes a vast multitude of such saints brought together in the glory of God's kingdom with robes washed white "in the blood of the Lamb" because they remained faithful, whether convenient or inconvenient, and kept their eyes fixed on the prize. They followed their crucified Lord, embracing suffering as he did, so now they wear the white robes that represent their purification and their new life in Christ.

The key to proclaiming a noble text like this is to read as if you were describing a real event that thrilled you with its magnificence and awed you with its power. The sound of your voice—echoing with wonder and delight—is as important as the actual words you speak. Adults don't let the fact that infants can't understand words stop them from speaking to their children, because they know the tone of their voices communicates the disapproval or love they wish to convey. Here, the unmistakable tone is one of celebration and triumph. Even if those listening understood none of your words, they should know you are describing a grand and touching scene—an assembly of saints we all hope to join one day.

They **prostrated** themselves before the throne,
    worshiped God, and exclaimed:
      "**Amen. Blessing** and **glory**, **wisdom** and **thanksgiving**,
        honor, **power**, and **might**
      be to our **God forever** and **ever**. **Amen**."

Then one of the **elders** spoke up and said to me,
    "Who **are** these wearing white **robes**,
      and where did they **come** from?"
I said to him, "My **lord**, **you** are the one who **knows**."
He said to me,
    "**These** are the ones who have **survived** the time
      of great **distress**;
    they have **washed** their robes
    and made them **white** in the **Blood** of the **Lamb**."

The "elder's" voice is kind, paternal and wise. He speaks with pride of those who survived persecution and trial.

The final comment tells us these multitudes have been made saints not by their own work but by the work of the "Lamb" whose blood has bleached their robes. What the Lamb could do for them he can do also for us.

READING II   1 John 3:1–3

A reading from the first Letter of Saint John

Beloved:
See what **love** the Father has **bestowed** on us
    that we may be called the **children** of God.
Yet so we **are**.
The reason the **world** does not know us
    is that it did not know **him**.
Beloved, we **are** God's children **now**;
    what we **shall** be has not yet been **revealed**.
We **do** know that when it **is** revealed we shall be **like** him,
    for we shall **see** him as he **is**.
Everyone who has this **hope** based on **him** makes himself **pure**,
    as **he** is pure.

Let this greeting set the tone.

Slow down only at the end of the sentence, setting off the final words "children of God."
Look right at the assembly as you make this assertion with joy and conviction.
Let the word "beloved" linger for a moment before you continue.
The tone is "This much we *do* know." Deliver these lines with joy on your face.

Pause, and then deliver the line slowly, making it both a prayer and an imperative.

READING II | This brief and very personal reading invites us to consider what it takes to become a saint. Twice you will address the assembly as "Beloved"; you will speak of the Father's "love" and of our status as God's "children," and you will exhort us to be as "pure" as God. Such a personal flavor challenges you to convey the depth of feeling without becoming syrupy. The best way to avoid that trap is to be convinced of the truth of what you say. Sentimentality is born of trying too hard. Real emotion always sounds authentic. So let your awareness of God's love for you, your desire to help the world "know him" better than it does, your longing to "be like him" in the world to come, infuse your reading with the sincerity that will keep it from lapsing into sentimentality.

God has claimed us as his "children," but the world fails to see it; we will eventually be changed, but we don't yet know into what; we do know this much—we will resemble Christ; this glimpse of our future destiny calls us to live a life as pure as Christ's. That's the totality of this text and because you have few words with which to deliver so important a message, you will need to work harder than usual to proclaim it well. You begin with wide-eyed wonder at God's goodness in naming us "children of God," then insist that is indeed our identity. But if we are to become like Christ, we must begin now, keeping ourselves "pure." The challenge of that declaration will be even more powerful if besides an announcement it is also a prayer.

GOSPEL   Matthew 5:1–12a

A reading from the holy Gospel according to Matthew

When Jesus saw the **crowds**, he went up the **mountain**,
    and after he had **sat** down, his **disciples** came to him.
He began to **teach** them, saying:

"**Blessed** are the **poor** in **spirit**,
    for theirs is the Kingdom of **heaven**.
Blessed are they who **mourn**,
    for they will be **comforted**.
Blessed are the **meek**,
    for they will inherit the **land**.
Blessed are they who **hunger** and **thirst** for **righteousness**,
    for they will be **satisfied**.
Blessed are the **merciful**,
    for they will be shown **mercy**.
Blessed are the clean of **heart**,
    for they will see **God**.
Blessed are the **peacemakers**,
    for they will be called **children** of God.
Blessed are they who are **persecuted** for the sake
        of **righteousness**,
    for **theirs** is the Kingdom of **heaven**.
Blessed are **you** when they **insult** you and **persecute** you
    and utter every kind of **evil** against you **falsely** because of **me**.
Rejoice and be **glad**,
    for your **reward** will be **great** in **heaven**."

Use these few lines to set the scene: The crowds have come to Jesus; he climbs the mountain, sits, and draws his disciples near. Then, he begins to teach.

You need never raise your voice for hilltop projection. A quiet intensity will serve the scripture better.

Look at individual faces as you speak, letting them draw out your desire to convince, challenge, and transform.

At certain points, you might imagine some of your listeners standing up and leaving—surely some left Jesus when he spoke. That image can add urgency to the Beatitude that follows.
Leave some space between each Beatitude for the words to make their impact.

Never rush; each Beatitude stands alone confronting worldly values.
This last Beatitude is the most direct. Make eye contact with the assembly and let your urgency flow from the knowledge you have of those who have endured injustice and calumny for the sake of the kingdom.
Note that the final sentence is an imperative.

GOSPEL   **Proclaiming the Beatitudes is more an act of faith and an exercise in prayer than it is a moment of instruction. These counterintuitive statements challenge us as we speak them and call us to surrender logic and objectivity to their mesmerizing poetry. In your preparation, you'll consider how these compare and contrast with Luke's version—reserved for the disciples, not the crowd, and delivered on the "plain," not the "mount"—that includes three "woes" among the "blesseds." You'll ponder Matthew's addition of "in spirit" to the first Beatitude and** wonder if he meant to exclude the poor who are not pious and faithful or to include anyone, of whatever economic status, who relies on God more than their wealth. You'll learn that the "Blessed are . . ." formula occurs elsewhere in scripture, that "the land" inherited by the meek has no earthly geography, but is found only in the kingdom, and you'll find comfort in the knowledge that every true disciple follows in the footsteps of Israel's persecuted prophets.

But your best preparation might require considering those people you know who exemplify the Beatitudes, so you can think of them as you proclaim. Your technical delivery can be simple and quiet, imbued with awareness of how life-altering each one is. Although you might use bravado when making a simple request of a friend, if you're asking for everything they've got, your tone will be hushed and humble. The Beatitudes ask everything of us. But they also comfort those who sorrow and infuse the weary with hope. They inspire the downtrodden and offer visions of a world where our hunger for justice is satisfied and mercy reigns.

COMMEMORATION OF ALL THE FAITHFUL DEPARTED

Lectionary #668

READING I   Wisdom 3:1–9

A reading from the Book of Wisdom

The **souls** of the **just** are in the **hand** of **God**,
    and no **torment** shall **touch** them.
They **seemed**, in the view of the **foolish**, to be **dead**;
    and their **passing** away was thought an **affliction**
    and their going **forth** from us, utter **destruction**.
But they are in **peace**.
For if in the sight of **others**, indeed they be **punished**,
    yet is their hope full of **immortality**;
chastised a little, they shall be greatly **blessed**,
    because God **tried** them
    and found them **worthy** of himself.
As **gold** in the **furnace**, he **proved** them,
    and as sacrificial **offerings** he took them to **himself**.
In the time of their **visitation** they shall **shine**,
    and shall dart about as **sparks** through **stubble**;
they shall judge **nations** and rule over **peoples**,
    and the **LORD** shall be their King **forever**.
Those who **trust** in him shall understand **truth**,
    and the **faithful** shall abide with him in **love**:
because **grace** and **mercy** are with his **holy** ones,
    and his **care** is with his **elect**.

The melodic opening line is the foundation for all that follows. Speak with joyful confidence.

Let your tone convey that here appearances don't match the reality.

This is another line to be delivered with utter conviction.

The purification that may come after death is not to be feared, but welcomed as God's gift that prepares one for final judgment. Speak with authority.

Here, the energy builds and the tempo quickens a bit as you offer the lovely image of souls shining like sparks.

The final sentence can be delivered at a slower pace, emphasizing the "grace," "mercy," and "care" that await God's elect.

Today options are given for the readings. Contact your parish staff to learn which readings will be used.

READING I   These sacred words from the Book of Wisdom have rained peace and comfort upon countless funeral liturgies. And no wonder. The text addresses many of the concerns we might have about a departed loved one: If they were just, we are assured they are with God; so they are not "destroyed," but in peace; and though death may have appeared a "punishment, it is, in fact, the door to "immortality."

Often applied to the martyrs, these verses speak also of the witness given by ordinary lives marked by the love of God and others. So the tone is peaceful and full of joy. Our eternal destiny is not a dark mystery; it is with God. In life God may chastise us a little so that for eternity we will be "blessed" because he has made us "worthy of himself." At the time the book of Wisdom was written, belief in an afterlife was far from settled, so the author's intent is to persuade as well as comfort. In our day, many hearts still need both comfort and persuasion, so let a serene conviction underscore your proclamation.

After assuring us of their fate, the writer describes the glory that is theirs: at the time of their judgment ("their visitation") they will "shine"; they will be "sparks" emanating from the rubble of earthly life. They will even "judge" nations. There is hopeful energy in these lines, but also some key words you must highlight. It is "those who trust" and "the faithful" who are assured "grace and mercy." Nothing is

Look right at the assembly and speak with confidence and joy. You'll be more convincing if you get in touch with the love of God in your own heart.

Marvel at the generosity of God.

The comparison serves to highlight God's mercy all the more and climaxes at the words "Christ died for us."

Renew your energy. Build on the previous point: If God loved us enough to save us while we were alienated, how much more will God bestow on us now that we have been reconciled through Christ!

Let your voice swell with boasting of the goodness of God!

READING II   Romans 5:5–11

A reading from the Letter of Saint Paul to the Romans

Brothers and sisters:
Hope does not **disappoint**,
    because the love of **God** has been poured out into our **hearts**
    through the Holy **Spirit** that has been **given** to us.
For **Christ**, while we were still **helpless**,
    died at the appointed time for the **ungodly**.
Indeed, only with **difficulty** does one die for a **just** person,
    though perhaps for a **good** person
    one might even find **courage** to die.
But God **proves** his love for us
    in that while we were still **sinners** Christ **died** for us.
How much **more** then, since we are now **justified** by his **Blood**,
    will we be **saved** through him from the **wrath**.
Indeed, if, while we were **enemies**,
    we were **reconciled** to God through the death of his **Son**,
    how much **more**, once **reconciled**,
    will we be **saved** by his **life**.
Not only **that**,
    but we also **boast** of God through our Lord Jesus **Christ**,
    through whom we have now received **reconciliation**.

Or:

guaranteed unless we have surrendered to God and become "his holy ones." But it is never too late to pray that those we love are among God's "elect."

READING II **ROMANS 5.** Most of the love we have experienced is conditional. Whether parents, spouse, or friend, there are often conditions connected to the love others give us. Sometimes, though, human love breaks those barriers and we see someone give his or her life for another. There, in that sacred space created by such selfless love, Paul tells us, is

where we find a model for the love God has for us! God's unconditional love is constant. We can rely on it. It doesn't come and go with changing circumstances. How do we know this? Because while we were still mired in the depths of sin, God sent his son to die for us. There was no, "If you do this, I will do that;" no waiting for us to change our ways before God mercifully intervened.

These are the words of an evangelist, of one in whom the Good News swells and demands to be shared. Paul's "hope" in the opening sentence is not something about

which we bite our nails and wonder if God will, in fact, deliver. No. It is assurance that flows from the Gospel promise that the Holy Spirit will help us give our hearts to God and to do God's will to the point that we come to resemble Christ and are his presence in the world.

We are loved by a God who took the initiative to love us, and completely transformed us with his love. God reached into the darkness of our sin and turned it into light. Now we are *justified* by faith and at peace with God. If God did all that *before* we were justified, Paul says, imagine how

READING II   Romans 6:3–9

A reading from the Letter of Saint Paul to the Romans

Brothers and sisters:
Are you **unaware** that we who were **baptized** into Christ Jesus
      were baptized into his **death**?
We were indeed **buried** with him through baptism into **death**,
      so that, just as Christ was **raised** from the dead
      by the glory of the **Father**,
      we **too** might live in **newness** of life.

For if we have grown into **union** with him through a **death**
      like his,
      we shall also be **united** with him in the **resurrection**.
We know that our **old** self was **crucified** with him,
      so that our **sinful** body might be done **away** with,
      that we might no longer be in **slavery** to sin.
For a **dead** person has been **absolved** from sin.
If, then, we have **died** with Christ,
      we believe that we shall also **live** with him.
We know that **Christ**, **raised** from the dead, dies **no more**;
      death no longer has **power** over him.

Paul's literary device is a rhetorical question. Let it sound like a question. Make eye contact and speak as directly as Paul writes.

Take the time to understand Paul's point: what happened to Christ will happen to us. He died and was buried, then rose. We die and are buried in Baptism; we, too, will rise to new (and eternal) life.

Paul develops the idea: we were made one with Christ by sharing a death (Baptism) like his; so we also will be made one with him in experiencing Resurrection.

Don't let this sound repetitive. Sustain the energy. Contrast "died" and "live."

"We know" means that we are convinced! "Dies no more . . . death no longer has power . . ." is the same idea stated twice: greater stress goes to the second statement.

---

much more God will do for us now that we live in the grace and reconciliation Christ won for us through his death.

ROMANS 6. At the Easter Vigil, when this text is also proclaimed, we hear these words in light of baptismal theology that tells us "death" and "burial" in the waters of Baptism are the path to "new life" in Christ. But for Paul, that new life starts here on earth—although here we only *taste* the fullness that won't be wholly ours till after death. Today these words speak of our ultimate destiny in Christ. Over and over, Paul compares our fate to Christ's:

we were buried with him in Baptism so that just as he was raised we, too, might live a new life.

"Are you not aware . . ." starts the passage with high energy, expecting a nod of the head as the words awaken realization in the hearer's heart. Paul expects us to already understand the dynamics of Christian life: "death" is good news, not bad, for it leads to glory with Christ. Although assurance of Resurrection is reserved to the saints we celebrated in yesterday's feast, today we rejoice in the

belief that whatever purgation comes after death will lead the faithful to living with Christ in full and endless glory.

Paul's message is full of hope that must be heralded in joy. "Death" and "burial" are not enemies when we die in Christ! Paul presents his reasoning with carefully balanced ideas: "If we have grown . . . through a *death* like his, we shall also be united . . . in the *Resurrection*." Proclaim joyously what "we *know*": we share in Christ's fate! As death had no power over him, it has no power over us. While we breathe, it's not too late to claim

GOSPEL   John 6:37–40

A reading from the holy Gospel according to John

Jesus said to the **crowds**:
  "**Everything** that the Father **gives** me will **come** to me,
  and I will not reject **anyone** who comes to me,
  because I came down from **heaven** not to do my **own** will
  but the will of the one who **sent** me.
And **this** is the will of the one who sent me,
  that I should not **lose** anything of what he **gave** me,
  but that I should **raise** it on the last **day**.
For **this** is the will of my **Father**,
  that everyone who sees the **Son** and **believes** in him
  may have eternal **life**,
  and I shall **raise** him on the last **day**."

Pause after the colon to shift into the attitude of Jesus. Though he's addressing the crowds, keep the tone personal and intimate.

Stress the word "this." His repetition of the previous line places extra focus on what will follow: "That I should not lose anything . . . ."

Once again, stress the word "this." God longs for our salvation more than we do. Stress the verbs "sees" and "believes."

Make eye contact as you deliver this comforting final line.

that victory, nor to pray for those who have already crossed the threshold of death.

GOSPEL Jesus speaks here with powerful clarity. He came not to pursue his own agenda, but the Father's. All God *intends* for him will *come* to him; and Jesus will reject no one who comes with open heart to him. In the spiritual life, so often it is more difficult to *know* God's will than to do it. "Just show me what to do," we find ourselves asking, "and I'll do it." Maybe it's a naïve claim,

but it does express the difficulty we often experience in discerning God's perfect will for us.

Jesus has no such problem: "*This* is the will of the one who sent me," he says. He knows with certainty because discernment becomes easier when we "live with God" on a daily basis; when we unite our hearts to his, desiring what God desires. Of course, desiring the will of God had becomes Jesus' daily bread; with every breath, Jesus inhaled the divine will even when, as in the garden, it was a knife that drew blood as it entered. God's will is that

Jesus lose none of those God draws to him and that he bring them to eternal life. Knowing Christ, truly knowing him, not just with the intellect but with the heart, so bonds us to him that his fate and ours are one. Such knowledge of Christ is eternal life. Jesus' life and death are his pledge that he will raise us and bring us to where he is. The same promise is made to all who have gone before us in full knowledge of and with faith in him.

31ST SUNDAY IN ORDINARY TIME

Lectionary #152

READING I   Deuteronomy 6:2–6

A reading from the Book of Deuteronomy

Moses spoke to the **people**, saying:
  "**Fear** the Lord, your **God**,
  and **keep**, throughout the days of your lives,
  all his **statutes** and **commandments** which I **enjoin** on you,
  and thus have **long life**.
Hear then, Israel, and be careful to **observe** them,
  that you may **grow** and prosper the **more**,
  in keeping with the **promise** of the Lord,
    the God of your **fathers**,
  to give you a **land** flowing with **milk** and **honey**.

"**Hear**, O Israel! The **Lord** is our **God**, the Lord **alone**!
Therefore, you shall **love** the Lord, your God,
  with all your **heart**,
  and with all your **soul**,
  and with all your **strength**.
Take to **heart** these words which I **enjoin** on you today."

Make sure Moses is clearly identified.

"Fear" of the Lord refers to appropriate awe and respect for God's sovereign majesty.

This is the second time Moses tells the people to keep the law. Speak with authority and awareness that their future depends on their obedience.

Employ your best energy for the recitation of the *Sh'ma*.

With energy and increased volume, render these words as prayerfully as you can.

Distinguish between "heart," "soul," and "strength." Together, they symbolize the totality of our being that we must surrender fully to the love and service of God.

The last line is not a threat, but we can hear an implied "If you know what's good for you" in the tone.

READING I   Certain words can define a relationship, a movement, even a nation. Whether it's the first "I love you" or "We hold these truths to be self-evident . . ." significant words find a place deep within us and take root. The ability to carry tremendous power is in the very nature of words, and so we put them in books, inscribe them on buildings, and hang them on our walls. This passage from Deuteronomy contains such a text and it is known as the *Sh'ma* (Hebrew for "listen")— "Hear, O Israel! The Lord is our God, the Lord alone!" These sacred words express the basic tenets of Judaism: fervent faith in one God and love of God with one's whole heart, soul, and strength. So sacred are these words that Deuteronomy mandates they be worn on the wrist and forehead and posted at the door posts of every home—still a common practice—in a small container called a "mezuzah." Jesus quotes these words in today's Gospel calling them the first and greatest commandment that encompasses the entirety of God's law.

Moses has gathered the people in solemn assembly to recite for them the entirety of the law. Here we glimpse part of the grand ritual and hear the great prophet and lawgiver address the people with solemn authority. Don't mistake solemn for "sad" or "lifeless." Though dignified and sacred, the tone also expresses urgency that the people keep God's commandment "throughout . . . [their] lives," because their growth and prosperity will depend on it. Knowledge that the nation's future rests on their willingness to embrace

This is the fifth of seven consecutive weeks we read from Hebrews.

"Levitical" priests were the priests of the Mosaic Law, all members of the tribe of Levi.

The former priests died and had to be replaced. Jesus' ministry lasts forever.

Jesus' "intercession" is not something added on to his sacrifice on the cross, but that very sacrifice eternally present before the throne of the Father.

Read these attributes of our ideal priest reverently, remembering each word names a unique quality.

You are contrasting Christ's intercession with that of the priests of old, exalting Christ's sinless preeminence.

"The law" is the *old* law, now superseded by the new covenant initiated through Christ's once-for-all death and Resurrection.

READING II   Hebrews 7:23–28

A reading from the Letter to the Hebrews

Brothers and sisters:
The **levitical** priests were **many**
  because they were prevented by **death** from remaining
    in office,
  but **Jesus**, because he remains **forever**,
  has a priesthood that does **not** pass away.
Therefore, he is always able to **save** those who approach God
    through **him**,
  since he lives **forever** to make **intercession** for them.

It was **fitting** that we should have such a high priest:
  holy, **innocent**, **undefiled**, **separated** from sinners,
  higher than the **heavens**.
He has no **need**, as did the **high** priests,
  to offer sacrifice **day** after **day**,
  first for his **own** sins and then for those of the **people**;
  he did that once for **all** when he offered **himself**.
For the **law** appoints men subject to **weakness** to be **high** priests,
  but the **word** of the oath, which was taken **after** the law,
  appoints a **son**,
  who has been made **perfect forever**.

and live God's law should help you give these words the urgency Moses must have given them.

READING II   Priests played a significant role in Jewish religion, and the high priest served the special role of making sin offerings in the Temple and each year entering the Holy of Holies to offer atoning sacrifice for his own sins and those of the people.

  For several weeks now, the author of Hebrews has been contrasting the Jewish, "Levitical" priesthood with the High Priesthood of Christ. Not only has Jesus' sacrificial death made Jewish ritual sacrifices unnecessary, the author argues, but Jesus has even rendered the Levitical priesthood itself meaningless, because he himself has become the one and only priest of the new covenant. That might sound odd, but in Christian faith, every priest shares in the one priesthood of Christ. They have no priesthood independent from his. Just as Christ's sacrifice, offered "once for all" on the Cross, is made present in every Eucharist, so the one priesthood of Christ is made present in every bishop and priest.

  Because Jesus is the eternal high priest, the new covenant he initiated has no need for the endless succession of priests required by the old law. Jesus has already accomplished for all time what the high priests had to repeat "day after day." Further, under Mosaic law, only men "subject to weakness," that is, sinners, could assume the mantle of priesthood. But Christ, who is "holy, innocent, and undefiled," has become our eternal priest, perfectly fulfilling "the word of [God's]

GOSPEL   Mark 12:28b–34

A reading from the holy Gospel according to Mark

One of the **scribes** came to **Jesus** and **asked** him,
  "Which is the **first** of all the **commandments**?"
Jesus replied, "The first is **this**:
  Hear, O Israel!
  *The Lord our **God** is Lord **alone**!*
  *You shall **love** the Lord your God with all your **heart**,*
  *with all your **soul**,*
  *with all your **mind**,*
  *and with all your **strength**.*
The second is **this**:
  *You shall love your **neighbor** as **yourself**.*
There is no **other** commandment greater than **these**."
The scribe said to him, "Well **said**, teacher.
You are **right** in saying,
  'He is **One** and there is no **other** than he.'
And 'to **love** him with all your **heart**,
  with all your **understanding**,
  with all your **strength**,
  and to love your **neighbor** as **yourself**'
  is worth **more** than all burnt **offerings** and **sacrifices**."
And when Jesus saw that he answered with **understanding**,
  he said to him,
  "You are not **far** from the kingdom of **God**."
And no one **dared** to ask him any more **questions**.

Introduce the scribe with a positive, upbeat tone.

Jesus speaks with instant certainty and authority.

You will read these words twice. The first iteration should be more measured and deliberate than the second.

Jesus adds a surprise addendum to his reply.

Given the great number of commandments in the Jewish law, Jesus' commentary is quite significant.

The scribe is sincere, not posturing, but his delivery is more brisk; he is reviewing, not lecturing as Jesus was.

The scribe adds his own commentary, which, again, is striking.

The narration and Jesus' final comment point to a significant moment in this encounter. Jesus does not speak idly; he has read the man's heart.

Deliver the final line in a way that says Jesus awed or intimidated them into silence.

oath"—"Like Melchizedek you are a priest forever" (Psalm 110:4).

GOSPEL   Matthew's version of this episode differs strikingly from Mark's in which the scribe is a much more sympathetic, in fact rather remarkable character. Impressed by Jesus' exchange with the Sadducees who were challenging belief in resurrection from the dead in the context of the "levirate law," the scribe asks a question, the answer to which he already seems to know. Jesus' response, as discussed in the commentary for the First Reading, is a recitation of the sacred *Sh'ma* that calls for belief in the one God and an undivided love of God. Though the scribe asks only for the "greatest" commandment, Jesus offers its compliment: "love your neighbor as yourself."

Jesus' teaching impresses the scribe all the more. Not only does he compliment Jesus and call him "teacher," but he parrots back Jesus' words as if he wants to underscore them either to impress them all the more upon himself or to etch them into the hearts of the crowd. In fact, he goes one step further; adding that love of neighbor "is much more than all burnt offerings and sacrifices." In Matthew the man's question is meant to "test," but here there seems to be no sinister intent and Jesus is clearly taken with the man's sincerity and "understanding," so he pays him a remarkable compliment telling him he is not "far from the kingdom of God." Some in the crowd may have had plans to test or embarrass Jesus, but his ability to read the man's heart makes them unwilling to interrogate him further.

32ND SUNDAY IN ORDINARY TIME

Lectionary #155

READING I 1 Kings 17:10–16

A reading from the first Book of Kings

In those days, **Elijah** the **prophet** went to **Zarephath**.
As he arrived at the **entrance** of the city,
   a **widow** was gathering **sticks** there; he called **out** to her,
   "**Please** bring me a small **cupful** of water to **drink**."
She left to **get** it, and he called out **after** her,
   "Please bring along a bit of **bread**."
She **answered**, "As the LORD, your God, **lives**,
   I have nothing **baked**; there is only a handful of **flour** in my jar
   and a little **oil** in my **jug**.
Just **now** I was collecting a couple of sticks,
   to go in and **prepare** something for myself and my **son**;
   when we have **eaten** it, we shall **die**."
Elijah said to her, "Do not be **afraid**.
Go and do as you **propose**.
But first make me a little **cake** and **bring** it to me.
Then you can prepare something for **yourself** and your **son**.
For the LORD, the God of **Israel**, says,
   'The jar of **flour** shall not go **empty**,
   nor the jug of **oil** run **dry**,
   until the **day** when the LORD sends **rain** upon the earth.'"

Zerephath = ZAYR-uh-fath

Elijah = ee-LĪ-juh

Be sure to clearly identify "Elijah the prophet."

Remember, God has told Elijah that a widow has been designated to care for him. His request is polite and measured; he is not "dying of thirst."

The request for bread is an afterthought; he must call out louder since she has turned away to fetch his water.

Don't make the woman pathetic in her need. She regrets her inability to offer proper hospitality, but she is not feeling sorry for herself.

Speak Elijah's injunction with authority and compassion.

Elijah's tone must not sound demanding or harsh. He is inviting her to a radical trust in God's providence. Speak the words with confidence and respect.

READING I If you are not moved by this story, you had best check your pulse. The poignancy of the woman's reply—"when we have eaten it, we shall die"—reaches out and grabs you by the collar. And yet, despite her impoverished state, Elijah, one of the most significant figures in Israelite history, doesn't hesitate to make a claim on her generosity and her meager rations. His boldness would border on insensitivity if, in the verse immediately preceding today's episode, Elijah had not received a divine command to go to Zerephath, where God has "designated a widow to provide for [him]." So, when Elijah asks, he is simply following orders, ignorant of the woman's destitute condition.

Once she makes him aware, however, Elijah responds with one of scripture's most consistent admonition: "Do not be afraid." Henri Nouwen has said "the Kingdom is where God provides for all we need . . . the realm of sufficiency where we are no longer pulled here and there by anxiety about having enough." Elijah is calling the widow into that realm of sufficiency, into a place of trust in God's provident care. That she can respond with trust, prepare the little she has, and share it with this stranger is miracle enough. That the jug and jar don't run dry is simply validation of a faith that doesn't rely on miracles. Because she trusted before she saw, the widow models the kind of faith Jesus singularly extols in today's Gospel where another widow's pennies are worth more than a treasury full of contributions.

First narrate her compliance with Elijah's wishes. Then announce the miracle. Rather than breathless amazement, let your tone suggest a deep satisfaction and gratitude to a God who provides so abundantly.

She **left** and **did** as Elijah had said.
She was able to eat for a **year**, and he and her son as **well**;
   the jar of **flour** did not go **empty**,
   nor the jug of **oil** run **dry**,
   as the LORD had **foretold** through **Elijah**.

READING II   Hebrews 9:24–28

A reading from the Letter to the Hebrews

Because your hearers won't have the benefit of the background you have on this text, read carefully and slowly so the parallels and contrasts are more apparent.

Don't assume a negative tone toward the former high priests—what they did was good; but what Jesus does is even better!

It's not that this would be ridiculous; it's just that it would be impossible.

The author's profound faith begins to emerge in these lines.

The logic of the comparison leads to the joyous declaration that ends the text. The final line describes the appropriate Christian stance: waiting *eagerly* for Christ's return!

Christ did not enter into a sanctuary made by **hands**,
   a copy of the **true** one, but heaven **itself**,
   that he might now appear before **God** on our **behalf**.
Not that he might offer himself **repeatedly**,
   as the **high** priest enters each year into the **sanctuary**
   with **blood** that is not his **own**;
   if **that** were so, he would have had to **suffer** repeatedly
   from the **foundation** of the **world**.
But now **once** for **all** he has appeared at the end of the **ages**
   to take away **sin** by his **sacrifice**.
Just as it is appointed that human beings **die** once,
   and after this the **judgment**, so also **Christ**,
   offered once to take away the sins of **many**,
   will appear a **second** time, not to take away **sin**
   but to bring **salvation** to those who eagerly **await** him.

READING II   Once a year, Israel's high priest entered the Holy of Holies, the sacred sanctuary of the temple in Jerusalem, to offer sacrifice that would atone for his sins and the sins of the nation. This sacred chamber was believed to be the earthly dwelling place of God, but as the author of Hebrews states, it was but a "sanctuary made with hands," a mere "copy of the true one." Now that Christ has assumed the role of eternal high priest, he has access to "heaven itself," not its earthly shadow, where he stands before God "on our behalf." A priest is an intercessor, an intermediary between God and humanity, and in Hebrew religion blood sacrifice was the means of atoning for sin. But when the high priest entered the sanctuary, it was the blood of animals, not his own blood, which he offered to atone for sin.

In a burst of fervor, the author enthuses that Jesus came "at the end of the ages" (Christ's coming initiated the "end times"!) to offer his *own* blood, not an animal's, as an unrepeatable sacrifice that will stand for all time, atoning for sins past, present, and future. Though the author uses logic to build his case, stacking ideas one upon the other, like bricks, underneath it all is great faith and feeling. The last sentence is a fine example: carefully balanced ideas make the point that just as we humans die once and then appear for "judgment," so Christ died once and will "appear a second time. . . ." But here's where the faith and fervor meet: Christ will appear again not to repeat his sacrifice, but to bring the *fruit* of his sacrifice—"*salvation* for those [us!] who eagerly await him."

There are two important details here: Jesus is "teaching" and he's addressing a "crowd," but he's in the temple, not on a hillside.

Within the temple area, these are bold and dangerous statements to make.

Perhaps the scribes' greatest crime: they consume the resources of the needy for their own selfish ends.

This is a harsh judgment that should not be compromised by your tone.

Narrate slowly, to suggest Jesus took some time to observe.

As you speak of the widow, your tone should immediately suggest she is a sympathetic character.

From the calm of his period of observation, Jesus announces this dramatic teaching: her little was greater than their plenty!

Make eye contact as you offer Jesus' explanation. She has given all—including her heart—to God.

GOSPEL   Mark 12:38–44

A reading from the holy Gospel according to Mark

In the course of his teaching **Jesus** said to the **crowds**,
    "Beware of the **scribes**, who like to go around in long **robes**
        and accept **greetings** in the **marketplaces**,
        seats of **honor** in **synagogues**,
        and places of **honor** at **banquets**.
They **devour** the houses of **widows** and, as a **pretext**
        recite lengthy **prayers**.
They will receive a very **severe** condemnation."

He sat down opposite the **treasury**
        and observed how the crowd put **money** into the treasury.
Many **rich** people put in **large** sums.
A poor **widow** also came and put in two small **coins**
        worth a few **cents**.
Calling his **disciples** to himself, he **said** to them,
    "**Amen**, I say to you, this **poor** widow put in **more**
        than all the **other** contributors to the treasury.
For they have all contributed from their **surplus** wealth,
        but **she**, from her **poverty**, has contributed all she **had**,
        her **whole** livelihood."

[Shorter: Mark 12:41–44]

GOSPEL   They are not the kind of criminals who capture the daily headlines, yet for these scribes Jesus pronounces a harsh judgment: "they will receive a very *severe* condemnation." Apparently the little things make a big difference between authentic and counterfeit devotion. But most important is to whom we give our hearts. The scribes have clearly not surrendered theirs to God for they serve their own egos through their public displays. Over and over we see Jesus revulsed by such hypocrisy. But Jesus is not simply critiquing the external piety and the inner corruption of the scribes; he is also warning his own disciples (and all of us) of the dangers inherent in the privilege and position that come with religious leadership.

To clarify his teaching, Jesus points to the poor widow. In contrast to the self-important posturing of the scribes, the widow demonstrates the spirituality of the *anawim*, the poor ones who recognize their total dependence on God and remain detached from the things of this world. The power of this story is found in contrasting not only the degree of generosity between the rich donors and the woman, but in who gets the focus. We sense that many made a grand show of their generous contributions while the widow quietly and humbly adds her "small coins." The ones who want attention and honor are forever frozen in a pose of shallow pretentiousness, while the woman becomes a portrait of the ideal disciple, giving not from her plenty but from her need, expecting nothing but the love of a God who already owns her heart.

33RD SUNDAY IN ORDINARY TIME

Lectionary #158

READING I   Daniel 12:1–3

A reading from the Book of the Prophet Daniel

Save the drama for Daniel's vision; the introductory statement can be low key.

In those days, I, **Daniel**,
   heard this word of the **Lord**:

Here you assume the voice of God, heralding a time of distress and deliverance.

"At **that** time there shall arise
   Michael, the great **prince**,
   guardian of your **people**;
it shall be a time **unsurpassed** in **distress**
   since nations **began** until **that** time.

Let this news ("your people shall escape") contrast with what went before.

At that time your people shall **escape**,
   everyone who is found **written** in the **book**.

Describe this scene as if you were witnessing the dead rise from their graves, and contrast those who will live with those who will be disgraced. This is scripture's first articulation of belief in life after death.

"Many of those who **sleep** in the dust of the **earth** shall **awake**;
   some shall live **forever**,
   others shall be an everlasting **horror** and **disgrace**.

A surge of energy fills this final sentence, but it is a solemn and measured energy that claims the power of God can turn human lives into shining stars.

"But the **wise** shall shine **brightly**
   like the **splendor** of the **firmament**,
and those who lead the many to **justice**
   shall be like the **stars forever**."

READING I   Written during a time of political and religious persecution, the book of Daniel attempts to do what all writing of this genre does—comfort and strengthen those enduring tribulation. Like the prophetic writings that preceded Daniel, this book looks toward the great and terrible day of the Lord, when space and time will cease. For Daniel, as for the prophets, God is sovereign lord of all of human history; through human events, God's will shall triumph.

As we end the liturgical year, the Church's readings focus us on the sobering reality that time and human history will come to an end, thus inviting us to consider our mortality and our readiness to encounter Christ both when our own life ends and when he returns in glory to judge all of humanity. Daniel's vision begins with the towering figure of Michael, the "guardian" of God's people. But his title contrasts with the "time" he ushers in that will be "unsurpassed in distress." As terrifying as that time will be, some will escape destruction—those whose names are written in God's book of the elect.

Even better news follows: the dead shall rise from their graves, some destined for eternal glory, others for eternal shame. But the "wise"—not in human terms, but in God's—who live with God in their daily lives, these shall light the sky with their glory. They have loved justice and virtue and God's life, so strong within them, will shine through them forever!

READING II   In this last of seven consecutive weeks that we have read from Hebrews, the author once again posits the superiority of Christ's high

This text is clearly written and well structured and loses little from being out of context. Though technical, you can find the emotions that, if not overtly articulated, are clearly implied.

Speak slowly, with deliberate precision.

Speak with mounting energy for, to you, the point is obvious: the former sacrifices did not remove sin; Jesus' sacrifice did! "This one" refers to Christ.

Don't "argue" this point; instead, express your gratitude for God's merciful love.

"These" refer to sins. Establish good eye contact as you explain that God has already forgiven and therefore no more sacrifices are needed.

READING II Hebrews 10:11–14, 18

A reading from the Letter to the Hebrews

Brothers and sisters:
Every **priest** stands **daily** at his **ministry**,
    offering **frequently** those same **sacrifices**
    that can **never** take away **sins**.
But **this** one offered **one** sacrifice for sins,
    and took his seat **forever** at the **right** hand of **God**;
    now he waits until his **enemies** are made his **footstool**.
For by **one** offering
    he has made **perfect** forever those who are being **consecrated**.

Where there is **forgiveness** of these,
    there is no longer **offering** for sin.

---

priesthood over that of his human counterparts in the Mosaic tradition. But the emphasis falls less on the insufficiency of the human sacrifices—although that is stated: every day priests offer animal sacrifices that don't really take away sin—and focuses much more on the efficacy of Christ's once and for all sacrifice offered on the altar of the cross. Jesus' self-sacrifice won him a seat at the right hand of God where now he intercedes for us. From that place, Christ reigns as sovereign lord and will eventually stretch out his legs and place his feet upon his enemies

who (what a striking image!) will become his "footstool.".

Review the passages from Hebrews read in recent weeks and see this as the summation of all that teaching. The writing is a bit technical and taken out of context, but don't let that dampen your confidence that this can be a moving proclamation. Gratitude should ring in your voice as you speak of the "one offering"—Christ's life—that yields grace in such abundance that it "perfects forever those (us!) who are being consecrated." Share that news slowly and tenderly. The final line is not spoken like a

courtroom argument, but like gentle advice coming from a friend or parent or counselor: the God of mercy truly does forgive, and once forgiven, "there is no longer offering for sin."

| GOSPEL | **Apocalyptic writing uses dark and startling imagery**, contrasted with a core message of consolation, to announce the victory of hope over despair. Mark masterfully weaves both elements in this passage. Frightening images and dire warnings are abundant, and they begin in the skies where the sun

GOSPEL   Mark 13:24–32

A reading from the holy Gospel according to Mark

Take a short pause after the introduction
to shift to the expansive tone of Jesus'
apocalyptic vision.

These are meant to be terrifying images
that you must not dilute.

Jesus said to his **disciples**:
"In **those** days after that **tribulation**
    the **sun** will be **darkened**,
    and the **moon** will not give its **light**,
    and the **stars** will be **falling** from the sky,
        and the **powers** in the heavens will be **shaken**.

Immediately, a sign of hope is introduced.
Take sufficient time to let these images
work. They counter the images of the
previous paragraph with light. "Son of
Man" is the term most often appropriated
by Jesus to himself.

"And **then** they will see 'the Son of **Man** coming in the **clouds'**
    with great **power** and **glory**,
    and then he will send out the **angels**
    and gather his **elect** from the four **winds**,
    from the end of the **earth** to the end of the **sky**.

Try to avoid a feeling of disconnect with
what went before. This image is offered
as an example that focuses us all the
more on what preceded.

The intensity of the warning grows in
these lines. Heeding these words is a
matter of eternal life or death.

"Learn a **lesson** from the **fig** tree.
When its branch becomes **tender** and sprouts **leaves**,
    you know that **summer** is near.
In the **same** way, when you see **these** things happening,
    know that **he** is near, at the **gates**.
Amen, I say to you,
    this **generation** will not pass **away**
    until **all** these things have taken **place**.
Heaven and **earth** will pass away,
    but my **words** will **not** pass away.

This is the solemn pronouncement of the
Lord of heaven and earth.

The final sentence has the feel of an
afterthought, as if saying: "But getting
back to what I said before . . . ."

Jesus' words call us to fix our eyes on
"heaven" and, at the ready, await the
Son, who will lead us to the Father.

"But of that **day** or **hour**, **no one** knows,
    neither the **angels** in heaven, nor the **Son**,
        but only the **Father**."

---

is "darkened," the moon yields no light, and the world, on the brink of utter collapse, can do nothing to save itself. But Mark soon offers an image of hope: "the Son of Man coming in the clouds." The mysterious term introduced by Daniel is used here to announce the return in glory of the risen Christ who comes amid clouds, a biblical sign of divine presence.

The triumphant Christ "send[s] out the angels" to gather and safeguard the "elect." No effort will be spared; they will scour "earth" and "sky" so none are left behind. This expansive imagery suggests God's

great love for all people, so speak the words with dignity and authority, and slow enough to suggest the great effort expended on the search.

To further explain the cosmic realities, Jesus unexpectedly shifts focus to the "fig tree," using it to teach the importance of being attentive and ready, to watch for and recognize the signs of the times. Adjust your tone for this momentary shift from cosmic to earthbound imagery, becoming more conversational and didactic. But soon the expansive mood returns as Jesus directs focus back to the skies

("when you see *these* things . . .") and explains their meaning: "he is near," at the very gates! Speak the lines with urgency, suggesting that without vigilance, salvation can be lost forever.

Jesus speaks of the enduring nature of "his words" with a note of finality. Heaven and earth will pass away; only his word will endure. But then, as if sensing an unspoken question from his disciples (in *every* generation), Jesus suggests the futility of seeking knowledge that is reserved to the Father.

OUR LORD JESUS CHRIST THE KING

Lectionary #161

READING I Daniel 7:13–14

Pause after "A reading from . . ." so that your listeners have time to settle and focus.

The opening line communicates that the story is already begun, and you are recounting "visions" that occurred at night (as a dream).

Immediately, your tone signals that this "Son of Man" is as much divine as human.

Don't list the attributes bestowed by the Ancient One as if reading a list of awards. Each should be a source of wonder.

This Ancient One draws all the people of the earth together into a lasting unity.

Make the final declaration with weighty conviction.

A reading from the Book of the Prophet Daniel

As the **visions** during the night **continued**, I saw
    one like a Son of **man** coming,
        on the clouds of **heaven**;
    when he reached the **Ancient** One
        and was **presented** before him,
    the one like a Son of man received **dominion**, **glory**,
        and **kingship**;
        all **peoples**, **nations**, and **languages** **serve** him.
His dominion is an **everlasting** dominion
    that shall not be taken **away**,
        his **kingship** shall not be **destroyed**.

READING I Daniel receives a vision in his sleep that terrifies him. He sees four beasts that represent the worldly powers of his day, all of which oppose the kingdom that God will establish for his people through the coming messiah. In the midst of his vision, Daniel sees a figure he calls "the Son of man," an enigmatic term that Jesus later appropriated to himself. Amid "clouds," an image that signifies the presence of divinity, the Son of man comes before the "Ancient One," that is, the Everlasting God, who lavishes on him glory,

authority, and—especially significant in light of today's solemnity—"kingship," making all people and nations subject to him. This royal leader will rule forever and his kingdom will never be destroyed.

Daniel is already in the midst of his story when we tune in. With expansive tone and high energy, he is concluding the narrative of his "visions during the night." Your assembly will not be as ready as you to jump into the middle of this story, so take the necessary time to establish the scene and develop a mood of sacred awe.

Imagine Bernadette or one of the visionaries of Fatima standing before the mysterious Lady of their visions, and let that inform your delivery of "I saw one like a . . . ." The list of titles conferred on him signifies the majesty of this Son of man," to whom so much is given and from whom nothing shall be "taken away." The humility and loyalty of a subject eager to serve the king echo in these lines. If you let the story fill you with awe, you won't have trouble filling the span of a minute with your telling.

READING II Revelation 1:5–8

A reading from the Book of Revelation

Jesus **Christ** is the faithful **witness**,
    the **firstborn** of the **dead** and **ruler** of the kings of the **earth**.
To him who **loves** us and has **freed** us from our sins by his **blood**,
    who has made us into a **kingdom**, **priests** for his God
        and **Father**,
to him be **glory** and **power** forever and **ever**. **Amen**.

    Behold, he is coming amid the **clouds**,
        and every eye will **see** him,
            even those who **pierced** him.
    All the peoples of the earth will **lament** him.
        Yes. Amen.

"I am the **Alpha** and the **Omega**," says the Lord God,
    "the one who **is** and who **was** and who is to **come**,
        the **almighty**."

You can't ease into this reading. From the start, it sings the praises of the risen Christ. Be sure to differentiate the aspects you extol in him.

Let there be gratitude as well as awe in your voice as you announce Christ's generous love.

Without any melodrama, increase your intensity as you proclaim, "Behold."
If the word were "beware," how would it affect your delivery?
This is a prophecy that those who reject Christ will rue their decision.

Here, the all-powerful God announces his identity. The "I am" statement signals divine self-identification. God says he is the beginning and the end (like A and Z of the alphabet); the sustainer of all things.

READING II Like the book of Daniel, Revelation is written by a visionary to comfort believers during times of persecution. Taken from the opening of the book, these lines exalt Christ, the one who has formed them into a people and sustains them with his love. More song than exposition, this short text sings the praise of Christ—all he is and was and ever will be. You have much to say of him here, so the challenge will be to keep the elements from blending together as undifferentiated expressions of approval.

Here is what you are given to share: Jesus is a "faithful witness": he was obedient unto death, doing all the Father asked him. He is "firstborn of the dead": though pierced and buried for our offenses, he rose again and lives forever. He "loves us" and "freed us from our sins": his blood is our drink, his body our nourishment; there is no greater love than that. Our only response can be to bend the knee and lift the voice: "glory and power forever."

What follows alludes to the classic prophecy from Daniel we hear in today's First Reading. The announcement of his

coming amid clouds rouses both those who loved him and those who pierced him. "All the peoples" refers to unbelievers who persecute the Church and are hostile to Christ. Their fate will be to mourn because of him. John punctuates that prophecy with: "Yes. Amen."

The final lines proclaim God's eternal sovereignty. God is the beginning and the end of all things. No matter the whims of earthly kings, no matter their designs against Christ's Church, the "one who is and who was" reigns even over them all.

In the Passion narrative the purpose of this scene is different from today's. Here, the scene harmonizes with the apocalyptic visions of Daniel and John that fix our eyes on the skies and clouds. Jesus reinforces that by telling us his kingdom doesn't belong to this world.

Pilate asks dispassionately, "Are you the King . . . ?" Today he is not a Roman official, but any person who seeks to understand Christ's identity.

Don't proclaim with Good Friday intensity. Pilate is less desperate; Jesus more philosophically muted.

When Jesus questions "Do you say this on your own . . . ?" he could be asking any one of us.

It's not the dialogue that matters here, but the image of a king who dies willingly for the sake of his subjects.

Pilate needs to pin him down . . . but fails. It's a question, not an accusation.

There is poetry in these lines and great dignity in this king who cares more about truth than saving his life. Memorize the final line and deliver it with eyes fixed on the assembly.

GOSPEL   John 18:33b–37

A reading from the holy Gospel according to John

Pilate said to **Jesus**,
   "Are you the **King** of the Jews?"
Jesus answered, "Do you say this on your **own**
   or have **others** told you about me?"
Pilate answered, "I am not a **Jew**, **am** I?
Your own **nation** and the chief **priests** handed you over to me.
What have you **done**?"
Jesus answered, "My **kingdom** does not belong to this **world**.
If my kingdom **did** belong to this world,
   my attendants would be **fighting**
   to **keep** me from being handed over to the Jews.
But as it **is**, my **kingdom** is not **here**."
So Pilate said to him, "Then you **are** a king?"
Jesus answered, "**You** say I am a king.
For **this** I was **born** and for **this** I came into the **world**,
   to **testify** to the **truth**.
Everyone who **belongs** to the truth **listens** to my voice."

GOSPEL   We are celebrating Christ's eternal kingship but the text we proclaim presents him sparring with a second rate governor of a less than second rate province who is about to condemn him to death. For today's solemnity, that the exchange occurs with Pilate is of little consequence. What matters is Jesus' characterization of his "kingdom" as an other worldly reality and his role as witness to the truth. Pilate, of course, can't grasp the significance of Jesus' assertion.

Jesus has become a troublesome, though fascinating, problem. Without realizing it, Pilate serves as Jesus' foil. For Pilate, it's a cat and mouse game that he is not winning. He needs Jesus to make a definitive statement, one way or the other, which will help convict or exonerate him. But Jesus is not cooperating. He already knows his fate and is not trying to avoid it. He won't give a direct response to Pilate's direct inquiry: "Then you are a king?" Emphasizing the initial pronoun in Jesus' reply ("You say that I am a king") suggests he would not have made the statement had Pilate not asked.

Jesus uses the opportunity to further his own agenda. This is who I am and why I was born: to testify to the truth. Since God is all that is good and beautiful and true, and since Jesus has previously said of himself that he is "the way and the truth," his assertion not only names his mission, but his very identity. Everyone who belongs to the truth, he says, that is to God, listens to his voice. It is the voice of a king whose crown is made of thorns and whose throne will be a cross on which he will stretch out his arms to die.